To
Micah 6:8

AMERICA

WHAT THE HELL WENT WRONG

AMERICA

Tom Newman

America: What The Hell Went Wrong

Cover Design by Ariel, Deitric Newman, Gordon (Kim) Maronde
Cover Photo by Deitric Newman

Published in the United States of America

ISBN:9781709448607

"Educate and inform the whole mass of people. They are the only sure reliance for the preservation of our liberty."

Thomas Jefferson

ACKNOWLEDGMENTS

I do not think anyone can write a book without help. That being said I would like to acknowledge and thank Nita Erlander for her assistance in grammatically editing my work, which made it readable. Gary Baldwin his conceptual editing of America: What The Hell Went Wrong. My son Deitric for the cover photo. And a good friend and incredible artist Gordon (Kim) Maronde for his help with the cover's final look. And as with all of my works, the Holy Spirt for His guidance, illumination and insight.

Table of Contents

PREFACE

There is something very wrong with America and American politics right now. Our Founding Fathers saw the history of failed democracies; from Rome to Greece to the Weimar Republic, they struggled to create an entirely new form of Government. Governments left unchecked are prone to corruption and an abuse of their powers. An abuse of power eventually leads to encroachments on the liberties of its citizens. The Founders designed a government based on a written Constitution, based on written law, not on the whims of a capricious government, or a king or monarchy. The Founders did not rely on man's law, but on God's revealed law. They designed a government that would protect the rights of its citizens, not work to limit those rights. The basic premise is that these rights are given to man from God, therefore they are unalienable, and cannot be taken from man by any government, so the Founders set about to create a government with the purpose of protecting the rights of its citizens. To be an American citizen it is important to understand the intent of the Founding Fathers. What issues they grappled with, what was their reasoning process and what was it they hoped to accomplish?

In a country ruled by law it is inevitable that environment will produce a plethora of attorneys, whom all are educated in the art of compromise. Compromises is essentially the art of give and take, however, we should never compromise on fundamentals like unalienable rights and God's law. Any compromise on fundamentals is a surrender because it is all give and no take.

It is also very difficult to find good, reliable and accurate information on American early history. The early history of America has been so

1

distorted by historical revisionists (those who rewrite history to reinterpret the motives and decisions of those involved to change our true history, if you change our history you change who we are) and political correctness. What you will find in *"America: What the Hell Went Wrong,"* is an honest, straight forward look at the first 200 years of America. From the first settlement to our Declaration of Independence. The Revolutionary War and the arduous process of forming an entirely new type of government to our second war of Independence, the War of 1812. And the state of America today and what the Hell Went Wrong.

INTRODUCTION

America: What the Hell Went Wrong, is essentially the first 200 years of Colonial American History. However, to understand what our Founding Fathers grappled with we have to understand history in general. The Founders considers the impact of some of the major events in history and the consequences those events meant for their country, government and their citizens. These events had an impact on the Founders and in their process of forming a nation, by creating a new form of government. That means we must consider the origins of major worldwide events: Christianity, the Catholic Church, The Protestant Reformation, the Inquisition, and the theory of evolution. There were also some very influential leaders; such as: Constantine, Charlemagne, Martell "The Hammer," King Jan Sobieski, Grand Vizier Kara Mustafa, Joan of Arc, Pope Leo I & X, Martin Luther, Fredrick the Wise, the kings of France and Britain, and Napoleon Bonaparte et al. The Founders also considered events that caused paradigm shifts across cultures that had a dramatic impact on the formation of nations; the 100 years' war, the Muslim invasion of Europe, the Thirty Years War, and the exploration and colonization of North and South America, as well as Africa, India and the islands of the Caribbean.

There were also people and events that shaped America from our founding's in the first colony at Jamestown, the relations with the Native Indians, the early colonial wars, the great awakening, our relationship with Britain, the French and Indian War, the Kentucky Rifle, the Battle of Saratoga, Captain Oliver Perry and the Battle of Lake Erie and Lieutenant Thomas Macdonough and the battle of Lake Champlain. There were major events within America that began to unfold in very important ways; British rule, a desire for independence which resulted in the Declaration of Independences. Which was followed by the eight-year Revolutionary War, where a fledgling new nation without an army or a navy engaged the most powerful military machine in existence at the time. Influential people as well, Jonathan Edwards, the Indian Prophet, Daniel Morgan, Pontiac, Andrew Jackson, Marquis de Lafayette, General Cornwallis, Thomas Jefferson and of course General and President George Washington The Founders then began the process of building a new nation and a new form of government. Only to fight a second Revolutionary War with the British thirty-six years after the first Revolutionary War, the War of 1812, the war that made America, America.

MAN'S CONQUEST OF MAN

The population of the earth began to grow, and people became tillers of the soil, farmers, herdsmen and shepherds. As families grew, they needed more land for farming, grazing and water. Since growth infringed on others the need developed for protecting one's property, which necessitated a need for defenders. The defenders did not contribute to the production of food, hence they needed to be provided for. This, in turn, created a need for food storage and a barter system. The need for equipment, tools and arms gave birth to tradesmen and metal workers. The natural evolution of civilization required yielding certain aspects of freedom in exchange for security.

As the population grew skills became more diversified. With larger populations the need for more security increased. Individual plots of land came under groups for protection. There became a need for order to manage the increasingly complex living arrangements. Groups or tribes would elect a person to manage or oversee the relationships within the local community, allocating resources and insuring the protection of those under his administration. This led to record keeping, establishing security, and eventually the building of walled cites for protection. As more kingdoms arose, the threat level correspondingly arose among existing communities. At the same time administrators of these communities began to gather wealth from the administration duties and collecting valuables for services rendered. Some of these administrators eventually became kings and forged alliances with surrounding kingdoms for mutual protection and defense. We can assume that some of these kingdoms pursued a path of production and prosperity while others struggled with success. Scripture warns of; "The lust of the flesh, the lust of the eyes and the pride of life."[1] When some were more successful because they spent more time on production and less on security they were perceived as a weaker neighbor and therefore more vulnerable to attack. Natural resources were not equally distributed, which lead to the success and wealth of some kingdoms while others struggled to provide for their population. As the population continued to grow, cites became more and more complex. Some lacked sufficient resources, and kings, not wanting to lose power and wealth, would attack and subjugate these cities to acquire slave labor and increase their own wealth. Eventually we see the development of dynasties.

The first dynasty was that of the Assyrians from 934 – 609 B.C. The first major conquest of the Middle East was executed by the Assyrians under Shalmaneser V in 722 B.C. in an attack on Israel. Shalmaneser was successful in his conquest and took some of the Jewish people into captivity. Israel's defeat was in large part to due to its weakened state which was caused by a lot of infighting amongst the Israelites.

The ten northern tribes of Israel had rebelled from Judah after the death of Solomon in 931 B.C. In 701 B.C. Assyrian King Sennacherib again, tried to subdue Israel and was defeated by God. In one night, God sent His Angel of Lord, (Christ) among the Assyrian army camp and slew 186,000 Assyrian soldiers.[2] In 609, the Assyrian Empire collapsed; the void created by their collapse was quickly filled by the Babylonians under King Nebuchadnezzar II. In 598 B.C. Nebuchadnezzar invaded Jerusalem; he destroyed the Temple, seized the Ark of the Covenant and drove most of the inhabitants into captivity in Babylon. From this time forward Israelites would be known as Jews. Unbeknownst to the Jews at the time their captivity produced a spiritual awakening in their faith. No longer was it necessary to have a physical temple or sacrifices, God's kingdom was not of this earth, and their faith flourished.

In 539 B.C. the Medes and Persians under Cyrus the Great conquered Babylon. God had said that Cyrus was His anointed one and commissioned Cyrus to allow the Jews to return to their land and rebuild the Temple. In 331B.C. Alexander the Great conquered Babylon defeating the Medes and the Persians. Upon the death of Alexander; his four generals divided up the empire. One of Alexanders generals, Seleucus I

---

[1] 1 John 2:16
[2] 2 Kings 19:35

controlled the Seleucids dynasty which covered most of Alexander's northern realm. During this time the Maccabees in Israel staged a revolt and for a time ruled Judea. In 60 B.C. Judah fell under the rule of the Roman Empire. The Roman Empire lasted until 476 A.D. in the west and until 1453 A.D. in the east.

In 70 A.D. Vespasian abandoned his conquest for Jerusalem to travel from Egypt to Rome to become the new emperor. He sent his son Titus to capture Jerusalem. Titus sailed from Alexandria in Egypt and launched his attack on Jerusalem from Syria. In 70 A.D. Titus used the Fifth and Tenth Legions that were already in Judah. He also employed the Fifteenth Legion from Turkey and the Third from Syria. The geography of Turkey and Syria represent the people who "the prince (the Antichrist) is to come from," referred to in the book of Daniel.[3] It may not be his country of origin, but it is where his seat of power will be.[4] Titus completely destroyed the Jewish temple and razed the city of Jerusalem to the ground. Titus took many of the Jews back to Rome to die as competitors in the arena in celebration of the victory. Jews not captured fled to other areas of the Mediterranean, and Northern Africa. The Christians and Jews living in Rome, Italy and Greece dispersed into Europe. This great migration of the Jewish people was called the diaspora or dispersal. Many of the Jews in exile gave up their ancestry and traditions and intermarried with the indigenous population. The Jews that went into exile are commonly referred to as the lost 10 tribes of Israel. Some Jews remained behind and continued the rebellion against Rome. The rebels were ultimately defeated in 135 A.D., teaching of the Mosaic Law was forbidden and what once had been the land of the Hebrews was renamed Syria Palaestina. The diaspora, along with the missionary, evangelical work and planting of churches by the Apostles stimulated the growth of Christianity throughout the Mediterranean, North Africa, Spain, and Europe. The Apostles Paul and Peter went as far as Rome, where they were both martyred for their faith in Jesus Christ.

.

---

[3] Daniel 9:26

[4] For a complete history of these evens see; *Things To Come: A Brief History of the Bible* by Tom Newman

THE BIRTH OF CHRISTIANTY

Historians pick different points in history to write about the beginning of the American experiment. However, there are major events all through history that played a part in the formation of America.

In ancient history, at about 100 B.C., Rome was the largest city in the world. It was governed by the Roman Senate as a Republic. The Republic became weakened by many wars, civil wars and corruption in the political leaders. In order to save the Republic, the Senate granted increasingly more authority to Julius Caesar, who was assassinated in 44 B.C. His adopted son, Octavian, took the throne. In 31 B.C. Octavian defeated Mark Antony and Cleopatra adding Egypt to the Roman Republic. In 27 B.C. the Senate formally granted Octavin overreaching powers and the new title Augusta making him the first Roman emperor which, in effect, ended the Roman Republic and transitioned it into the Roman Empire. Augustus then subdued Spain, France, the Balkans and North Africa. The Roman Empire was taking shape at the time of the birth of Jesus Christ. The Roman Empire had many pagan gods that were usually paired as male-female couples: Jupiter – Juno, Neptune – Minerva, Mars – Venus, Vulcan – Vesta and Mercury – Ceres. There were also many other pagan gods in different parts of the Empire.

In 30 A.D., after the crucifixion and resurrection of Jesus Christ the disciples following the charge of Christ and began their missionary work.; "Go therefore and make disciples of all the nations, baptizing them in the name of the Father and the Son and the Holy Spirit, teaching them to observe all that I commanded you; and lo, I am with you always, even to the end of the age,"[5] The disciples began establishing churches throughout the Roman Empire. By the end of the 3rd century there were churches and bishops in every mid-to large city from Morocco, Algeria, Libya, Egypt, the Arabian Peninsula, Spain, Persia, Turkey and Europe. The Disciples and their followers were heavily persecuted in the Roman Empire. They worshipped an unseen God, they professed Christ as Lord and would never say, "Caesar is Lord." The Christians were blamed for any and all misfortune that befell civilization because they would not worship their pagan gods. Hence, the pagan gods would then extract their punishment on the populace. The Christians were considered cannibals because at their secret meetings, they would "drink blood and eat flesh," which, of course, were actually the sacraments of communion. In spite of the persecution by the authorities, Christianity grew in number because of their excitement about telling others about Jesus, the influence of the Holy Spirit and the actions of Christians. The Christians practiced moral restraint. They retrieved unwanted children who had been abandoned in the forest to be eaten by wild beasts. They buried the dead so that a person created in the image of God would not be desecrated. They tended the sick, widows, and orphans when others would not. They pioneered hospice care, which would later give name to our hospitals. Christians behavior was a constant condemnation of the pagan way of life which naturally produced resentment and persecution.

The church in Rome came to permanence because it was the largest church. It was also the wealthiest and located in the most densely populated area, resultantly it had the most influence of all the churches. The church in Rome took the position that Christ had commissioned Peter as the founder of the church. When Christ asked the disciples; "But you, whom do you say Me to be?" Peter answered, "You are the Christ, the Son of the living God." To which Christ replied; "Flesh and blood did not reveal this to you but My Father who is in heaven, on this rock I will build My church."[6] Christ's intended meaning was that He as the Son of God would be the foundation of the church. The church in Rome, however, took it to mean the church would be built on Peter, a man, commissioned by Christ to lead the church. The church developed a theology that was based on the apostles more than on the teachings of Christ or the God of the Old Testament. This gave the church more leeway in the interpretation of Scripture, which then gave the church and the pope particularly, the power

---

[5] Matthew 28:19-20 NASB
[6] Matthew 16:13-17

9

of God on earth. Christ's words to His disciples, "If you forgive anyone his sins, they are forgiven..." were interpreted to mean that man can forgive the sins of another. However, the clear message of the gospel is the absolute truth that the way a person has their sins forgiven is by having faith in Jesus Christ as his or her Lord and Savior and by repenting of their sins, "who can forgive sins, but God alone".[7]

An apostolic approach gave the church power on earth and a path to great wealth. The church took on the role for forgiving sin, something only God can do, and created indulgences and the sacrament of penance to create greater wealth. There were people with the gift of healing, granted by the Holy Spirit. The people so gifted would often heal the local population of their infirmities and illnesses. In response to this the Catholic Church wrote and issued a doctrine on healing for all the priests and bishops to follow. The bishops now would assume the role of the Holy Spirit. If you read the church manual you could perform healing. If your healing failed it was because of the weak faith of the recipient. The church assumed the miracle of healing, ignoring that the ability to heal is a gift from the Holy Spirit.

In about 100 A.D., the church in Rome took on the name The Holy Roman Catholic Church, meaning the universal church. Christians continued to be heavily persecuted, especially under Emperor Diocletian (285-305AD) and his successor Galerius. Diocletian thought the Roman Empire was impossible for a single emperor to manage from a single location. He divided the empire into four parts and established co-regents to manage the imperial courts in the other regions. Constantius Chlorus, Constantine's father, was the co-regent in Western Europe, which encompassed all of Europe from Britain to Russia and south to Spain. It was understood that when Constantius' reign ended his son Constantine would replace him. However, in 305, Diocletian and Maximian stepped down and named their sons as Caesar: Severus and Maximinus. Upset with the outcome, Constantine went north to be with his father. They engaged in a few battles together and Constantine demonstrated himself as a true warrior. When Constantius died in 306 the officers and legions declared Constantine their emperor.

---

[7] Mark 2:7, Luke 5:21

EMPEROR CONSTANTINE

The persecution of Christians continued under Roman authority until Constantine became Emperor. The account of Constantine's conversion comes from *The Life of Constantine* by Eusebius of Caesarea. The account describes one of the most important events for the growth of Christianity. Constantine (274-337 A.D.) had been declared Caesar by his troops. Just before the battle of the Milvian Bridge near Rome in 312 A.D., as the army prepared to engage his rival, they witnessed a miracle. Constantine said; "about noon, when…he saw with his own eyes the trophy of a cross of light in the heavens, above the sun, and bearing the inscription; "Conquer by This." At this sight Constantine was absolutely shocked, his army on the expedition with him saw the miracle as well.

I have read several different accounts of Constantine's conversion. As expected, there are many accounts trying to discredit Constantine's Christian faith. This is a common theme amongst historical revisionists; if you cannot discredit the belief, discredit the man. In an attempt to find the truth, I went to the source. Eusebius Pamphilus of Caesarea was a theologian and historian who wrote, *The Life of the Blessed Emperor Constantine.* Constantine died in 337 A.D. Eusebius began writing Constantine's biography just after his death. Eusebius died in 339 A.D. before completing the biography.

The following account are extracts from Eusebius' biography of Constantine, quoting;

"…the design of my present undertaking being to speak and write of those circumstances only which have reference to his religious character.

11

And since these are themselves of almost infinite variety, I shall select from the facts which have come to my knowledge such as are most suitable, and worthy of lasting record, and endeavor to narrate them as briefly as possible. Henceforward, indeed, there is a full and opportunity for celebrating in every way the praises of this truly blessed prince, which hitherto we have been unable to do, oh the ground that we are forbidden to judge any one blessed before his death, because of the uncertain vicissitudes of life. Let me implore then the help of God, and may the inspiring aid of the heavenly Word be with me, while I commence my history from the very earliest period of his life…

…At a time when four emperors shared the administration of the Roman empire, Constantius (Constantine's father) alone, following a course of conduct different from that pursued by his colleagues, entered into the friendship of the Supreme God. For while they besieged and wasted the churches of God, leveling them to the ground, and obliterating the very foundations of the houses of prayer, he kept his hands pure from their abominable impiety, and never in any respect resembled them. They polluted their provinces by the indiscriminate slaughter of godly men and women; but he kept his soul free from the stain of this crime…

On the other hand, Constantius conceived an expedient full of sagacity, and did a thing which sounds paradoxical, but in fact was most admirable.

He made a proposal to all the officers of his court, including even those in the highest stations of authority, offering them the following alternative: either that they should offer sacrifice to demons, and thus be permitted to remain with him, and enjoy their usual honors; or, in case of refusal, that they should be shut out from all access to his person, and entirely disqualified from acquaintance and association with him. Accordingly, when they had individually made their choice, some one way and some the other; and the choice of each had been ascertained, then this admirable prince disclosed the secret meaning of his expedient, and condemned the cowardice and selfishness of the one party, while he highly commended the other for their conscientious devotion to God. He declared, too, that those who had been false to their God must be unworthy of the confidence of their prince; for how was it possible that they should preserve their fidelity to him, who had proved themselves faithless to a higher power? He determined, therefore, that such persons should be removed altogether from the imperial court, while, on the other hand, declaring that those men who, in bearing witness for the truth, had proved themselves to be worthy servants of God, would manifest the same fidelity to their king, he entrusted them with the guardianship of his person and empire, saying that he was bound to treat such persons with special regard as his nearest and most valued friends, and to esteem them far more highly than the richest treasures...

On the death of Constantine's father.

Nor did the imperial throne remain long unoccupied: for Constantine invested himself with his father's purple, and proceeded from his father's palace, presenting to all a renewal, as it were, in his own person, of his father's life and reign. He then conducted the funeral procession in company with his father's friends, some preceding, others following the train, and performed the last offices for the pious deceased with an extraordinary degree of magnificence, and all united in honoring this thrice blessed prince with acclamations and praises, and while with one mind and voice, they glorified the rule of the son as a living again of him who was dead, they hastened at once to hail their new sovereign by the titles of Imperial and Worshipful Augustus, with joyful shouts. Thus, the memory of the deceased emperor received honor from the praises bestowed upon his son, while the latter was pronounced blessed in being the successor of such a father. All the nations also under his dominion were filled with joy and inexpressible gladness at not being even for a moment deprived of the benefits of a well...

Thus, then the God of all, the Supreme Governor of the whole universe, by his own will appointed Constantine, the descendant of so renowned a parent, to be prince and sovereign: so that, while others have been raised to this distinction by the election of their fellow- men, he is the only one to whose elevation no mortal may boast of having contributed.

How he resolved to deliver Rome from Maxentius.

While, therefore, he regarded the entire world as one immense body, and perceived that the head of it all, the royal city of the Roman empire, was bowed down by the weight of a tyrannous oppression; at first, he had left the task of liberation to those who governed the other divisions of the empire, as being his superiors in point of age. But when none of these proved able to afford relief, and those who had attempted it had experienced a disastrous termination of their enterprise, he said that life was without enjoyment to him as long as he saw the imperial city thus afflicted, and prepared himself for the overthrowal of the tyranny.

That after reflecting on the Dawn fall of those who had worshiped Idols, he made Choice of Christianity.

Being convinced, however, that he needed some more powerful aid than his military forces could afford him, on account of the wicked and magical enchantments which were so diligently practiced by the tyrant, he sought Divine assistance, deeming the possession of arms and a numerous soldiery of secondary importance, but believing the co-operating power of Deity invincible and not to be shaken. He considered, therefore, on what God he might rely for protection and assistance. While engaged in this enquiry, the thought occurred to him, that, of the many emperors who had preceded him, those who had rested their hopes in a multitude of gods, and served them with sacrifices and offerings, had in the first place been deceived by flattering predictions, and oracles which promised them all prosperity, and at last had met with an unhappy end, while not one of their gods had stood by to warn them of the impending wrath of heaven; while one alone who had pursued an entirely opposite course, who had condemned their error, and honored the one Supreme God during his whole life, had formal l him to be the Saviour and Protector of his empire, and the Giver of every good thing. Reflecting on this, and well weighing the fact that they who had trusted in many gods had also fallen by manifold forms of death, without leaving behind them either family or offspring, stock, name, or memorial among men: while the God of his father had given to him, on the other hand, manifestations of his power and very many tokens: and considering farther that those who had already taken arms against the tyrant, and had marched to the battle-field under the protection of a multitude of gods, had met with a dishonorable end (for one of them had shamefully retreated from the contest without a blow, and the other, being slain in the midst of his own troops, became, as it were, the mere sport of death; reviewing, I say, all these considerations, he judged it to be folly indeed to join in the idle worship of those who were no gods, and, after such convincing evidence, to err from the truth; and therefore felt it incumbent on him to honor his father's God alone.

How, while he was praying, God sent him a Vision of a Cross of Light in the Heavens at Mid-day, with an Inscription admonishing him to conquer by that.

ACCORDINGLY, he called on him with earnest prayer and supplications that he would reveal to him who he was, and stretch forth his right hand to help him in his present difficulties. And while he was thus praying with fervent entreaty, a most marvelous sign appeared to him from heaven, the account of which it might have been hard to believe had it been related by any other person. But since the victorious emperor himself long afterwards declared it to the writer of this history, when he was honored with his acquaintance and society, and confirmed his statement by an oath, who could hesitate to accredit the relation, especially since the testimony of after- time has established its truth? He said that about noon, when the day was already beginning to decline, he saw with his own eyes the trophy of a cross of light in the heavens, above the sun, and bearing the inscription, CONQUER BY THIS. At this sight he himself was struck with amazement, and his whole army also, which followed him on this expedition, and witnessed the miracle.

How the Christ of God appeared to him in his Sleep, and commanded him to use in his Wars a Standard made in the Form of the Cross.

He said, moreover, that he doubted within himself what the import of this apparition could be. And while he continued to ponder and reason on its meaning, night suddenly came on; then in his sleep the Christ of God appeared to him with the same sign which he had seen in the heavens, and commanded him to make a likeness of that sign which he had seen in the heavens, and to use it as a safeguard in all engagements with his enemies.

The Making of the Standard of the Cross.

AT dawn of day he arose, and communicated the marvel to his friends: and then, calling together the workers in gold and precious stones, he sat in the midst of them, and described to them the figure of the sign he had seen, bidding them represent it in gold and precious stones. And this representation I myself have had an opportunity of seeing.

15

A Description of the Standard of the Cross, which the Romans now call the Labarum.

Now it was made in the following manner. A long spear, overlaid with gold, formed the figure of the cross by means of a transverse bar laid over it. On the top of the whole was fixed a wreath of gold and precious stones; and within this, the symbol of the Saviour's name, two letters indicating the name of Christ by means of its initial characters, the letter P being intersected by X in its centre: and these letters the emperor was in the habit of wearing on his helmet at a later period. From the cross-bar of the spear was suspended a cloth, a royal piece, covered with a profuse embroidery of most brilliant precious stones; and which, being also richly interlaced with gold, presented an indescribable degree of beauty to the beholder. This banner was of a square form, and the upright staff, whose lower section was of great length, bore a golden half-length portrait of the pious emperor and his children on its upper part, beneath the trophy of the cross, and immediately above the embroidered banner.

The emperor constantly made use of this sign of salvation as a safeguard against every adverse and hostile power, and commanded that others similar to it should be carried at the head of all his armies.

How Constantine received Instruction, and read the Sacred Scriptures.

These things were done shortly afterwards. But at the time above specified, being struck with amazement at the extraordinary vision, and resolving to worship no other God save Him who had appeared to him, he sent for those who were acquainted with the mysteries of His doctrines, and enquired who that God was, and what was intended by the sign of the vision he had seen. They affirmed that He was God, the only begotten Son of the one and only God: that the sign which had appeared was the symbol of immortality, and the trophy of that victory over death which He had gained in time past when sojourning on earth. They taught him also the causes of His advent, and explained to him the true account of His incarnation. Thus, he was instructed in these matters, and was impressed with wonder at the divine manifestation which had been presented to his sight. Comparing, therefore, the heavenly vision with the interpretation given, he found his judgment confirmed; and, in the persuasion that the knowledge of these things had been imparted to him by Divine teaching, he determined thenceforth to devote himself to the reading of the Inspired writings.

Moreover, he made the priests of God his counselors, and deemed it incumbent on him to honor the God who had appeared to him with all devotion. And after this, being fortified by well-grounded hopes in Him, he hastened to quench the threatening fire of tyranny.

Of the Adulterous Conduct of Maxentius at Rome.

For the who had tyrannically possessed himself of the imperial city, had proceeded to great lengths in impiety and wickedness, so as to venture without hesitation on every vile and impure action.

For example: he would separate women from their husbands, and after a time send them back to them again, and these insults he offered not to men of mean or obscure condition, but to those who held the first places in the Roman senate. Moreover, though he shamefully dishonored almost numberless free women, he was unable to satisfy his ungoverned and intemperate desires. But when he assayed to corrupt Christian women also, he could no longer secure success to his designs, since they chose rather to submit their lives to death than yield their persons to be defiled by him.

How the Wife of a Prefect slew herself for Chastity's Sake.

Now a certain woman, wife of one of the senators who held the authority of prefect, when she understood that those who ministered to the tyrant in such matters were standing before her house (she was a Christian), and knew that her husband through fear had bidden them take her and lead her away, begged a short space of time for arraying herself in her usual dress, and entered her chamber. There, being left alone, she sheathed a sword in her own breast, and immediately expired, leaving indeed her dead body to the procurers, but declaring to all mankind, both to present and future generations, by an act which spoke louder than any words, that the chastity for which Christians are famed is the only thing which is invincible and indestructible. Such was the conduct displayed by this woman.

Massacre of the Roman People by Maxentius.

All men, therefore, both people and magistrates, whether of high or low degree, trembled through fear of him whose daring wickedness was such as I have described, and were oppressed by his grievous tyranny. Nay, though they submitted quietly, and endured this bitter servitude, still there was no escape from the tyrant's sanguinary cruelty. For at one time, on some trifling pretense, he exposed the populace to be slaughtered by his own body-guard; and countless multitudes of the Roman people were slain in the very midst of the city by the lances and weapons, not of Scythians or barbarians, but of their own fellow-citizens. And besides this, it is impossible to calculate the number of senators whose blood was shed with a view to the seizure of their respective estates, for at different times and on various fictitious charges, multitudes of them suffered death.

Magic Arts of Maxentius against Constantine; and Famine at Rome.

BUT the crowning point of the tyrant's wickedness was his having recourse to sorcery: sometimes for magic purposes ripping up women with child, at other times searching into the bowels of new-born infants. He slew lions also. and practiced certain horrid arts for evoking demons, and averting the approaching war, hoping by these means to get the victory. In short, it is impossible to describe the manifold acts of oppression by which this tyrant of Rome enslaved his subjects: so that by this time they were reduced to the most extreme penury and want of necessary food, a scarcity such as our contemporaries do not remember ever before to have existed at Rome.

Defeat of Maxentius's Armies in Italy.

Constantine, however, filled with compassion on account of all these miseries, began to arm himself with all warlike preparation against the tyranny. Assuming therefore the Supreme God as his patron, and invoking His Christ to be his preserver and aid, and setting the victorious trophy, the salutary symbol, in front of his soldiers and body-guard, he marched with his whole forces, trying to obtain again for the Romans the freedom they had inherited from their ancestors.

And whereas, Maxentius, trusting more in his magic arts than in the affection of his subjects, dared not even advance outside the city gates, but had guarded every place and district and city subject to his tyranny, with large bodies of soldiers, the emperor, confiding in the help of God, advanced against the first and second and third divisions of the tyrant's forces, defeated them all with ease at the first assault, and made his way into the very interior of Italy.

Death of Maxentius on the Bridge of the Tiber.

And already he was approaching very near-Rome itself, when, to save him from the necessity of fighting with all the Romans for the tyrant's sake, God himself drew the tyrant, as it were by secret cords, a long way outside the gates. And now those miracles recorded in Holy Writ, which God of old wrought against the ungodly (discredited by most as fables, yet believed by the faithful), did he in every deed confirm to all alike, believers and unbelievers, who were eye-witnesses of the wonders. For as once in the days of Moses and the Hebrew nation, who were worshipers of God, "Pharaoh's chariots and his host hath he cast into the sea and his chosen chariot-captains are drowned in the Red Sea," --so at this time Maxentius, and the soldiers and guards with him, "went down into the depths like stone," when, in his flight before the divinely-aided forces of Constantine, he essayed to cross the river which lay in his way, over which, making a strong bridge of boats, he had framed an engine of destruction, really against himself, but in the hope of ca-snaring, (a flag, standard or banner) thereby him who was beloved by God. For his God stood by the one to protect him, while the other, godless, proved to be the miserable contriver of these secret devices to his own ruin. So that one might well say, "He hath made a pit, and digged it, and is fallen into the ditch which he made. His mischief shall return upon his own head, and his violence shall, come down upon his own pate." Thus, in the present instance, under divine direction, the machine erected on the bridge, with the ambuscade concealed therein, giving way unexpectedly before the appointed time, the bridge began to sink, and the boats with the men in them went bodily to the bottom. And first the wretch himself, then his armed attendants and guards, even as the sacred oracles had before described, "sank as lead in the mighty waters." So that they who thus obtained victory from God might well, if not in the same words, yet in fact in the same spirit as the people of his great servant Moses, sing and speak as they did concerning the impious tyrant of old: "Let us sing unto the Lord, for he hath been glorified exceedingly: the horse and his rider hath he thrown into the sea. He is become my helper and my shield unto salvation." And again, "Who is like unto thee, O Lord, among the gods? who is like thee, glorious in holiness, marvelous in praises, doing wonders?"

Death of Maximin, who had attempted a Conspiracy, and of Others whom Constantine detected by Divine Revelation.

WHILE he was thus engaged, the second of those who had resigned the throne, being detected in a treasonable conspiracy, suffered a most ignominious death. He was the first whose pictures, statues, and all similar marks of honor and distinction were everywhere destroyed, on the ground of his crimes and impiety. After him others also of the same family were discovered in the act of forming secret plots against the emperor; all their intentions being miraculously revealed by God through visions to His servant.

For he frequently vouchsafed to him manifestations of himself, the Divine presence appearing to him in a most marvelous manner, and according to him manifold intimations of future events. Indeed, it is impossible to express in words the indescribable wonders of Divine grace which God was pleased to vouchsafe to His servant. Surrounded by these, he passed the rest of his life in security, rejoicing in the affection of his subjects, rejoicing too because he saw all beneath his government leading contented lives; but above all delighted at the flourishing condition of the churches of God.

He surpassed all Preceding Emperors in Devotion to God.

STANDING, as he did, alone and pre-eminent among the Roman emperors as a worshiper of God; alone as the bold proclaimer to all men of the doctrine of Christ; having alone rendered honor, as none before him had ever done, to his Church; having alone abolished utterly the error of polytheism, and discountenanced idolatry in every form: so, alone among them both during life and after death, was he accounted worthy of such honors as none can say have been attained to by any other; so that no one, whether Greek or Barbarian, nay, of the ancient Romans themselves, has ever been presented to us as worthy of comparison with him."

20

End of quotation from Eusebius

With this victory Constantine became the first Christian Roman emperor. Constantine went on to defeat Licinius in 324 A.D. and became the sole ruler of the empire. Constantine established a second capital city in Byzantium, which he renamed Constantinople. Byzantium was located on a narrow strip of land between the Mediterranean and the Black Seas. This area was a major trade route between Asia and Europe. Constantine thought the Christian religion could provide the common denominator for all of his citizens and keep them together in unity. However, the church must be in unity first. Constantine commissioned the first Ecumenical Council to meet in Nicaea in 325 A.D. to iron out the divisions in theology. The primary issues were the true nature of Christ; God or man and an understanding of the Holy Trinity. The result of the council was the creation of the Nicene or Apostle's Creed used in all Christian denominations to this day. The Trinity was seen as God with three personal disclosures. A date was also set for the celebration of Easter apart from the Jewish calendar and Passover. Easter was set as the first Sunday after the first full moon that falls on or after March 21st, which is the usual day of the vernal equinox. Twenty canons (Biblical rules) were also established having to do with church governess.

Arian, a minister under Bishop Alexander of Alexandria, disagreed that the Holy Spirit was a personal disclosure of God and that both the Holy Spirit and Christ were subservient to God. When the bishop protested, Constantine, foreseeing further unrest, sent him into exile and had him excommunicated from the church. Arian, whose position became known as Arianism, thought the Holy Spirit proceeded from the Father, not from the Father and the Son. Arian held that only God is God. This difference in the understanding of the Son as God eventually lead to a complete split between the East and the West in 1054, known as "The Great Schism." The real issue of The Great Schism was that the pope, for clarity, added "and the Son," to the Nicene Creed. The patriarchs in the East maintained that only a council can change the Creed. Hence, the real issue was the pope trying to assert his authority over both halves of the Catholic Church. The East was not having any part of it. So, the popes excommunicated each other. The significance of Constantine's involvement set the precedent for secular authorities to establish Christian doctrine. For the first time there was a merger between church and state with the state having a central concern over the rightness of church doctrine. This also set the stage for the continuing clashes for ultimate

21

authority between the emperor and the pope and later with kings and the pope, clashes which would last for a thousand years. This split in The Great Schism resulted in the church of Western Roman Catholicism and the church of Eastern Orthodoxy, both still in existence today.

The original version of the Apostle's Creed from 325 A.D. reads;

> We believe in one God, the Father Almighty, Maker of all things visible and invisible.
>
> And in one Lord Jesus Christ, the Son of God, begotten of the Father the only-begotten; that is, of the essence of the Father, God of God, Light of Light, very God of very God, begotten, not made, being of one substance (ὁμοούσιον) with the Father; by whom all things were made both in heaven and on earth; who for us men, and for our salvation, came down and was incarnate and was made man; he suffered, and the third day he rose again, ascended into heaven; from thence he shall come to judge the quick and the dead.
>
> And in the Holy Ghost.
>
> But those who say: 'There was a time when he was not;' and 'He was not before he was made;' and 'He was made out of nothing,' or 'He is of another substance' or 'essence,' or 'The Son of God is created,' or 'changeable,' or 'alterable'—they are condemned by the holy catholic and apostolic Church

The original version was revised in 381 A.D. to read as follows;

> We believe in one God, the Father Almighty, Maker of heaven and earth, and of all things visible and invisible. And in one Lord Jesus Christ, the only-begotten Son of God, begotten of the Father before all worlds (æons), Light of Light, very God of very God, begotten, not made, being of one substance with the Father; by whom all things were made; who for us men, and for our salvation, came down from heaven, and was incarnate by the Holy Ghost of the Virgin Mary, and was made man; he was crucified for us under Pontius Pilate, and suffered, and was buried, and the third day he rose again, according to the Scriptures, and ascended into heaven, and sitteth on the right hand of the Father; from thence he shall come again, with glory, to judge the quick and the dead; whose kingdom shall have no end. And in the Holy Ghost, the Lord and Giver of life, who proceedeth from the Father, who with the Father and the Son together is worshiped and glorified, who spake by the prophets. In one holy catholic and apostolic Church; we

acknowledge one baptism for the remission of sins; we look for the resurrection of the dead, and the life of the world to come. Amen.

Constantine gave Christians special considerations. He allowed Christian ministers exemption from paying taxes, he outlawed crucifixions and he stopped the battles of the gladiators as punishment for crimes. He stopped Christian persecution and he made Sunday a public holiday. He also put an end to temple prostitution among the pagan religions. These actions even brought about persecution of the pagan residents. With the designation of Constantinople as the capital of the Roman Empire, divisions developed between the western half with Rome as the capital and the eastern half governed by Constantinople. The bishop in Constantinople declared himself as pope, or as the patriarch as the pope was called in the Eastern half. The Pope in Rome refused to relinquish his title or recognize the church in Constantinople as anything but subservient to Rome.

THE CATHOLIC CHURCH

The relationship between the pope and secular rulers was in a continual state of instability. When the barbarians were sieging Europe, there were times when there was not an effective monarchy. In these instances, the pope interceded on behalf of the population and for the preservation of the church. There were also times when the secular ruler, having allied himself with the church, expected the church to do the king's bidding. And during the crusades the pope was dependent on the European monarchies to fill the ranks. There also were dominating figures that had a tremendous influence on the course of history and the balance of power between rulers and popes, such as Constantine, Charles "The Hammer" Martel, Charles the Great, AKA Charlemagne, Justinian, Charles V, and several popes: Pope Leo I, Gregory III, (the Great), Leo III, Innocent III, and Leo X.

Constantine set a precedence early on by evolving Rome into a religious monarchy. The emperor served as the connecting link between God and the world, while the state was the earthly reflection of divine law. Constantine's reasoning for this was that he was led to victory under the sign of the cross. The popes, however, thought that they were God's regent on earth and did not answer to any secular authority. Pope Leo I (440-461 A.D.) laid the theoretical foundation for papal primacy. Leo I maintained that Christ promised to build His church on Peter, the rock, and the bishops are his successor. However, when Christ asked Peter who He was Peter answered, "You are the Christ, the Son of the living God." To which Christ responded; "Blessed are you, Simon Barjona because flesh and blood did not reveal this to you, but My Father who is in heaven. I also say to you that you are Peter, and upon this rock I will build My Church;

24

and the gates of Hades will not overpower it." The interpretation of this passage of Scripture has divided the Catholic Church from all other Christian religions. Catholicism interprets this to mean that Christ will build his church on a man, Peter. Christians believe the correct interpretation is that the church will be built on the firm foundation of; "You are the Christ, the Son of the living God." Christ is the head of the church, not man. Often cited by Christians is 1st Timothy 2:5 "For there is one God, and one mediator also between God and men, the man Christ Jesus." Innocent III (1198 – 1216) would later proclaim that he was, "established as a mediator between God and man, below God but beyond man, less than God but more than man, who shall judge all and be judged by no one." In the West, the pope was the head of the Holy Roman Catholic Church. His position became greatly enhanced because there were no definitive or strong rulers for centuries. In the East, the pope or patriarch, as he was called, was appointed by the Emperor, so there was little debate about who was in charge.

There were important events in history that forced changes in the composite of the developing civilization in Europe and elsewhere that provided valuable lessons for America's Founding Fathers. In 455 A.D. the Vandals, a migrating tribe from Scandinavia captured Rome with almost no resistance and looted the city for fourteen days. This is where we get the term "vandalism." In 476, Germanic war lord Odoacer sacked Rome and declared himself king of Italy. This has been set as the date of the fall of the Western Roman Empire. However, the subsequent rulers in Rome and elsewhere in Europe managed to survive thwarting threats from Barbarians, warlords, Vikings and Muslims, to preserve Europe. There is a transition from rulers and popes in competition for dominance over the people to rulers of state and the pope ruler of the ecclesiastical. Briefly, this transition looks like this: Odoacer, of German descent, captured Rome and declared himself king. In 453 A.D. Attila the Hun died and Odoacer began to expand his territory, into what was once controlled by Attila, Central and Eastern Europe. In 493 A.D. Theodoric, king of the new Ostrogothic coalition, sliced Odoacer in half and completed his control of Italy, the Adriatic coast of Dalmatia, Sicily, Hungary, southern France and most of Spain. Upon his death the leadership in Constantinople encouraged the kingdoms of Europe to separate and establish Gothic kingdoms of their own in Italy and Spain. In 532 A.D. Emperor Justinian sent his General Belisarius to the Hippodrome to break up a gathering of folks calling for his removal from office. A riot ensued and thousands were killed. This was known as "The Massacre at the Nika Riots." Justinian then sent Belisarius to North Africa. Belisarius won a spectacular victory over the Vandals and Carthage falls. Justinian continued his conquests and captured Italy, Dalmatia, southern Spain and parts of North Africa. It is important to note that whenever people from one culture move into lands of another culture the result is often the spread of disease. In 541 A.D. there was an outbreak of the bubonic plague. The plague was called the Justinian Plague because Justinian was the emperor at the time. However, forensic evidence identifies the bacterium responsible for this pandemic as Yersinia Pestis, the same bacterium that caused the Black Death plague of 1331 – 1353 A.D. The estimated death toll was 25 million people. The church historian from the time, Evagrius Scholasticus records that he was affected with the buboes associated with the disease but survived. He also notes that the plague occurred for more times in his lifetime.

THE ISLAMIC CONQUEST

In 632 A.D. Muhammad died and the great Islamic conquest, or jihad began, with the invasion of the Near East, North Africa and most of Spain. The Muslims completely destroyed Persia, thereby denying Constantinople much of its territory and a significant part of its tax base. Constantinople's power, wealth and influence were greatly diminished, and Constantinople no longer dominated the Mediterranean and its trade routes. Twelve years after Mohammed's death in 644 A.D. Muslim jihadists conquered Spain, Syria, Palestine, Eastern Anatolia, Armenia, Upper Egypt, Lower Egypt and North Africa. The Muslim pirates then terrorized the Mediterranean, severely disrupting trade. This caused an economic disaster in Europe by diminishing products moving East to West. Without trade the businesses, farm producers and merchants suffered greatly. It is said that the cities along the Mediterranean and on the islands in the Mediterranean were reduced to villages. The disruption in trade was a foremost aspect of bringing about the Dark Ages. It took ten days to sail from Carthage (North Africa) to Italy. By land, the same trip took one hundred and forty days. Shipping a ton of grain from Egypt to Rome cost the same amount as shipping it seventy-five miles by ox cart. There would be as many as 500 ships in the harbor in Constantinople at any one time.

The Muslims desired to conquer Constantinople not only as the gateway to Europe but also to secure all of the Mediterranean trade routes and access to the Black Sea and its trade routes. Muslims attacked Constantinople from 674 to 678 A.D. but were unsuccessful in their attempt to capture the city. The Muslims again tried in 717 to 718 A.D. to take Constantinople and again failed, both attempts ended in disaster for the Muslims. The Muslims built siege towers along the walls protecting the city and waited for the navy to arrive to blockade the city's ports. The Byzantine navy employed a completely new weapon, "Greek Fire" and destroyed the Muslim ships. There is no definitive explanation of what Greek Fire is, other than the speculation that fire was somehow propelled from the Byzantine ships to set the Muslim ships on fire. The Muslim army, without its navy and weakened by famine and disease, retreated and were ambushed in their retreat. Of the 120,000 Muslims sent to capture Constantinople 30,000 returned to Persia. Two Muslim fleets were sent as reinforcements. One in 674 A.D. was destroyed after the Egyptian Coptic Christian crews defected from the ships. The other fleet, in 718 A.D., on its return, after the army abandoned the siege of Constantinople, was almost completely destroyed in a storm. The ships that escaped the storm were set on fire from the ashes coming from the erupting, Santorini volcano. Of the 1,800 ships sent to siege Constantinople five returned. As Ben Franklin said, "God governs in the affairs of men."

In 711 A.D. the Moors, Moroccan Muslims, invaded Spain, overpowering the Germanic Visigoths. The Muslim Moors tried to advance into southern France and were defeated by Charles "The Hammer" Martel in 732 A.D in the "Battle of Tours." Charles was the Duke and Prince of the Franks and assumed these positions after the death of his father, Pepin of Herstal. The Hammer restored centralized government in France and after several military successes he re-established the Franks as the undisputed ruler. Charles Martell was a Christian and ruler of France, western Germany, Switzerland, Belgium and the Netherlands and was the dominate Christian power in western Europe at the time. Martel used Christian missionaries to convert the primarily pagan German tribes to Christianity as a means of uniting his kingdom, much in the same way Constantine had done.

This defeat of the Muslim army at the "Battle of Tours" stopped the Muslim conquest of southern Europe and preserved Christianity for all of Europe. This was at a time when the Muslims were aggressively spreading Islam in the remains of the old Roman and Persian Empires. Martell's army of 15,000 was mostly infantry. The tactical advantage in the battle initially fell to the Muslims' heavy Calvary which they had developed by the use of stirrups where Martell's army had not and remained primarily as an army of infantry on foot. The mounted heavy Calvary would charge the infantry, break their ranks on the first charge, and slaughter the infantry soldiers as they broke and ran. This is one of the primary reasons the Muslims were so effective in early battle engagements against Europe. The Muslim army of 100,000 was primarily heavy Calvary. From their base in Spain the Muslims had been pillaging and plundering advancing north into France. Martell rushed his army to meet the threat and to obtain the high ground. The armies faced off for six days, the Muslims not wanting to attack higher ground and Martell with a much smaller army did not want to abandon his defensive position which offered him a decisive advantage against heavy Calvary. The difference in this battle, the Franks were men of courage and held their line. A Medieval Source Book gives this account. "And in the shock of the battle the men of the North seemed like North a sea that cannot be moved. Firmly they stood, one close to another, forming as it were a bulwark of ice; and with great blows of their swords they hewed down the Arabs. Drawn up in a band around their chief, the people of Austrasians carried all before them. Their tireless hands drove their swords down to the breasts of the foe." On the second day Martell sent scouts into the Muslim camp to free the slaves and plunder their booty. Some of the Muslims became aware of the raid and rushed to camp to protect their plunder and slaves. Others seeing the men returning to camp thought it was a retreat and they also fled. Abd er Rahman, the Muslim commander, was surrounded by Franks and killed. On the next day a repeated attack was not forthcoming. Martel sent scouts to the Muslim camp, only to find it deserted, they had fled during the night and returned to Spain.

In 800 A.D. Charlemagne ascended to power and was crowned Emperor by Pope Leo III in St. Peters. The transformation is slowly evolving. Rulers will govern their kingdoms and the pope oversees all ecclesiastical matters.

In 1346 A.D. the world was devastated by the Black Death, which started in the Far East; China, and India, and spread to Persia, Syria and Egypt. The Black Death spread to Europe killing one of every three people. The death toll for Europe is estimated at 20 million and 74 to 200 million worldwide. The Black Death had severe ramifications both culturally and religiously. The plague was called the "Scourge from God", and the laity tired of not getting an answer to their question, "How can God allow this to happen?" Hearing from clergy that it was all their fault caused them to lose confidence in the church. Culturally, the economy of many regions, including Europe collapsed. There were few workers. Productivity, farming and trade virtually came to a standstill. The plague was responsible for the elimination of serfdom, where workers gave their services for food, housing, protection and very little money in return for a month of military

29

service and a plot of land to farm. Now, workers were in huge demand. With fewer laborers their bargaining power was greatly enhanced. There were also several peasant uprisings.

The Muslim Ottoman Turks, anticipating Europe would be greatly weakened by the plague, again attacked Constantinople and finally captured the city in 1453. The Islamic destruction of Constantinople allowed the restoration of the Empire in the West on a European powerbase. Other forces also attacked Constantinople, including the capture of the city by the fourth crusade in 1202. With Constantinople, the gateway to Europe, in Muslim hands, Muslims advanced into Europe, invading the Balkans and the southern part of Greece. With the invasion of Greece, the nobles' scholars, philosophers and the wealthy fled with all of their valuables to Greece and France. This huge influx of art, books, music and brain power actually started the Renaissance Period in Europe.

Another major historical event occurred around this time in the Roman Catholic Church; the mid-evil Inquisitions. A couple groups of believers took issue with the way the Catholic Church was conducting itself in matters of orthodoxy. One group in the mid-1100's, the Cathars, which means pure, believed the Roman Catholic Church's sacramental system was evil and they were not teaching God's message. They felt that Scripture was the inerrant word of God and if a teaching was not in Scripture, to teach it was apostasy. They also thought that punishment of Christians by secular authorities was sin. Scripture clearly defines how discipline is to be conducted within the church for believers.[8] Some of the beliefs of the Cathars were also far from sound Scriptural understanding. For instance, they believed spirits were the spirits of angels trapped in human bodies being reincarnated until they reached perfection. In 1208, Pope Innocent III called for a crusade against the heresy of the Cathars. Pope Innocent III offered spiritual favors, or indulgences for anyone that would join his crusade and hunt down the Cathars, which just about wiped them out.

Another group that were considered heretics by the church like the Cathars were the Waldensians. The Waldensians received the gospel of Christianity from Paul. The Waldensians were a very peaceful people, whose only mission was to spread the Gospel message. Under the extreme persecution of Nero (54 – 68 A.D.) towards all Christians the Waldensians moved into the Piedmont Valley in the northwest mountains

---

[8] Matthew 18:15-17

30

of Italy. Like all Christians, they again went through severe persecution under Emperor Diocletian (284 – 305 A.D.). Historically this is referred to as "The Great Persecution," with over 20,000 Christians being killed. This forced the Waldensians deeper into the valley. Evangelicals of today would have had tremendous support for the Waldensians who, in a sense, were the first Protestants. The Waldensians held with a strict interpretation of the Bible and the Bible was the only rule of faith. They abhorred the Catholic Church as they thought it retained much of the pagan influences from before Christianity. They refused the doctrine of transubstantiation, where the Catholic Church maintains that the bread and wine of communion actually become the blood and body of Christ. They also would not treat the pope with veneration, nor did they believe that one could only come to faith in Christ through the sacraments and a priest. They saw none of this in Scripture. They would make copies of the Bible and portions of the Bible and hand them out telling people to read it for themselves. Twice, Italy and France sent armies into the valley to rid it of the heretics. With the reformation the Waldensians joined the Protestant Church. Persecution continued in Europe against the new heretics, the Protestants. Twenty-nine Waldensians, like many other Protestants, fled to the New World. The Waldensians that sailed to America founded Valdese in North Carolina.

Initially the internal persecution, or crusades, were against the Cathars and the Waldensians, both of which professed reading Scripture for oneself. Later the inquisitions were directed against the Protestants and Lutherans who also professed people should read the Scripture for themselves and form a personal relationship with God through Christ, not the pope or the church. There were two phases to the inquisition: the mid-evil phase of Europe and the Spanish Inquisition.

The Spanish inquisition was started when King Ferdinand and Queen Isabella asked Pope Sixtus IV for permission to conduct an inquisition in 1492. At the outset, bishops would travel within the Holy Roman Empire and make "inquires" regarding one's faith, looking for heretics, which was anyone that did not follow Catholic Church doctrine. Civilian authorities picked up the cause as a means of increasing and consolidating their power in society by enforcing orthodoxy. Eventually the bishops were replaced by monks, as the inquisitors, primarily from the order of the Franciscan and Dominican Monasteries. It's difficult to find good information on the actual number of deaths, and persons imprisoned or tortured during the inquisitions. Records from the time are hard to come

31

by and there is a wide range in the estimates of people actually killed, imprisoned and tortured, depending on the tapestry one is trying to weave. Some sources are obviously trying to minimize the extent of this tragic time and there are those whose numbers seem unrealistically high. In 1184 A.D. Pope Lucius III called for an inquisition stating, "To abolish the malignity of diverse heresies which are lately sprung up in most parts of the world, it is but fitting that the power committed to the church should be awakened, that by the concurring assistance of the Imperial strength, both the insolence and mal-pertness (impudent) of the heretics in their false design may be crushed... We likewise declare all, be liable to the same sentence...unless by adjuring his heresy and making satisfaction he immediately returns to the orthodox faith, we decree him to be left to the sentence of the secular judge, to receive condign (deserved) punishment according to the quality of the offense." We will never know how many people were killed during the inquisitions, but we can understand its origin and the ramifications for civilization. Religion was the prominent influence in most people's lives. People of faith were not as concerned about this life as much as they were concerned about the next life. That focus did not change until the Age of Enlightenment, or The Age of Reason and later with an even greater impact in the 19th century with the advent of Darwin's book "The Origins of Species," evolutionary biology.

From the time of Constantine, Medieval Christians were the common link throughout European cultures. Denial of any of the truths of doctrine emanating from the church or disregarding the divine appointment of the pope was a grievous offense; in fact, the bases of heresy. Regarding heresy, the church had two primary motives for the inquisition; to convert the heretic and to safeguard Christian society. The Catholic Church chose to be apostolic, where a church puts an emphasis on the apostle's interpretation of Scripture. Being apostolic, the church could continue the tradition of interpreting Scripture for its congregation. The mass would be read in Latin and then the priest would interpret the Scripture. This method was preferred for rendering interpretations, as opposed to teaching God's word from the Old Testament or Christ's teaching from the New Testament, both of which leave very little room for interpretation. Left to their own interpretations, they could wield the congregation's beliefs to whatever best served the purposes of the church or the pope. This is why the Catholic Church was so adamantly opposed to the laity having their own Bibles and reading the word of God for themselves. How could the Catholic Church defend indulgences when commoners would read verses such as; Psalms 49: 7 "A man cannot at all redeem a brother, nor give to God a ransom for him?"

The Spanish Inquisition was primarily directed against Jews and Muslims who professed that they had given up their previous beliefs and had returned to Catholic orthodoxy. The inquisitors were seeking those who had made this profession, yet secretly continued in their former beliefs. After Spain's experience of 700 years of domination by Muslims, Ferdinand and Isabella wanted all but Catholics and Christians expelled from their country. If one was found guilty, they were "relaxed," probably one of the first accounts of political correctness. To be "relaxed" meant to be turned over to the civilian authorities to be burned at the stake. Anyone found guilty of heresy was imprisoned or burned at the stake. Most of those imprisoned died during their imprisonment. The church confiscated all assets of those found guilty of heresy. The last person executed in an inquisition was in 1826.

The Catholic Church's practice of indulgences was first introduced by Pope Urban II to recruit warriors for the First Crusade in 1095, calling all Christians in Europe to war against Muslims in order to reclaim the Holy Land. The call was, "Deus vult", God Wills It. His offer was, "Whoever for devotion alone, but not to gain honor or money, goes to Jerusalem to libertate the Church of God can substitute this journey for all penance." The penance offered remission of temporal punishment for any participants. It didn't take long for the practice of indulgences to be misused by clergy prone to lust for greed, power and influence, the three human incessant motivations that can be traced all through human history as the primary factors in the fall of civilizations worldwide, and almost all wars. The practice of indulgences went through a resurgence against the Cathars, the Waldensians and again with Pope Leo X, (1513-1521) as he contemplated ways to finance building St Peter's Basilica.

There was a process that became known as "Simony", which had its origins in the book of Acts, Chapter 8 verses 9 through 21. 18 "Now when Simon saw that the Spirit was bestowed through the laying on of the apostles' hands, he offered them money, saying, 'Give this authority to me as well, so that everyone on whom I lay my hands may receive the Holy Spirit.' But Peter said to him, "May your silver perish with you, because you thought you could obtain the gift of God with money! "You have no part or portion in this matter, for your heart is not right before God." Simony became the process of a person of wealth or position buying a position within the church. It certainly is hypocritical for the Catholic Church to condone this portion of Scripture, which condemns the process, and allowed this practice to take place. Critics of Christianity lay claim that religion is the cause of most wars and human suffering. However, the truth remains that human suffering is caused by evil people in positions of power and their continual lust and greed, for more power, wealth and influence.

Albert of Mainz bought the position of bishop and a second archbishop position in addition to Mainz. (Incidentally, holding two offices is against canon law.) This situation was overlooked by Leo X. Albert proposed to Leo X that he would sell indulgences to pay off the debt he had incurred in buying his positions and would send half of the profits to Leo X for the construction of the church of St Peter. Leo X agreed but thought they should keep the agreement secret as it may reflect negatively on the church. Albert, not wanting to be involved with anything that may tarnish his position or prestige, hired friar Johann Tetzel to sell the indulgences. It should be remembered there was no effective way of communicating until recent history. Word would have to travel by ship, on foot, or horse, hence many activities were conducted unobserved and surreptitiously. Without the rule of law how does a commoner challenge injustice? They cannot, they are subject to the capricious whims of someone above their station.

Tetzel expanded the importance of indulgences. Not only could paying a monetary indulgence replace performing penance to recompense a sinner for his sin, a sin that had already been confessed and forgiven, an indulgence could reduce the amount of time a loved one or family member would spend in purgatory. Tetzel was famous for giving a fire and brimstone sermon and concluding by saying, "As soon as the gold in the coffer rings, the rescued soul to heavens springs." In the Catholic tradition purgatory is a place a person goes after death to undergo purification so they may enter heaven. The two verses the church cites as proof of the existence of purgatory are 1 Corinthians 3:15, "If the work is burned up, the builder will suffer lose; the builder will be saved, but only as through fire." Thus, a person in purgatory is in a perpetual firestorm. The second verse is taken from 2 Maccabees 12:45; "But if he was looking for the splendid reward that is laid up for those who fall asleep in godliness, it is a holy and pious thought, therefore he made attornment for the dead, so that they might be delivered from their sin." This is one of the reasons the Books of 1st and 2nd Maccabees is included in the Catholic Bible and not in other translations.

The sacrament of penance works like this in the Catholic Church: a person is baptized as soon as possible after birth and enters a state of grace. It is through the sacrament of baptism that we receive the Holy Spirit and become members of the people of God, of the body of Christ, which is the church. A person is washed, cleaned and the devil is cast out. However, sin pulls you out of the system of grace. A person sins and must confess their sins to a priest. There are mortal sins and there are venial sins. A venial sin can be considered a minor sin, yet it is still an offence to God. Mortal sins are of such a grievous nature that a person who commits one can kill the grace allotted to believers by Christ's sacrificial death on the cross. There are seven mortal sins; lust, gluttony, greed, sloth, wrath, envy and pride. The Catholic Church teaches that mortal sins cannot be forgiven and must be absolved by a priest. However, even after the sin has been absolved the Christian must make satisfaction for the sin they have committed, and this is where the sacrament of penance comes in. After confession a person must be genuinely sorry for the sin they have committed and must resolve to not repeat the sin. After confession the priest will assign a penance. A penance can be a lot of things-reading Scripture for a certain amount of time for a certain length of time, saying the rosary x number of times, saying prayers x amount of times, fasting, or doing something nice to your enemy. The penance is usually associated with the sin. The priest will then offer a prayer of absolution. If a person cannot perform the penance, or chooses not to, money may be offered instead. None of which is in Scripture. It does not take much for one to see that this system is vulnerable to abuse. The reoccurring theme we see through all of mankind through all of history is fallen man's proclivity toward lust for greed, influence, wealth and power. It has not changed since the Garden of Eden. The desire for significance, "you will be as God," people do not want God to be God they want to be god. The rationale behind giving money for penance was that the money provided would finance the recipient so they could continue to work as God has called them. Not everyone agreed with the idea of monetary remuneration as part of the sacrament of penance.

Indulgences were not the only situation that caused a strain in the relationship between the Roman Catholic Church, the clergy and the laity. The composite of several world changing events facilitated the acceptance for the timing of Luther's Reformation. The Black Death prompted people to look for the meaning of life. Simony was seen as the corruption within the church. In 1309 Clement V was elected the first French pope. It was thought by many that Philipp the IV of France was instrumental in securing Clements papacy. These situations resulted in a very stressful atmosphere in Rome for Clement V, hence he chose to move the papacy to Avignon in France. Most of the men Clement V appointed as Cardinals were French and, since the Cardinals elect the pope, the next seven popes were French. All, of whom, chose to remain in Avignon. Catherine of Siena and St. Bridget of Sweden persuaded Gregory XI to move back to Rome. He did so in 1377, but he died in 1378 and was succeeded by Urban VI. Urban VI was so hostile to the cardinals that thirteen of them went on to elect another pope. For the next four decades there were two popes and two papal curiae; - one in France and one in Rome. There was also a brief time when there were three pope's indicative of the need for significance; lust, greed, power, wealth and influence. This situation quite naturally caused a lot of confusion. With whom would the rulers address their issues? The French pope would favor French issues and the Roman pope would favor Italian issues. The rulers of Scotland, England, the Netherlands, Germany and Denmark were at a loss as to whose decrees they were to follow. This division would also come to be known as "The Great Schism," because of the ramifications it held for the church. The Schism greatly reduced the authority of the popes and the church. The laity lost confidence in the church and the pope, which had already been weakened by the Black Death; if they could no longer manage their own affairs how could the people be confident, they can manage theirs? The schism also gave the rulers more power and authority as the people began to look to their leaders for leadership. With the weakening of the affiliation with the church, people and rulers began to think it terms of nationalism. It meant more to be German or English rather than Catholic. The population grew weary of the brutality of the inquisitions. People were also horrified by the brutal jihad of the Muslims who issued an ultimatum to convert to Islam or be killed. In the final analysis people came to view Islam and Catholicism as slavery. If your father was Muslim, then you were Muslim at birth. In the Catholic faith, you were baptized as soon as possible after birth and a Catholic for life. Both religions told people what to believe and how to live their lives, which amounts to a form of slavery.

None of this history escaped the notice of the Founding Fathers of America. Freedom became a basic tenant of America's unalienable rights. A man must be free to choose his brand of Christianity. The Founding Fathers were only interested in Christianity, as is evidenced by the

Mayflower Compact and the state charters of the original thirteen colonies, which we will get to later.

EUROPEAN INFLENCES

Populations continued to grow, and technology continued to improve, as did living conditions; however, war and disease continued to exert forces against peaceful progress. From 1337 to 1776 A.D. there were six events that would completely transform the world and all of humanity, including; four important events in Europe that reshaped Europe and had profound implications on the New World: the 100 Years War, 1337-1453 A.D., the Protestant Reformation, the Thirty Years War from 1618 – 1648 A.D. and the Muslim invasion. These were followed by the French and Indian War in America, Europe and Canada, and the American Revolution.

First, a little background. At the beginning of the first century most of the occupied land and peoples lived within the Holy Roman Empire. There were other small kingdoms and provinces that were outside the borders of the Roman Empire. Records show that in the year 1A.D. there were an estimated 170,000,000 people living on the planet and 50 to 90%, which means nobody knows, were living in the Holy Roman Empire. There was also the Han Dynasty in China. Most regions of the globe were populated by various tribes as was made possible by the breakup of the supercontinent after Noah's flood, according to Dr. Brown's theory,(explained later in this text). The tribes were of a specific ethnicity and often an ethnic group had many different tribes. As a reference, no one knows for sure how many Native Americans lived in the U.S. prior to 1492, but there were an estimated 562 tribes. As the population grew, tribes expanded their territories - which usually meant conflict. The Zhu-Zhu in China expelled the Huns from what is now Mongolia. The Huns went in search of a new homeland. The first tribes to fall to the Huns were

38

the Alans of Southern Russia. Under the warrior chief Attila, they aggressively moved west, forcing the tribes of Germany into areas of the Holy Roman Empire. Germans originally came from the North German Plain and Southern Scandinavia. They were known as Goths (Ostrogoths and Visigoths,) Vandals, Franks, Saxons, Lombard's, Burgundians and Angels. The people of the German tribes were primarily hunters and shepherds. Very few were farmers.

In 375 A.D. the Huns defeated the Ostrogoths and the Visigoths. The Roman Army attempted to push the fleeing Germans back but were defeated by the Ostrogoths and the Visigoths. The Germans were brutal fighters and liked to press the battle into close hand-to- hand combat. The Romans now had to settle with the Goths. The Romans agreed to let them live within the borders of the Empire under their own rulers. The Romans also enlisted the brave German fighters into their ranks to fend off further advances from the Huns and other barbarians. Then the grievances began. The Romans passed a law that Germans could not marry citizens of the Empire. The Germans were not able to buy land within the Empire as they were promised. The German soldiers also thought they were being treated as second class citizens. Alaric, king of the Visigoths was a very accomplished strategist and soldier. He led his troops, both German and Roman to many victories. When he did not get the promotion, he thought was due him because of his leadership, he revolted. In 410 A.D. he led his army into Rome, the slaves joined his ranks, and the city was sacked. This is the point many historians call the beginning of the end of the Western Holy Roman Empire. The Visigoths settled in Southern France, which was called Gaul at the time. Gaul was a Celtic Territory which was later called Francia, meaning, "country of the Franks." The Visigoths continued south into Spain. An alliance of German tribes defeated Atilla and his army in 455. The Saxons and Angels settled in England, hence the term Anglo-Saxton for that era. The name "England" has its origins in an older word Englaland, which means land of the angels. It was named after one of the Germanic tribes, the Angels, occupying the island.

THE 100 YEARS WAR

The Hundred Years War, which was actually 116 years, was a series of conflicts fought between England and France. The war actually had its beginnings in 1066 when William the Conqueror invaded Britain. William the Conqueror, or the Duke of Normandy, can trace his lineage to the Vikings. The Vikings originated from Denmark, Norway and Sweden. In 845 A.D. the Vikings sacked the city of Paris. The French king Charles the Simple, in order to make peace with the Vikings and to stave off further raids, gave the area of France, known as Normandy (Norman, men of the north) to the Vikings as a permanent settlement in 911. When William the Conqueror invaded Britain he declared himself king of England. This declaration resulted in many revolts, which in many cases resembled a civil war by the local population-primarily Angels and Saxons. The Hundred Years War lasted through five kings in both France and England. The core issue was that, with the collapse of the Holy Roman Empire, people gave their allegiance to their king and country. The king of England was French and had land holdings in France. For four generations the claims of land in France, and who would rule France sparked many conflicts and battles cumulatively called the Hundred Years War. In 1328 A.D. Charles IV of France died, leaving no heirs to the throne. The closest male blood relative was Edward III, king of England, who laid claim to the throne. The French considered this inconceivable and appointed a distant cousin of Charles, who became Philip VI of France. Philip VI began taking control of English land in France which prompted Edward III to reassert his claim to the French throne. By 1337 A.D. the only English holding left in France was Gascony, and Philip VI laid claim to that as well. England sent its army to France to protect its land holdings. With its better army, initial English victories at Crécy, Poitiers and Agincourt encouraged the English and convinced them to continue funding the war effort. The English were also incorporating new battle tactics that the French had a hard time adjusting to. The introduction of the long bow by the English allowed them to engage the enemy at greater distances. The arrows from the longbow, with greater speed than conventional arrows, were able to pierce armor. The ultimate culmination in battle was decided by who was victorious in the inevitable hand-to-hand combat, each side trying to inflict more casualties than the opposing army. The long bow was able to engage the enemy at greater distance, giving the archers more time to reduce the enemy's numbers before the hand-to-hand fighting began. Troops also began to develop the Light Cavalry, which were mounted troops that would take up positions in front of the army, a vanguard-on the flanks, and as a rear guard. They served as scouts-a buffer between armies-and if the opportunity presented itself as a quick strike force, referred to as a skirmish. The English also began a strategy of occupation, occupying lands they had taken. The French troops wondered how soon they would be trained to counter this new warfare.

Once again, we see the providence of God in the affairs of human history and the callousness of man. At the age of thirteen Joan of Arc began to hear a voice from God telling her to rid France of the English and see Charles VII crowned as king. Charles VI died in 1422 and Charles VII could not be crowned king because the coronations always took place in the city of Remis, which was controlled by the English. By this time the English controlled half of France. Joan rode five hundred miles to see Charles the Dauphin (a title given to a prince waiting to be crowned as king). Joan explained her visions to the captain of the guard, and he turned her away. Joan returned the following year and the captain of the guard impressed by her piety and persistence, allowed her to see Charles the Dauphin. Charles was very skeptical and reluctant to see Joan. He placed an imposter on the throne and hid among the court personnel. Joan was not deceived and walked straight to Charles. The members of Charles's court demanded proof of her claims. She told them to contact the prelates at the Church of Saint Catherine in Fierbois and deliver to her the sword behind the altar. They responded that there was no sword behind the altar. Joan told them to dig - the sword was found and inlaid with five crosses. The legend of the sword with five crosses is that Charles Martel, "The Hammer," grandfather of Charlemagne and the one who halted the Muslim invasion of Europe founded the church of Saint Catherine, buried his sword under the altar, for the next person God would send to find it and save France. Charles the Dauphin had Joan interrogated by his theologians, and upon their advice he granted Joan an audience. Joan told Charles to give her an army and she would rid France of the English and see him crowned king. She told Charles that the French were losing the battle at Orleans and with a small army she could assure a victory. (She would have had no way of knowing that in fact the French were losing the battle.) Then Joan approached Charles and whispered something in his ear. There is no record of what Joan said to Charles but he immediately commissioned Joan as a captain and gave her an army to lead – well, co-lead.

On her path to Orléans Joan's army freed many towns and villages from the English. Not one of the battles were lost. As Joan and her army approached Orléans the French were attacking from the west. Joan entered the city unopposed, from the east, bringing much needed food and medical supplies. As in all the other towns, Joan was treated as a saint. There were prophecies and folklore about a virgin maiden that would save France; the people believed this to be Joan. Joan led a charge against the English and was shot with an arrow. She quickly was bandaged and returned to the fight. The French troops were inspired. The English troops were dismayed however, because they had proclaimed that they had sent Joan to hell. The English defenses failed, and the city was taken by the French. Joan and her army went deep into enemy territory, 150 miles, to Reims and liberated the town from English control. Now, Charles was able to travel to Reims to be crowned king of France.

After the coronation the French wanted to press on to liberate Paris; however, Joan had not received any messages from God about Paris. Again, many battles were fought in towns and villages on the way through the English occupied lands. Joan was captured by the Burgundians, a Germanic tribe that inhabited Burgundy. They offered her to Charles VII for a ransom. Charles VII, aware of the intense popularity of Joan and fearing her power and influence could threaten his throne, refused to pay the ransom. The Burgundians then ransomed Joan to England. England paid the ransom and subjected Joan to an inquisition. Not finding any concrete evidence against her, and unable to trip her up in her testimony, they charged her with heresy from a passage in Deuteronomy about a woman wearing a man's clothing. She had adorned men's clothing as battle dress because there was no battle dress designed for women- and she had cut her hair short. (Deuteronomy 22:5). Found guilty, the English burned Joan at the stake. It was a revenge murder - pure and simple - for her leading the French to victory.

The 100 Years War brought many changes to Europe. During the middle ages most land was governed under the feudal system, in which Noblemen, would make a land grant to a peasant who would farm the land and was usually required to give a month of each year in service to the noblemen in military service. Most of the service included participating in wars that the noblemen were engaged in but unwilling to fight themselves. The Black Plague virtually eliminated the Feudal system, the 100 Years

War eliminated it for good. Other major changes effecting society included most of the countries that were now forming with the absence of the Holy Roman Empire developed their own standing armies. These armies were well trained, and the soldiers were disciplined. Mercenaries were given ultimatums for joining the military or being hunted down. The mercenary armies exacted a heavy toll on the civilian population and would no longer be tolerated. They had little regard for the countries or the population of foreign lands, and often treated the population horribly by; looting, burning and raping. A sense of nationalism developed, and countries began to take shape. Some of the first among these were the Dutch Republic, Switzerland, Portugal, Spain, France, England, Germany, Denmark, Poland, Norway, and the Ukraine. There were also major changes in military equipment and strategies; the longbow and light cavalry in particular and fighting skirmishes rather than army-to-army confrontations.

MARTIN LUTHER

One of the most significant contributing historical events that lead to the Protestant Reformation was a monk, friar, priest and professor named Martin Luther. Proverbs 20:24 says; "Man's steps are ordained by the Lord; How then can man understand his way?" Keep in mind that in the early 1500's there were many grievances against the church: Simony, two and three popes, the inquisitions, the Black Plague, the persecution of the Cathars, and the Waldensians, whose brutal repression resulted in riots.

Martin Luther was constantly beleaguered with guilt. How could he ever be good enough to be granted eternal life? Mankind incessantly falls into sin, even those with the best intentions. Most people will unintentionally violate one or more of the seven mortal sins repeatedly. Luther never felt forgiven, and even when he had been absolved of his sin, he wasn't sure that in his heart he was truly emotionally sorry or that he was sanctified. He struggled with his will. A person must truly feel convicted, not just satisfied because some tradition was followed. In 1515, Martin was studying Scripture and came across several verses that would change his life and change the world forever and would forever remove the papacy as the organizing principle of the church. Romans 1:17 "For in it the righteousness of God is revealed from faith to faith; as it is written, 'But the righteous man shall live by faith.' The general understanding of the verse, according to the Catholic Church, was that righteousness was tied up with merit; the good works of a Christian manifested in their behavior throughout their life. Additionally, Ephesians 2:8 "For by grace you have been saved through faith; and that not of yourself, it is the gift of God; not as a result of works..." And Romans 4:5 "But to the one who does not work, but believes in Him who justifies the ungodly, his faith is credited as righteousness." This changed everything for Luther. Our righteousness is

44

the righteousness of Christ, and if we, in faith, believe that Christ's sacrificial death on the cross atoned for our sins, then we receive our righteousness from Christ. A gift not because of anything we have or will do - it is a gift. Luther called this the "Great Exchange." Christ took our sins and gave us His righteousness. Because of God's grace we will receive that which we do not deserve - righteousness. And because of His mercy we will not receive the thing we do deserve - judgment. This understanding is what Luther comes to call "Justification by Faith." Because of our faith in what Christ has accomplished on the cross, and if we truly believe that, then we are just before God. By faith alone, not by any thing we do. Especially not by buying favors, which amounts to bribery. As close as we can tell this new understanding came to Luther in about 1515. Usually when we have these life changing revelations it takes a while before we can fully acclimate to our new understanding and the implications of it, especially if the revelation is contrary to currently accepted doctrine.

There had been a long tradition in Wittenberg within academia that if someone wished to invite a debate, they would post the questions or assertions on the door of the All Saints Church. Luther famously posted his 95 Theses on the door of the church on October 31, 1517, All Saint Day, (AKA All Hallows' Day). The month before, Luther also posted 97 theses, inviting debate. These 97 were very theological in nature. Thesis five stated, "It is false to state that man's inclination is free to choose between either of two opposites. Indeed, the inclination is not free, but captive." Thesis ten read; "One must concede that the will is not free to strive toward whatever is declared good." Number seventeen read; "Man is by nature unable to want God to be God. Indeed, he must himself want to be god, and does not want God to be God." It is unknown if any debate occurred regarding his 97 theses, but it is clear that Luther was trying to formulate a new theology that was contrary to current church doctrine. Martin Luther was a professor of moral theology at the University of Halle-Wittenberg in the cities of Halle and Wittenberg in Saxony-Anhalt, Germany. This is also where friar Johann Tetzel was hawking indulgences. We can imagine, that as Luther was working through his undeveloped theology and concluding that works contribute nothing to your salvation, then buying your way to heaven was even more grievance. Luther's 95 Thesis focused on the practice of indulgencies and was not directed at the Catholic Church. Thesis twenty-one reads; "Thus those indulgence preachers are in error who say that a man is absolved from every penalty and saved by papal indulgences."

Thesis twenty-seven states; "They preach only human doctrines who say that as soon as the money clinks into the money chest, the soul flies out of purgatory." It is important to keep in mind how difficult communication was at this time. Luther, in his naiveté, was calling out "those indulgence preachers," not fully understanding that this current resurgence of collecting indulgences was sanctioned by Pope Leo X and he did not anticipate the hostile response he would receive. Luther sent a copy of his 95 Theses to Albert of Mainz, who sent a copy to Pope Leo X. A copy was also translated from Latin and printed in Germany. Many copies were handed out to the local population, which created widespread discontent. The pope had no choice but to respond. Most debates or attempts to resolve challenging and controversial subject matter are hidden in camouflage and subterfuge, as was certainly the case in the pope's response to Luther's 95 Theses. Always, there are two factors at play – the stated grievance, and the true, unspoken issue.

The pope first sent Sylvester Prierias, the chief theologian in Rome, to review Luther's theology. Prierias told Luther that papal authority was supreme and if he persisted in pressing the issue, he could be branded a heretic. Failing in his mission, Leo X sent Cardinal Cajetan to pressure the local prince, Fredrick the Wise, to send Luther to Rome. Luther refused to go to Rome, so Cajetan and Luther met in Augsburg. The net result was that Cajetan affirmed the supremacy of the pope and Luther would not budge on his position that, given a push between the pope and Scripture, Scripture supersedes the pope. Luther came to understand that the practice of indulgences is not something carried on only by some of the local preachers but rather is a broad practice within the church, sanctioned by the pope. The issue of indulgences transitioned into one of Luther challenging the pope's authority to promote or enforce indulgences. It became a matter of challenging the pope's infallibility; if Luther is right, the pope can be wrong. If that is the case, the pope has no right to rule on doctrine or interpret Scripture, so all we must rely on is Scripture and the Holy Spirit guiding our understanding through enlightenment. Therefore, every person should possess and be able to read the Bible and understand what it means for themselves.

In June of 1520, the pope issued a papal bull (public decree) citing forty-one beliefs of Luther, which deviated from Roman Catholic Church doctrine and regarded as heresy. The real nucleus of the bull was that it accused Luther of attacking the church's practice of indulgences and called his attack unwarranted and unjustified. The second major point is that Luther has attacked the authority of the papacy, attempting to lessen the church's role in the lives of everyday believers. The bull declared Luther a heretic and threatened him with excommunication from the church if he did not respond. Luther could not believe that no one in the church supported him and from this point on referred to the pope as the anti-Christ. He was not just name calling; he really believed this; furthermore, if the clergy could not see the obvious Scriptural interpretation of justification by faith, the church must be under the influence of Satan. At this time in history heretics were still put to death for heresy. The church would never execute anyone on their own, because they did not want the blood on their hands, so heretics were turned over to the local authorities for execution. On Dec 10, 1521, Luther responded in defiance by burning the bull. It is a rather dramatic scene of lighting a bonfire and casting the bull into the fire. The pope responded by issuing another bull on Jan 3, 1522, excommunicating Luther from the church and branding him a heretic. Luther must now appear before the civilian authorities. If they agree with the pope's bull for heresy, Luther will be executed.

At this time Charles the V was the Holy Roman Emperor, which was an elected position. He was certainly the most powerful man in the empire. However, the empire was governed by 300 princes. The emperor, on occasion, would call a congress, which was called a "Diet," where the emperor and all the princes would gather for issues of governance of all the providences. The Diet of 1522 was being held in the city of Worms, and Luther was summoned to the Diet of Worms. The trial was held and if the majority agreed with the pope Luther would be executed. Charles the V told Fredrick the Wise of Saxony to deliver Martin Luther to the Diet to determine his guilt or innocence. Fredrick asked Charles for a decree of safe passage for Luther, which meant that if Luther was found guilty, he would not be immediately executed but could return to Wittenberg for execution. Charles the V granted Fredrick's request.

A prominent figure in the life of Luther was Johann Eck, a major theologian at the time from the University of Leipzig. It was Eck who debated Luther at both the Heidelberg and Leipzig Disputations. Eck was a defender of the Catholic faith and a highly respected Dominican friar. It was also Eck that presented the case against Luther at the Diet of Worms. When Luther entered the Diet there was a table holding all of the writings of Luther. Eck asked Luther if the writings were his. Luther reviewed the literature and said that they were his. Eck then asked Luther to recant all of his writings. Luther replied that he wanted the night to think about it. Luther thought it unfair to be asked to recant all of his writings. There was much of his theology that was not at issue with the church; by recanting it all he and his theology would stand for nothing. From Luther's own testimony it was a night of doubt, prayer and Scripture. His stance had been 'Am I alone wise?" Now he had to decide if he was willing to die for his beliefs.

The next morning Eck repeated his questions and Luther's response has become famous: "Unless I am convinced by proofs from the Scripture or by plain and clear reason and arguments, I cannot and will not retract, for it is neither safe nor wise to do anything against conscience. Here I stand, I can do no other. God help me, Amen!" On May 25th it was decided the pope was right. Luther was a heretic, declared an outlaw, and was to be arrested and executed as soon as the safe conduct expired. Luther immediately left for Wittenberg. As he was traveling, he was kidnapped by employees of Fredrick the Wise and taken to Wartburg Castle. Fredrick the Wise told his men to find a safe place for Luther to ride out the storm, but they were not to tell him where they had taken him. When Fredrick the Wise was asked by the pope and Charles V, on several occasions, where Luther was Fredrick replied, without lying, that he had no idea as to Luther's location.

It took a good deal of courage for Fredrick the Wise to align himself against the two most powerful men in the Empire at the time. Fredrick got his courage from a dream he had the night before Luther hung his 95 Thesis on the Door of All Saints Church. He shared his dream with his brother.

"Brother, I must tell you a dream which I had last night, and the meaning of which I should like much to know. It is so deeply impressed on my mind, that I will never forget it, were I to live a thousand years. For I dreamed it thrice, and each time with new circumstances."

Duke John: "Is it a good or a bad dream?"

Fredrick the Wise: "I know not; God knows."

Duke John: "Do not be uneasy at it; but be so good as tell it to me."

Fredrick: "Having gone to bed last night, fatigued and out of spirits, I fell asleep shortly after my prayer, and slept calmly for about two hours and a half; I then awoke, and continued awake to midnight, all sorts of thoughts passing through my mind. Among other things, I thought how I was to observe the Feast of All Saints. I prayed for the poor souls in purgatory; and supplicated God to guide me, my counsels, and my people according to truth. I again fell asleep, and then dreamed that Almighty God sent me a monk, who was a true son of the Apostle Paul. All the saints accompanied him by order of God, in order to bear testimony before me, and to declare that he did not come to contrive any plot, but that all that he did was according to the will of God. They asked me to have the goodness graciously to permit him to write something on the door of the church of the Castle of Wittenberg. This I granted through my chancellor. Thereupon the monk went to the church and began to write in such large characters that I could read the writing at Schweinitz. The pen which he used was so large that its end reached as far as Rome, where it pierced the ears of a lion that was crouching there and caused the triple crown upon the head of the Pope to shake. All the cardinals and princes, running hastily up, tried to prevent it from falling. You and I, brother, wished also to assist, and I stretched out my arm; — but at this moment I awoke, with my arm in the air, quite amazed, and very much enraged at the monk for not managing his pen better. I recollected myself a little; it was only a dream.

"I was still half asleep, and once more closed my eyes. The dream returned. The lion, still annoyed by the pen, began to roar with all his might, so much so that the whole city of Rome, and all the States of the Holy Empire, ran to see what the matter was. The Pope requested them to oppose this monk, and applied particularly to me, on account of his being in my country. I again awoke, repeated the Lord's prayer, entreated God to preserve his Holiness, and once more fell asleep."

"Then I dreamed that all the princes of the Empire, and we among them, hastened to Rome, and strove, one after another, to break the pen; but the more we tried the stiffer it became, sounding as if it had been made of iron. We at length desisted. I then asked the monk (for I was sometimes at Rome, and sometimes at Wittenberg) where he got this pen, and why it was so strong. 'The pen,' replied he, 'belonged to an old goose of Bohemia, a hundred years old. I got it from one of my old schoolmasters. As to its strength, it is owing to the impossibility of depriving it of its pith or marrow; and I am quite astonished at it myself.' Suddenly I heard a loud noise — a large number of other pens had sprung out of the long pen of the monk. I awoke a third time: it was daylight."

Duke John: "Chancellor, what is your opinion? Would we had a Joseph, or a Daniel, enlightened by God!"

Chancellor: "Your highness knows the common proverb, that the dreams of young girls, learned men, and great lords have usually some hidden meaning. The meaning of this dream, however, we shall not be able to know for some time — not till the things to which it relates have taken place. Wherefore, leave the accomplishment to God, and place it fully in his hand."

Duke John: "I am of your opinion, Chancellor; 'tis not fit for us to annoy ourselves in attempting to discover the meaning. God will overrule all for his glory."

Fredrick: "May our faithful God do so; yet I shall never forget, this dream. I have, indeed, thought of an interpretation, but I keep it to myself. Time, perhaps, will show if I have been a good diviner.

While at Wartburg Castle, Luther took the name Junker George. He formalizes his complete separation from the Catholic Church and set about to dissolve Catholic dogma. He solidified his theology and translated the Bible from Latin, Greek and Hebrew into German. With the advent of the printing press, Luther's work was broadly distributed. He accomplished what he had envisioned since 1515. He put the Scripture in the hands of the laity. With the advent of the printing press he was able to accomplish this very central part of his new system of beliefs Protestant Theology. Jan Hus, (the old goose of Bohemia) who a hundred years before Luther had similar complaints, concerns and ideas, but, without broad support that Luther achieved through broad distribution of his work, Hus was burned at the stake. John Wycliff was also burned at the stake for translating the Bible into English and professing that every man has the right to examine the Bible for himself. The church was particularly vindictive of Wycliff's belief that," Every man, priest or layman, holds an equal place in the eyes of God." People who began to follow Luther's brand of Christianity came to be called Lutherans. Luther said that he had done nothing, that Christ had done it all; they should therefore call themselves Christians.

Martin Luther's primary beliefs for which he was accused of heresy, because they contradicted Roman Catholicism, can be summarized as follows:

Luther could never reconcile himself to his sin. There were times when he would spend up to six hours in the confessional. His moral dilemma was wondering how he, a sinful, fallen man could ever live up to the holiness of God. His breakthrough came when he realized, "For by grace you have been saved through faith; and that not of yourselves, it is the gift of God." Luther's conclusion was that all that is required for us to be just before God is to have faith in the incarnation of Jesus Christ, and that His death on the cross was sufficient for our propitiation. The Catholic Church maintained that works were still needed, which, in effect, said that Christ's death on the cross was not enough.

Justification by faith, was of course, in direct opposition to the doctrine of indulgences. The Catholic Church taught that because of the work of Christ and the meritorious deeds of the saints, the church has access to a "treasure of merit," - a great spiritual reservoir. Priests could draw from this to aid Christians who have insufficient merit of their own or for friends and family members in purgatory. The dominion of earth was not enough for the Catholic Church it spread its influence on prayers for the dead and ministering to suffering souls in purgatory, neither of which are found in Scripture. The Protestant Christian belief was that all believers were saints and that indulgences were works and detracted from justification by faith. Jesus Christ bridged the gap between God and man. Man has been reconciled through Christ. Another point of contention was Luther's assertion that the sole source of authority was Scripture, not the pope or traditions, moreover, Scripture does not have to be read by the pope - every man, women and child should be able to read Scripture for themselves. As it was, the priest read a portion of Scripture at mass in Latin and then interpret the passage for the congregation.

Luther's stance was; by faith alone, in Christ alone, by grace alone. This was in direct contradiction to the claim of the Catholic Church, that the pope was the judge of the world, "set in the midst between God and man, below God and above man." However, now, with the Bible in the hands of the laity, they could read for themselves that, "There is but one God and one Mediator between man and God," Christ - not the pope. There was also an issue with the Catholic doctrine of transubstantiation, in which the church maintains that at communion the bread becomes Christ's actual flesh and the wine His actual blood. Luther avowed that these were symbols of His body and blood, not actual physical elements. The bread and wine, Luther asserted, served as a symbolic memorial so we would not forget Christ's command, as Scripture says, "Do this in remembrance of Me."

Luther also took issue with celibacy. He thought marriage and children were a gift and blessing from God and should be available to everyone. He could find no justification for celibacy in Scripture, and Scripture does say children are a gift from God - the fruit of the womb is a reward (Psalms 127:3). Many monks and nuns left their monasteries and nunneries to be married. Luther married a nun and they had six children and adopted an additional four more. To the laity, Luther's theology made a great deal of sense. It was understandable, verified in Scripture, and a believer could have a relationship with God through Christ - not the pope, or an institution. A personal relationship, not a buffer, through an intermediator. Many people left the Catholic church to become followers of Lutheranism, which caused a great deal of concern with the church, the pope and the bishops. The Catholic church's response, of course, suppressed their heresy.

John Calvin, a professor at the University of Paris, went to Switzerland and was persuaded to stay. He wrote The Institute of the Christian Religion, which formalized reformed theology and made it available to the laity. His writings taught people to know themselves and God through the word of God. When a person reads the Bible for themselves it opens them up to a personal relationship with Christ through illumination by the Holy Spirit. There were other reformers too. Felix Manz taught that the Lord's Supper should be performed in the native tongue of the congregation, not in Latin, so the people could understand. He also taught the supremacy of Scripture, for which he was burned at the stake. William Tyndale, who translated the Bible into English, was also burned at the stake.

In 1545 A.D. Pope Paul III called for the Council of Trent. The purpose of this assembly was so that the bishops and cardinals could address the challenges that had arisen within the church as a result of the Lutherans heresies. They had two main goals: to address abuses in the church, and to clarify teachings in order to meet the Protestant challenge. The Council was professed to be an internal reformation. They met twenty-five times over the course of eighteen years under three different popes. The council found that the church is the ultimate interpreter of Scripture. Also, church traditions were equally authoritative and carried as much weight as Scripture. In spite of the fact that Christ says in the book of Mark,

"Neglecting the commandment of God, you hold to the traditions of men."[9] The council challenged Luther's "justification by faith alone," with specific canons;

Council of Trent, 1545, Canon 9, 11, 12, 17, 23, 24, 32. Quoting directly.

- "If anyone says the sinner is justified by faith alone, let him be damned.

- "If anyone says that men are justified by the sole imputation of the righteousness of Christ, let him be damned."

- "If anyone says that justifying faith is nothing else than confidence in divine mercy which remits sins for Christ's sake, let him be damned."

- "If anyone says that the grace of justification is shared by those only who are predestined to life, let him be damned."

- "If anyone says that a man once justified can sin no more nor lose grace and that therefore he that falls and sins was never truly justified, let him be damned."

- "If anyone says that the righteousness received is not preserved and increased before God through good works, let him be damned."

- "If anyone says that the good works of the one justified are in such a manner the gifts of God that they are not also the good merits of him justified, let him be damned."

Damnation is the very thing that the New Testament teaches regarding salvation. Salvation is by grace alone, through faith alone, in Christ alone,

---

[9] Mark 7:8

apart from works. Some of the above Canons directly contradict Scripture; 9, 11, 17, 24, 32.

In short, works were alive and well after the Council of Trent. Most major conflicts throughout human history have seldom been reconciled, because of mankind's incessant desire for camouflage and subterfuge not ever wanting to tell the truth - to identify the real issues. For the pope and the church, it was all about lust, greed, power, wealth and influence. Pertinent issues were debated under the guise of differences in theology and doctrine. If the pope was deemed fallible that would be a tremendous loss of power and influence, which would affect the financial wellbeing of the church. There would also be significant repercussions for the Church's control over the congregation and their ability to extract funds and control their thinking.

To soften the controversy of indulgences the pope said they were to be thought of as alms, that is just giving extra beyond what was required, as a good work. Alms for the poor there is plenty of justification in Scripture to take care of the poor. The doctrine of transubstantiation was also affirmed at Trent and the church would continue to be the authority on interpretation of Scripture. The church preached if everyone read the Bible and had their own understanding, how could anything be known for certain. The church billed the Council of Trent as "internal reform," so Lutherans could come back into the fold. However, Lutherans "protested" and were outlawed in some areas. Thus, the evolution of the name "Protestants." Accordingly, there was a resurgence of the practice of inquisitions and Protestants were tortured, jailed and executed. This history did not escape the notice of the Founding Fathers, who believed that people should not be killed or tortured for their beliefs. Each man was free to read Scripture and worship God as he was led by his conscience.

This rational line of reasoning, not dominated by the lust of greed, power, wealth and influence, gave birth to the many Christian denominations within America. The Anabaptists did not see infant baptism in Scripture, so they baptized at the age of reason. They had all been baptized as infants but that was not Scriptural. Ana means again, hence they were again baptized when they could make a profession of their faith in Jesus Christ. With the freedom of religious expression rather than the threat of being branded as heretics,' people with a different understanding of Scripture could start a new denomination. All denominations were considered united under a common understanding of the universal church with Christ at the head. This was unique to America. "Congress shall make no law respecting an establishment of religion..." (First Amendment). The Founding Fathers held freedom in such high regard because Christ granted us freedom and the people had to be free to make the choice about what to believe - not a king or the pope or the Iman.

King Henry VIII broke with the Catholic Church because Pope Clement VII would not grant him an annulment from his wife, who was also his sister-in-law. He started the Anglican Church of England, which differed little from the Catholic traditions. When his daughter Mary I took the throne, she wanted Europe to be more Catholic. Her persecutions of Protestants including burning 288 at the stake earned her the name "Bloody Mary." Many Protestants were imprisoned, tortured and executed all across Europe. To escape persecution and the idea of being accused of being a heretic for your Protestant beliefs during the inquisition many Protestants fled to the "New World," - America. This is why historical revisionists, progressives, liberals, globalists and evolutionists try to discredit the Founding Fathers and refer to them as criminals and convicts. Many of the early colonists were imprisoned in Europe for their Protestant faith. In the late 1600s 98 percent of the colonists were Protestant, 2 percent were Catholic and there were about 200,000 Jews. It is interesting to note that when congress was trying to decide which day would be the Sabbath, as Jews celebrated the Sabbath on Saturday and the Protestants honored the Sabbath on Sunday, they decided both Saturday and Sunday would be holy days. This is why, at the time, America was the only country with a five-day work week and a two-day weekend - two days to honor the Sabbath according to your faith.

An early Baptist dissenter who died in London's Newgate Prison was Thomas Helwys, who wrote in 1612: "The king is a mortal man, and not God, therefore he hath no power over the mortal soul of his subjects to make laws and ordinances for them and to set spiritual Lords over them." John Leland wrote in 1791 *"Rights of Conscience Inalienable": "*Every man must give an account of himself to God, and therefore every man ought to be at liberty to serve God in a way that he can best reconcile to his conscience. If government can answer for individuals at the day of judgment, let man be controlled by it in religious matters; otherwise let men be free.

MUSLIM INVASION

The Muslim conquest of Europe resurfaced in 1529. The Muslims, trying to expand their foothold on Europe under the command of Suliman the Magnificent, attacked Vienna with a force of 70,000 soldiers. The Muslim Ottoman soldiers spread desolation as they marched to Vienna, burning villages, beheading men and raping women.

Peter Stern notes in his Chronicle of 1529; "Many thousands of people were murdered or dragged into slavery. Children were cut out of their mothers' wombs and stuck on pikes; young women abused to death, and their corpses left on the highway."

Sermons being preached in Europe were calling Suleiman the anti-Christ. Martin Luther was preaching that the Muslim Ottomans were servants of the devil trying to topple God's kingdom. Providentially early heavy rains made the roads impassable for Suliman's' heavy artillery, much of which he had to leave behind - and much of their gunpowder got wet and was ineffectual.

From the diary of Sultan Suleiman's secretary: "It rained so heavily that some of the horses and camels were swept away by the water. Men climbed up trees and spent two days and nights there."

Without the bigger pieces of artillery, the smaller guns couldn't breach the walls. Suleiman had his soldiers' tunnel under the wall and placed kegs of gunpowder to blow breaches in the walls. Some of the powder was wet and did not ignite. The Viennese, using water barrels to detect where they were digging under the walls, found and defused the kegs of powder. The Viennese set the water barrels around the walls and watched for ripples made by the underground tunneling. Then an early winter set in and Suliman was forced to retreat. Before he left, he beheaded his 4,000 Christian captives.

The invasion had been stopped. The narrative became "God is on our side." A special hymn was written, based on Psalm 127:1 "Unless the Lord guards the city, The watchman keeps awake in vain."

A generation later the Grand Vizier Kara Mustafa mustered the Muslim Ottoman army again for an attack on Vienna. Again, the Ottomans ravaged the countryside on their way to Vienna, killing, burning and raping. Mustafa had 200,000 soldiers. There were 15,000 Viennese soldiers inside the walled city under the command of General Ernst Rüdiger Graf Von Starhemberg. The walls had been rebuilt since the last siege in a star shaped configuration, which deflected cannon balls and made the walls nearly impregnable. Earlier in 1683 the Treaty of Warsaw had been signed By Leopold I, Holy Roman Emperor and Jan III Sobieski, King of Poland. The treaty was for mutual defense; if Krakow in Poland was attacked Leopold I would come to Jan's defense and likewise if Vienna was attacked.

Mustafa arrived at the outskirts of Vienna on July 14th, 1683. He offered terms to Starhemberg: surrender, convert to Islam, and you may live peacefully. Resist and you will be slaughtered young and old. Starhemberg was aware that, en route to Vienna, Mustafa had made the same terms to the governor of Perchtoldsdorf. The governor accepted the terms and Mustafa's men slaughtered the entire inhabitants of the city anyway. Starhemberg refused the terms to capitulate knowing that Mustafa could not be trusted. Mustafa began his two-month siege. The Ottoman cannons were ineffective against the star shaped walls and again the plan was to tunnel under the walls and plant mines, kegs of black powder. The Viennese held out against every attack launched by the Muslims and pushed back the attackers. Again, the Muslims tunneled, and again the Viennese, using the water barrels, detected every mine and defused them. Leopold I and Jan III assembled their troops - 70,000 in all - against Mustafa's 200,000.

Jan III was put in overall command and split their forces to attack on both flanks. As the army's engaged one another on the flanks, Jan III lead a cavalry charge down an embankment directly into the middle of the camp of Mustafa's army. Jan III lead 18,000 of his famed "Winged Hussars" in the largest cavalry charge in history. The battle was over in two hours and the Muslim Ottoman's were completely rousted. The Muslim Ottomans abandoned the battlefield and fled south. Jan III is quoted as having said; "I came, I saw, God conquered." Jan III and his men pursed in what turned out to be a sixteen-year purge of the Muslims out of southern Europe in the west. The defeated Ottoman army returned home and as is customary for anyone who has failed the sultan, Mustafa was publicly strangled. The Muslim Ottoman Empire never recovered from this defeat, which actually proved to be a significant factor in their decline as a world power.

After the death of Christ, the apostles set out upon Christs' great commission; "Go therefore and make disciples of all the nations, baptizing them in the name of the Father and the Son and the Holy Spirit." By 500 A.D. Christianity had spread from Israel as far West as Morocco, Spain and Portugal, across Northern Africa to Syria, Iraq, Turkey, southern Europe and as far as Brittan. From 622 until 1683 Islam waged 548 Jihads against Christianity.

Mike Konrad in an article in the American Thinker states, "Though the numbers are not clear, what is obvious in that Islam is the greatest murder machine in history bar none, possibly exceeding 250 million dead. Possibly one-third to one-half or more of all those killed by war or slavery in history can be traced to Islam; and this is just a cursory examination."

A host of Islamic slavery was sexual in nature, with a preference for women, as opposed to young boys. There was a standing order for 1,000 blond virgins to be delivered to Bagdad every year. The men who were captured were castrated and either sold or used for forced labor. Ships would travel to Africa to procure slaves from the Muslim slave market. Muslims captured people for slaves from all over Africa and along the Atlantic coast as far as Norway. Muslim contributions to civilization have been the slave industry, and the institutionalizing of sex slaves. The destruction of commerce in the Mediterranean causing the Dark Ages. The real destroyer of classical civilization were the Muslims

.

THE THIRTY-YEARS WAR

Few events have as dramatic of an impact on civilization, nations and rulers as war. Another major world-changing event was the Thirty Years War from 1618 – 1648, which altered the balance of power, reshaped Europe and had a profound impact on the Founding Fathers of America. The Thirty-Years War was the most destructive war the world had ever seen, up to this point in time, leaving over eight million dead, predominately civilian casualties of war, famine and disease. A disproportionate number of the casualties were residents of Germany where most of the battles were fought.

The war involved all of the major powers at the time and should really be considered the first world war. The origin of the conflict can be traced back to the Peace of Augsburg signed in 1555 by Charles V, (House of Habsburg, a Dynasty) emperor of the Holy Roman Empire, and representatives of the Schmalkalden League. The League was a military alliance between Lutheran princes within the Holy Roman Empire, predominately in Germany. To come to one another's aid should any member come under attack by Charles V. The Peace of Augsburg ended the Christendom established by the Holy Roman Empire that had ruled Europe for a thousand years. It also ended the struggle between Catholics and Lutherans, allowing individual rulers to choose between Catholicism and Lutheranism for their province. The stanchly Catholic Habsburg Dynasty of Spain and Austria, originally from Switzerland, was a formidable world power from 1279 until the end of WWI in 1918. The Catholic Church was the largest landowner at the time. The House of Habsburg controlled the lands of the Holy Roman Empire - other lands the church was acquiring as it continued to expand its authority through marriages and the appointment of relatives to rule in other provinces. The lands they controlled were modern countries of Austria, Belgium, Bosnia Herzegovina, Croatia, Czech Republic, France, Germany, Hungary, Italy, Poland, Romania, Serbia, Switzerland, Ukraine, Slovakia, Slovenia, Luxemburg, Netherlands, and Liechtenstein. France, although Catholic, was very concerned about the encroachment and continued expansion of the House of Habsburg. Although the pretense of the Thirty-Year War was 'Protestants against Catholics,' which it certainly was, the real motivation of the war was between France and the House of Habsburg for European political pre-eminence. Spain, after the defeat of the Spanish Armada by England in 1587, was no longer the foremost naval force of the world. As we have seen repeatedly the underlying issues are man's lust for greed, power, wealth and influence. The Catholic Empire, however, was losing power and influence because of the largely Protestant princes in Germany.

The war was precipitated by the election of Ferdinand II as the Holy Roman Emperor who began imposing religious uniformity within the Holy Roman Empire by forcing Catholicism on its people. These actions were in direct violation of the 1555 Peace of Augsburg. The Northern Protestant States banded together to form the Protestant Union. The Protestant Bohemians, seeing these actions as a grave threat revolted. Ferdinand II sent a delegation to Prague to try and calm the waters, which resulted in the Defenestration of Prague. Defenestration means to throw someone out of the window and that is exactly what the Bohemians did, they threw the delegation out of the fifth story window of the castle. The Protestant Bohemians then ousted the Habsburgs and elected a Calvinist, Frederick V, as the new king of the Kingdom of Bohemia. The relatively new theology of Calvinism was regarded by most as an extreme form of Protestantism and was treated with a lot of skepticism. Frederick V took the offer of being king without support of the Protestant Union, which, as a Calvinist, he probably would not have received in any case.

The southern states, mainly Roman Catholic, were enraged as they had not been consulted when a Calvinist was put on the throne. Led by Bavaria, the southern states formed the Catholic League to expel Frederick V in support of the Emperor. The Empire dealt a crushing blow to the Protestant Union in a decisive battle at White Mountain. Their victory was followed up by the execution of many of the leading Bohemian aristocrats. There was an outcry over the execution atrocities and Saxony gave its support to the Protestant Union. Bohemia and Saxony decided to fight back against the Emperor. Sweden at the time, with the first army that underwent extensive training and drilling was a rising military power. In 1630, under the superior leadership of their King Gustavus Adolphus, the Swiss also joined with the Protestant Union.

This action set the stage for a major confrontation between the Protestant Union and Habsburg's Holy Roman Empire. The Emperor's attempt to curb the growing tide of Protestantism was turning into a full-scale European War. Spain, who had for a long time been battling with the Dutch opposition to their rule in the Netherlands and the Dutch Republic, entered the escalating confrontation under the pretext of helping their Habsburg ally, Austria. However, their real motive for becoming involved was to crush the Dutch rebellion. France, seeing the opportunity for the House of Hapsburg to grow in power and influence, although Catholic, entered the coalition on the side of the Protestant Union to counter the Hapsburgs. Many of the soldiers and some whole armies were mercenaries with little regard for the people or counties they would occupy. Mercenaries commonly subsidized their wages with stealing, pillaging, raping, torturing and burning homes if there was no booty.

The Thirty-Years War had a devastating effect on the population of Europe, especially in Germany, Italy, Bohemia and the Southern Netherlands. Ninety percent of the eight million deaths were civilians mostly peasants and farmers. With no personal possessions of firearms, the population had no means of defending their homes and protecting their families, they just watched everyone die. The mercenaries and the soldiers of the armies looted and extorted tribute from the occupied territories, forcing many of the kingdoms into bankruptcy. Without a sophisticated supply line, the countryside and crops were devastated resulting in famine and disease in many areas of occupation. Disease usually follows famine as undernourished people have a weakened immune system and are therefore vulnerable to disease and infection. England, Italy and Spain all had epidemics of the plague.

The clear winner of the Thirty-Years War was the Dutch Republic who were freed from the domination of the Habsburgs at the end of the revolt against Spain. After the war the Dutch Republic experienced a time of great prosperity and development. This era is known as the Dutch Golden Age. The Dutch Republic became one of the world's foremost economic, colonial and naval powers. France also benefited in becoming a major player in the world stage, particularity by the significant decline in the power and influence of the House of Habsburg and the rise of the French House of Bourbon. Sweden, for a time maintained its military preeminence.

It is easy to see how the history of Europe would lead to the American's Constitutional first and second amendments. Amendment I: "Congress shall make no law respecting an establishment of religion or prohibiting the free exercise thereof; or abridging the freedom of speech, or of the press; or the right of the people peaceably to assemble, and to petition the Government for a redress of grievances." As well as the second: "A well-regulated Militia, being necessary to security of a free State, the right of the people to keep and bear Arms, shall not be infringed.

"

A WORLD DIVIDED

To understand the origins of America and the original thirteen colonies we must consider two things: activities in North America before the first British Colonies were established, and the historical events in Europe during the 1500s.

Christopher Columbus contracted with King Ferdinand and Queen Isabella, of Spain, to finance his journey to Asia. The Portuguese were sailing around Africa and Columbus thought across the Atlantic would be a much shorter route. Columbus negotiated to keep 10 percent of all the gold and silver he found. His desire was to finance a crusade to free the Holy Lands.

After Columbus first discovered the New World in 1492, there was a lot of exploration of the Americas, Mexico and the Caribbean islands before the British Colonies were established in the early 1600s. Much of this early exploration was conducted by Spain, France, the Dutch, Portugal, and England. There was also exploration of India, Africa, Australia and Indonesia.

Spain and Portugal signed a treaty in 1494, whereby Portugal could explore Africa, Asia, and India. Spain had exclusive rights to the Americas. With the improvements in ship building and navigation, European nations looked for alternate sea routes to the east to avoid the Muslim Barbary Pirate's aggression in the Mediterranean and the Black Sea. Nations were looking to increase their power and wealth and they saw trade as the best way to accomplish that. The quest was for trade routes, gold, silver, spices and other valuables. Also, paramount was the European desire to Christianize the world, and Spain and France to spread Catholicism.

France established the colony of New France in Canada in 1534 and established the city of Quebec in 1608. French colonists, mostly fur trappers, populated the banks of the Mississippi and around the Great Lakes region of Lake Ontario, Erie, Champlain, and the Ohio River Valley. The population of New France (French population) was 3,215 in 1665, 16,000 in 1700 and 55,000 in 1754. New France was ceded to the United Kingdom in 1763 after the French were defeated by the British in the French and Indian War, also known as the Seven-Years' War in Europe. Up until 1763, France controlled three-quarters of the total land mass of North America. In 1867, the Providence of Canada was joined with two other British colonies, New Brunswick and Nova Scotia, through a confederation forming a self-governing entity named Canada under British rule. The Queen of England is still the Queen of Canada. The Spanish controlled the Caribbean Islands, half of South America, all of Central America, and much of Southern and Western North America, including Florida. The population of the thirteen colonies was 75,058 in 1665, 250,800 in 1700 and 1,170,760 in 1754. This population disparity put the French at a great disadvantage in colonization, as it meant there were fewer men available for military service, industry, trade, production and agriculture.

EARLY EXPLORATION

Spain began exploring the Americas and the Caribbean islands in the early 1500's. Initially, Spain was not interested in colonizing North America. They were searching for resources like; gold, silver, and the fountain of youth in Florida. They also, captured Indians as slaves to be sent to the plantations on the Caribbean islands. The Spanish also brought missionaries with them, with the intent of converting indigenous populations to the Catholic religion. The missionaries built many Missions across the Americas. The Spanish found plenty of gold in Mexico and South America where they enslaved the local population as miners. The gold sent back to Spain provided the country with great wealth, which they used to assemble a very large army and many ships-of-war for their navy to defend its treasure ships and to build new treasure ships, which they used to bring the gold and silver back to Spain. This began the formation of the famous Spanish Armada. The treasure ships carried 181 tons of Gold and 16,000 tons of silver back to Spain. The first permanent settlement in North America was established at St. Augustine on the coast of Florida by the Spanish to protect their treasure ships from pirates, in the passage between Cuba and Florida. The pirates were primarily from England, France and the Dutch from the Netherlands. These were not rogue pirates but agents of the countries they represented. The Spanish Conquistadors made their way into Florida, and after not finding any of the aforementioned treasures gave up their quest, and turned to slavery, capturing members of the indigenousness Indian tribes as slaves for work in Cuba, Haiti, Puerto Rico and the Dominican Republic.

Cortés arrived in Hispaniola (Haiti, Dominican Republic) in 1504 and served in a number of government positions, ending as mayor in the capital of Cuba. He was commissioned to colonize the mainland (Mexico) in 1519. The charter was rescinded by the Governor of Cuba, but Cortés went anyway, essentially, he mutinied. Cortés landed on the Yucatan Peninsula, home of the Mayan people. The Yucatan Peninsula was sparsely populated with many divergent tribes. Subsequent studies and archeological digs have found that Maya was once a very sophisticated and highly developed civilization. They were the only civilization in the Americas with a written language. They also had art, architecture, mathematics, a calendar and an astronomical system. No one knows for sure what caused their demise; however, the usual causes are typically warfare and disease. Scientists have recently discovered that epidemics follow a rainy season that follows an extended drought. They identify these cycles by the growth rings in trees.

Dr. Rodolfo Acuna-Soto, a Harvard-trained infectious disease specialist at the National Autonomous University of Mexico in Mexico City, said it made no sense that a deadly outbreak of European origin could occur so long after the Spanish arrived, because the natives who survived previous plagues would have passed on their immunities. Exhaustive diaries kept by Francisco Hernandez; the surgeon general of New Spain witnessed the second catastrophic epidemic in 1576. The first occurred in 1545. Hernandez described a highly contagious and lethal scourge that killed within a few days, causing raging fevers, jaundice, tremors, dysentery, abdominal and chest pains, enormous thirst, delirium and seizures. "Blood flowed from the ears," the physician observed, "and in many cases blood truly gushed from the nose."

These are classic symptoms of viral hemorrhagic fever spread by the urine of the Vesper Mouse. The smallpox, spread by Cortés men, had a devastating impact on the indigenous population as well. The subsequent hemorrhagic fever also took a huge toll. No one knows how many people were killed as there was no census at the time. We do not know how many people there were. What history has told us is that epidemics can absolutely devastate the population of cites or countries. It is thought that the Black Plague, which occurred three times, killed a third of the world's population. The Mayan civilization was in serious decline and there remained just a small remnant of what had once been a great civilization.

It is theorized that the hemorrhagic fever may be what decimated the Mayan civilization as they were in full decline before the Spaniards arrived. The Conquistadors did establish colonies in South America and

Mexico to extract the wealth from these lands. The Spanish would later establish colonies in California, Arizona, New Mexico and Texas; however, these were primarily missions and served as a buffer to protect Mexico from other world powers.

The first Spanish colonies were in Central and South America. Hernando Cortez, a Conquistador, while exploring Mexico, came upon the city of Tenochitlán which was the largest city in the Americas. It was the home of the Aztecs, who possessed great wealth, primarily in gold. The Spanish were shocked by the regular practice of the Aztecs of performing large scale human sacrifices. Those who were sacrificed were captured warriors from other tribes. The heart was extracted from the captive while the person was still alive and the blood from the heart was smeared on the image of their deity. The arms and legs were then severed from the body and cooked over a fire for consumption by the sacrifice's participants. Cortez used the sacrifices as a justification for his violent conquest of the Aztecs, and I'm sure the prevalence of gold played a major role in his motivation. A further justification is that this is also the era of the Catholic Church's inquisitions, the rigorous enforcement of its doctrines and the war against heretics. Cortez with 600 soldiers and 1,000 warriors from other tribes were the force against the Aztecs. Natives from other tribes were willing to join Cortés as many of the human sacrifices were taken from among their villages. Initially, Cortés was beaten back and lost several hundred men in his retreat. Some report as many as 800 were killed. Upon reaching the coast Cortés was reinforced by additional troops from Cuba and they were able to defeat the Aztecs.

The King of the Aztecs was Montezuma. He was considered by his people to be a God. When he was killed by Cortez the population was thrown into a panic and the resulting chaos left them ineffective to defend themselves. The belief among many ancient civilizations was that whichever side won the battle must have a stronger god, which caused many conversions. This could very well be the case of the Aztec's that survived, and why they disappeared, the same may be said of the Inca's.

Another Conquistador, Francisco Pizzaro González, a distant cousin of Cortez, infatuated with the successes of Cortez, embarked on his own explorations. He is most well-known for his conquest of Peru and the defeat of the Incas. After two unsuccessful attempts in 1524 and 1526, he returned to Spain and received support from King Charles I. In 1530 he returned and began his campaign to conquer the Inca region and its people. In November of 1532, at the battle of Cajamarca, the Spanish forces defeated the Incas. Pizzaro ordered the execution of the Incan emperor Atahualpa, for which he was harshly criticized by King Charles I. Having captured Peru and claiming the land for Spain, along with the largest silver mine in the Americas, he founded the capital of Lima on the coast.

Aside from the military conquests of the Conquistadors, diseases took a heavy toll on the indigenous people of America, Mexico and the Caribbean Islands. Europeans brought smallpox, measles and the flu. As the indigenous slave labor began to die off slaves were purchased from the Muslim slave traders in Africa and brought in as replacements and they brought with them; malaria, diphtheria, yellow fever and typhus. What few eyewitness accounts there are of epidemics are very localized and do not provide the scope necessary to understand the magnitude of an epidemic. An event that best puts this in perspective is the flu epidemic of 1918, which placed the death toll at 20 to 50 million, but then again, we really have no idea. I think it is also interesting that native Americans are called "Indians" because Columbus thought he had made it to India.

One of the reasons the indigenous people of the Americas and Mexico were so vulnerable to disease is their frail immune systems. Our intestines are full of bacteria, some of it is beneficial and some of it can cause illnesses, disease and death. We are, of course, immune to the bacteria in our own system because our body has built up anti-bodies for all of the hurtful bacteria in our system. Humans get most of our diseases from other vectors - domesticated animals, rodents, insects (especially mosquitoes), ticks, fleas, midges, mites, lice and flies. Our exposure to domesticated animals introduces a broad spectrum of diseases to humans. We get sick, our immune system fights off the disease and we survive or if our immune system fails to defeat the threat we die. If we survive, we now have an immunity to that disease because our bodies have built anti-bodies for that agent that caused the disease. Animals also carry a host of bacteria in their intestines which are flushed out in their feces, and that is the source of contamination to the human population - to those working with livestock or soil and water contamination. The people in the Old World had exposure to at least five types of domesticated mammals which killed many but also provided for the ability to establish anti-bodies against diseases, pigs, chickens, cattle, goats, and sheep are the source of many diseases that afflict mankind. [10] Camels are another source for disease

---

[10]   https://www.fli.de/en/services/national-reference-laboratories/list-of-animal-diseases/

but, they are not as proliferate.

Our best defense is cooking our foods and practicing good personal hygiene. Some of the diseases we contract from animal parasites, pathogens, bacteria or viruses, called zoonoses are measles, smallpox, tuberculosis, malaria, crypto, mad cow diseases (bovine spongiform encephalopathy), hookworm, rabies, E coli O157:H7, plague, anthrax, Hendra virus, salmonella, campylobacter jejuni, and listeriosis, to name a few. The reason this is important is the only domesticated animal the Indians had were dogs. The Spaniards brought horses, pigs and goats, and the English brought cattle, chickens and sheep to the Americas. The Indians never had a chance to be exposed to the myriad of pathogens that Europeans were. There were no anti-bodies in Native Americans for the diseases brought to the New World. This is also paralleled by most armies of invading forces, which either brought new diseases or contracted diseases in the countries they invaded. All armies of the world suffered this fate until the advent of vaccinations and antibiotics. It wasn't just smallpox and it wasn't just the Indians all were plagued by multiple epidemics throughout the age of discovery.

EARLY NORTH AMERICAN SETTLEMENTS

In England in the early 1500s the primary source of Scripture was "The Great Bible," the first authorized Bible, and it was the Bible of the Church of England. There were about 150 copies which were primarily in the churches, none of which were readily available to the general public. In 1579 the Geneva Bible, the first mechanically printed massed produced Bible, was becoming readily available directly to the public. The Geneva Bible was the first Bible to have verse citations and each chapter began with a summary of the content of the book. It was also the first translation taken directly from the Hebrew Bible. It contained maps, tables, margin notes and woodcut illustrations. The tone of the Geneva Bible was plain, forceful and vigorous. It was very well received by the general public. The Bible carried a Calvinist slant to its theology and many of the margin notes were decidedly anti-Catholic. This is the Bible that was brought to America by the early settlers.

The Geneva Bible was a great concern to the rulers in England, as it was so contrary to the "Great Bible." King James I was concerned that his people may believe the margin notes making it more difficult for him and his church to convey to the congregation the interpretation they preferred. This was the dream of Martin Luther and the Protestant Reformation - a Bible readily available for any and all to read. In 1603, King James I commissioned the writing of an official Bible, the Bible of England. He instructed the translators to use the "Kings English."

The first settlement by the English in America was on Roanoke Island, North Carolina called the Roanoke Colony - also called the "Lost

Colony." This is a very interesting part of our history and explains much of the early interactions between the Native Americans and the colonists. Queen Elizabeth I issued a charter to Sir Walter Raleigh stating that he was to "Discover, search, find out and view such remote heathen and barbarous lands, countries and territories…to have, hold, occupy and enjoy." The Queen wanted to establish a presence in the New World to make a claim of the land for England. The charter also instructed Raleigh to establish a base to send privateers on raids against the treasure ships of Spain and to counter - act the activities of the Spaniards claiming Florida. In 1584, Raleigh dispatched an expedition to the eastern coast of North America led by Arthur Barlowe. They arrived at Roanoke Island, did some exploring, and met with local natives - the Secotans and the Croatans. Barlowe returned to England with two Croatan Indians, Manteo and Wanchese, and left 107 settlers behind. The Indians gave Raleigh local intelligence about tribes, geography, politics and the culture of the Indians. In 1586, Sir Francis Drake, after completing a successful raid on Spanish treasure ships, stopped by the settlement and offered to take the settlers back to England. Some of them accepted the offer. The Roanoke colonists brought back with them tobacco, maize (corn) and potatoes, introducing these items to England. Shortly after Drake's departure, the relief fleet from England arrived only to find the settlement abandoned. Grenville, the ship's captain, left a detachment of fifteen men behind to maintain England's claim to the land. In 1587, Raleigh dispatched a new group of 115 colonists to settle at Chesapeake Bay. They were instructed to stop by Roanoke and collect the fifteen men that had been left there. Upon their arrival they found the post abandoned. The captain of the ship made the 115 disembark and maintain the claim of the land for England. At this time in history Spain enjoyed naval supremacy with its famous Spanish Armada. England was developing a formidable navy of its own.

Just after the discovery of the Americas the English were again at war. With the advent of the Anglo-Spanish War all English ships were needed for the war effort. It would be another three years before a return trip would be made to the Roanoke Colony. On August 18th in 1590, Sir Francis Drake arrived at the Roanoke Colony, only to find it deserted. There was no trace of the 90 men, 17 women and 11 children who had made up the colony. There was no sign of a struggle or battle either and the fate of the "Lost Colony" remains a mystery to this day. However, it is not hard to figure out what happened. The colony had to survive for three years without being resupplied because of the Anglo – Spanish War.

Rather than face extinction it is reasonable to assume the colonists were cared for and probably joined the Croatan Indian Tribe. Two Croatan Indians had already displayed their willingness to align with the colonist when Manteo and Wanchese offered to accompany Barlowe on his return to England. There were eyewitness accounts and diary entries of people seeing Croatan Indians with grey eyes and less than completely black hair. Perhaps a relationship developed between the colonists and the Croatan Indians and they cohabitated. Others speculate that the colonists were wiped out by the local native tribes. To the Indians, the newcomers were white and there was probably no distinction between English, Spaniards and the French. Stories may have spread of the whites - slave trade, sickness, disease and perhaps even the slaughter of the Aztec and Inca tribes. DNA testing has not been to able confirm or rule out the idea of cohabitation of the Roanoke settlers and the Croatan Indians. In 1993, Hurricane Emily uncovered numerous relics in the area of the Croatan capital, gun flints, copper farthings produced in the 1670s, and a signet ring. The crest on the ring was traced and indicates it belonged to Master Kendall who was recorded as one of the occupants of the Roanoke Colony. Because of heavy erosion at the site of the island colony of Roanoke little else remains as evidence. Further evidence of this hypothesis can be gleaned from the second colony established in the New World at Jamestown.

In 1585, an undeclared war broke out between Spain and England. There are two causative issues that resulted in the Anglo – Spanish War - religion and privateering. King of England Henry VIII, having been excommunicated from the Catholic Church by Pope Clement VII because he divorced his wife, Catherine of Aragon to marry his mistress, Anne Boleyn, was the first monarch to introduce a new state religion separate from the Catholic Church. Henry and Anne had one child, Mary, and there was also a son by Henry and Jane Seymore, Edward. Edward VI was king upon Henry's death and when he became ill, he tried to have Mary removed from the line of succession. He was convinced that if Mary were to become Queen, she would turn back his father's religious reforms in the kingdom and return England to Catholicism. Upon Edwards death Mary did became Queen of England. She became known as Bloody Mary because of her harsh suppression and persecution of Protestants, 288 of whom she burned at the stake. Phillip of Spain was also dealing with a protestant uprising that eventually turned into outright rebellion. Queen Mary and King Phillip of Spain married as a means of solidifying the Catholic faith in

Europe. Mary died five years into her reign and was succeeded by Queen Elizabeth I, who restored authority to the Angelic Church of England started by Henry VIII.

The Netherlands and Ireland were also dealing with rebellions of a religious nature. Spain and England began to take sides. The relationship between Phillip and Elizabeth I became strained over these religious differences and the ongoing struggles with the Catholic Church as it tried to exert more control. The protest was sometimes violent against reformers. The situation was exacerbated further by the continual English privateering against Spanish treasure ships. English ships were seized in Spanish ports, and England launched a campaign against Spanish fishing in the waters off Newfoundland. This caused England to join the Eighty-Years War on the side of the Protestant Dutch in their fight for independence from Spain. Sir Francis Drake, in a preemptive, strike sacked the Spanish city of Santo Domingo, then sailed to St. Augustine in Florida. This is when Drake stopped at the Roanoke Colony.

King Phillip finally sent his famed Spanish Armada against England, not only to destroy their navy but soldiers to invade England itself and put a Catholic on the throne. The two navies fought a couple of small skirmishes in the English Channel. At night the Spanish Armada anchored off the coast of Calais in a crescent formation. Drake set eight ships on fire and sent them into the formation. The sailors, in a panic, cut their anchor lines and scattered. In a subsequent battle the English navy inflicted a defeat on the Armada, forcing it to sail northward in more dangerous stormy waters. Along the coast of Scotland stormy weather forced many of the ships aground. Without anchors they were helpless. There was a repeat of very bad weather along the coast of Ireland as well, with the loss of more ships and men. The Armada's failure was seen as divine intervention from God and direct support from God of the Protestant Reformation in England. A commemorative medal was designed for the English victory that bore the inscription, "Yahweh blew, and they were scattered." Over half of the 130 ships of the Armada were destroyed and 20,000 of the 30,000 soldiers and sailors were killed. Upon hearing the news King Philip said, "I sent my ships to fight against men and not against the winds and waves of God." Two years later a second Armada was sent against England. This fleet was destroyed at sea by storms and had to be recalled. With the defeat of the Spanish Armada and many of its soldiers and sailors Spain was no longer the premier naval world power. That position was now taken over by England. Had God not intervened in the

Anglo-Spanish War by the defeat of the Spanish Armada the American colonies could very well have been Spanish and not English.

There are few things that impact a society, civilization, or a country, as the transformational effects of war. The two most significant wars that directly affected the formation of America were the French and Indian War, and naturally, the Revolutionary War. By no means, however, were these the only two wars fought in the emerging republic, the American Experiment, and American Exceptionalism.

The Vikings from Iceland, who colonized Greenland, were the first to establish a colony in North America on the island of Newfoundland. The year is not known but thought to be about 1000 A.D. The colony was unable to sustain itself or to be properly resupplied and all that remains are the remnants of the settlement. European expeditions began in earnest by 1497. John Cabot, an Italian immigrant to England, landed on Newfoundland and claimed it for England. Between 1534, and 1542, Jacques Cartier made three voyages across the Atlantic on order of King Francis I of France. He was charged with finding gold, spices and a direct route to Asia. On June 9, 1534, Cartier sailed into the waters of the St. Lawrence River in eastern Canada, planted a cross on the shore, and declared the land for France. Several attempts at colonization followed but they failed. From 1604, to 1608, three colonies were established by the French that would survive: St Croix Island (Maine), Port-Royal in Arcadia (Nova Scotia), and Quebec. The first Dutch settlement in 1615, was Fort Nassau on Castle Island on the Hudson River, near present day Albany, New York. The fort was strictly used for fur trading with the Lenape tribe.

Noah Webster in his 1828 *"American Dictionary of the English Language,"* defines providence as "the care and superintendence which God exercises over His creatures. He that acknowledges a creation and denies a providence, involves himself in a palpable contradiction; for the same power which caused a thing to exist is necessary to continue its existence...A belief in divine providence, is a source of great consolation to good men. BY divine providence is often understood God Himself."

THE EARLY COLONIAL WARS

1610-1614, 1622-1646 The Powhatan Wars
1629 – 1701 The Iroquois's Beaver War
1637-1636 The Pequot War
1643-1644 The Dutch and Indian War
1675 – 1678 King Philip's War
1168-1697 King William's War
1676 -Bacon's Rebellion
1702 – 1713 Queen Anne's War
1722-1725 -Dummer's War
1744 – 1748 King George's War
1749 – 1755 Father Le Loutre's War
1754 – 1763 The French and Indian War – The War that Formed America

The royal colonies in America were ruled directly by the English monarchy. The king granted state charters and appointed a governor for a track of land to be colonized and claimed for the crown of England. Investors would form a holding company, such as the London Companies and the Hudson Bay Company. These holding companies would make an investment by financing the voyage, supplies and settlements. For them it was a business venture and they expected the settlers to return a profit. The settlers, for the most part, were Protestants willing to take the risk to escape religious persecution, the inquisitions and establish communities free of the politics and religions of Europe. Those that could not afford the price of a ticket went as indentured servants and worked as laborers until their debt was paid, usually in five to seven years.

Initially there were two groups of people: Separatists, who wanted to completely separate themselves from the Catholic and Church of England, and Puritans, who gave up on trying to purify the Church of England and sailed to begin a New England.

Dishonest historical revisionists portray a slanted view of history. David Barton from WallBuilders, LLC, maintains that American history revisionists began rewriting American history in the 1900s. If you want an actual portrayal of American history look for writings from before that time. However, we must be careful, as many subsequent editions have been revised. Another great source is in the archives of the Congressional Record. The Congressional Record is a substantially verbatim account of the remarks made by senators and representatives while they were on the floor of the Senate and the House of Representatives. It also includes all bills, resolutions, and motions proposed, as well as debates and roll call votes.

The original charters of the colonies give us a clear understanding of the settler's intent, and their faith and trust in God's providence for their undertakings in colonizing America. Historical revisionists lay claim that the founding of America was the work of Deists, not the work of profoundly religious men.

The preamble for the, "Original Constitution of the Colony of New Haven, June 4, 1639"

"THE 4th day of the 4th month, called June, 1639, all the free planters assembled together in a general meeting, to consult about settling civil government, according to GOD, and the nomination of persons that might be found, by consent of all, fittest in all respects for the foundation work of a church, which was intended to be gathered in Quinipiack. After solemn invocation of the name of GOD, in prayer for the presence and help of his spirit and grace, in those weighty businesses, they were reminded of the business whereabout they met, (viz.) for the establishment of such civil order as might be most pleasing unto GOD, and for the choosing the fittest men for the foundation work of a church to be gathered. For the better enabling them to discern the mind of GOD, and to agree accordingly concerning the establishment of civil order, Mr. John Davenport propounded divers queries to them publicly, praying them to consider seriously in the presence and fear of GOD, the weight of the business they met about, and not to be rash or slight in giving their votes to things they understood not; but to digest fully and thoroughly what should be propounded to them, and without respect to men, as they should be satisfied and persuaded in their own minds, to give their answers in such sort as they would be willing should stand upon record for posterity."

Query 1 WHETHER the scriptures do hold forth a perfect rule for the direction and government of all men in all duties which they are to perform to GOD and men, as well in families and commonwealth, as in matters of the church? This was assented unto by all, no man dissenting, as was expressed by holding up of hands. Afterwards it was read over to them, that they might see in what words their vote was expressed. They again expressed their consent by holding up their hands, no man dissenting.

Charter of Delaware March 4, 1680

BECAUSE no People can be truly happy, though under the greatest Enjoyment of Civil Liberties, if abridged of the Freedom of their Consciences, as to their Religious Profession and Worship: And Almighty God being the only Lord of Conscience, Father of Lights and Spirits; and the Author as well as Object of all divine Knowledge, Faith and Worship, who only doth enlighten the Minds, and persuade and convince the Understandings of People...AND that all Persons who also profess to believe in Jesus Christ, the Saviour of the World, shall be capable (notwithstanding their other Persuasions and Practices in Point of Conscience and Religion) to serve this Government in any Capacity, both legislatively and executively..."

Agreement of the Settlers at Exeter in New Hampshire, 1639

"Whereas it hath pleased the Lord to move the Heart of our dread Sovereigns Charles by the Grace of God King &c. to grant Licence and Libertye to sundry of his subjects to plant themselves in the Westerlle parts of America. We his loyal Subjects Brethren of the Church in Exeter situate and lying upon the River Pascataqua with other Inhabitants there, considering with ourselves the holy Will of God and o'er own Necessity that we should not live without wholesomne Lawes and Civil Government among us of which we are altogether destitute; do in the name of Christ and in the sight of God combine ourselves together to erect and set up among us such Government as shall be to our best discerning agreeable to the Will of God professing ourselves Subjects to our Sovereign Lord King Charles according to the Libertyes of our English Colony of Massachusetts, and binding of ourselves solemnly by the Grace and Help of Christ and in His Name and fear to submit ourselves to such Godly and Christian Lawes as are established in the realm of England to our best Knowledge, and to all other such Lawes which shall upon good grounds be made and enacted among us according to God that we may live quietly and peaceably together in all godliness and honesty. Mo. 8. D. 4. 1639 as attests our Hands."

Charter of Carolina March 24, 1663

"…being excited with a laudable and pious zeal for the propagation of the Christian faith, and the enlargement of our empire and dominions, have humbly besought leave of us, by their industry and charge, to transport and make an ample colony of our subjects, natives of our kingdom of England, and elsewhere within our dominions, unto a certain country hereafter described, in the parts of America not yet cultivated or planted, and only inhabited by some barbarous people, who have no knowledge of Almighty God."

After the Roanoke settlement between 1607 and 1622, seven more settlements were established. The king wanted to stake a claim in America as the French and Spanish already had a presence in the Americas and Mexico. In some instances, some of the investors would be a part of the settlement. The first undertaking would be to build a fort and dwellings. First a wall would be constructed of upright timbers, then the house of worship was built, which would house up to twenty men. Individual dwellings were then constructed as women and families arrived. As more settlers arrived, homesteads were set up outside the fort and eventually towns were formed, the church was the center piece of all settlements. The church served as the gathering place. The church bells would warn of danger and the settlers would gather at the church.

Jamestown and the Powhatan War

The first permanent settlement was at Jamestown in 1607, named after King James I of England. The settlement would prove to be a horrendous ordeal for the 104 men and boys who first arrived, thirteen years before the Pilgrims arrived at Plymouth. Jamestown was a poor choice; the land was poor for farming and contained a lot of marshes. The settlement was on an island in the James River in eastern Virginia. It was selected because it could be easily defended and had a deep-water port for anchorage. The location of Jamestown was in the midst of the chiefdom of a powerful Powhatan chief and his 14,000 Algonquian speaking Indians. The first resupply ships destined for Jamestown were lost in a storm, so the settlers

78

had to wait for new ships to be built. This period was called "The Starving Time -" forty of the settlers died of starvation, disease and warfare with the Indians. The arrival of the settlers at Jamestown coincided with the end of a seven-year drought. Food was in short supply, which caused tensions between the Indians and the settlers. Some of the settlers that ventured out of the fort for food were slain by the Indians. All of the horses brought from England were eaten during the winter. All was but lost when the replacement resupply ships arrived. On what the settlers called "The Day of Providence." They were spared from extinction.

Initially, as the settlement developed, settlers got along with the Indians of the Powhattan Confederacy; however, they continued to encroach on the Indian lands as the colony grew, straining their relationship. Several tribes would unite for defensive protection against other tribes. These were called confederations. There were two basic Indian groups - agricultural, who were relatively passive, and the more aggressive hunter tribes. Most tribes were involved in both of these activities, some just had more emphasis on one over the other. Hostilities eventually broke out at the Jamestown settlement. There were brief clashes between the Powhatan Confederacy and the settlers of Jamestown. Initially the settlers did not know what to expect from the indigenous population. There were accounts from the Spaniards and the Portuguese of the brutal savagery of the occupants of South America and Mexico. Some of the claims by the early explorers may have been exaggerated to justify their brutal treatments of the Aztec's and the Inca's. However, two things to keep in mind; this was the early-1600s, the time of the Catholic Inquisitions, accusations of heresy and ruthless enforcement of Catholic beliefs. No Christian religion would tolerate idol worship, cannibalism or human sacrifices as were common among the Aztecs and the Incas. Accessorial records conclude that the original occupants of North Americas were from Mongolia and western China and arrived via land bridges formed after the flood and the dispersal of people after the Tower of Babel.

The early settlements were predominantly Protestant Christians. In addition to establishing their settlements their charge was to bring Christianity to the New World. Evangelizing for the colonists was a completely different story than in Mexico and South America. The Indians that the early settlers encountered had a completely different religion, the religion of the Great Spirit. The colonists also worshiped and relied on help and salvation from a Great Spirit, but theirs had a name. The Indians also believed that everything had a spirit, either good or bad, and referred to as good or bad medicine for a person, place or thing. Native Americans also believed that the Great Spirit gave each person a medicine, a unique spiritual gift or talent, which also coincided with the Christian's view of the Holy Spirit and the spiritual gifts He imparts to believers. Indians, at times, would take captives to replace warriors lost in battle to maintain the spiritual strength of the tribe. Captives were sometimes tortured; the women and children of the tribe would participate in the torturing as it was more humiliating. If a captive was very brave, he or she may be assimilated into the tribe. Some captives were run through a gauntlet, where the captive would run between two rows of Indians with clubs and be beaten to break their spirit. If a captive fell and could not get up, he was immediately killed. At the end of the gauntlet was a pole where a captive may be burned alive or shot with arrows. The longer it took a person to die the stronger the spirt was in the person. There were some tribes where a warrior would eat the liver or heart of a brave captive so that he could absorb his spiritual strength or courage. Mohawk means flesh-eater in the Algonquin language.[11] Most of the Powhatan tribe, as well as Pocahontas, were converted to Christianity.

English settlements tended to attract people of like theologies, such as Puritans, Quakers, Angelic, Separatists, Baptists, etc. The colonists learned their lesson from Europe, the Catholic Church and the Inquisition. Christians in America did not kill people for having a different belief. The Protestant Reformation taught people to have the freedom to read Scripture and form a relationship with God based on their conscience. Liberty comes from God and is a right of all men. "Now the Lord is the Spirit, and where the Spirit of the Lord is, there is liberty."[12] The American colonies were the birthplace of many Christian denominations. The understanding was that no one really knows for sure which exact theology is right as long as your faith is built on God as the Creator His Son the Incarnate Jesus Christ as your Savior, the inspiration and illumination of the Holy Spirit and the infallibility of Scriptures. All believers belong to one church body in which Christ is the Head.

In the Jamestown settlement, after a few skirmishes with the Powhatan Indians, Samuel Argall captured Matoaka (aka Pocahontas). Chief Powhatan's daughter and he agreed to a peace treaty in exchange

---

[11] References; Narrative of the Life of Mrs. Mary Jemison, The Jesuits Relations, The Explorations of Raddison
[12] 2 Corinthians 3:17 NASB

for her safety. Pocahontas traveled to England where she died of an unknown disease. Her father also died that year.

The first representative form of government was at Jamestown when The House of Burgesses was convened. The general assembly was called at the request of settlers who wanted a say in the laws and rules that were going to be established to govern the settlement. The sentiment was that Christians did not need laws, as they abide by the teachings of Scripture. However, some may arrive that are not Christian, and they wanted to have laws and rules of conduct established prior to their arrival. The laws were then established on Biblical principles. Some of the common laws of Britain were also adopted. The laws reflected many of the teachings of the Bible, as it is authored by God, "all Scripture is inspired by God and profitable for teaching, for reproof, for correction, for training in righteousness;"[13] and is was the essential foundation of truth. God made man; we are therefore accountable to Him; hence, we adopt His statues as our rules for living. The 10 Commandments, as truth from the Bible, define appropriate behavior as do the 613 statutes found in the first five books of the Bible, called The Torah. Although all of the statutes are Biblical in origin, they are behavioral parameters in execution. "The sum of Your word is truth, And every one of Your righteous ordinances is everlasting."[14] Between 1607, and 1624, six-thousand settlers arrived at Jamestown of which only three thousand four hundred survived. Deaths were due to starvation, diseases and warfare with the Indians.

The Jamestown settlement only flourished when John Rolfe, who had married Pocahontas, planted some untested tobacco seeds he had from Bermuda. Tobacco flourished and was readily purchased by England as Englishmen took to smoking. The tobacco required expansion of the tobacco fields, which alarmed Chief Opchanacanough. (brother of Chief Powhatan), who assumed leadership of the Confederacy upon Powhattan's death. Chief Opchanacanough was concerned that every year brought more settlers. He wanted to eliminate the English colony. In March of 1622, he and warriors of the Confederation attacked plantations and settlements along the James River in what became known as the "Indian Massacre of 1622." Over 300 of the settlers were killed - about a third of the settlement's population. Christianized natives warned other settlers, which saved many lives. The colonists would send out militia to hunt for warriors of the Powhatan tribe. This went on for years, during

---

[13] 2 Timothy 3:16 NASB
[14] Psalm 119:160

which time the colonists built three more forts, pushing out their boundaries and forming alliances with the Accohannock and Patawomeck tribes. Finally, a meeting was arranged to talk of peace. However, the militia poisoned the wine they gave to the Indians in revenge for the 1622 massacre. After an unsteady cease fire that lasted for twelve years. Settlers continued to arrive and once again Opchanacanough, now 92, wanted to resume tribal raids to rid his lands of the settlers. The ensuing raid on the settlements resulted in the death of 500 settlers. The militia responded and in the ensuing battle Opchanacanough was captured. While in captivity he was killed when a guard shot him in the back. The resulting peace treaty established boundaries between Powhatan and the colonists, ending the Powhatan Wars, 1610 - 1614, and 1622 - 1646. Under the new treaty one could only cross the boundary on official business, and they had to be in possession of a pass.

The Pilgrims

The next notable settlement was that of Plymouth, Massachusetts. The two ships that began the voyage were the Mayflower and the Speedwell. The Speedwell proved to be unseaworthy and after several delays the supplies and passengers were loaded onto the Mayflower. There were strong westerly winds in the unanticipated Gulf Stream. There was also a design flaw on the ship, as the quarterdeck was too high and provided resistance against the wind. The return trip took half as much time.

The Plymouth Colony was founded by "Pilgrims," who were members of a Puritan religious group known as the Separatists. The most notable achievement on this settlement was establishing self-government through the creation of the Mayflower Compact, which represents America's origins in democracy and the first Constitution. Through an act of providence, the Mayflower did not land on the property specified in their charter. Their settlement would not be under British governmental oversight. They took it upon themselves to establish their own document for governing the settlement. It is also the site of the first celebration of Thanksgiving. The Puritans of the Mayflower signed the Mayflower Compact onboard just before making landfall on November 11, 1620. The first order of business was planting a cross on the shore. The Compact, in today's English, reads as follows;

"In the name of God, Amen. We, whose names are underwritten, the Loyal Subjects of our dread Sovereign Lord, King James, by the Grace of God, of England, France and Ireland, King, Defender of the Faith, e&. Having undertaken for the Glory of God, and Advancement of the Christian Faith, and the Honor of our King and Country, a voyage to plant the first colony in the northern parts of Virginia; do by these presents, solemnly and mutually in the Presence of God and one of another, covenant and combine ourselves together into a civil Body Politick, for our better Ordering and Preservation, and Furtherance of the Ends aforesaid; And by Virtue hereof to enact, constitute, and frame, such just and equal Laws, Ordinances, Acts, Constitutions and Offices, from time to time, as shall be thought most meet and convenient for the General good of the Colony; unto which we promise all due submission and obedience. In Witness whereof we have hereunto subscribed our names at Cape Cod the eleventh of November, in the Reign of our Sovereign Lord, King James of England, France and Ireland, the eighteenth, and of Scotland the fifty-fourth. Anno Domini, 1620."   The purpose for establishing the colonies as first recorded in the Mayflower Compact was for the glory of God and the advancement of the Christian faith. The Compact was also written to establish just and equal laws for the good of the settlement. It bound the men to form a government and submit to the will of the majority. The belief among the Puritans was that, contrary to a monarchy, a majority vote would reflect the will of God. This is the beginning of the idea of self-rule, governed by the consent of the governed, and that God has sovereignty over His creation. The idea was that all men are created equal and have an equal say. The king or monarch was not divine, he or she was no different than any other man or woman. The principle established by the Mayflower Compact was that government rests on the consent of the governed, and decisions should be made democratically rather than imposed by an authority. The idea of a political body to make laws to govern by the consent of the governed sprang from the idea that Protestants and others of the Christian faith did not need laws as they all lived by God's natural laws found in Scripture, but there would have to be laws for others to guide their behavior. It is interesting to note that this was the same line of reasoning of the first governing body at Jamestown thirteen years earlier and now was represented in the first formal document.

Unfortunately, the 107 Pilgrims that landed at Providence Bay, as they named it, on November 11, 1620, arrived at the outset of winter. They remained on board the next day, Sunday, for prayer and worship. There would be no time to plant crops. They scouted the landing area for three days and decided to build their settlement on the site of an abandoned Indian village. The women and children remained on board while the men constructed the walls of the fort and the house of worship to get them through the winter. By the end of January everyone disembarked to take up residence in the settlement. They all lived in the house of worship until individual dwellings were built.

On March 16, 1621, a Native American, Samoset, boldly walked into the settlement and proclaimed, "Welcome Englishmen." Samoset had learned English from fisherman off the coast of Maine. He introduced the settlers to Massasoit, Chief of the Wampanoag and to Squanto. Squanto had been abducted by some Dutch sailors and worked as an indentured servant. He escaped and made his way to England. After five years he returned to his native homeland as a guide. When he returned, he found that his village had been wiped out by disease. He joined the Wampanoag Confederacy. Chief Massasoit and Governor Martin, governor of the settlement, signed a peace treaty ensuring they would bring no harm to one another, establish trade with one another and would come to the aid if either were attacked. They both saw the advantage of trade rather than war. The settlers needed food; deer, ducks, fish and the Indians wanted European goods - metal tools instead of stone, guns, and ammunition primarily for hunting and having an advantage over unfriendly tribes. Not all tribes got along. Some chiefs wanted to form confederacies out of multiple tribes, and some tribes wanted to remain independent, such as the Mohicans. The settlers also bought land from the Indians on an ongoing basis. Squanto took up residence in the settlement and showed the Pilgrims how to survive in winter, and how to hunt and fish. In the spring he showed them how to plant corn, potatoes and squash. Squanto also arranged an exclusive trading pact with the settlers and the Wampanoag for trading primarily beaver pelts. This trading pact cut out the French who had been trading with the Wampanoags but had lost much of their esteem with the Wampanoags after they were severely weakened by the "Beaver War." The French were no longer viable partners. Each year more settlers would arrive to America. Some brought cattle. In 1610 there were 350 settlers, all in Virginia. By 1620 there were 2,302 in Virginia and the Plymouth Plantation. By 1630 there were 4,646. After the "Great Migration" of 1630-1640 26,643 settlers had arrived and by 1650 there were 50,368. By 1700 there would be a quarter of a million people in the colonies.

When settling New England, the Puritans (Pilgrims) created self-governing communities of religious congregations of farmers and their families. The whole settlement made up the church's congregation. Understanding they could not purify the church of England they named their first colonies New England. In the early colonies they created the Congregational Church; however, their belief that God singled out only a few specific people for salvation tended to restrict membership. A person that wanted to join the Congregational Church had to prove that he or she was saved. Also, under heavy persecution in England, the Protestants also chose America. Protestants were the first followers of Martin Luther and established the Lutheran religion in America.

From the early 1600s English colonies along the Atlantic seaboard, with plentiful sea access, became richer and more populated than New France. In 1628, the Massachusetts Bay Colony was established in present day central New England, and would eventually include portions of Massachusetts, Connecticut, New Hampshire, Maine and up through Nova Scotia at the time known as Arcadia. Initially, settlements were in Boston and Salem. The Dutch colonists of New Netherlands, who founded their colony in 1611, disputed much of the claim for land advanced by the Bay Colony. New Netherlands covered portions of New York, New Jersey, Connecticut, Pennsylvania and Delaware. The Dutch only occupied small areas of these regions, areas close to or on the water for navigation in conducting their fur trade with the Indians. By 1700s the English colonies had become firmly established from Maine to Georgia. Both the French and English were heavily involved in the lucrative fur trade industry. In 1670 King Charles II of England granted the Hudson Bay Company exclusive trading rights over the watershed draining into Hudson Bay. For the next 100 years the Company competed with– Montreal based traders. England and the France were both staking claims in what would become Canada, and both were very interested in fur trading with the Indians. Most of the fur–bearing animals had been over–hunted in Europe, yet, there remained a huge demand for fur from beaver pelts–for making hats, coats and other garments. To get an idea of how important beaver pelts were to commerce, between 1700 and 1770, twenty-one million hats made from beaver felt were exported to England. Beaver pelts were the first great American trade commodity. Although the British Colonists were not involved in the "Beaver War" it does have ramifications for the development of the colonies.

The Iroquois's Beaver War

The combatants in the war in 1629 were the Iroquois Confederacy made up of several tribes: Mohawk, Oneida, Onondaga, Cayuga, and the Seneca, all inhabitants of the area around upper New York to the eastern edge of the Great Lakes of Ontario, Erie, Huron, Lake Champlain and the Ohio River Valley. The great Chief Hiawatha united the five tribes as their continual warring with each other threatened them into extinction. The Iroquois Confederacy dominated all of the other tribes in northeast America and Canada. Their reputation was one of ruthless cruelty, especially in their torture of captives, and cannibalism. The cannibalism centered around eating the hearts and liver of combatants that were exceptionally brave. The Indians thought that by consuming these organs they would gain possession of the bravery and courage of their fallen enemy. Their adversaries were the French Colonists and the Indian tribes that had aligned themselves with the French, the Algonquins and the Hurons. In 1754 the Iroquois Confederacy would become allies with the Colonists in the French and Indian War. The British Colonists were much better trading partners for the Iroquois because the supply ships could arrive at settlement ports, meaning better, cheaper and a broader variety of goods. The French were remotely located in the inner parts of Canada and along the Mississippi River and very poorly supplied. The Iroquois placed a high value on arms and ammunition from the settlers, both for hunting and warfare with their enemies, other tribes and, in this instance, the French. The Iroquois also traded for iron tools, axes, plows, farming tools, and clothing. It is easier to fell a tree with a steel ax than one made of stone. The Iroquois wanted to become the sole purveyor of pelts and other furs to the British and Dutch Colonists. Beavers were becoming scarce in the lands of the Iroquois and to realize their monopoly they would have to expand their territory, taking over the trading posts operated by the French. They would also have to dislocate some of the other tribes in the Great Lakes region. The French had established treaty relationships for trade and mutual defense with the Huron and the Algonquin Tribes. The battles and wars to gain the fur monopoly became known as the "Beaver Wars," of 1629.

By 1600 South America and Mexico were largely controlled by Spain and Portugal. England and France, long standing rivals in Europe, were vying for dominance of North America. This need to colonize by bigger and stronger populations would cause tensions with the Indians, as the ever-increasing numbers seemed an ominous threat. A major cultural difference that would add to the tensions was that the settlers would buy the land from the Indians, but the Indians did not understand the idea of land ownership. They thought they were selling the use of the land. If you were strong enough to hold onto your land, it was yours for living, hunting and planting. As the Iroquois began their expansion some tribes fled because of the ferocity of Iroquois warriors, especially the Mohawks. Some tribes stayed and defended their land. Several tribes were virtually wiped out–the Huron, Neutral, Erie, Susquehannock, and the Shawnee. The result of the Beaver Wars was that the Dutch virtually abandoned their claim to North America and the French position was greatly weakened.

The Pequot War - 1637

The Dutch had established a trading relationship with the Pequots. The population and government of the Bay colony were strongly Puritan. The colonists initially had good trading relationships with the local Indian tribes; however, as seems customary, tensions eventually developed. A kind of pattern seemed to emerge with most of the settlements. Initially there was mutually beneficial trade between the two parties; then, as the population of the settlements begin to grow and more land was needed, the Indians became concerned about becoming a minority in their home territory. Tribes also wanted to establish trading monopolies and discouraged other tribes from trading, which caused tensions among many of the tribes. The tensions grew, and by 1636 erupted into the Pequot Wars, which lasted until 1638. The tribes that traded with British colonists were at a great advantage over other tribes with their newly acquired firearms, gunpowder and metal tools. These tensions emerged as King Philips War in 1675 and lasted until 1678.

There was not a clear understanding between cultures of land payments. The Indians thought the land payments were for recognition of common rights to the use of the land, in return for friendly relations and mutual defense. The settlers' understanding was that they had purchased the land, and it was now theirs. The settler's idea of land ownership was that you owned the land so it could be developed. If the land was not yours anyone stronger or more numerous could take it, so what would be the point of building or developing the land. The Indians' belief was that no one can really own land–it is for everyone. The initial colonists established settlements called Massachusetts Bay and Saybrook and they had allied themselves with the Narragansett and the Mohegan tribes. The Chief of the Pequot was Sassacus and he wanted to expand his trading with the Dutch and saw the new colonists as a threat to his trading enterprise. He began expanding his territory, pushing the Wampanoags to the north, the Narragansetts to the east, the Mohegans to the west and the Lenape Algonquian to the south. Just prior to the settlers' arriving there had been some kind of a plague in this part of New England that apparently started in the early 1600s and ran for many years, by the best estimates. The plague had weakened all of the tribes and created a power vacuum of sorts, which in turn created the need for tribes to band together. With the Indian belief of "it is your land if you can hold onto it" the Narragansetts began to expand their territory. This situation forged a strong alliance with the Dutch and the Pequot and between the English and the Mohegans.

A fur trader by the name of John Oldham and some of his crew were murdered while on a trading voyage. This was done by members of the Pequot tribe to discourage the English from trading with the Mohegans and the Narragansetts. Endecott, the Governor of the Massachusetts settlement, with his militia raided a nearby village. Most of the villagers escaped so they burnt the village. This set off a series of raids by Sassacus, Chief of the Pequot, on the settlements for the next several months. Governor Endecott commissioned Captain John Mason and his militia of ninety and seventy Mohegans, to attack Chief Sassacus's Fort Mystic. John Underhill, with twenty militia and 200 Narragansetts from Saybrook joined with Mason for the attack. This would result in the May 26th, 1637 "Mystic Massacre." The Pequot's fort was surrounded by wood pickets. Twenty of the militia breached the gates and went inside. The accompanying Indians surrounded the fort, and soon, upon entering the militia, were besieged from an onslaught of arrows. Many of the militia were wounded. To create chaos and effect an escape, some of the militia set some of the wigwams on fire. A prevailing wind quickly pushed the fire through the whole fort. The militia escaped, but most of the Pequot inside the fort died. The militia then moved in on a second camp. The Pequots fled and became trapped in the Sasqua swamp. The women and children were allowed out of the camp before the battle began. It is uncertain how many casualties there were on either side, however some of the Pequot escaped along with Sassacus. One hundred and eighty Pequots were captured. As was customary at the time, among Indians, the captured Indians were divided out among the victorious tribes. Those that would assimilate became part of the tribe, and those that would not were either used as laborers or sold into slavery. The Pequots sought refuge with the Mohawks; however, the Mohawks killed the Pequots, beheaded Sassacus and sent his head to the colonists. The Pequot Wars virtually eliminated the Pequot tribe.

Settlements

When the colonies were first established residents had small farms. The men worked the farm or tended livestock. The role of women was to tend to the household and to raise and nurture healthy children, which they did. Many pioneer women had six to eight children. Life expectancy was about sixty years; however, many children died of disease before they were five years old, thus the big families. The women spun yarn from wool to make clothing, knitted, cooked and made candles and soap. New England parents, upon the marriage of their children, helped their sons establish farms of their own, giving them gifts of land, livestock or farming equipment. Women would receive household goods, farm animals or cash. Because of the abundance of wood most farmhouses were one and a half stories and made from lumber. The half story was the loft where the children slept. Family life revolved around the fireplace, used for cooking, lighting for chores, activities and warmth. Alternate light sources were homemade candles, kerosene lanterns were not commonplace until the mid-1850s. Daily life centered on chores, farming, tending a couple of animals and gathering protein from hunting or fishing. If you wanted to sweep the floor, you first had to make the broom, as with most things, out of shredding a tree branch and tying back the strands. There were schools in towns, most settlements relied on home schooling with the New England Primer. Boys did the outside chores, chopping firewood, fetching water, girls were inside weaving, soap and candle making. Aside from chores there were games, some established others just made up from adolescent creativity. The day usually closed with Scripture reading around the fireplace by the head of the household. Through their faith, strong work ethic and determination, the American family was born free, democratic and decidedly Christian.

Colonizing North America was a vastly new lifestyle from Europe. When they arrived there were no roads, no cities, no structure or supplies. Everything had to be built, farmed, made or shipped from developed countries, primarily England. Women working outside the home was a vastly new idea. The idea of female independence has its origins in the early years of colonization, as did American independence, perseverance, entrepreneurship, and American exceptionalism. In three hundred years Americans went from candles and ox carts to the first man on the moon. Women often worked alongside their husbands in the fields, growing crops. They also received full title to the property the family owned upon the death of the man of the house, a concept unheard of in the rest of the world.

Although the idea of the separation of church and state is nowhere in the Constitution, the understanding of the concept has been changed by revisionists from its original intent. The early settlers-built schools in every community. The idea carried over from the Protestant Reformation that everyone should be able to read the Bible and form their own understanding as it was given to them from the Holy Spirit. In order to affect that concept in the New World, schools were built so that every child would be taught to read so they could read the Bible for themselves. The literacy rate in the colonies was 70 percent, whereas it was 0 to 40 percent in the rest of the world. The idea was also held that governing laws, regulations and statutes were to have their origins from Scripture. When legislation was proposed the discussion would start with the question, "and where do you find a basis for that in Scripture?" The Catholic Church dominated the rulers of Europe for the most part and the Church of England was an extension of the government. The intent of the founders of the colonies and of the Founding Fathers was that government should be based on God's natural law and the Federal Government had no right to interfere with the church. God's law, not mans, would set the precedence of how Americans would be governed. The unalienable rights given to us by God would be kept secure under the authority of God's law, which in turn keeps us free. The "separation" was that government would be established on Biblical principles and the government would have no say in religious matters. The First Amendment reads; "Congress shall make no law respecting the establishment of religion or prohibiting the free expression thereof; or abridging the freedom of speech, or of the press; or the right of people to peacefully assemble, and to petition the government for a redress of grievances."

The objective of the Spaniards was gold, obtained with superior firepower and converting the people of the New World to Catholicism. The French sought to colonize North America and Canada, establish trade, and convert the indigenous population to Catholicism. The Dutch were primarily interested in trade and profit. The English looked to colonize North America, establish trade, create agriculture and convert the tribes of North America to Christianity. "For the glory of God and the advancement of the Christian faith." And to expand English presence on the worlds stage.

The Anglican Church was the state church of Virginia. Their charter was established in 1606.

Virginia declaration of rights.

"That religion, or the duty which we owe to our Creator and the manner of discharging it, can be directed by reason and conviction, not by force or violence; and therefore, all men are equally entitled to the free exercise of religion, according to the dictates of conscience; and that it is the mutual duty of all to practice Christian forbearance, love, and charity towards each other."

January 1639, The Fundamental Order of Connecticut. "Forasmuch as it has pleased Almighty God by the wise disposition of His Divine Providence so to order and dispose of things that we the inhabitants and residents...and well knowing where a people are gathered together the Word of God requires thast to maintain the peace and union of such a people there should be an orderly and decent government established according to God, to order and dispose of the affairs of all the people at all seasons as occasions shall require."

Massachusetts, with a charter date of 1629, officially proclaimed its recognized religion to be Congregationalist, primarily Puritans. The Puritans established their colony primarily seeking freedom from religious persecution in England. The freedom they sought, however, was for themselves and not for others. The Puritans felt called by God to establish 'new Israel,' a holy commonwealth based on a covenant between God and themselves as the people of God. Though there were separate areas of authority for church and state in Puritan Massachusetts, all laws of the community were to be grounded in God's law and all citizens were expected to uphold the divine covenant...

American politics gained another footing with the outbreak of the civil war in England from 1642-1651. Parliament was becoming more Protestant and increasingly at odds with king Charles I, a Catholic. Charles disbanded Parliament and ruled without it for a decade. The disparity soon became a battle over control of the government of England. Charles believed in the divine right of kings to rule, which stated that his right to rule came from God. Parliament wanted to put restrictions on the power of the king, especially for taxing the citizenry. As tensions increased Charles formed an army, as did Parliament. In essence, neither side was winning the civil war. Seeking an upper hand in the civil war, Charles allied with the Irish and Parliament with the Scots, thus dragging them into war. The end result was that Charles was tried for treason and beheaded on January 30, 1649. Charles the II, who was in exile in France, was invited to take the throne. However, the precedent had been set the monarch could not rule without the consent of Parliament–and the nation was becoming a parliamentary monarchy. This also dispensed with the idea of kings having a divine right to rule. The American colonies, under the control of England, would now be ruled by Parliament, not just by the king.

The Dutch and Indian War - 1643

In 1643 there was the Dutch and Indian War, although this war did not involve the English colonists; there were repercussions for the English. The Dutch were not as interested in establishing colonies as they were in profiting from the fur trade. They had a group of investors, the Dutch West India Company, that were not connected with the government, so they had a lot of leeway in conducting their business, which was building trade routes worldwide to become the dominant force in world trade. The Dutch colonies were in New Netherlands. Willem Kieft was the governor of New Netherlands, which was one of the only nonprofitable ventures of the Dutch West India Company. Kieft decided to make up his shortfall by taxing the local Indian tribes of the Lenape population. They, of course refused. The population of New Netherlands tried their best to dissuade Kieft from actions against the local Indians, with whom they had lived peaceably with for two decades, becoming partners, employers and employees of one another's adventures. Kieft sent militia against one of Lenape camp to show them he was serious. There are no real reliable accounts of what happened other than to acknowledge that the plans of battle often turn into chaos in the execution. The result of this venture was a massacre of one of the Lenape camps. This action caused the Algonquians to form an alliance with the Lenape tribe. There were several raids on the settlers of New Netherlands, and many were killed.

The Dutch did not fare well in their engagements with the local tribes. Their primary Native American ally, the Pequot, had been annihilated in the Pequot Wars. Kieft decided to fortify the main fort so he replaced the wood wall with one made of stone, and thus today we have wall street. In 1643 a force of 1,500 natives invaded New Netherlands. Many settlers were killed, and villages and farms were destroyed. Kieft hired Captain John Underhill, who had defeated the Pequots, to come to his aid. Underhill assembled a militia and his forces killed more than 1,000 Natives, including the 500 or so that were killed in the Pound Ridge Massacre. Many of the Dutch settlers, disturbed by Kieft hostility towards the Indians returned to Holland. Kieft was recalled by the Dutch West India Company to be held accountable for his actions; however, the ill will created by his actions would not be forgotten. Kieft died in a shipwreck on the way home. In 1664 English King Charles II awarded the colony of New Netherland to his brother, the Duke of York. Four English ships sailed into the New Amsterdam's harbor and demanded that the Dutch surrender. The new governor of New Amsterdam, Peter Stuyvesant, surrendered without a fight. The name of New Netherlands was changed to New York after the Duke of York.

King Phillip's War - 1675

In 1675 another war erupted between the colonists and the local Indian population. It was called "King Philip's War." Chief Metacomet was the leader of the Wampanoag Indian tribe. Metacomet adopted the name of King Philip because of the friendly relationship between his father Massasoit and the Mayflower Pilgrims. The friendship between the two peoples lasted through the leadership of Chief Massasoit, and his oldest son Wamsutta, called Alexander by the colonists. Massasoit's youngest son, Metacomet, became the Chief at the death of Alexander. A lot had changed since Massasoit had helped the Pilgrims through their first winter. Many more colonists had arrived, and new settlements had developed at Windsor Connecticut, (1633), Newbury Massachusetts, (1635), Hartford Connecticut, (1636), Springfield Massachusetts, (1636), Northampton Massachusetts, (1654), and Providence Rhode Island, (1636). Metacomet saw his territory and influence being slowly eroded by the ever-increasing number of new arrivals. He was determined to drive the colonists from America.

As the colonies were forming, men of military age were required to have a firearm, powder and ammunition and to join the local militia. The militia were trained by local soldiers with experience and all were expected to participate in any threat to the settlement or any adjacent farms or towns. John Sossamon, an Indian convert to Christianity was called the "Praying Indian." John heard of the plans Metacomet had to send raiding parties into the settlements in an effort to drive them out. John was an early graduate of Harvard College and served as a mediator between the two peoples, although he did not declare an allegiance to either. John reported Sossamon's plans to the governor of Plymouth Colony. Metacomet was called before the governor and, though nothing could be proven, he was warned not to begin an uprising, or his land and firearms would be confiscated. John Sossamon was found dead shortly thereafter. Based on the testimony of an Indian witness, Plymouth county officials arrested three Wampanoags that were lieutenants of Metacomet. The lieutenants were found guilty of murder by a jury that contained six Indian elders. They were executed by hanging on June 8, 1675.

A band of the Wampanoag, the Pauquunaukit, attacked some settlements around the town of Swansea, then besieged the town and burnt it to the ground. Militia from Plymouth and Massachusetts Bay colonies responded to the attacks and destroyed the Wampanoag village at Mount Hope. The Podunk and the Nipmuck tribes then joined the Wampanoags. In the summer of 1675 the Indians attacked Middleborough, Dartmouth, Mendon, Brookfield, Lancaster, Deerfield, Hadley and Northfield. In response, the Massachusetts Bay Colony, Plymouth Colony, New Haven Colony and the Connecticut Colony formed the New England Confederation and declared war on the Indian nation of the Wampanoags. On September 12, 1675 a supply train of wagons securing food for the winter was ambushed by members of the Nipmuck tribe, killing 57 of the 79 men in the wagon supply train and confiscating all of the supplies. Next, the Indians attacked the largest settlement in Connecticut at Springfield on October 5, 1675, burning it to the ground. The Plymouth Colony sent their militia, numbering about 1,000, with 150 Indian allies from the Mohicans. They caught up with the Narragansett, one of the tribes participating in the raids, at the fort in what was called the "great swamp." The battle became known as the "Great Swamp Fight." Most of the Indians escaped. It is unknown how many were killed. Seventy of the militia were killed and 150 were wounded.

Indian attacks continued throughout the winter of 1675-1676 on twenty-two more settlements, in an effort to annihilate the colonists. In the spring of 1676 other settlements were attacked, and Providence was burned to the ground. Some of the colonists were captured and were tortured as part of the Indians' ritual for captured enemies. The same treatment tribes used on one another as captives were used on the Europeans as well. Treatment varied from one tribe to another, according to the culture of each tribe. Captives were either killed, tortured, assimilated or enslaved. In April, when Sudbury was attacked, the militia marshalled to their aid; however, they were ambushed in route. Captain Wadsworth was killed along with thirty of his sixty-man company. Tired of the continual bloodshed Metacomet's men began to desert him. By July, over 400 had surrendered to the colonists.

After the disastrous defeat of General Braddock, with over a thousand English Grenadiers killed in battle, London realized America represented a completely new type of warfare. England commissioned the formation of Ranger Companies. The militia began to form units of rangers. They were better trained and gave their Indian allies more say in the strategies. The rangers were paid by the British government and represented the first permanent military presence in America. Initially they ranged in the frontier from post to post, protecting settlers from Indian attacks. Their name comes from this activity of "ranging." They were recognized by the common green uniforms. They also were well versed in guerilla warfare–common with the Indians. They engaged in target practice, which England thought was a waste of ammunition, they trained in fighting tactics and strategies for attacks and ambushes. They also employed Indians as scouts, guides and interpreters. The rangers traveled light; a rifle, powder, ball ammunition, water, a knife and a tomahawk. They carried very little food and lived off the land. The most notable of the rangers was Roger's Rangers because of their extensive involvement in so many of the battles in the French and Indian War.

Metacomet took refuge in a swamp near Providence that was raided by the rangers. On August 12, 1676 an Indian guide for the rangers, named John Alderman, shot and killed Metacomet. Metacomet was beheaded, drawn and quartered–a traditional treatment of Europe for traitors in this era. "Drawn" meant to be tied to wood planking and drawn by horse to where you were to be hung, almost to the point of death, emasculated, disemboweled, beheaded and quartered, chopped into four pieces, arms and legs cut off.

In 1665-1666 there was the "Great Plague of London" which took the lives of 100,000 Londoners. The plague spread to France in 1668, then resurfaced in Spain in 1676. In 1687 there was a measles outbreak in Boston, Massachusetts, followed by an outbreak of Yellow Fever in New

York in 1690. Yellow Fever caused thousands of deaths in the colonies. It was brought to North America by mosquitoes from Barbados, first appearing in 1668. In 1721 a smallpox epidemic broke out in Boston. The entire population fled the city as it was so severe. This exodus from Boston spread smallpox to all of the other colonies. Malaria was also a new disease in the colonies, which killed many settlers from Europe where malaria was very rare, and few had immunities for it. Every five years there was an outbreak of measles in Boston. Most of these diseases came to be called childhood disease because they affected mostly children. When a person first contracted a major life-threatening disease, they either recovered or died. Those that survived the outbreaks now had an immunity to the disease. When a disease would resurface it would only effect children who did not yet have immunity.

King William's War - 1688

As part of King Philip's War there was also fighting further north in Maine. It was called "King Williams War," which was actually an extension of King Phillip's War. The reason for the continuation was that the terms and agreements from Philip's War were not adhered to. This fighting was motivated by the French to attack the English Colonists that were expanding further and further North. The French were not very aggressive in colonizing. Their population remained sparse, with few from France, willing to venture to New France. French interests remained more in fur trade, fishing for cod and forcing Catholicism on the Indians. The French saw the English as an encroachment into their territory and a threat to their beaver pelt trade and cod fishing. They instructed the Indians to conduct raids on the English settlements and bring them scalps as proof they had killed Englishmen, for which they were then paid. The fighting in Maine and Arcadia never really came to an end. After about four-hundred settlers were killed, the colonists pulled back to New England. The continual warring between the French, Indians and the American colonists left the area in a constant state of disarray without any real civilized development. The American colonists withdrew from Arcadia. The French fishing industry had been destroyed and the fur trading never recovered from the continual warring. The tenuous relationship the Indians had with the French was rapidly deteriorating. The hostilities that begun in 1688 lasted until 1697. The fighting consisted of raids on French or English towns, settlements or ports and then retaliatory raids. A lot of settlers were killed and there were no real major battles. This era ended with the Treaty of Ryswick, another ill-conceived treaty that would lead to the next war, Queen Anne's War in 1702.

Queen Anne's War - 1702

Queen Anne's War, also known as the "War of Spanish Succession in Europe," is the third of what would become known as the French and Indian Wars, fought by French and English Colonies, along with their respective Indian allies for control of North America. Queen Anne's War was an extension of the war in Europe between France, England and Spain, who had allied with France. By 1700 the English colonies, with about 250,000 residents, spread from Massachusetts in the north to the Providence of Carolina in the south, which at the time included Georgia. All of the settlements were east of the Appalachian Mountains, aside from some fur trading posts. North of Boston and into Maine and Nova Scotia, called Acadia at the time, was an area of land in dispute between the French, Indians and the English and had been in a semi state of war since 1675. To the south of Carolina in Florida was land claimed by the Spanish crown. The Spanish were building missions in the south and were very aggressive in converting the Indians to Catholicism. The colonists who had fled religious persecution in England were very aware and very defensive against the Catholic French in the north and the Catholic Spanish to the south.

The French established a trading post in New Orleans on the Mississippi and built a fort at Biloxi Mississippi. This created a good deal of concern among the English colonists. They were also concerned about the French trading posts being established along the Mississippi. Both the colonists and the French knew that the Mississippi would be vital to the fur trading industry. In the south the French had begun trading with and allied with the Choctaw Indians, who happened to be enemies of the Chickasaw who in turn had allied themselves with the English. Before war broke out in Europe in 1702 the Spanish allied with the Apalachee and planned to raid the English trading centers in the back country of Carolina. This was Carolina before it split into North and South Carolina and included parts of northern Georgia. The English got word of the impending raids and waited in ambush for the raiding parties at the head of the Flint River. The English and their allies, the Chickasaw, routed the Spanish forces and drove them back to Pensacola. The English, anticipating continued hostilities, also allied with the Muscogee (Creek) and the Yamasee. After this encounter Carolina's Governor Moore, in a preemptive action with a militia of 500 men and 300 Indian allies captured and burned St. Augustine, Florida. Governor Moore's forces were unable to take the main fortress Castillo de San Marcos, the oldest masonry fort in the United States, and is a National Park today. When a Spanish fleet arrived from Cuba, Moore called off the siege and returned with his forces to Carolina.

In 1704 Moore conducted numerous raiding expeditions with his militia and Indian allies into Florida, which devasted the population of the Apalachee and the Timucua tribes. The action would come to be known as the "Apalachee Massacre of 1704." Most of the population was either killed, captured, fled to Spanish and French outposts or joined the English. Many of the Indians that joined the English did so because they were poorly treated by the Spanish, being used as forced labor and there was also concern among the tribes about Indians being used to shed Indian blood. Moore resettled the Apalachee Indians along the Savannah River. The Creek however, continued to raid the Spanish and their allies for the next couple of years. There were no major consequences of these battles other than a greatly diminished Spanish presence, a loss of life for the Spanish colonists, Apalachee, Creek, and the resettlement of the Apalachee from Florida to Carolina, today Georgia. The Savannah River is the present-day border between Georgia and South Carolina.

Queen Anne's War in the north was a replay of King William's War–raids on English settlers by the French and their allies, the Wabanaki Confederacy, which consisted of the Mi'kmaq, Maliseet, Passamaquoddy, Abenaki and Penobscot tribes and reciprocal raids of reprisal. The raids were quick, often surprising the settlers, many of whom were killed or captured. An emerging feature of this conflict, however, was the capitalization of human trafficking. When the settlements were raided the settlers that were not killed were taken captive and held for ransom. When 50 French Canadians, 250 Abenaki and Caughnawaga Indians raided and destroyed the Deerfield settlement in the Province of Massachusetts Bay all the settlers that were not killed were taken captive. The children that survived the raid were adopted by the Mohawks and the adults were held for ransom. This worked so well that adult captives became a new commodity for the Indians. Communities would take up collections to buy back their captured neighbors. Several major campaigns were planned but when the naval support failed to arrive the plans were abandoned.

An interesting development of this war was that the English were reluctant to make a full-scale commitment because they did not want to disrupt the fur industry. The Iroquois chose to remain neutral during the war, focusing as well on the fur trade industry. The Iroquois also believed Indians should not shed Indian blood for the sake of the settlers. The French put certain settlements off limits, as they did not want to incite the Iroquois into battle. They were more afraid of the Iroquois than they were of the English.

Adding to these ingredients for conflict was the death of the childless king Charles of Spain. Claims for the throne were made by his closest heirs' members of the Austrian Habsburg, which was also the throne of the Holy Roman Empire. Charles also had heirs in the House of Bourbon, who ruled in France. There was a potential for a significant shift in the power structure of Europe depending on who would be seated on the throne in Spain. At this time in history Spain was one of the largest empires in the world with land possessions in Asia, Italy, Spanish Netherlands, the Philippines and the Americas. Spain had sent its Spanish Armada with an invasion force to England previously, and France and England had been involved in mutual hostilities for decades. With the potential power shift the king of England and the parliament declared war on France and Spain in 1702. The dates of Queen Anne's War were from 1701 – 1714. By 1710 the fighting was at a stalemate. French forces had been driven back into France and the Allies, Austria and Spain, were unable to occupy France. In 1711 Britain withdrew from the conflict, forcing the warring factions to make peace, resulting in the 1713 Treaty of Utrecht.

The only real conclusive outcome of the war in Arcadia came as a result of the terms of the treaty signed in Europe between England and France. In the 1713 Treaty of Utrecht, Britain gained Arcadia, which they renamed Nova Scotia, and sovereignty over Newfoundland and the Hudson Bay region; however, once again, England and France failed to include the Indians in the treaty talks and the treaty itself. The treaty defined lands and set borders regardless of Indian territories. The colonists made agreements with their allies and set borders. The lands allocated to the Indians were called reservations. But the French and their allies would not honor the English agreements, and neither would the English honor the agreements between the French and their allies. By the time this treaty was signed there had been four wars in the area of Arcadia, Massachusetts and the Hudson Bay area. The treaties were ill defined, usually formulated in Europe, ambiguous, and always left out the Indians. The treaties did not stop the fighting, it only slowed it down, and the fragile peace remained intact until the occurrence of some grievous affront by one of the parties. The continual violation of treaties by opposing parties left the overriding impression that the treaties, once signed, were never honored. Unfortunately, this practice would continue and left very little confidence for the Indian in any treaty that was signed. Additionally, there were people such as Father Sébastien Rale who was constantly encouraging the Norridgewock tribe to attack English settlements. The Governor of Massachusetts, Joseph Dudley, became so infuriated with the attacks he offered a reward for the capture of Rale.

There were two fundamental issues that went unresolved and were the underlying cause of most of the hostilities. First, it was the trade. Trading relationships were established and as long as they remained equitable the fragile peace held. However, hostilities would eventuate as Indians, French and the Americans would try to form fur monopolies. The trading competition created friction over land and trade agreements. The Indians did not necessarily honor exclusive trading with one partner, it was whoever gave them the better deal. This form of trading pitted the French against the Americans. Secondly, as the colonists continued to arrive a chief would come to power, see the encroachment of settlers as more of a threat than the benefit of trade, and try to expel the newcomers.

The immigration, of course, was not going to stop. This sentiment continued throughout the settling of North America. Great Apache warrior chiefs like Geronimo and Cochise fought the U.S. Government as immigrants settled in the southwest U.S. There were many great chiefs, including Lakota chiefs, Crazy Horse and Sitting Bull, who also fought the US Calvary. Additionally, there was the continual unresolved issue of land use versus land ownership. This idea was further complicated by the Indian custom of taking land if you needed it. Whoever was stronger would hold onto it. Much in the manner the Iroquois expelled neighboring tribes when they wanted a monopoly of the fur trade. Wars are never fought over a right and a wrong; both parties involved think they are in the right; hence, wars are fought between two rights and that is why disagreements erupt into war.

Drummer's War - 1722

The peace from the Treaty of Utrecht signed in 1713 lasted until 1722. In the treaty Arcadia, renamed by the English as Novia Scotia, transferred from French rule to English. When the English signed treaties with the Indians they expected the Indians to then be British subjects. Most of the Indians that understood this rejected the claim or any attempts to administer such claims. They belonged to no one.

The war that began in 1722 has been called "Drummer's War" named after Lt. Governor Drummer of Massachusetts. It was a war in Arcadia between the New England Colonists and the Wabanaki Confederacy, consisting of the Mi'kmaq, Maliseet, and Abenaki tribes. When the Wabanaki tribes realized that Nova Scotia had been seceded to the British by the French the Abenaki tribe sought a treaty with the English. The English and Abenaki tribe signed a treaty; however, the Mi'kmaq would have nothing to do with a treaty. Instead they began raiding parties against settlements and fishing towns along the coast of Maine and Nova Scotia. This takes on a very familiar pattern, Indian raids on settlements are followed by raids of reprisal by the colonists. The raids were conducted in Maine, Nova Scotia and along the borders of Massachusetts and New France (Canada). The Indians were led by Father Sébastien Rale who, it was later discovered, was working as an agent for the French to ensure continued raids on the English by the Indians. There were no major battles, just a series of raids and reprisal skirmishes. The result of the war was that the English had a more secure position in Maine.

King George's War 1744

The peace held for twenty years until 1744, when king George's War broke out, in roughly the same area. This war was also the consequence of war in Europe between England and France called the "Austria War of Succession" in Europe. When the French in Canada at Fort Louisbourg received news of the war in Europe they immediately began plans to attack the English garrison at Fort Anne. The French were delayed in their offensive as the Mi'kmaq and the Maliseet under Father Jean-Louis Le Loutre decided to attack on their own. Their attack in July proved unsuccessful. They were unable to take the Fort. The French tried without aid from the Indians in August and were also unsuccessful in their attempt.

Had they remained united there may have been a different outcome.

In 1745 the English were able to capture Fort Louisbourg from the French, after a six-week siege. In retaliation the Wabanaki Confederacy began attacking settlements in Arcadia and fishing villages along the coast. When French King Louis XV heard that the fort had fallen, he dispatched reinforcements to retake the fort. King Louis XV put his Admiral Jean-Baptiste Louis Frédéric de La Rochefoucauld de Roye in command of the largest force ever sent to the New World. The force included 11,000 soldiers and sailors and a fleet of 64 ships. This is the sixth time the French had tried to retake Arcadia over the last fifty years.

As the fleet set sail, it was caught in adverse winds and a severe storm, all which extended their time at sea. The fleet then ran into a dead calm which was followed by another storm. Lightning set several of the ships on fire, in one exploding the munitions, killing thirty of those on board. They were still over a thousand miles from Nova Scotia when typhus broke out amongst the crews. As they approached land they were opposed by another storm, which damaged several ships. The damaged ships were forced to return to France.

Jean-Baptiste Nicolas de Ramezay lead a force of 700 soldiers from Quebec to rendezvous with the French fleet. Ramezay's forces were joined by 300 Abenaki and 300 Mi'kmaq Indian warriors. The fleet arrived three months after leaving France. There were 44 left of the original 64 ships, and thousands of men had died of typhus and typhoid fever. The admiral died of a heart attack six days after their arrival. Constantin-Louis d'Estourmel was put in charge of the expedition. He sent a force of 1,500 men to rendezvous with 300 soldiers from Quebec, d'Estourmel then attempted suicide. No one seems to know why. He came down with a fever and relinquished his command to rear-admiral Taffanel La Jonquiere, who was a passenger aboard the fleet and was to be governor general of Canada. La Jonquiere mustered a portion of his fleet for an attack off Cape Negro, Nova Scotia. Two days later he changed his mind, called off the attack, sent word to Ramezay to withdraw and took the fleet back to France. La Jonquiere inherited a fleet of 42 ships and 41 percent of the soldiers and sailors that had not died of disease. La Jonquiere, considering his diminished force, probably thought it was better to be the governor general of Canada than to potentially die in battle. He returned the flowing year as the governor general of Canada. Again, nothing was resolved by this conflict. Tensions remained high. Skirmishes and raids continued and would eventuate in 1749 as Father Le Loutre's War.

Arcadia, now called Nova Scotia, had been ceded to the English, at the end of King William's War. However, the Mi'kmaq did not acknowledge the legitimacy of this agreement. The English sent 3,229 Protestants to settle in Nova Scotia. The Mi'kmaq became very concerned about the huge influx of settlers and began a series of raids on the settlements. The response of both the French and English was to construct forts. The forts, although not very large, served as staging areas for retaliatory strikes against the Indians and a position of defense and protection. The Arcadians were descendants of French colonists who settled Arcadia (Nova Scotia) during the 17th century. The Arcadians also did not acknowledge British rule over what they considered their land, regardless of what agreements were reached in a treaty, and they certainly would not take an oath of loyalty to the English crown. The English began deporting Arcadians. Father Le Loutre began paying Mi'kmaqs for English scalps. The war actually began when Edward Cornwallis arrived from England with thirteen transports with the intent of establishing a fort and settlement at Halifax. The French immediately saw this as a threat to their supply line, the St. John River, which would also give the English direct access to Quebec, an immediate threat. The French immediately responded by building three forts along the river. The Mi'kmaq thought establishing Halifax was a direct treaty violation, however, that was a treaty they had with the French. The English continued to deport Arcadians as they knew they were helping the French with communications, logistic support and aiding and abetting. The English attacked and took control of the three river forts. Le Loutre resigned to this fate. Without the ability to be resupplied he had little chance of success.

The deportation of Acadians continued. English settlers took their place throughout Maine. Some of the Acadians returned to France and others resettled in French New Orleans, expecting to remain French. The Louisiana population contributed to the founding of the modern Cajun population. The French word "Acadien" changed to "Cadien" then to Cajun. The Cajun today occupy parishes in Lafayette, New Iberia, St Martin, St Mary and Vermilion in southwest portions of Louisiana

The Great Awakening

During the late 1730s and early 1740s the American colonies experienced a religious revival called "The Great Awakening." The sentiments and issues that arose were much like the underpinnings to the Protestant Reformation inspired by Martin Luther. A new kind of preaching arose by clergy like Jonathan Edwards and his famous emotional and intense delivery of a sermon called; "Sinners in the Hands of an Angry God." If you were to attend one of Edward's sermons you would have heard a theology that expressed;

"But man being the highest of this lower creation, the next step from him is to God. He therefore is made for the service and glory of God. This is the whole work and business of man; it is his highest end, to which all other ends are subordinate."

Edwards once preached; "So the subordinate end of the husbandman in ploughing and sowing, and well manuring his field is, that it may bring forth a crop. But his more ultimate end is, that food may be provided for him and his family. Therefore, through his inferior end be obtained, and his field bring forth ever so good a crop, yet if after all it be consumed by fire, or otherwise destroyed, he ploughed and sowed his field as much in vain, as if the seed had never sprung up. So, if man obtain his subordinate ends ever so fully, yet if he altogether fails of his ultimate end, he is wholly a useless creature. Thus, if men be very useful in temporal things to their families, or greatly promote the temporal interest of the neighborhood, or of the public; yet if no glory be brought to God by it, they are altogether useless."

This is the heart and mind, the worldview of Americans, in the formative years of our beginning and our accountability to God. There were also very charismatic preachers like George Whitfield and Charles and John Wesley, who held large outdoor preaching events called revivals. Women and slaves attended these events in a very untraditional type of religious setting. It brought a new understanding of the Holy Spirit as an abstract but perceptible force that brought understanding to the individual through a commitment to the Father and His incarnate Son. It brought emotion and the ability to feel an intimacy with God. Colonists realized that the Holy Spirit resided within the individual, an indwelling. With this came the understanding that an established church or religious authority was not necessary for one's salvation. God's will is understood by reading Scripture and being guided by the Holy Spirit and one's conscience, not by the government or a king or state–religion all with ulterior motives that did not favor the individual. Religion is very personal.

The Great Awakening gave birth to many new denominations, including Methodists and Baptists. There was an increased interest in education, too. Princeton University was built to train ministers. Dartmouth College was started to educate Native Americans about Christianity. Harvard's rules and precepts upon its founding were; "Let every student be plainly instructed, and earnestly pressed to consider well, the main end of his life and studies, to know God and Jesus Christ which is eternal life (John 17:3) and therefore lay Christ at the bottom, as the only foundation of all sound knowledge and learning." The founding statement for Princeton was "Cursed is all learning that is contrary to the cross of Christ" The Great Awakening also bore the seed that political power does not and should not reside in the hands of a monarchy, or from England for that matter. The power of politics, of government belongs to the people. Faith was not a matter of the clergy but a matter of the individual, just as government does not belong in the hands of England but in the hands of the American people. John Adams credited the Great Awakening as the motivating force behind the revolution.

THE WAR THAT MADE AMERICA

The fourth and final French and Indian War from 1754 – 1763, was called "The Seven Years War" in Europe and "The French and Indian War" in the colonies. Historians refer to this war as the war that made America, America. It was also the first World War. It involved all of the great powers of Europe: Great Britain and France, of course, but also Austria, Sweden, Russia, Saxony, Prussia, Hanover, Spain, and Portugal. The war also involved Africa, India, South America, the Philippines, the Caribbean Islands, North America and Canada.

The war in America was fought from 1754 until 1760, from the beginning to the end of the fighting. The war in Europe was fought from 1756 until 1763 from the declaration of war against France in 1756, until the signing of the Paris Peace Treaty in 1763. There are several distinguishing characteristics of the French and Indian War of 1754 - 1763. Firstly, the other French and Indian Wars; King Williams War 1688 – 1697, Queen Anne's War 1702 – 1713, King George's War, 1748 – 1754 could all be considered a 75-year war. These are the names of the wars in the colonies in Europe they were called, respectively: The Grand Alliance, The War of Spanish Succession, The War of the Austrian Succession and the Seven Years War. The first three wars started in Europe and bled over to the colonies. The French and Indian War started in the colonies. Although the preliminary events transpired in Europe.

In 1740 Charles the VI, Emperor of the Holy Roman Empire, died. He was succeeded by his daughter, Maria Theresa, who inherited his kingdom, and became Queen of Hungary, Croatia, Bohemia and was the Archduchess of Austria. Fredrick the II (the Great) of Prussia challenged

106

the legitimacy of her crown. However, Fredrick' s real motivation was to challenge the House of Habsburg, (Austria). Fredrick II declared war against Austria who was allied with France, Saxony, Sweden and Russia. Fredrick seized control of a region of Austria called Silesia. Fredrick II of Prussia was allied with Hanover and Great Britain. This was the deadliest war fought in the 18th century.

However, our focus is on the American Colonies. The French and Indian War was the culmination of the efforts of France and England for dominance of North America. Hostilities, skirmishes, battles and wars had been ongoing for seventy-five years. When the English took control of Maine and Nova Scotia the French began expansion west of Quebec and Montreal into the Ohio River Valley, present day New York State, Pennsylvania and Virginia. The French built forts to protect trade with the Indians. The English wanted to expel the French from what they saw as land granted in their charters. The charters were fairly ambiguous, specifying land grants with no good maps of North America and Canada to specify specific boundaries.

With increasing population due to large families and immigration, land became a premium. The obvious solution was territorial expansion. Others abandoned the farm with the increasing population other forms of livelihood became available, blacksmiths, ship building, transportation of goods by water or on land, stores and shops. Taverns and lodges were built along the roads that went from town to town to support the budding transportation activities. Most of the transactions between people were on a barter system, as those that gave up farming needed food. For the most part early Americans had a good relationship with the indigenous population. That relationship would be drastically changed by the French and the British, frankly because they did not give a damn about the Indians or the Colonists.

The French and Indian Wars were so named because of the major importance of native Americans' participation in these conflicts. The Iroquois Confederacy, or Haudenosaunee (Long-house), was allied with the English and consisted of the Native American tribes of the Mohawk, (People of the Flint), Oneida (People of the Standing Stone), Onondaga (People of the Hills), Cayuga (People of the Great Swamp), and the Seneca (People of the Great Hill). The French were allied with the enemies of the Iroquois, the Hurons from the region around the valley of the Ottawa River, Quebec, and Ontario. They were also allied with the tribes of Acadia, the Algonquins, consisting of the Penobscot, Abenaki, Mi'kmaq,

Passamaquoddy, and the Maliseet. Also, members of the Wabanaki Confederation; Ojibwa, Ottawa, Shawnee and Wyandot. Fighting took place along the frontiers between New France and the British Colonies, from Virginia to Newfoundland.

In the 1740's and 1750's British and French-Canadian traders increasingly encountered each other in the upper watershed of the Ohio River in what is now western Pennsylvania and Ohio. As they represented competition to one another in the fur trading industry, each side was looking to gain preeminence. The beaver pelt industry had been going very strong for a hundred years. As the beaver population thinned, trappers moved west. In the Ohio River Valley English trappers began running into French trappers moving south from Canada. There were no formal treaties and both sides claimed the land for either France or England. In some instances, it was nothing other than putting up a sign that read, "this land belongs to England." The British, with better, more and cheaper goods, were becoming the trading partner of preference with the Indians.

During the late 1740's, William Trent, an English trapper, had a fur trading enterprise with Indians in the Ohio River Valley. He built a trading post at the headwaters of the Ohio River. It was an ideal location at the center of three rivers. The trading opportunities were especially promising as the rivers provided easy access far into the forest and to many different tribes, as where there were no roads. In 1754 a French military force captured Trent's outpost and began building Fort Duquesne. They also ran off other traders in western Pennsylvania. To formalize their land claims New France in 1754 began building other fortifications. The fortifications not only alarmed the British but the Indian tribes as well. A Mingo chief known as "Half-King" set a meeting with Paul Marin de la Malgue, commander of the French construction force. During the meeting Malgue yelled at Half-King, threw his gift to the ground and insulted him. Half-King, of course, was greatly angered by this outburst and had been humiliated in front of his men. Malgue contracted an illness and died soon afterwards. He was replaced by Jacques Legardeur de Saint-Pierre. Both commanders sent from France to construct the fortifications had never been to New France and were completely unaccustomed to working with Indians. They thought they were savages and held them in contempt.

Fort Necessity

In December of 1753, Virginia Royal Governor Robert Dinwiddie sent militia Major George Washington into the Ohio Valley with instructions and a letter informing the French to leave. Washington met with Saint-Pierre, who was in charge of the French fort constructions. Saint-Pierre told Washington the letter should have been addressed to his superiors and he had no intention of leaving.

In March of 1754, Dinwiddie ordered Lieutenant Colonel Washington back into the Ohio Valley with the instruction to "act on the defensive, but in case any attempts are made to obstruct the works or interrupt our settlements by any person whatsoever, You are to restrain all such offenders, and in case of resistance to make prisoners of or kill and destroy them." Dinwiddie's instructions were issued without the knowledge or direction from the British government. By the time Washington set out on April 2nd, he had a force of 160 men. On his march Washington was joined by Captain Trent and his militia. Captain Trent told Washington that the French were advancing toward his position. He also told him he had a message from Half-King, that he and his warriors would assist the British against the French. Washington continued to a point about 37 miles from the fork in the river and began building a fortification. On May 23rd, Joseph Coulon de Villers de Jumonville was sent to see if Washington was building a fortification. He also had a summons ordering Washington and his troops out of New France territory. On May 27, Christopher Gist, a settler who had accompanied Washington on his 1753 expedition, told Washington that a Canadian troop of about 50 men was in the area. Washington sent 75 men with Gist to find the Canadians.

That evening Washington received a message from Half-King that he had found the Canadian camp. Washington, with a detachment of 40 men, met with Half-King and his 12 warriors. They decided to approach the camp so that Washington could read his letter from the governor. Most of the Canadians in the camp were asleep, Washington and Half-King's men encircled the camp. One of the Canadians, surprised by their presence, fired his musket and Washington ordered his men to fire. They swarmed into the camp. Fourteen of the Canadians had been killed and Jumonville was wounded. Half-King took out his tomahawk and split Jumonville's head open and scalped him. Washington was appalled. Military code of conduct stipulated that soldiers wounded in battle were to be cared for, not summarily executed, he was also surprised at the savagery of Half-King.

However, he also knew better than to call out or reprimand his new ally. Washington and his men returned to finish construction on the fortification, Fort Necessity. On July 3rd, 1754, a combined force of 600 French, Canadian and Indians, commanded by Jumonville's brother, captured Fort Necessity in the Battle of the Great Meadows. Washington negotiated a withdrawal under arms and signed a capitulation document in French, stipulating that Jumonville and his men had been assassinated. Washington did not know the French language and was unaware of what he had signed.

After the defeat and surrender by Washington, Ben Franklin proposed that the colonies unite and form a national military consisting of an army and a navy. His plan was called the "Albany Plan" and was rejected by the colonies who did not want a central government and thought this would be the first step in the formation of one. The colonists were content to have thirteen separate state governments and not risk the scourge of Europe brought by a king or a monarchy.

The Battle of Monongahela

In 1755 news of the two battles reached the Duke of Newcastle in England. He decided to send an expeditionary force to the Colonies. He selected Major General Edward Braddock to force the French from English colonial lands. From France, King Louis XV sent an even larger force. He had intelligence of the size of the English force, and his aim was to try and counteract the effectiveness of the new English presence in the colonies. British Admiral Edward Boscawen, on June 8, 1755, fired on the French ship Alcide, capturing her and two troop ships heading for New France. Military engagements began to escalate both on the seas and on the land until in the spring of 1756, when France and Britain declared war on each other, which is the official beginning of the Seven Years War.

In 1755, General Braddock arrived at the colonies and met with the colonial governors and planned four coordinated attacks on New France. Massachusetts governor William Shirley was to fortify Fort Oswego, then attack Fort Niagara. Sir William Johnson was to capture the fort at Crown Point, New York, and Fort Frédéric. Lieutenant Colonel Robert Monckton was charged with capturing the fort between Nova Scotia and Acadia, Fort Beauséjour. General Braddock was planning to take Fort Duquesne, located at modern day Pittsburg. The fort was located where the Allegheny

River and the Monongahela joined the Ohio River.

The most notable of these attacks was the Battle of the Monongahela or, more aptly, the "Battle of the Wilderness." This was the fort built on the previous location of Trent's trading post. It was a crucial transportation juncture for the Ohio Valley, consisting of Pennsylvania, Virginia, Ohio and west to Lake Erie. General Braddock, with a force of 2,400 British Grenadiers, was accompanied by volunteer Lieutenant Colonel George Washington and his 400 militia. The formation was preceded by 300 ax men to widen the trail to accommodate the troops, wagons, artillery and camp followers. Camp followers were wives, and single women who served by cooking, cleaning, tending the wounded. There were also craftsmen: blacksmiths, leatherworkers and gunsmiths. The Camp followers were usually a couple of miles behind the army. Most of the women that accompanied the army did so because they would be safer with the army than being left at home alone while their husbands were away. In the first week they had only traveled twenty-two of the 100 miles to Fort Duquesne. Almost a month later as they neared the Monongahela River Braddock split his forces and went ahead with 1,400 of his Grenadiers and Washington with his militia.

The Potawatomi and Ottawa, who were allied with the French, had been watching Braddock's movement west from the shadows of the forest. As Braddock came within a few miles of the fort the Indian scouts informed the French of the army's presence. The commander of the French fort did not think he could withstand such a large force and decided his only chance was to ambush Braddock's army at the river. Braddock's scout saw the enemy approaching and informed Braddock. Braddock put his Grenadiers in formation, six to a line, because of the dense forest, and advanced on the enemy. The French also had a traditional European force of French Regulars in similar formation. The French formation actually served as a blocking force as the two armies began to engage each other. The Indians from concealed positions poured gunfire onto the British. Washington deployed his men into the woods, but Braddock would not hear of fighting in such a cowardly fashion. The artillery proved ineffective in the heavy wooded cover, especially with the enemy so broadly dispersed. Chaos ensued and the Grenadiers broke rank and ran into the woods. Abandoning their defensive position, they became targets for the Indians. Braddock was wounded in the chest from a musket ball. The British began a retreat and ran into their rear guard which caused more confusion. After three hours over a thousand of Braddock's Grenadiers were dead with a loss of only twenty-one to the French. Every officer on horseback was shot, except Washington. All fifty-four women were taken captive. Some were later ransomed and returned from Canada. The Indians did not pursue the British but remained to gather honors of battle from the fallen. Honors of Battle were whatever the Indians could collect from the dead or wounded, including scalps, to show their bravery back in their village. Although not in charge Lieutenant Colonel Washington achieved hero status by preventing the British from complete annihilation. Braddock's field desk was captured, revealing the British plans, providing the French with field intelligence for the upcoming battles at Fort Oswego, Fort William Henry and Fort Carillion.

After the battle George Washington wrote from Fort Cumberland to his brother, John Washington on July 18, 1755. The letter reads; "As I have heard, since my arrival at this place, a circumstantial account of my death and dying speech, I take this early opportunity of contradicting the first, and of assuring you, that I have not as yet composed the latter. But by the All-Powerful Dispensations of Providence, I have been protected beyond all human probability or expectation; for I had four bullets through my coat, and two horses shot under me, yet escaped unhurt, although death was leveling my companions on every side of me."

The Indian Prophet

Fifteen years after the Battle of Monongahela, George Washington was in the same vicinity of the Ohio River Valley, where the battle took place, surveying for some land he planned to acquire. He was met by an old chief who spoke with Washington through an interpreter.

"I am a chief and ruler over my tribes. My influence extends to the waters of the great lakes and to the far blue mountains. I have traveled a long and weary path that I might see the young warrior of the great battle.

It was on the day when the white man's blood mixed with the streams of our forest that I first beheld the Chief. I called to my young men and said, mark yon tall and daring warrior. He is not of the red-coat tribe he hath an Indian's wisdom, and his warriors fight as we do, himself alone exposed. Quick, let your aim be certain, and he dies.

Our rifles were leveled, rifles which, but for you, knew not how to miss. Twas all in vain, a power mightier far than we, shielded you. Seeing you were under the special guardianship of the Great Spirit, we immediately ceased to fire at you.

I am old and soon shall be gathered to the great council fire of my fathers in the land of shades, but ere I go, there is something bids me speak in the voice of prophecy. Listen! The Great Spirit protects that man and guides his destinies, he will become the chief of nations, and a people yet unborn will hail him as the founder of a mighty empire.

I am come to pay homage to the man who is the particular favorite of Heaven, and who can never die in battle."

General George Washington went on, over eight years of the Revolutionary War, to lead America to victory over the British is spite of generals that tried to unseat him, congress that doubted him, and a militia that was trying to figure out what an army was, and how to go to battle. As we have seen through history, there are people, at times, that are called by God to do the miraculous, and they step up to the challenge, those that don't, we have never heard of.

The Battle of Fort Beauséjour

Robert Monckton had been charged with taking Fort Beauséjour. The fort was built in 1751 to serve as a buffer between French Arcadia and British–occupied Nova Scotia. Monckton, with a force of 2,000 combined Grenadiers and American militia, set siege to the fort in June of 1755.The fort, thought to be impregnable, was lightly staffed with only 162 French troops. One of the first artillery rounds to strike the fort killed six of the French officers The French withstood the siege for thirteen days, then surrendered the fort. The new British governor of Nova Scotia, Charles Law, immediately began the deportation of the Arcadias. He was convinced they were aiding and abetting the French. This was a very important victory for the British, as they now controlled the entrance to the St Lawrence Seaway, which led directly to Québec.

Shirley and his Niagara expedition had been in competition with William Johnson and his Crown Point expedition for supplies and men in Albany. With the news of Braddock's defeat and additional information that the French had been reinforced with thousands of new troops from France, Shirley postponed his expedition until the spring of the next year. Shirley was recalled to England to give an accounting of his lack of progress on his assigned mission. He was replaced by John Campbell, who immediately cancelled Shirley's plans for Oswego, present day Oswego, New York.

The Battle of Lake George

In September of 1755, William Johnsons' expedition with 3,500 men finally got underway to Fort Frédéric at Crown Point on the south end of Lake Champlain. En route, Johnson's force constructed Fort Edward on the Hudson River. Johnson wanted a staging area and, if the battle did not go well, a place to retreat to. The French officer in charge of Fort Frédéric was Jean-Armand Dieskau, whose scouts informed him of the British presence and the construction of Fort Edward. Dieskau had a force of 3,000 men and decided to go on the offensive and attack Fort Edward while it was still under construction. He took a force of 1,500 men composed of two hundred French Regulars, six hundred irregular Canadian militia and seven hundred Indian warriors. Johnson set up camp on Lake George while the fort was being built. Dieskau's Indians refused to attack Fort Edward. The main fortifications were complete, and there was a large force working that could defend the fort. Dieskau convinced his Indian allies that with the element of surprise they could attack Johnson's base camp on Lake George instead. The Indians agreed. Johnson had scouts as well and he was thereby informed of Dieskau's plans to attack Fort Edward. Johnson immediately sent 1,000 troops and two-hundred Mohawks to help defend the fort. The two forces ran into each other en route, Dieskau's men fell into formation, and Johnson's men dispersed into the forest, retreating to the camp. The encounter was very brief. Dieskau's men pursued the British and colonial militia. When Dieskau's forces arrived at the camp the Indians again refused to attack a well-fortified encampment. The Canadian militia agreed. Frustrated, Dieskau ordered his two hundred French regulars to attack the camp. The regulars were virtually annihilated by musket and cannon fire. Dieskau was wounded and taken prisoner. The Indians and Canadians broke into groups and began working their way back to Fort Frédéric. When the soldiers at Fort Edward heard the battle, the commander sent a detachment of two hundred to reinforce the camp. A scout for the detachment came upon four hundred Canadians and Indians resting. He returned to the detachment and they planned and coordinated a surprise attack. They encircled the resting forces and sprung their attack. All four hundred were either killed or captured. Neither of the forces continued hostilities, Johnson did not press onto Fort Frédéric, and the French remained in control of Lake Champlain and built Fort Carillon located between Lake George on the north end of the lake and the southern end of Lake Champlain. Johnson built Fort William Henry on the south end of Lake George to protect the road to Albany. Although Johnson and his forces won the battles of Lake George, they failed in their mission to take Fort Frédéric.

The Battle of Fort Oswego

The next year, 1756, in May, Britain declared war on France. With opposing forces on either end of Lake George, French and British patrols frequently ran across each other's path, resulting in brief skirmishes. Since Britain had declared war, both sides were increasing their troop strength in North America.

In May of 1756, the Marquis de Montcalm arrived in Canada from France with six regiments of regulars–about 4,000 men. The Canadian governor, Pierre de Rigaud, Marquis de Vaudreuil, was in command of 1,500 marines and 14,000 Canadian militia. Responding to the declaration of war, Montcalm decided to take the initiative against the British and attack Fort Oswego. With a force of 3,000 French regulars, Canadian militia and Indian allies, they marched towards Fort Oswego. The British, aware of the advancing army, retreated from Fort Ontario to Fort Oswego where they planned to make their stance. Montcalm, with the cannons captured from General Braddock's army, began an artillery bombardment of the fort. The British commander was killed by an artillery shell in the opening salvos. Many of the troops in the fort were suffering with illnesses. Greatly outnumbered and under heavy fire, the British surrendered the fort. Montcalm had lost thirty men and gained 121 cannons and 6 armed sloops, and had 1,700 prisoners, including laborers, shipbuilders, women and children. Montcalm turned twenty of his prisoners over to the Indians to compensate them for their losses. The 1,700 was the largest group of prisoners of war in North America up to this point in time. Montcalm marched the prisoners to Montreal. He allowed the Indians to loot the forts, the Indians scalped and killed the sick and wounded who had been left behind. He then burnt both forts to the ground, hoping to encourage the

Indians to stay loyal to the French cause. This action had Montcalm's desired effect as the Seneca and Oneida allied themselves with the French after the battle.

The Battle of Fort William Henry

The following year, in August, Montcalm set his sights on Fort William Henry. The British General Daniel Webb visited Fort William Henry but left after his visit to return to Fort Edward, leaving Lieutenant Colonel George Munro in charge. Fort Edward was on the Hudson River about sixteen miles east of Fort William Henry. Fort William Henry could only accommodate 500 soldiers and there were already 2,200 men stationed there. The balance of Munro's force was entrenched in a camp to the southeast of the fort. Montcalm, with a force of 6,200 regulars, Canadian militia and 1,800 Indian allies marched to Fort William Henry. Some of Major Israel Putman's Rangers discovered the force moving towards Fort William Henry and informed Munro. Munro sent a messenger to Webb asking for reinforcements. The fort, constructed with thirty-foot-thick earthen and wood walls, was surrounded on three sides by a dry trench. The northern wall faced the lake. Although the fort was formidable, it was built to defend against Indian attacks and would not withstand an attack by artillery. The fort had withstood an attack by the French in March primarily because the French lacked any artillery. When Montcalm reached the fort with his force of 8,000, he immediately asked Munro to surrender the fort. Munro rejected the offer.

The following day Montcalm began an artillery bombardment of the fort. After two days of artillery fire Montcalm again asked Munro to surrender, which again was refused. Montcalm's men intercepted a messenger coming from Webb telling Munro he would not be able to send reinforcements and that he should seek the best possible terms for surrender. Under a white flag Montcalm delivered the message from Webb to Munro. The fort had been badly damaged by the artillery bombardment and there were several gaps in the wall surrounding the fort. There was also a smallpox outbreak amongst Munro's troops. The commanders agreed to garrison terms for the surrender. Munro's accompaniment of soldiers would be able to keep their muskets and one cannon, but no ammunition. They were not to take up arms against the French for eighteen months. They would also be provided with a French escort to Fort

Edward. The Indians looted the fort and killed the wounded and ill soldiers they found inside. Concerned with the Indians ferocity, Montcalm and Munro decided they better leave for Fort Edward immediately. At dawn on the next day, August 10th, the column, which included women and children, formed and was provided with a 200-man escort. As the column began its journey the Indians began to attack the column. Some of the French soldiers tried to halt the attack but to no avail. Not wanting to alienate their Indian allies, they offered little resistance. Many in the column broke from the formation and tried to make their way to the fort on their own. The original compliment of Fort William Henry was 2,308 by the end of the month 1,783 had made it to Fort Edward, leaving 525 missing in action. The French escort, on their return to Fort Carillon dismantled and destroyed Fort William Henry. There was a lot of tension between the French and their Indian allies after the battle. The Indians decided they had had enough and departed. Montcalm, without his Indian support, did not press on to siege Fort Edward but instead returned to Fort Carillon. Webb was recalled to London to give an accounting of his inability to reinforce Fort William Henry.

A Change in Leadership

The new accountability of military leadership was the work of the new English Secretary of State William Pitt the Elder, who would later become Prime Minister of Britain. Britain was involved in the Seven Years War in Europe and the French and Indian War in America. It is reported that Pitt was quoted as saying; "I am sure I can save this country, and no one else can." Pitt had a very bold strategy for both America and Europe. He ordered three attacks for his forces in America: to take Louisbourg on Cape Breton Island, which would protect the entrance to the St Lawrence River, gateway to Quebec. Secondly, capture Fort Duquesne at the fork of the Ohio River, to take command of the waterways. The French forts in the Ohio Valley were there to protect the land that France had declared as theirs, which included Québec, Ontario, Michigan, Ohio, Indiana, Wisconsin, and Illinois. Thirdly, the British were to capture Fort Carillon on Lake Champlain protecting the lakes and rivers in the Ohio Valley, essential to supplying the troops. For the latter mission Pitt chose Lord George Howe as commander. However, for political considerations the command was given to Major General (2 stars) James Abercrombie. Howe was given the rank of Brigadier General (1 star), second in command. Pitt also provided Frederic II of Prussia with generous funding for his war against France in Europe. Pitt saw North America, not Europe, as essential in the expansion of Britain's Empire. His generous funding of Fredrick II of Prussia was so they could handle the bulk of the conflict in Europe leaving British forces, ships and resources for the war in North America.

The Siege of Louisbourg

Louisbourg, named after Louis XIV of France, was actually a fortified city. It was founded in 1713 to capitalize on the very profitable fishing industry of the Grand Banks of Newfoundland. The French began fortifying the city in 1720 to protect the fishing industry and the entrance to the Gulf of St Lawrence. The St Lawrence River was a direct access to Québec and Montreal. The fortification was completed in 1740 with thirty-foot-high walls spanning over two miles in length. It was the largest and most expensive fort in all of North America. There were also two smaller garrisons constructed on Cape Breton Island. American colonists captured the city in 1745; however, it was returned to France in the treaty that ended Queen Anne's War, which also gave the American colonists Nova Scotia and Newfoundland. There were some drawbacks to the location of Louisbourg from a military defensive position. Its location was in a low-lying area surrounded by hills, which would give an attacking army a decisive advantage. Its construction was primarily designed for a sea-based assaults, leaving the land facing portion in a weak position. It was also fairly isolated and a long way from either France or Québec should reinforcements or resupplying essentials for war be needed.

In preparation for the siege of Louisbourg, Pitt commanded Admiral Edward Boscawen to form a flotilla of 40 ships-of-the-line, and a hundred troop and supply transports. His combined force was 12,000 sailors and marines. He commissioned Major General Jeffery Amherst (2 stars) to be in charge of ground operations under the direction of Brigadier General James Wolfe (1 star) whom Pitt was familiar with from his operations in the European theater. Wolf led his men, 9,000 British regulars, and a detachment of 600 Roger's Rangers who were under the command of Rogers himself. The British troops were divided into three divisions: Red was under the command of Wolfe, White under General Whitmore and Blue under General Lawrence. They marched into Nova Scotia and spent the month of May training for the attack. Louisbourg was manned by 3,500 soldiers, 3,500 sailors and marines, 11 ships and 800 cannons. The commander of Louisbourg, Chevalier de Drucour, ordered five of the ships scuttled in the harbor to prevent British ships from gaining entry to the Gulf of St Lawrence. The sailors and cannons were off loaded onto the fortification. The commander was aware of the British intentions. The most logical and only strategic place for an offensive landing would be at Gabarus Bay. Drucour sent 2,000 troops to the bay to build fortifications and mount cannon emplacements, to serve as a defensive position.

On June 8th, Admiral Boscawen began his voyage north with Brigadier General Wolfe and his accompaniment of soldiers and rangers. As the flotilla neared Louisbourg General Whitmore staged a feint against Flat Point and General Lawrence staged a feint at White Point. General Wolfe deployed with his men in whaleboats to Gabarus Bay. However, due to the onslaught of cannon fire from the Bay they were forced to turn around. Some of the boats the rangers were in, by providence, were blown east. They spotted a small landing area sheltered from French cannon fire by giant granite boulders. They secured a small beachhead and Wolfe ordered the remaining troops to follow the rangers. Once everyone was on shore the rangers and light infantry attacked the French from the flank and the rear. The French broke and ran to Louisbourg. Some were killed and some taken prisoner. The British began unloading their cannons, powder and ammunition. Wolfe took a detachment of the rangers and 600 men he hand-picked and moved to capture Lighthouse Point.

By June 12th, the point was under his control and he had his men construct a battery on the point from which to shell the walls of the fortification and any of the French vessels that came within range. By June 19th, the cannons were in place and the bombardment commenced. The cannon fire from the British was met by cannon fire from the French. British ships began firing on Louisbourg and the French ships sailed in to neutralize the cannons on Lighthouse Point. One of the French ships was struck by cannon fire from the Point. The cannon ball hit the powder on board and the explosion set the ship on fire. The fire soon spread to the two other ships that had moved in unison to engage the Point. The British had moved portable furnaces onto the Point for the purpose of heating the cannon balls. This produced what was called "hot shot." When the cannon balls were heated, they could very easily set wooden war ships on fire, as well as buildings, and ignite munitions. (May be something of Greek Fire here). When the hot shot was fired into Louisbourg it set the King's Bastion on fire. The building was the headquarters of the fortress and the largest building in North America. Next, the Queen's Bastion was set on fire from hot shot. On July 25th, in the early morning fog, Boscawen dispatched a cutting out party to capture or destroy the two remaining French ships. One of the ships was set on fire and the other was taken captive and sailed to the British flotilla.

Drucour was besieged by the population to surrender before the walls were breached and they would be in the middle of hand-to-hand combat. Drucour knew the British now had full and free access to the harbor and saw no alternative but to surrender. Drucour asked for honors of war as terms for his surrender. With the memory still fresh in his mind of the slaughters at Fort Oswego and Fort William Henry, Amhurst refused the request and demanded unconditional surrender. Drucour reluctantly agreed and surrendered all firearms, ammunition, equipment, and colors. Amherst had lost 172 killed, and 355 wounded. The French lost 102 killed, 303 wounded and the rest taken prisoner. The way to Québec was now wide open.

The Battle of Fort Carillon

At the same time Amherst was executing his charge to take Louisbourg, Major General James Abercrombie was preparing to take Fort Carillon, situated on the north end of Lake George. Although Abercrombie was an untested officer his second in command was the very experienced and well-respected field general, Lord George Howe. The fort was built by the French in 1755, in response to their defeat at the Battle of Lake George. The fort was under the command of Montcalm with a force of 3,600 soldiers. Howe assembled a force of 9,000 colonial militia, 6,000 British regulars and a detachment of rangers at the southern edge of Lake George. Loudoun had a terrible relationship with the colonists. He treated them as second-class citizens and made demands, never asking for men, money and supplies. He threated to use force for their lack of compliance. When Loudoun demanded that Massachusetts provide 2,100 troops they refused. Under Amhurst, who was Loudoun's second in command and aware of Loudoun's disrespect for the colonists, took a much different approach. The change in policies and procedures were welcomed and appreciated by the colonists, which was evidenced by the support they provided him. When Amhurst asked Massachusetts for militia the citizens voted to send him 7,000.

When Montcalm received word of the British advance, he sent his men out to construct a wall from felled trees with shooting platforms along the top. His men also felled trees on the approach that would act as barriers to the advancing troops. The French sharpened the end of the branches on the felled trees to form an abatis. As the soldiers would navigate the felled trees they would be slowed or stopped, which would make them easy targets. For the first time neither force had an Indian element in their ranks. The Indians involved in several of the previous engagements preferred to attack settlements rather than engage in major operations. They suffered very few losses and the booty was easily obtained. Settlements offered very little resistance, plenty of booty, and they were not under the scrutiny of a military of a different culture. The French, to encourage attacks on settlements, continued to reward the Indians with payments for scalps, and continued trading for arms and ammunition.

In July Howe's forces used one thousand boats to travel from the south end of Lake George to the north end. The boats, used in the inland lakes of the Ohio River Valley, were called "bateau," which is French for boat. More commonly, in English, they are referred to as a jon boat. They can be anywhere from 24 to 50 feet long and 5 to 8 feet wide with a flat bottom. The flat bottom made them very stable and able to traverse in very shallow water. An average jon boat could carry twenty soldiers or 12 barrels of supplies. They are pointed at both ends, powered by oars–occasionally a sail, and had a single oar aft to serve as a rudder. The larger boats could be equipped with a small cannon on the front bow.

Once on shore on the north end of the lake, as the camp was being established, Howe took a small force to reconnoiter Fort Carillon. En route, they ran into a French patrol which resulted in a brief skirmish; however, Howe was killed in the exchange of gunfire. The inexperienced Abercrombie took command. He was very cautious and indecisive, changing plans several times. His scouts reported to him that the fort was only manned by several thousand troops. The march to the fort would have only taken a couple of hours, but because of Abercrombie's indecisiveness it took two days to begin moving on the fort. This delay gave the French time to ready their defenses. There was a hill adjacent to the fort and Abercrombie's engineers encouraged him to set artillery on the hill and bombard the fort before they made an assault. It is uncertain why Abercrombie chose to disregard this council; he did not put the artillery into use. Abercrombie's plan, despite the French defenses, was a frontal assault on the fort; overwhelm the defenses and take the fort. The rangers thought the plan foolhardy and refused to participate. They told Abercrombie that if he refused to use the artillery then they should just encircle the fort, cutting off any attempt at resupplying Carillon, wait for Montcalm to run out of food and supplies, and surrender. The colonial militia, taking their cue from the rangers, also refused to participate. Abercrombie sent wave after wave of British Regulars against the fort, many of whom were killed trying to make their way over the abatis. After many failed attempts to take the fort, Abercrombie was forced to call off the attack and retreat to the lake, leaving 1,907 British Regulars dead and wounded on the battlefield. The following morning Abercrombie loaded his troops back into the boats and returned to the south end of the lake. The British lost 551 killed, 1,356 wounded and 37 missing. The French casualties were 106 killed, 266 wounded.

The Battle of Fort Frontenac

Abercrombie received a lot of criticism for his conduct of the battle for Fort Carillon and lost all respect from his men. He would be relieved of his duties in September.

Abercrombie was approached by one of his junior officers, Lieutenant Colonel John Bradstreet, with a plan to attack Fort Frontenac. Eager to win back favor, and because he would not be involved in the fight, he approved the plan. Fort Frontenac was located on the east end of Lake Ontario. The fort was built in 1673 by Comte de Frontenac, governor of New France. It was constructed on the northwest corner of Lake Ontario with easy access to the headwaters of the St Lawrence River. Frontenac hoped to control the lucrative fur trade throughout the Great Lakes region from this location. In the early to mid-1700s the fort served as the main supply hub for all of the French forts to the west and for the French fleet that sailed on Lake Ontario. Taking the fort would remove the supply line, enabling the French forts and ships to be easily defeated once their supplies ran out. The French may even surrender without a fight.

Bradstreet took 5,000 men in jon boats up the Mohawk River in a feint to appear to be rebuilding Fort Bull which had been destroyed by the French in 1756. When he reached the location, they cut north and headed straight across the lake to Fort Frontenac. They put ashore near the fort and established a beachhead. The troops unloaded the canons and placed them in position to fire on the fort. All were surprised by the lack of a response from the fort. The following day the bombardment of the fort commenced. After a few hours a white flag was hoisted over the fort. There were only a hundred defenders in the fort. The balance of the fort's accompaniment had departed at Montcalm's request as reinforcements for the attack on Fort Carillon. The fort, however, was loaded with supplies and equipment to be sent west. The troops loaded as much as they could into their boats and allowed the fort's occupants, which included women and children, to depart for Montreal. Knowing that the reinforcements may soon be returning, Bradstreet ordered the forts destruction and quickly departed.

The Battle of Fort Duquesne

Fort Duquesne was the last objective in the plans devised by Secretary of State Pitt. Fort Duquesne was built on the confluence of the Allegheny and Monongahela rivers formed by the Ohio River. This was the location of Trent's Trading Post. It was strategically important for the British, as it would be used for controlling the Ohio country for both settlements and trade. As it was in 1758, the fort prevented any expansion into the Ohio River Valley by the English. This was the intended objective of General Braddock when his army was defeated.

General Forbes was commissioned to capture the fort with his force of 6,000 soldiers, including Colonel George Washington and Indians from the Cherokee and Catawba tribes. Washington urged Forbes to use the road that had been cleared by General Braddock; however, Forbes insisted on cutting a new road. Washington cautioned against this because the time to build a new road would allow the French to fortify the fort. As Forbes' army neared the fort, he sent Major James Grant of the Scottish 1st Highlanders to reconnoiter the fort. Grant took his 850 Highlanders through the woods, arriving at the fort just before nightfall. Grant sent fifty men to scout out the fort. They set a storehouse on fire and returned, informing Grant there were no troops outside the fort or any other encampment. Grant estimated there were only 200 defenders of the fort and planned an attack for the morning.

In the morning Grant positioned 400 of his men for an ambush and held 300 in reserve to dispatch when he knew the course of the fighting.

He had a company of his Highlanders with drums and flute approach the fort. When the inhabitants of the fort came out to attack, he would spring his ambush. It is curious as to why they set the storehouse on fire, alerting the French to their presence. It was also poor military strategy to leave a fortification and attack an oncoming foe. Traditionally, defenders in a fort have a three-fold advantage over an attacking force.

The commander of the French fort was Francois-Marie Le Marchand de Lignery. The size of his force is really unknown. In the morning the soldiers in the fort were overwhelmed by the show of force as they marched on the fort. Lignery's Indian allies had surrounded the ambush force, and when the soldiers from the fort attacked the oncoming formation, the Indians, from their concealed position, ambushed the ambush. The Highlanders broke and ran, leaving 342 casualties on the battlefield. Grant and thirty of his Highlanders were taken captive. When the Indian allies of the French learned the size of Forbes' forces, they abandoned Lignery. Lignery ordered the fort destroyed and set on fire. He and his men boarded jon boats and escaped up the river. When Forbes' men arrived at the smoldering fort, they were shocked to find the heads of the captured Highlanders impaled on wooden stakes with their kilts laid at the base of the stakes. General Forbes ordered the fort rebuilt and named it Fort Pitt after the Secretary of State that was bringing victory for the British. The fort was located at what is today Pittsburg.

The Battle of Fort Carillon (Ticonderoga)

The British, under Secretary Pitt, began putting more emphasis on removing the French from North America altogether. France and England had been fighting with each other for decades in Europe and he did not want to have the same situation in America. The English poured more resources and soldiers into North America and they raised taxes on their citizens to help finance the war effort both at home and abroad. Britain was also fighting France in Africa and India. Fort Carillon still remained in French hands as the gateway to the west.

In 1759, a major new offensive was launched against New France. It was set as a two-pronged attack so that French forces would be divided between two fronts. This would prevent the French from marshalling their reinforcements as a cohesive unit. General James Wolfe, who was promoted to Major General after his victory at Louisbourg, was to travel up the St. Lawrence River to lay siege to Québec. General Amherst, who replaced Abercrombie after his loss with an army of 16,000 against Montcalm's force of 3,500, was to capture Fort Carillon, then travel north and rendezvous with Wolfe for the siege on Québec. The French, based on intelligence they had received from their Indian scouts, informed Montcalm of British activity. The French, in an attempt to counteract the offensive against Québec, ordered Montcalm to leave Fort Carillon with a contingence force, and bring the rest of his men to Québec. Further intelligence received by Montcalm informed him that Amhurst had a force of 11,000 men. Montcalm knew his forces, numbering about 3,000, would be over-whelmed by Amhurst. Montcalm then instructed Brigadier General Francois-Charles de Bourlamaque to destroy Fort Carillon and, in a slow advance, head towards Québec–but more importantly act as a delaying force so that Amhurst does not reach Québec to rendezvous with Wolfe. This decision prevented the soldiers from Fort Carillon to provide additional support for the upcoming battle for Québec on the Plains of Abraham. Amherst, with his men in jon boats and the rangers and light infantry at the lead in whaleboats, formed a single-file line to work through the narrows on their approach to the fort.

It took several days to place the cannons, and on July 23rd, the bombardment of the fort began. Montcalm's artillery returned fire. By the 26th, Montcalm had his plan in place. He would depart heading to Fort Frédéric (Crown Point), to see to its destruction and act as a delaying force as his army worked its way to Québec. He left 400 men behind to destroy the fort and set a fuse to the powder magazine. The remnant of soldiers left the fort at 10 PM and at midnight the powder magazine exploded. The explosion set many of the buildings on fire; however, the walls of the fort were relatively undamaged. The following morning Amhurst occupied the fort. He instructed his men to put out the fires and begin restoring the fort and to salvage what they could. Before Amhurst left he destroyed the French ships that remained on Lake Champlain. He also dispatched Brigadier General John Prideaux to capture Fort Niagara. These activities prevented Amhurst from joining with Wolfe for the siege of Québec.

The Battle for Fort Niagara

The area between Lake Ontario and Lake Erie traversed by the Niagara River was recognized by the earliest European explorers for its strategic value. La Salle constructed a small fortification there in 1670 called Fort Conti. Poor relations with the Iroquois and the remote location made it difficult to sustain. The fort alternated between being occupied and being abandoned. In 1726 the French, with the permission of the Iroquois, constructed a more permanent structure located on a bluff above the Niagara River and called it Fort Niagara.

Prideaux was accompanied by 3,000 regulars, colonial militia and Sir William Johnson with 1,000 Iroquois. The forces rendezvoused at the destroyed the fort at Lake George. Prideaux left a contingent behind, under the command of Lieutenant Colonel Fredrick Haldimand to rebuild the fort. Prideaux and Johnson continued on to Fort Niagara in jon boats, traveling along the south shoreline of Lake Ontario. They were able to avoid being detected by the French fleet that patrolled the lake. They put ashore three miles from the Fort at the mouth of Little Swamp River. Niagara was commanded by Captain Pierre Pouchot with a garrison force of 486 soldiers. Prideaux, having achieved the element of surprise, portaged his boats into the woods to a ravine called La Bell Famille. He then began moving his artillery ashore and constructed a battery at Montreal Point. Pouchot sent a message to Captain Francisco-Marie Le Marchand de Lignery that he was in desperate need of reinforcements. The British–allied Iroquois were able to convince the French–allied Seneca that the battle would be easily won by the numerical superiority of the British forces. The Seneca left under a white flag. On July 17th, British howitzers began fire missions from Montreal Point on the fort. Three days later Prideaux was killed when he was struck in the head by a fragment of an exploding mortar barrel. Johnson, holding the rank of colonel, assumed command.

An Iroquois scout informed Johnson of the approaching Lignery with 1,600 soldiers. Johnson instructed Lieutenant Colonel Massy to set an ambush on the portage trail on the clearing at La Bell Famille. Massy took several hundred of the regulars and six-hundred Iroquois. He had his troops build an abatis across the road. He positioned one-hundred of his men behind the abatis. He then deployed the rest of his men along the sides of the trail concealed in the underbrush. Massy positioned the Iroquois at the extreme end of the ambush formation. When Lignery's troops saw the abatis, they began firing their muskets at the soldiers who were manning the barricade, reloading as they advanced. Massy's men held their fire until the French were within 35 yards. Most of the volley from the troops behind the barricade found their mark. The flanking ambush was sprung from both sides as the French suffered a withering firestorm. They turned, and in confusion and chaos ran back up the trail. The 600 Iroquois sprang from their cover and inflicted heavy losses. Lignery was wounded and taken prisoner. The French forces suffered 334 killed and 96 wounded, Massy lost 12 killed and 40 wounded. Pouchot would not believe Johnson that his reinforcements had been defeated en route in an ambush. Johnson brought out some of the captive officers who told Pouchot of the ambush. Pouchot surrendered the fort. The British were now in control of the entire western frontier.

A Change in the Balance of Power

A very important naval battle took place in Europe that had a direct impact on the French and Indian War. France was not doing well in several fronts against England. Nearly bankrupt and losing battles with Britain, they were seeking a dramatic reversal of fortunes in what can only be considered an act of desperation. Louis XV of France made plans to invade Britain. Choiseul Frances Foreign Minister was charged with the task.

In 1759 the British, under Sir Edward Hawke, maintained a tight blockade around France in an effort to prevent France from suppling New France with troops, supplies, provisions and other war goods necessary in the conduct of war. Britain had committed 50,000 troops to America while France had only been able to send 12,000. There was also an enormous disparity in the population differences between the sparsely populated New France and the continually growing British colonies, which has a tremendous impact on the size of each army's militia. Britain's blockades, in an effort to hinder France's war efforts, extended to French ports in America, Africa, India, and the West Indies. France's naval forces were split between the Atlantic Ocean and the Mediterranean Sea and must be united for the invasion of Britain. Admiral Edward Boscawen, with fourteen ships-of -the-line, was blocking the French port of Toulon, and its large navel and military bases.

A "ship-of-the-line" is the designation of a ship of war that is used to pull up broadside to an enemy vessel for the purpose of cannon engagement. In a battle, several ships would form a line to engage the enemy ships, hence, the name "ship-of-the-line." The larger the ship the more guns it could carry. This is what usually defined the victor in a battle. The one exception to this was speed and maneuverability. Early on in ship development a single–layered ship would have raised platforms aft and at the bow so that archers could fire arrows down into an opposing ship. These castles eventually evolved to two-and three-story ships. Ship layers meant bigger ships which allowed for more and bigger cannons. A ship-of-the-line could have between sixty to 110 cannons, depending on the size of the ship. Speed, being an important element in battle necessitated the need for small fast ships. These were called frigates. Frigates had a single line continue gun deck, with thirty to forty guns and usually three masts. They were often used as escort ships, patrolling and rapid fast attacks.

After a brief encounter with a French ship-of-the-line, Boscawen sailed to Gibraltar for repairs and to resupply with food and water. Commander of the French fleet, Comte de La Conflans, took this opportunity to leave with his twelve ships-of-the-line and three frigates from Toulon to rendezvous with the rest of the French fleet at Cadiz. However, his ships were spotted by one of the Boscawen lookouts and they took chase. Conflans, not wanting to be blockaded in the Spanish port of Cadiz; his original destination, changed course at dusk, and headed out to open sea. Seven of the captains on Conflans ships noticed the course change and followed. Eight did not and continued on to Cadiz. Boscawen's ship and seven others chased after Conflans. Boscawen told the other ships to delay and then catch up. Boscawen knew Conflans would be looking for his other eight ships. He sailed ahead with eight ships entrusting that Conflans would think the eight distant sails were the rest of his fleet, until it would be too late. Conflans saw the sails and stopped to wait. When he saw the rest of Boscawen's ships appear on the horizon, he realized his error and tried to flee. The British ships were faster and overtook the French fleet. One of the French ships was destroyed. As night set in, two French ships managed to escape, two others were captured, and two were forced aground and destroyed.

Sir Edward Hawke, with 24 ships-of-the-line, formed a blockade on the French coast near Brest. Choiseul gave orders to Conflans to escape the blockade and rendezvous with the navy's transport ship, and to proceed to Scotland for the invasion. During the first week of November in 1759 gale–force winds (39-54 mph sustained surface winds) forced Hawke to break his blockade and seek shelter. Hawke left Captain Robert Duff with five smaller ships-of-the-line and nine frigates to maintain watch on Conflans. Conflans took this opportunity to break free from the harbor and the blockade and head for the open sea. Having cleared the harbor and still battling gale force winds, Conflans decided to put up in Quiberon Bay. Before reaching his destination, he saw seven sails in the distance realizing that this could not be Hawke and his fleet but a much smaller fleet. He gave chase. Duff split his ships, half going south and the other half north. The French fleet split as well. Hawke's main fleet began to catch up as the British ships were faster and, because they were newer, they had certain navigational advantages. The French fleet broke off their pursuit but were scattered in disarray. Hawke gave the signal for his ships to form abreast. Conflans decided to run. He would head for Quiberon Bay and doubted that Hawke would follow him in as the bay's shoals and reefs were treacherous, especially if you were unfamiliar with the bay. Hawke gave orders for his first seven ships to be online and full speed ahead in pursuit. Hawke's ships were gaining on the French fleet and as Conflans was turning to enter the bay, Hawke's lead vessels began firing on the rear guard on Conflans ships. Of the rear guard one ship surrendered, one capsized and sank, one ran aground on the reef and one was badly damaged, and unseaworthy–it too ran aground. During the night eight French ships managed to slip away. The remainder jettisoned their cannons and ammunition in an attempt to lighten the ship to be able to sail over the sandbar at the bottom of the Villaine River when the tide came in. However, the first ship to make the attempt ran aground and trapped the rest of the ships. They sat in the water defenseless. Britain was now the world's premier naval power, which meant there would be no or very little aid to New France. As this battle determined the fate of New France the next battle, the battle for Québec, is the battle that determined the fate of the 13 colonies and America.

The Siege of Québec

After the British victory at Louisbourg Pitt began plans for the capture of the city of Québec. He commissioned Major General James Wolfe to lead the ground offensive and Admiral Sir Charles Saunders to command the naval fleet consisting of 49 ships-of-the-line and 140 smaller crafts–frigates, jon and whaleboats. Wolfe had to leave 3,500 of his men behind as they were suffering from a measles outbreak. He departed with 8,500 soldiers. Admiral Saunders was very apprehensive of sailing the uncharted waters of the St. Lawrence River. He pulled the Union Jacks down and hoisted French flags on his vessels. As they approached, French harbor men rowed out to meet them to act as guides to get them through the treacherous waters. The harbor men did not know the true identity of the sailors until they were on board; then, under gunpoint, they complied with the ship Captain's request for safe navigation. Once the ships were entering the harbor at Québec, the flags were exchanged. The French flags came down and the Union Jacks went up. Montcalm was taken totally by surprise not only had he been deceived but the British arrival from the east was totally unexpected. He had anticipated the attacks would come from the south or west.

The surprise arrival caused Montcalm to dispatch 4,500 of his militia, as a defensive line, along a seven mile stretch of the north shore of the St Lawrence River from Québec to the Montmorency River under the command of Colonel Louis-Antoine de Bougainville. They were to build fortifications and defend the shoreline against an invasion force. Montcalm had no intention of engaging the British; he just had to wait until October and the navy would be forced to leave or be stranded when the river iced over. Montcalm did not need to fight the British in order to claim victory–he could do that when they left. Wolfe landed with part of his force on the north shore, east of the Montmorency River. Wolfe formed his men to cross the Montmorency River and attack the east end of Bougainville's defensive line. He planned to attack up the line, where the line was only a few men abreast as they were spread out along the seven miles of shoreline. He anticipated a vigorous attack would cause the men to break and run in confusion, not being able to form a defensive line. As Wolfe's men crossed the river the French had massed a company on the river's bank and ambushed Wolfe's troops as they tried to cross. A severe thunderstorm broke out, unable to keep their gunpowder dry, Wolfe was forced to call off the attack. It had been a costly attempt. Wolfe lost 450 troops to France's sixty. He pulled his troops out, rowed across the St. Lawrence, and set up on the Island of Orleans.

Saunder's fleet sailed past the fort, firing their cannons at the city as they moved. They also were looking for a place where they could land an invasion force. Wolfe moved west along the river's edge to Point Levi, directly across the river from Québec, and established an artillery battery. Québec was a fortified city; in essence, a city surrounded by a wall with defensive capabilities. The wall was built to protect the inhabitants of Québec from Indian attacks. Québec is located on a precipice overlooking the St. Lawrence River. Wolfe was not going to attack from the east again as he anticipated the same result. The shelling of the city went on into October without any sign of Montcalm surrendering.

Wolfe was becoming desperate as cold weather would set in soon and the river would ice over. He sent raiding parties out into the settlements around the city, forcing settlers to flee and burning their buildings, all in an attempt to get Montcalm to come out and fight. Wolfe finally found a small cove at Anse-au-Foulon, west of Québec, and sent out a scouting party to see if it would be a location from which they could launch an attack. His scouts reported that the cove could only hold a small force. It was at the foot of a 175-foot cliff. There was a road that lead up to the Fields of Abraham, which was a broad, open area in front of the walls of Québec. However, there was a small garrison that housed probably forty to fifty men protecting the road. Wolfe determined under the cover of darkness he would send a small force of volunteers to scale the cliff and take the garrison from the rear. Then he would land his main force, they would take the road up to the Fields of Abraham, and Wolfe would have his troops formed up in the field as daylight broke. Wolfe sent twenty-four volunteers across the river while the rest of his force prepared to board their transports across the river. Saunders set out to feign an invasion on the shore to the east. With cannons blazing, he came as close to shore as he dared. The Fort returned fire and had the desired effect. All were watching Saunders. The twenty-four volunteers scaled the cliff and took the garrison with ease. Most of the men were sleeping or drunk, as no one expected an attack on the cliff side of the city. One of the French soldiers escaped and tried to warn of the French officers; however, by providence, he was dismissed as being delusional. In another act of providence there was a mounted patrol that watched the western edge of the city wall; however, two of the horses were lame and someone had stolen the third. As such there was no mounted patrol that night.

The boats ferried 5,000 troops across the river and, using the narrow road, they marched up and assembled on the Plains of Abraham. Wolfe formed his troops across the plains in a horseshoe configuration, two troopers deep. He kept a reserve unit that was positioned in the middle of the horseshoe, making that portion three deep. Montcalm was informed of the British presence. He wanted to engage immediately before Wolfe's troops could fortify and establish a position. In very poor judgement he chose not to wait for Bougainville who could have simultaneously attacked Wolfe's formation from the rear. He immediately formed his 3,500 soldiers abreast, outside of the wall, three deep. As Montcalm's soldiers advanced, they began firing and Wolfe told his troops to lie down in the tall grass. Wolfe instructed his troops to load two rounds of ammunition down the barrel. Montcalm's soldiers continued to advance firing as they moved. Wolfe instructed his troops to fix bayonets. When the French soldiers were within forty yards Wolfe told his troops to rise. He held their fire until the French were within thirty-five yards and commenced firing. The first round of double shot was devastating. The front line dropped to one knee to reload. The second line fired their double shot. So many solders fell that Wolfe ordered a bayonet charge. In all of the carnage and chaos the French soldiers broke and ran for the cover of the walls of Québec. Wolfe was struck in the thigh and chest and died on the battlefield. Montcalm was also struck in the chest and would die later that night. The British lost 58 killed and 596 wounded. The French lost 200 killed and 1,200 wounded.

Brigadier General George Townshend assumed command and immediately began to besiege the fort. Bougainville arrived with his soldiers. He was surprised to see that Montcalm had been forced back into the city walls. There was a brief firefight with the British and then Bougainville withdrew his forces. On September 18th, the commander of the Québec garrison, Jean-Baptiste-Nicolas-Roch de Ramezay, surrendered the city to Townshend and Saunders. Townshend gave the Canadians generous terms of surrender. The citizens would be allowed to remain in the city if they swore an oath of loyalty to Great Britain. Townsend left 7,000 troops behind under the command of Brigadier General James Murry to hold Québec over the long winter. Townsend and the rest of the troops joined Saunders and sailed up the St Lawrence and out to sea. Montcalm died not knowing that reinforcements and supplies would not be coming to relieve him and his garrison as the French fleet had been destroyed at Quiberon Bay.

In spring, Chevalier de Levis, Montcalm's replacement arrived, at Québec with 7,000 soldiers. General James Murry, having lost 3,200 of his troops to disease through the winter, thought he did not have enough troops to defend Québec. He moved his remaining troops and twenty cannons onto the field. Being under strength, he thought it best to take the initiative and attack. His cannons got bogged down in the muddy field and his troops, after fighting illness and a long winter with not enough food, were not up to the fight. After a brief encounter, Murry retreated into the city. Having lost 1,100 of his troops to Levis 850 killed or wounded. Levis was unable to take the fort, when British ships arrived with reinforcements, he retreated to Montreal.

On September 8th, 1760 the British army moved to take Montreal. They advanced from three directions: Murry's army of 3,600, reinforced and refitted, came up the St. Lawrence River from Québec. Haviland, with 3,400, troops arrived by the Richelieu River, and Amherst, with an army of 11,000, came by the St Lawrence from Lake Ontario. Levis, with a force of 2,100 surrendered without a fight. Britain was now in control of all of Canada and America from the Atlantic coast to the Mississippi River.

When king George III would become king of England, he would appoint new political leaders and advisors that will follow stricter polices towards America. Prime Minister George Greenville was replaced by Lord Bute, the former First Lord of the Treasury. Bute wanted to take a stronger position with the Americans—they were British subjects, and if subjects in Great Britain were paying for the war, the colonists should as well. The French and Indian War was settled in 1763 when the Treaty of Paris was signed. France lost all claims to Canada and gave Louisiana to Spain. Britain received Spanish Florida.

Pontiac's Rebellion

As a reward for his military successes Amherst was appointed governor general of British North America. He began repairing and rebuilding the Forts in the Ohio Valley, then his troops began occupying all of the French forts and building new ones. This alarmed the Indian population. If the French had been defeated, why was the army increasing in size and why were more forts needed? Forts meant occupation, not trade.

The French population at the end of the war was about 68,000. Their presence did not represent a threat to the Indians or to the colonists. After The French and Indian War, the French were in Canada and the Ohio River Valley primarily for hunting and trapping. They also encouraged the Indians to continue their attacks on colonial settlements. They took Indians for wives and many were adopted into local tribes. The Indians were very concerned by the loss of their relationship with the French. They also were very dismayed at being told they were now subjects of the king, a claim many refused to acknowledge. Amherst came with a completely different attitude and strategy for dealing with the Indians.

England had doubled its national debt in the French and Indian War, and in Europe with the Seven Years War. Amhurst did not continue the French and British tradition of annual gift giving to the chiefs of the tribes, which they would distribute among their people, giving them prestige and fostering a working relationship between France, Britain and their Indians allies. The Indians considered the gifts as a symbol of a desire for peaceful relations. Amherst thought England could no longer afford these niceties. The French cultivated a relationship with the Indians. Because of their small numbers they knew they would need Indian support if hostilities broke out with the British. Amherst thought with the wars end he no longer needed Indian support. In 1761, the Cherokees rebelled against their British allies, but the fighting came to an end when the Indians ran out of gunpowder. Amherst also, not trusting some of the tribes because they had been loyal allies with the French, and because of the Cherokee's Rebellion, severely restricted the number of guns, powder and ammunition that could be traded with the Indians. This had an adverse effect on the Indian's ability to acquire fur for trade and food for their tribes. The Indians were also greatly concerned that now with the French defeat there would be a continual influx of settlers onto their lands.

The Ottawa Chief Pontiac held a war council trying to persuade the other tribes to join him in a war against the British. This would come to be known as "Pontiac's Rebellion." Historians are not clear as to whether the rebellion was a unified attack or if once other tribes heard of Pontiac's raid on Fort Detroit, they then joined the rebellion. The Indians raided settlements and captured eight British Forts where they killed and scalped the inhabitants. Amhurst sent out two expeditions to stop the rebellion. Bradstreet was sent to the Great Lakes regions where he negotiated peace treaties with the Indians. However, he overstepped his bounds, as he was only authorized to make a truce. These treaties would not be honored, which would cause further distrust and tensions between the Indians and the British. On the second expedition Colonel Bouquet, with the aid of William Johnson, was able to negotiate a truce with the Indians of the Ohio Valley. Johnson also secured the release of 200 captives. As fall set in the Indians moved to their winter grounds. The remainder of the war over the next two years was mostly negotiations and little fighting. The end result of the rebellion was; 400 British Regulars killed, 50 captured, 2,000 settlers killed. 4,000 displaced, and 200 Indians warriors killed.

There was also the issue of the Paxton Boys, for all intent and purpose, was nothing more than a gang of vigilantes from the town of

Paxton Pennsylvania. The slaughter of settlers continued during Pontiac's rebellion. A schoolteacher in Pennsylvania and her ten students were killed and scalped, which set off a fervor of resentment. Fifty men from Paxton thought not enough was being done by the government so they took matters into their own hands. They heard a war party was in the Indian village of Conestoga, the residents of whom were mostly Christian. They raided the village and killed six Susquehannock's. Pennsylvania officials put the remining sixteen Susquehannocks in protective custody. However, the Paxton Boys broke into the safe house and killed most of the Indians who were taking refuge there. Governor John Penn put a bounty on them, but no one came forth. The raiding stopped. At the end of the war settlers began moving west, using the two roads built by Braddock and Amherst. The Indians perceived the influx of new settlers as a direct threat to their lands. They conveyed their concerns to Johnson as the leading Indian agent for the colonies. However, Johnson was powerless. England was the government of the colonies.

By September of 1760, the British controlled Canada, the Atlantic seaboard, the Ohio River Valley, Nova Scotia, and Newfoundland. The war and most of the fighting was over. The Treaty of Paris, signed in 1763, set the terms for France's capitulation. Under the treaty France was to surrender all of her American possessions to the British and the Spanish. When the war ended so did the cultural and political influences of France. England gained massive amounts of land on the new continent, greatly strengthening its position on the world's stage. The war's victory and the presence of the British troops greatly strengthened England's hold on the colonies. However, their conduct and treatment of the Indians had done irreparable harm. Britain continued to build forts in the Ohio Valley. The Indians, upset with the colonists, saw this as an even bigger threat, they made no distinction between the British and the settlers. Forts only meant one thing–a military presence, and if the war was over who were they going to fight against?

TAXES – THE CORNERSSTONE OF DISSENTION

In July of 1651, Parliament passed the Navigation Act regulating trade with the colonies. The Navigation Act stipulated that all products going to the colonies had to first go to England and then be transferred onto English cargo ships. A duty was collected in England and again in the colonies. This act, of course, greatly increased smuggling by the Americans with their trading partners, especially the Dutch. These trade restrictions were wholly illegal; however, America was powerless to stop them. The competition in trade between England and the Dutch erupted into several wars over twenty years, known as the Anglo-Dutch Wars.

Important differences began to develop between the Colonies and Great Britain, as it was now named after Britain and Scotland, united in 1760. Each colony had as its administrator a Royal Governor who was appointed by the king of England. The colonists had long established that an individual in good standing in the community and in the congregation had a responsibility to be involved in town meetings where policy and laws were established. This in contrast to Great Britain, where a person's wealth or family status determined their station in life and their ability to legislate for the majority. In the colonies anyone could attend Town Hall Meetings, but only land-owning male church members were allowed to vote. By the end of the 1600s, any man who owned property could vote. This included blacks who had come over as indentured servants, paid off their debt and acquired land. It also included blacks who had earned their freedom and land by volunteering for service in the military. Each free, land–owning male was expected to participate in his civic duty of participation in the local town hall meetings. They believed it was up to the community to establish rules of commerce, to establish a stable currency, to levy taxes, and to standardize weights and measures. They also took it upon themselves to develop roads, canals, harbors, postal centers and other communication systems. Most important to the colonies was the responsibility to establish trade, collect taxes, build schools and provide for a militia. Each state acted independently from one another. The colonists believed the government's role was very limited, with only three primary responsibilities: protection against foreign invaders, protection of citizens from wrongs committed against them by other citizens, and the building and maintenance of public institutions. Great Britain asked the colonists to find a means of helping with its war debt and the cost to maintain the residual British forces in the colonies. With the defeat of the French the colonists saw no need for the presence of British troops on American soil. The colonies had developed a formidable militia over the course of the Seven Years War and were confident in their ability to defend themselves. They saw no reason to pay for Great Britain's occupation.

Great Britain meanwhile was struggling with how to pay off its war debt. Pontiac's Rebellion was another costly war–time event. With British colonies now in America, India, Africa and the Caribbean Islands a less costly means of governing and administering the new protectorates had to be devised. The French and Indian War and the Seven Years War cost Britain 70 million pounds. That is 14 trillion in today's currency. The 70 million doubled Britain's debt to 140 million. England was already taxing its citizenry to the point of excess and riots of protest were breaking out in London. Great Britain thought the American Colonies should pay their fair share of the cost of the French and Indian War and for governing and protecting the new land possessions. Great Britain also now had a standing Army of 10,000 troops in the colonies for protection against further hostilities with the Indians and to maintain control over the colonists. They also now had to maintain law and order among the Catholic French Canadians who were refusing to consider themselves British loyal subjects. The Treaty of Paris was signed on February 7, 1763. In October of 1763, King George signed the "Royal Proclamation of 1763." The Proclamation established an Indian reservation from the crest of the Appalachian Mountains to the Mississippi River and from Louisiana to Québec. No English settlements were allowed on the reservation. There were, of course, many challenges with the Proclamation. Many settlers had been forced to flee from the Indian attacks on settlements, and they of course, wanted to return. At the war's end new settlers were crossing the Appalachian Mountains in search of farmland. Colonial militia had been promised land if they rendered military service in the French and Indian War; this arrangement was now cancelled. However, English soldiers were allowed to have settlements on the reservation. It's obvious the reasoning behind this was that if England could establish enough veteran settlers, they, in effect would have a militia, a military presence without the cost. There is another ominous part of the Proclamation. It outlawed the private purchase of Indian land. All future land purchases were to be made through the Crown. Selling any of the land and allowing English soldiers to settle was already a violation of the treaty with the Indians; however, this was a means for Great Britain to acquire revenue to help towards retiring its war debt, by keeping the money that belonged to the Indians. Land was sold to land speculators in England and to a lesser extent to some colonists who had made significant contributions to the war effort.

A typical family in the colonies had six to eight children. Large families were common because of the high incidence of infant mortality from epidemics. As communities grew, more land was needed. All males were expected to serve eight months in the militia. For this they would be paid eighty pounds, and a signing bonus anywhere from one to eight months' pay, depending of the military's needs. A soldier, if he did not want to wait for his land by inheritance, could buy his own land once out of the military. If he wanted a settlement close to his family, where the land was in high demand, with 15 pounds he could buy thirty acres in or around the community. If he wanted to venture out into new lands, with 15 pounds he could buy a hundred and fifty acres. This was a strong motivation for expanding and creating new settlements. Great Britain looked to the growing wealth of the Portuguese and the Dutch in how they were conducting world affairs. They relied almost solely on trade, rather than colonization, and rarely engaged militarily with their trading partners, much as the model of the Dutch in North America in the mid-1600s.

King George III shifted his worldly strategy towards enhancing revenues through trade and capitalizing on his significant land holdings in North America. Part of this strategy was the Proclamation of 1763. King George III wanted the colonies to expand south into newly acquired Georgia and Florida and north into Maine and Nova Scotia. This would keep new settlements on the coast to build trade with England, (customers). Settlers inland would be mostly self-sufficient and not very good trading partners. The Proclamation of 1763 was not about preserving Indian rights to the land, rather the intent was to give England a monopoly on all future land transactions and expand Britain's customer base. The revenues from land sales would go to the Crown, not to the Indians. This only increased the animosity the Indians had for the British– their land was being stolen. From 1768 to 1770, Great Britain modified the reservation boundaries with the Indians in three separate treaties, which opened West Virginia and Kentucky to settlements.

George Greenville, who was named prime minister of England in 1763, designed the American Revenue Act. Commonly known as the "Sugar Act" it replaced the "Sugar and Molasses Act." The Sugar Act went into effect in April of 1764. The former Act levied a six pence per gallon tax on Molasses coming from The French and Dutch West Indies. Molasses was a key ingredient for rum–making which was a significant business in the colonies, being the favored social libation of the day. A gallon and a half of rum requires 160 ounces of molasses and 12.5 pounds of raw cane sugar. The tax had a severe impact on colonial distilleries and put the price of the beverage out of reach to the lower end of the socio-economic scale. The tax was put in place to discourage trade with the French and Dutch West Indies and to drive business for the British West Indies. Molasses and cane sugar from the British West Indies were significantly more expensive than from the West Indies of other nations. The new tax was less– only three pence per gallon, but Greenville, thought with more stringent enforcement, he could collect more money. The new tax also included lumber, which the Americans could only sell to Great Britain. The six-pence tax resulted in smuggling, bribes and intimidation of custom officials. The new act also empowered custom officials to use the Vice Admiralty Courts, where the magistrates would determine the fate of those charged. Prior to the Admiralty Courts, cases of a maritime concern were tried in a general court with a jury. Greenville thought the jurors were far too lenient on other colonists. In response to the Sugar Act, Boston merchants boycotted English luxury goods. Also, in 1764, Parliament passed the Currency Act. There was no gold or silver mines in America at this time, so lenders would use land or mortgages as collateral for their Bills of Credit. The Currency Act put Parliament in charge of America's monetary system. The act prohibited the issue of any new bills and the reissue of existing bills. Americans protested this act vehemently. There was already a trade deficit with Great Britain and this monetary manipulation would exacerbate the situation. The British pound sterling would be the only acceptable currency. The Currency Act put a tremendous burden on merchants, many of whom went out of business. The Sugar Act was a primary causative factor in the post– war recession in the colonies. The Americans took this act as a direct assault on their rights.

In March of 1765, Parliament passed the Stamp Act, which was the first direct tax on the Americans. The new tax was to be affixed to any official document on paper purchased from London and embossed with the revenue stamp–wills, newspapers, contracts, marriage licenses, and even playing cards. The Stamp Act also included the Quartering Act. The act mandated that food and lodging be provided for by the colonists to British soldiers. If there was not enough room at the Inn, taverns, barns, stables, or other public buildings then the troops would have to be quartered in private homes. The reaction to the Stamp Act was immediate and very forceful. This took Parliament by surprise. Why would the colonies refuse a tax that British subjects had been paying for fifty years? This was the beginning of "no taxation without representation." Patrick Henry, in the Virginia House of Burgess, proposed the "Virginia Resolves."

Virginia Resolves

On May 29, 1765, the House of Burgesses of Virginia came to the following resolutions:
Resolved, That the first adventurers and settlers of this his majesty's colony and dominion of Virginia brought with them and transmitted to their posterity and all others, his majesty's subjects since inhabiting in this is majesty's colony, all the privileges and immunities that have at any time been held, enjoyed, and possessed by the people of Great Britain.

Resolved, That by the two royal charters granted by King James the First, the colonists aforesaid are declared entitled to all privileges of faithful, liege (owing allegiance to a lord), and natural born subjects, to all intents and purposes, as if they had been abiding and born within the realm of England.

Resolved, That his majesty's liege people of this his most ancient colony have enjoyed the right being thus governed by their own assembly, in the article of taxes and internal police; and that the same have never been forfeited or any other way yielded up, but have been constantly recognized by the kings and people of Great Britain.

Resolved therefore, That the general assembly of the colony, together with his majesty or his substitute have in their representative capacity the only exclusive right and power to levy taxes and impositions on the inhabitants of this colony and that every attempt to vest such a power in any person or persons whatsoever other than the general assembly aforesaid is illegal, unconstitutional, and unjust, and ahs a manifest tendency to destroy British, as well as American freedom."

The two that were removed but published in the newspapers read;

"Resolved, That his majesty's liege people, the inhabitants of this colony, are not bound to yield obedience to any law or ordinance whatsoever designed to impose any taxation whatsoever upon them, other than the laws and ordinances of the general assembly aforesaid."

"Resolved, That any person who shall by speaking or writing maintain that any person or persons other than the general assembly of this colony have any right or power to impose or lay any taxation whatsoever on the people here shall be deemed an enemy to this his majesty's colony."

Many of the newspapers in other colonies picked up the story and it became widely circulated. By 1765, eight other colonies had adopted similar documents expressing the same sentiments. This by no means was the limit to the colonial protests. There were riots, effigies of tax collectors were hanged, some tax collectors were tarred and feathered, many tax collectors out of fear refused to take their posts. The colonists, with their frustration over Britain's refusal to acknowledge grievances from independent colonies, decided a new course of action was necessary. In 1765 James Otis suggested an intercolonial conference involving all of the colonies to decide on a united course of action.

The Stamp Act Congress

The Stamp Act Congress, the first Congress of the American Colonies, convened in New York between October 7 and 25, 1765, to address Britain's Stamp Act. The congress was represented by 27 representatives from nine colonies. They drafted fourteen points and called the document the "Declaration of Rights and Grievances." They also decided that the most effective tool they had was to boycott British goods. The declaration began with an assertion of their loyalty to the king, and the resounding message, again, was "no taxation without representation." The document was sent to the king, the House of Commons and the House of Lords. The boycott began immediately. In March 1766, Parliament repealed the Stamp Act, more in response to the boycott than any legal claims by the Americans. Parliament also passed, on the same day, the "Declaratory Act," which affirmed the right of Parliament to pass laws over the colonies, "in all cases whatsoever." During the debate George Grenville, who was the prime minister when the Stamp Act was passed and now a member of Parliament, inquired, "Great Britain protects America; America is bound to yield obedience. If not, tell me when Americans were emancipated?" William Pitt, a proponent of America's rights replied, "I desire to know when they were made slaves?" As concerns in the colonies began to crystalize, colonists came to recognize a need for cohesion amongst the colonies so the "Committees of Correspondence" were formed so that a communication link was opened between representatives of the thirteen colonies so they could all be on the same page, as it were, with news of the day.

In 1766, Charles Townshend was appointed as the head of the Treasury in Great Britain. When New York refused to obey the Quartering Act in 1766, which was part of the Stamp Act, Parliament passed the Townshend Act with three provisions. Firstly, the act suspended the New York legislature until they agreed to the Quartering Act. Secondly, included was the Revenue Act, which was designed to raise revenue by putting new import duties on lead, glass, paints and tea. Thirdly, was the Board of Customs Act to enforce the duties imposed by the Revenue Act and establish new Admiralty Courts in Boston, Philadelphia, and Charleston, with jurisdiction throughout the thirteen colonies.

In 1766, a shadow government began to form with members in each colony with the purpose of organizing resistance against the increasing encroachment upon colonist's rights and to address the issue of taxation without representation. One such Group was The Sons of Liberty. The organization spread and soon there was a chapter in each colony. Many women joined the cause as The Daughters of Liberty. Sentiments within the group were, "if we are not involved in Parliamentary decisions on taxation how will they know what we can bear, and what would be the best means of raising such revenue? They also stated, "only colonial assemblies have the right to tax, the colonies, and trial by jury is a right." The use of Admiralty Courts was abusive and denied the colonists of a trial by jury. Colonists possessed all of the rights of Englishmen but did not have voting rights. They felt Parliament could not represent the colonist's interest from 3,000 miles away.

Because of American emphasis on community and congregation, it was already forming as a very participator process for self-rule. In Great Britain the process that evolved with all the focus on aristocrats and landowners, only ten percent of the population was involved in the decision-making process. America was intentionally heading in the direction of a participatory from of rule, as ninety percent of colonists were landowners and involved in the governing process. In Britain aristocrats would never make concession of the elite sharing power with the masses. The protest groups within the colonies organized a boycott against buying British goods. The boycott increased the amount of smuggling, which in turn increased the authoritative activities of the British troops in the colonies under the authority of the Royal Governor. The merchants in Britain put a lot of pressure on Parliament to ease the burdens on the colonies. In 1770, Parliament rescinded the Townshend duties except the tea tax, which was maintained to demonstrate Parliament's sovereignty over the colonies. Britain stationed troops in all major colonial ports to enforce tariffs, and taxes and to curtail smuggling. This led to confrontations between colonists and the British soldiers. There were a couple of armed conflicts in some of the ports resulting in the deaths of two Americans, one of whom was a ten-year old boy. This all culminated in March 5, 1770, in what has come to be known as the "Boston Massacre," where British troops fired into an angry mob killing five colonists and wounding six. Britain allowed the soldiers to be tried in the colonies. John Adams defended the British saying there was no crime, as the soldiers were defending themselves from bodily harm by an angry mob. Six of the eight soldiers were acquitted and two were found guilty of manslaughter. The two soldiers charged with manslaughter escaped hanging because of a legal clause at the time called the "benefit of clergy." This exempted clergy and men with the ability to read or recite Biblical passages from the customary sentencing guidelines, in the secular courts. Both men were able to recite Bible verses at their sentencing hearing. Their punishment was to be branded on the thumb with an "M" for manslaughter.

One of Britain's most successful trading companies was the British East India Company. India was also involved in the Seven Years War. The conflict was between the French and the British over land possession and trade in India. India had incurred a war debt; as did Britain for its military support to protect India. As with the colonies, Britain wanted India to help pay her war debt, however, India was nearly bankrupt. The large sum of money requested by Britain was significantly contributing to India's money problems. In May of 1773, to help India out of its financial trouble, Parliament passed the Tea Act. The act eliminated the customs duty of India's tea and allowed them to ship directly to the North American colonies. Parliament reasoned that by removing the duty, India tea would be cheaper than the smuggled Dutch tea. Colonists would then buy India tea and Britain could collect the tea tax that had been circumvented by the colonies buying the smuggled Dutch tea. The colonial perspective was that Britain was covertly trying to force them to pay British taxes and to break the boycott. The primary concern for the colonies was that if they bought the tea Britain would think they were not really all that serious about the constant claims of no taxation without representation.

Patriots in the Sons of Liberty and the Liberty Boys boycotted the harbors and refused to let ships carrying India tea dock, forcing them to sail to England. However, three ships were able to dock in Boston Harbor and the Royal Governor made plans to offload the tea. Protests have a way of escalating if the protesters are not seeing results from their efforts. Worldwide, there was a high regard for property rights, hence some patriots decided to up the ante. Members of the Sons of Liberty dressed up as Mohawk Indians, boarded the three ships, in the Boston Harbor and threw 342 chests of tea overboard. Parliament, the British people, and Loyalists in the colonies were all shocked at the destruction of private property. Many of those that were still sympathetic to the colonial cause began changing their minds and those that were equivocating between colonial rights and colonial independence hardened their resolve against the patriotic colonists. Instead of repealing the Tea Act, as the colonists had hoped, Britain responded quickly by punishing the people of Boston and Massachusetts. Britain passed a series of five acts known in the colonies as the "Intolerable Acts" and in England as the "Coercive Acts."

On March 30, 1774, the "Boston Port Act" was passed. This act closed the port of Boston until the East India Company and Britain were reimbursed for the tea and lost taxes. Bostonians would have to reimburse both Britain and India, paying for the tea twice. The Boston Port Act was viewed as being very unjust as it punished the whole population of Massachusetts not just the people responsible for the destruction of the tea. King George III thought the colonies needed a stern message and would send a show of force. On May 13, 1774, General Thomas Gage was sent as commander of all British troops in the colonies, arrived in Boston with 4 regiments (each regiment at the time was about 800 soldiers) and stationed his troops in the colonial port cities of Boston and New York.

On May 20, 1774, Parliament passed the Massachusetts Government Act, which stipulated that Boston's Executive Council would no longer be represented by elected officials, but its members would be appointed by the king. All other elected officials, including judges and marshals, would be dismissed and replacements would be appointed by the Royal Governor. A portion of the act reads, "the governor, for the time being, …without the consent of the council, shall have full power and authority to nominate and appoint the persons to succeed to the said offices, who shall hold their commission during the pleasure of his Majesty…"

Patriots formed the Massachusetts Provincial Congress, outside of Boston, in order to continue self-rule and decide how to respond to this new threat. The First Continental Congress met from October 5th through the 26th of 1774, in response to the Intolerable Acts. The Second Continental Congress met in May of 1775 and ran until 1781. It wrote, passed and in 1776, announced to the world, "The Declaration of Independence." After the Declaration of Independence was declared America had to set up some form of government to replace British Rule. The First Continental Congress, as a ruling body, bled into the Second under the Articles of Confederation from 1775 through 1781. Which in turn bled into the Congress of the Confederation which ran from 1781 until 1789, establishing the Constitution of the United States.

A brief timeline for clarity: The Declaration and Resolves were issued on October 26, 1774. The Battle at Lexington and Concord occurred on April 19, 1775, starting the Revolutionary War. On July 4, 1776, the Declaration of Independence was announced to the world, as a nation under the providence of God. March 2, 1781, the Articles of Confederation were drafted. In 1783 the Revolutionary War ended with the signing of a treaty with Britain. September 17, 1787, the U.S. Constitution was ratified, only after the first ten amendments had been added, The Bill of Rights.

THE ARTICLES OF CONFEDERATION

The Articles of Confederation served as the written document that established the functions of the national government of the United States. Ben Franklin drew up the plan for the Articles of Confederation and Perpetual Union. The Articles represented the first Constitution of the United States after its Declaration of Independence. The delegates, or representatives, from twelve states, (Georgia did not attend), drafted a document that was over–zealous in protecting the citizenry from, as history had taught them, arbitrary judges and capricious monarchies. In order for the Articles to take affect all of the states had to ratify the document. America had just concluded a war to end what they considered the tyrannical rule of a strong government. Leary of the monarchies that dominated in Europe, the colonists were apprehensive about a strong national government. Under the Articles of Confederation, a legislative Congress was the sole branch of a national government, but it had no power to force states to do anything against their will. The Articles were ratified on March 1, 1781; however, no amendments could be made to the document unless there was a unanimous consent of all thirteen states. Although the Articles referred to "The United States of America", they committed the states only to "a firm league of friendship with each other for their common defense, the security of their liberties, and their mutual and general welfare." They thought of themselves as a confederation of sovereign states, rather than the creation of a nation.

The Articles of Confederation (spelling and punctuation are as is in original document)

"To all to whom these Presents shall come, we the undersigned Delegates of the States affixed to our Names send greeting.

Articles of Confederation and perpetual Union between the states of New Hampshire, Massachusetts-bay Rhode Island and Providence Plantations, Connecticut, New York, New Jersey, Pennsylvania, Delaware, Maryland, Virginia, North Carolina, South Carolina and Georgia.

I.

The Stile of this Confederacy shall be
"The United States of America."

II.

Each state retains its sovereignty, freedom, and independence, and every power, jurisdiction, and right, which is not by this Confederation expressly delegated to the United States, in Congress assembled.

III.

The said States hereby severally enter into a firm league of friendship with each other, for their common defense, the security of their liberties, and their mutual and general welfare, binding themselves to assist each other, against all force offered to, or attacks made upon them, or any of them, on account of religion, sovereignty, trade, or any other pretense whatever.

IV.

The better to secure and perpetuate mutual friendship and intercourse among the people of the different States in this Union, the free inhabitants of each of these States, paupers, vagabonds, and fugitives from justice excepted, shall be entitled to all privileges and immunities of free citizens in the several States; and the people of each State shall free ingress and regress to and from any other State, and shall enjoy therein all the privileges of trade and commerce, subject to the same duties, impositions, and restrictions as the inhabitants thereof respectively, provided that such restrictions shall not extend so far as to prevent the removal of property imported into any State, to any other State, of which the owner is an inhabitant; provided also that no imposition, duties or restriction shall be laid by any State, on the property of the United States, or either of them.

If any person guilty of, or charged with, treason, felony, or other high misdemeanor in any State, shall flee from justice, and be found in any of the United States, he shall, upon demand of the Governor or executive power of the State from which he fled, be delivered up and removed to the State having jurisdiction of his offense.

Full faith and credit shall be given in each of these States to the records, acts, and judicial proceedings of the courts and magistrates of every other State.

V.

For the most convenient management of the general interests of the United States, delegates shall be annually appointed in such manner as the legislatures of each State shall direct, to meet in Congress on the first Monday in November, in every year, with a power reserved to each State to recall its delegates, or any of them, at any time within the year, and to send others in their stead for the remainder of the year.

No State shall be represented in Congress by less than two, nor more than seven members; and no person shall be capable of being a delegate for more than three years in any term of six years; nor shall any person, being a delegate, be capable of holding any office under the United States, for which he, or another for his benefit, receives any salary, fees or emolument of any kind.

Each State shall maintain its own delegates in a meeting of the States, and while they act as members of the committee of the States.

In determining questions in the United States in Congress assembled, each State shall have one vote.

Freedom of speech and debate in Congress shall not be impeached or questioned in any court or place out of Congress, and the members of Congress shall be protected in their persons from arrests or imprisonments, during the time of their going to and from, and attendence on Congress, except for treason, felony, or breach of the peace.

VI.

No State, without the consent of the United States in Congress assembled, shall send any embassy to, or receive any embassy from, or enter into any conference, agreement, alliance or treaty with any King, Prince or State; nor shall any person holding any office of profit or trust under the United States, or any of them, accept any present, emolument, office or title of any kind whatever from any King, Prince or foreign State; nor shall the United States in Congress assembled, or any of them, grant any title of nobility.

No two or more States shall enter into any treaty, confederation or alliance whatever between them, without the consent of the United States in Congress assembled, specifying accurately the purposes for which the same is to be entered into, and how long it shall continue.

No State shall lay any imposts or duties, which may interfere with any stipulations in treaties, entered into by the United States in Congress assembled, with any King, Prince or State, in pursuance of any treaties already proposed by Congress, to the courts of France and Spain.

No vessel of war shall be kept up in time of peace by any State, except such number only, as shall be deemed necessary by the United States in Congress assembled, for the defense of such State, or its trade; nor shall any body of forces be kept up by any State in time of peace, except such number only, as in the judgement of the United States in Congress assembled, shall be deemed requisite to garrison the forts necessary for the defense of such State; but every State shall always keep up a well-regulated and disciplined militia, sufficiently armed and accoutered, and shall provide and constantly have ready for use, in public stores, a due number of filed pieces and tents, and a proper quantity of arms, ammunition and camp equipage.

No State shall engage in any war without the consent of the United States in Congress assembled, unless such State be actually invaded by enemies, or shall have received certain advice of a resolution being formed by some nation of Indians to invade such State, and the danger is so imminent as not to admit of a delay till the United States in Congress assembled can be consulted; nor shall any State grant commissions to any ships or vessels of war, nor letters of marque or reprisal, except it be after a declaration of war by the United States in Congress assembled, and then only against the Kingdom or State and the subjects thereof, against which war has been so declared, and under such regulations as shall be established by the United States in Congress assembled, unless such State be infested by pirates, in which case vessels of war may be fitted out for that occasion, and kept so long as the danger shall continue, or until the United States in Congress assembled shall determine otherwise.

VII.

When land forces are raised by any State for the common defense, all officers of or under the rank of colonel, shall be appointed by the legislature of each State respectively, by whom such forces shall be raised, or in such manner as such State shall direct, and all vacancies shall be filled up by the State which first made the appointment.

VIII.

All charges of war, and all other expenses that shall be incurred for the common defense or general welfare, and allowed by the United States in Congress assembled, shall be defrayed out of a common treasury, which shall be supplied by the several States in proportion to the value of all land within each State, granted or surveyed for any person, as such land and the buildings and improvements thereon shall be estimated according to such mode as the United States in Congress assembled, shall from time to time direct and appoint.

The taxes for paying that proportion shall be laid and levied by the authority and direction of the legislatures of the several States within the time agreed upon by the United States in Congress assembled.

IX.

The United States in Congress assembled, shall have the sole and exclusive right and power of determining on peace and war, except in the cases mentioned in the sixth article -- of sending and receiving ambassadors -- entering into treaties and alliances, provided that no treaty of commerce shall be made whereby the legislative power of the respective States shall be restrained from imposing such imposts and duties on foreigners, as their own people are subjected to, or from prohibiting the exportation or importation of any species of goods or commodities whatsoever -- of establishing rules for deciding in all cases, what captures on land or water shall be legal, and in what manner prizes taken by land or naval forces in the service of the United States shall be divided or appropriated -- of granting letters of marque and reprisal in times of peace -- appointing courts for the trial of piracies and felonies commited on the high seas and establishing courts for receiving and determining finally appeals in all cases of captures, provided that no member of Congress shall be appointed a judge of any of the said courts.

The United States in Congress assembled shall also be the last resort on appeal in all disputes and differences now subsisting or that hereafter may arise between two or more States concerning boundary, jurisdiction or any other causes whatever; which authority shall always be exercised in the manner following. Whenever the legislative or executive authority or lawful agent of any State in controversy with another shall present a petition to Congress stating the matter in question and praying for a hearing, notice thereof shall be given by order of Congress to the legislative or executive authority of the other State in controversy, and a day assigned for the appearance of the parties by their lawful agents, who shall then be directed to appoint by joint consent, commissioners or judges to constitute a court for hearing and determining the matter in question: but if they cannot agree, Congress shall name three persons out of each of the United States, and from the list of such persons each party shall alternately strike out one, the petitioners beginning, until the number shall be reduced to thirteen; and from that number not less than seven, nor more than nine names as Congress shall direct, shall in the presence of Congress be drawn out by lot, and the persons whose names shall be so drawn or any five of them, shall be commissioners or judges, to hear and finally determine the controversy, so always as a major part of the judges who shall hear the cause shall agree in the determination: and if either party shall neglect to attend at the day appointed, without showing reasons, which Congress shall judge sufficient, or being present shall refuse to strike, the Congress shall proceed to nominate three persons out of each State, and the secretary of Congress shall strike in behalf of such party absent or refusing; and the judgement and sentence of the court to be appointed, in the manner before prescribed, shall be final and conclusive; and if any of the parties shall refuse to submit to the authority of such court, or to appear or defend their claim or cause, the court shall nevertheless proceed to pronounce sentence, or judgement, which shall in like manner be final and decisive, the judgement or sentence and other proceedings being in either case transmitted to Congress, and lodged among the acts of Congress for the security of the parties concerned: provided that every commissioner, before he sits in judgement, shall take an oath to be administered by one of the judges of the supreme or superior court of the State, where the cause shall be tried, 'well and truly to hear and determine the matter in question, according to the best of his judgement, without favor, affection or hope of reward': provided also, that no State shall be deprived of territory for the benefit of the United States.

All controversies concerning the private right of soil claimed under different grants of two or more States, whose jurisdictions as they may respect such lands, and the States which passed such grants are adjusted, the said grants or either of them being at the same time claimed to have originated antecedent to such settlement of jurisdiction, shall on the petition of either party to the Congress of the United States, be finally determined as near as may be in the same manner as is before prescribed for deciding disputes respecting territorial jurisdiction between different States.

The United States in Congress assembled shall also have the sole and exclusive right and power of regulating the alloy and value of coin struck by their own authority, or by that of the respective States -- fixing the standards of weights and measures throughout the United States -- regulating the trade and managing all affairs with the Indians, not members of any of the States, provided that the legislative right of any State within its own limits be not infringed or violated -- establishing or regulating post offices from one State to another, throughout all the United States, and exacting such postage on the papers passing through the same as may be requisite to defray the expenses of the said office -- appointing all officers of the land forces, in the service of the United States, excepting regimental officers -- appointing all the officers of the naval forces, and commissioning all officers whatever in the service of the United States -- making rules for the government and regulation of the said land and naval forces, and directing their operations.

The United States in Congress assembled shall have authority to appoint a committee, to sit in the recess of Congress, to be denominated 'A Committee of the States', and to consist of one delegate from each State; and to appoint such other committees and civil officers as may be necessary for managing the general affairs of the United States under their direction -- to appoint one of their members to preside, provided that no person be allowed to serve in the office of president more than one year in any term of three years; to ascertain the necessary sums of money to be raised for the service of the United States, and to appropriate and apply the same for defraying the public expenses -- to borrow money, or emit bills on the credit of the United States, transmitting every half-year to the respective States an account of the sums of money so borrowed or emitted -- to build and equip a navy -- to agree upon the number of land forces, and to make requisitions from each State for its quota, in proportion to the number of white inhabitants in such State; which requisition shall be binding, and thereupon the legislature of each State shall appoint the regimental officers, raise the men and cloath, arm and equip them in a solid-like manner, at the expense of the United States; and the officers and men so cloathed, armed and equipped shall march to the place appointed, and within the time agreed on by the United States in Congress assembled. But if the United States in Congress assembled shall, on consideration of circumstances judge proper that any State should not raise men, or should raise a smaller number of men than the quota thereof, such extra number shall be raised, officered, cloathed, armed and equipped in the same manner as the quota of each State, unless the legislature of such State shall judge that such extra number cannot be safely spread out in the same, in which case they shall raise, officer, cloath, arm and equip as many of such extra number as they judeg can be safely spared. And the officers and men so cloathed, armed, and equipped, shall march to the place appointed, and within the time agreed on by the United States in Congress assembled.

The United States in Congress assembled shall never engage in a war, nor grant letters of marque or reprisal in time of peace, nor enter into any treaties or alliances, nor coin money, nor regulate the value thereof, nor ascertain the sums and expenses necessary for the defense and welfare of the United States, or any of them, nor emit bills, nor borrow money on the credit of the United States, nor appropriate money, nor agree upon the number of vessels of war, to be built or purchased, or the number of land or sea forces to be raised, nor appoint a commander in chief of the army or navy, unless nine States assent to the same: nor shall a question on any other point, except for adjourning from day to day be determined, unless by the votes of the majority of the United States in Congress assembled.

The Congress of the United States shall have power to adjourn to any time within the year, and to any place within the United States, so that no period of adjournment be for a longer duration than the space of six months, and shall publish the journal of their proceedings monthly, except such parts thereof relating to treaties, alliances or military operations, as in their judgement require secrecy; and the yeas and nays of the delegates of each State on any question shall be entered on the journal, when it is desired by any delegates of a State, or any of them, at his or their request shall be furnished with a transcript of the said journal, except such parts as are above excepted, to lay before the legislatures of the several States.

X.

The Committee of the States, or any nine of them, shall be authorized to execute, in the recess of Congress, such of the powers of Congress as the United States in Congress assembled, by the consent of the nine States, shall from time to time think expedient to vest them with; provided that no power be delegated to the said Committee, for the exercise of which, by the Articles of Confederation, the voice of nine States in the Congress of the United States assembled be requisite.

XI.

Canada acceding to this confederation, and adjoining in the measures of the United States, shall be admitted into, and entitled to all the advantages of this Union; but no other colony shall be admitted into the same, unless such admission be agreed to by nine States.

XII.

All bills of credit emitted, monies borrowed, and debts contracted by, or under the authority of Congress, before the assembling of the United States, in pursuance of the present confederation, shall be deemed and considered as a charge against the United States, for payment and satisfaction whereof the said United States, and the public faith are hereby solemnly pleged.

XIII.

Every State shall abide by the determination of the United States in Congress assembled, on all questions which by this confederation are submitted to them. And the Articles of this Confederation shall be inviolably observed by every State, and the Union shall be perpetual; nor shall any alteration at any time hereafter be made in any of them; unless such alteration be agreed to in a Congress of the United States, and be afterwards confirmed by the legislatures of every State.

And Whereas it hath pleased the Great Governor of the World to incline the hearts of the legislatures we respectively represent in Congress, to approve of, and to authorize us to ratify the said Articles of Confederation and perpetual Union. Know Ye that we the undersigned delegates, by virtue of the power and authority to us given for that purpose, do by these presents, in the name and in behalf of our respective constituents, fully and entirely ratify and confirm each and every of the said Articles of Confederation and perpetual Union, and all and singular the matters and things therein contained: And we do further solemnly plight and engage the faith of our respective constituents, that they shall abide by the determinations of the United States in Congress assembled, on all questions, which by the said Confederation are submitted to them. And that the Articles thereof shall be inviolably observed by the States we respectively represent, and that the Union shall be perpetual.

In Witness whereof we have hereunto set our hands in Congress. Done at Philadelphia in the State of Pennsylvania the ninth day of July in the Year of our Lord One Thousand Seven Hundred and Seventy-Eight, and in the Third Year of the independence of America.

Agreed to by Congress 15 November 1777 in force after ratification by Maryland, 1 March 1781."

A revision of the 1765 Quartering Act was passed by Parliament on June 2. The act expanded the types of buildings that could be occupied by troops. It did not, however, include private dwellings. The act also removed the requirement that Americans had to provide provisions for the soldiers. On June 22, 1774, Parliament passed the Québec Act. The Québec Act granted permanent government status to the provincial government of Canada and made the Catholic religion the religion of state. It also gave the Ohio River Valley to Canada−land that had been granted to the colonies under their original charters. In passing these acts Lord North hoped to isolate the troublemakers and demonstrate to the Americans who was really in charge. However, to the Americans, with five new acts in four months, wondered if it would ever end. They saw their autonomy being destroyed. This was going way beyond "no taxation without representation." This was tyrannical treatment of its own subjects. Their charters and very rights as citizens were being slowly eliminated. Parliament arbitrarily gave portions of the colonies to Canada, land they were already developing. All of this culminated in the meeting of the First

Continental Congress in Philadelphia on September 5th to October 26, 1774. The congress agreed to boycott all British goods and to halt all exports to Britain if the Intolerable Acts were not repealed in a year. The strategy of Britain to isolate and divide had the opposite effect on the Americans–it brought them together with a common enemy, a common purpose, and a common resolve.   In 1775 John Hancock, while president of congress, wrote the Declaration of the Cause and Necessity of Taking Up Arms; extracts from the document;

...If it was possible for men, who exercise their reason to believe, that the divine Author of our existence intended a part of the human race to hold an absolute property in, and an unbounded power over others, marked out by his infinite goodness and wisdom, as the objects of a legal domination never rightfully resistible, however severe and oppressive, the inhabitants of these colonies might at least require from the parliament of Great-Britain some evidence, that this dreadful authority over them, has been granted to that body. But a reverence for our great Creator, principles of humanity, and the dictates of common sense, must convince all those who reflect upon the subject, that government was instituted to promote the welfare of mankind, and ought to be administered for the attainment of that end...

...We are reduced to the alternative of chusing an unconditional submission to the tyranny of irritated ministers, or resistance by force. — The latter latter is our choice. — We have counted the cost of this contest, and find nothing so dreadful as voluntary slavery. — Honour, justice, and humanity, forbid us tamely to surrender that freedom which we received from our gallant ancestors, and which our innocent posterity have a right to receive from us. We cannot endure the infamy and guilt of resigning succeeding generations to that wretchedness which inevitably awaits them, if we basely entail hereditary bondage upon them...

...Our cause is just. Our union is perfect. Our internal resources are great, and, if necessary, foreign assistance is undoubtably attainable. — We gratefully acknowledge, as signal instances of the Divine favour towards us, that his Providence would not permit us to be called into this severe controversy, until we were grown up to our present strength, had been previously exercised in warlike operation, and possessed of the means of defending ourselves. With hearts fortified with these animating reflections, we most solemnly, before God and the world, *declare*, that exerting the utmost energy of those powers, which our beneficent Creator hath graciously bestowed upon us, the arms we have been compelled by our enemies to assume, we will, in defiance of every hazard, with unabating firmness and perseverance, employ for the preservation of our liberties; being with one mind resolved to die freemen rather than to live slaves…

…With an humble confidence in the mercies of the supreme and impartial Judge and Ruler of the Universe, we most devoutly implore his divine goodness to protect us happily through this great conflict, to dispose our adversaries to reconciliation on reasonable terms, and thereby to relieve the empire from the calamities of civil war…

   …

FIRST BLOOD

Historical revisionists often omit a very crucial issue contributing to our war with Great Britain. After thirteen years of various taxes being levied against the colonists, they became increasingly resentful of the British taxing the colonies without any colonial representation in Parliament. Patrick Henry wrote his famous "Give me Liberty or Give me Death" speech in response to the widely held belief that Britain plainly meant to subjugate the Colonies by force. Henry proclaimed, "The millions of people, armed in the holy cause of liberty, and in such a country as that which we possess, are invincible by any force which our enemy can send against us." The Convention, whose members included Patrick Henry, George Washington and Thomas Jefferson, resolved "that every Man be provided with a good Rifle and every Horseman be provided with a pistol, holster, a carbine or other flintlock." The militiamen pledged that each would keep a flintlock, six pounds of gunpowder and twenty pounds of lead in their homes.

In February, the British Parliament declared the colony of Massachusetts to be in open rebellion and authorized British troops to kill the violent rebels. The Americans saw the Intolerable Acts as wholly unnecessary and very repressive. The Americans saw the deployment of General Gage and his troops as a means to enforce the Intolerable Acts. General Gage, who had been in America earlier and fought with General Braddock at the Battle of Monongahela, thought he understood the Americans and could put down the rebellion. The Americans thought, "if we are capable of self-rule, as our history has demonstrated, since 1624, why are the British troops here?" The Patriots of Lancaster County, PA resolved, "That in the event of Great Britain attempting to force unjust laws upon us by strength of arms, our cause we leave to heaven and our rifles."

The Royal Governor of Massachusetts, British General Thomas

157

Gage had forbidden town hall meetings. When a town hall meeting was assembled Gage sent Redcoats to break up the meeting in Salem. The Redcoats were met by 3,000-armed militia and hastily retreated. Military rule would be difficult to impose on an armed populace. On September 1, 1774, 260 of Gage's Redcoats covertly sailed up the Mystic River and seized hundreds of barrels of powder from the Charleston powder house. The tone of the militia was that if the British used violence to seize arms or powder, the Americans would consider such actions an act of war and would take up arms. Governor Gage then directed Redcoats to begin warrantless searches for arms and ammunition along with smuggled contraband.

On October 26, 1774, the Colonial Provincial Congress condemned Gage for unlawful seizure and retention of powder and arms in the Boston arsenal. The Provincial Congress declared that everyone who did not already possess a firearm should get one and start practicing diligently. In October of 1774, King George III blocked importation of arms, powder and ammunition to America, so we started making our own.

In December of 1774, the midnight ride of Paul Revere was to warn the militia in Lexington and Concorde that two British ships were headed to Fort William and Mary to seize firearms, cannons and gunpowder. Revere, made famous by Longfellow's poem, was a member of the Sons of Liberty, a courier for the Committees of Correspondence, and had several accomplices. Most notable of his companions was Wentworth Cheswell, a free African American, and Sybil Ludington, the sixteen-year old daughter of Colonel Henry Ludington. Revere was captured by the British and did not complete his ride; however, his accomplices were able to make it to their destinations, alerting all militia along the way.

The militia at Lexington emptied the armories of all of their munitions. The American War of Independence began on April 19, 1775, when 700 Redcoats left Boston to seize Colonial arms at Lexington and Concord, at the orders of British General William Howe who had replaced General Gage. Actually, the Revolutionary War was started over taxes and gun control. It is obvious why we have a second amendment and provisions against illegal search and seizure. The Constitution was designed such that no government would, ours or others, be able to perpetuate the kind of injustices or the denial of our unalienable rights that had provoked the Revolutionary War.

The 700 Redcoats left at night under the command of Major John Pitcam so they could arrive at Lexington just before dawn. John Parker,

Captain of the Lexington militia, having been warned by the midnight ride, gathered his seventy minutemen and took a position on the village green. He told his men not to fire first, telling them God would bless them in a defensive war not in an offensive one.

History does not record who fired the first shot, "the shot heard round the world," but when it was over five minutemen were dead and three would die later from their wounds. One British Regular lay dead. Major Pitcam then ordered his troops to proceed to Concord. Upon arriving they found all of the store houses and the armory empty. Pitcam ordered them all burned. He then ordered his men back to Boston.

The Minutemen saw the smoke from the burning store houses and thought the British had set fire to Concord. The church bells began ringing, raising the alarm. The Minutemen began forming in small groups and traveling through the woods paralleling the British troops sniping at them all the way back on their eighteen-mile march, killing and wounding 267, and themselves losing forty-nine.

The first battle with the British was an American victory. Although many of the battles were fought in the traditional European style, the adaptation of guerrilla tactics by the Americans would prove to be a decisive tactical advantage. The first American's to die in the battle for America's freedom were John Brown, Samuel Hadley, Caleb Harrington, Jonathon Harrington, Robert Munroe, Isaac Muzzey, Asahel Porter and Jonas Parker. Among the wounded was Prince Estabrook, a black slave earning his freedom by volunteering for military service.

There are a recorded 1,547 known military engagements that occurred during the Revolutionary War. In many of the battles, skirmishes and naval gunfights the causality figures are very light, which is primarily due to the inaccuracy of the smoothbore musket. The Continental Army and militia lost 8,000 soldiers killed in action. 17,000 died of diseases and 25,000 were wounded. The British lost 9,372 killed in action 24,000 wounded and 27,000 died of disease. The British also lost 1,243 sailors in combat operations and an additional 18,500 sailors that died of disease. The Loyalists who fought as militia for the British in America lost 1,700 in combat operations and 5,300 that died of disease. The German Hessian Mercenaries lost 1,800 in combat operations and 4,888 to disease.

American forces; 8,000 killed, 25,000 wounded, 17,000 died of disease. British, all forces, 14,000 killed, 24,000 wounded, 55,688 died of disease. During the eight years of the Revolutionary War a total of 22,115 soldiers were killed in battle, 72,688 died of diseases and about 50,000 were wounded. It is my considered opinion that many of the British reported as having died of disease were in fact killed on the battlefield. The British Generals were very apprehensive of reporting true war fatalities lest they be called back to London in disgrace as General Howe had been. General Washington's marksmen had the ability to shoot the enemy out to 300 yards.

The British soldier could not fire effectively until he was within 50 yards or close enough to use his bayonet. In most engagements the American Rifle devastated the British Infantry.

Interesting to note about the German Hessians, after the war 7,000 chose to remain in America, as did many British soldiers.

At this time in history Germany was not a country; there were 300 principalities ruled by German princes. The largest of these was Hesse-Kassel, whose soldiers were world renowned as fierce warriors. The prince of Hesse-Kassel readily provided his solders as mercenaries, for hire, to any country willing to pay the price, thus, the term Hessian for German mercenaries.

I cannot emphasize enough the tremendous effect the rifle had on the Revolutionary War and on the way, war would be fought in the future. The accuracy of the rifle compared to the smoothbore musket changed warfare forever. Just as when the smoothbore rifle was introduced and could pierce body armor the days of the Knights ended. For all intents and purposes, the rifle put an end to line-of-line formations for engaging the enemy. By the time America was in the Civil War soldiers would build earthen works or use redoubts to protect themselves from enemy fire. A redoubt is an earthen barrier made of earth, logs and stone as a defensive position that soldiers may fire on the enemy without being fully exposed. The redoubt was usually constructed to be about chest high and allow protection yet provided the ability for soldiers to fire upon approaching troops. Artillery would weaken the defensive position of the enemy and when it was thought the enemy had been sufficiently decimated by artillery fire the infantry would advance. This is not an apple to apples comparison; however, a comparison worthy of notice. There were a lot more soldiers involved in the American Civil War; however, the war only lasted four years, not eight like the Revolutionary War. With the introduction of the rifle, and by the time of the Civil War, accuracy had been increased from 75 yards with a smoothbore musket to 600 yards with a rifle. As revolutionary as rifling was for accuracy the next game changer was the repeating rifle and firepower. During the Civil War warfare saw the introduction of Sharp's repeating rifle, capable of firing seven consecutive shots. In 1860, Benjamin Tyler Henry introduced his Henry repeating rifle. The Henry was a breech loading, lever-action rifle capable of holding 16 rounds in its tubular magazine. There were 214,938 soldiers killed in action, 450,000 wounded and 445,881 that died of disease. The accuracy of the rifle and increased firepower drastically increased the lethality of firearms.

Most of what I see or read about the American Revolutionary War soldier is pretty bleak. The Continental Army was ill-equipped, untrained, unorganized, and had intermittent pay days. There is also a lot said about soldiers not having shoes, and starving, boiling leather to eat because there was no food.

We should put things into perspective. We have to first understand the motive behind historians in the highly subjective nature of interpreting past historical events. First of all, the officers and most of the sergeants in the Continental Army had experience in combat during the French and Indian War, they were experienced. Any soldier worth his mettle will teach as much as he can to the new recruits that join the ranks from local militia units, the point of battle is to win. The new soldiers that joined Washington's Continental Army were all minutemen and militia men from their local community. For the most part the local pastor organized the militia and minutemen from the local congregations. Veterans from previous wars, weather the French and Indian War or the continual battles with the Indians, trained the men entering the militia. They were men of faith–church goers. This was the time when everyone had a Bible–they were able to read and read their Bible. They were every mindful of God's council to Joshua before going into battle; "Have I not commanded you? Be strong and courageous! Do not tremble or be dismayed, for the Lord your God is with you wherever you go."[15] And equally important; "But for the cowardly and unbelieving…and immoral persons…their part will be in the lake that burns with fire and brimstone, which is the second death."[16] These early American soldiers were motivated by their love of God, Country, and an intense desire for liberty. In actuality the colonies had been self-governing since the mid-1600s. The only impediments to self-rule were the taxes imposed by England, the decrees of the Royal Governor and the ever-present English soldiers. The English soldiers, however, were only stationed in a few port cities, primarily Boston and New

---

[15] Joshua 1:9
[16] Revelation 21:8

York. For the most part the Royal Governors interfered very little in local governments; trouble arose occasionally when England intervened in American affairs.

American soldiers put up with the hardships because they believed in their cause, something bigger than themselves. Some left, some deserted, as in any war; not everyone is suited for battle. Not every soldier is devastated by war or scarred for life. There are those who we say have a warrior's heart. On the positive side they endure the hardships and the carnage of war because they know the only way to preserve the Judeo-Christian values into the next generation is to understand that these ideas are worth fighting for and, if need be, dying for in order to guarantee their preservation. On the negative side they are fighting against injustice, oppression and oftentimes just plain evil. Americans enjoyed and appreciated their religious freedom, self-government and the liberty of their culture. What do soldiers do when they are not fighting? They train. Any soldier that wants to come home is going to do all he can to learn as much as he can before ever going into combat.

Most of the fighting during this era was called "European Style," where armies would form up in ranks and face off against each other. All of the American soldiers that had fought in the French and Indian War were very familiar with the guerrilla tactics employed by the Indians, as well as the European style of warfare. In George Washington's third battle of the French and Indian War at Monongahela he deployed his troops into the woods as guerrilla fighters, not in formation as Braddock had done. Braddock would not resort to such a cowardly form of fighting, and his rank and file lost 1,000 men to the unconventional guerrilla tactics of the French and Indians.

The Ranger Companies in America were developed during this time and they used guerrilla tactics exclusively. I'm a little skeptical of historians, that have never been in combat yet think they are authorities on how soldiers think, feel, act and what motivates them. A person's worldview is central to how they will portray historical events. I have heard so many times, "They had no shoes." I live in Minnesota. If you do not have a pair of boots you would not last a day in the winter without freezing your feet. "Their boots were wrapped in rags." Every winter war army has had soldiers wrap their boots in cloth for extra warmth, right up until there was such a thing as insulated boots. You must understand the motivation of any historian, aside from the facts—dates, times, places and recorded words. Much of historical interpretation is very subjective. Do they have a version they want to portray and then slant their interpretation to prove their point? Are they evolutionist, anti-war, secular or atheists? My perspective is that of a Christian, as I believe God created the heavens and the earth and that He does involve Himself in the daily affairs of individuals, governments and nations. I believe we are fallen creatures and in need of a Savior, who is Jesus Christ.[17] I am also a combat veteran. I understand battle, carnage, death, miracles and how soldiers think, behave and believe.[18] I also believe in the sanctity of human life and that when a soldier is killed, he is a father, brother, husband or a friend. I also understand that sometimes the only way to stop someone from committing horrible acts is to kill them.

British soldiers came to America expecting to fight a European style of war, but what they found themselves involved in was entirely different. In European style of warfare, the opposing sides face each other in rows–sometimes platoon size (40 men), sometimes company size (150 men). The rows are usually two, and sometimes three deep. As the soldiers form up cannons and howitzers will fire on opposing sides. The two forces advance on each other until they are about 100 yards apart; then, the first row fires their smoothbore musket, all at once, and exchange volleys of musket balls. The second row will step forward while the first row, kneels and reloads preparing to fire their next volley. The emphasis is on reloading as quickly as possible to be ready for the next order to "fire." I know this seems crazy to stand in the open and fire weapons at each other. However, this style of warfare was dictated by the weapons in use at the time. The weapon used in Europe and in most of the world was officially called the Long Land Pattern Musket, known as "Brown Bess," by the troops. Matchbox muskets produced before Brown Bess were bare steel. Chemicals were used on the metal of the Brown Bess to reduce rusting and the chemicals turned the metal brown, and with the wooden stock, it was the Brown Bess. The term has its origins from the German version of their long gun called a strong gun, or in German, braun buss. Brown Bess is a flintlock smoothbore musket. Usually the barrel was .75 caliber, firing a .69 caliber musket ball. Gun powder would be poured down the barrel or a premeasured portion would be used; then the musket ball was dropped down the barrel and a ramrod shoved down the barrel, seating both in position opposite the flash pan and flintlock. The muskets used black powder, which caused a lot of fouling in the weapon. That is

---

[17] Things To Come: A Brief History of the Bible by Tom Newman
[18] See Just War: A Soldier's Revelation by Tom Newman

why the musket ball was actually smaller than the bore. Generally, after firing about ten musket balls, the weapon would need some cleaning. The reason the soldiers stood face to face is because the smoothbore musket was incredibly inaccurate. The Brown Bess did not have sights. Soldiers were not taught how to aim; they were told to point and shoot or point at the horizon and shoot. Because the musket ball was so loose in the barrel there was very little control of the round's trajectory. The musket ball could miss its target by three feet at 75 yards. This was about the limit of its relative effective range. The idea was more like firing a shotgun as opposed to a rifle. A shotgun will propel hundreds of bbs over a broad range called a pattern, in the hopes of hitting something. Whereas a rifle fires a tight-fitting musket ball down a barrel with riffling. Because of the tight fit the ball is in constant contact with the riffling and the twist in the riffling imparts a spin on the ball, giving the ball more accuracy. The tight fit also insures all of the powder from the charge will ignite giving the ball more force and it will travel a greater distance at a greater speed. A marksman is now able to place a single well aimed shot out to 3 or 400 yards. The Brown Bess weighted about ten pounds and were five to six feet long.

The point was to send a volley of musket balls at the enemy and hope that some of them found a target, repeat firing volleys until you were within charging distance of the enemy. Then the primary weapon of the infantry would be used, the seventeen-inch bayonet attached to the end of the barrel of the five or six-foot-long musket. The bayonet lug on the top of the barrel could be used as a front sight but there was no rear sight for sight alignment. Some of America's militia used smoothbore muskets, primarily city dwellers. However, the weapon of choice for American militia was the American Long Rifle. Settlers, pioneers, trappers and backwoodsmen relied on the rifle for protection against Indians and for collecting food for themselves and their families. You had to hit what you were aiming at, the first time, and sometimes from as much as two or three hundred yards away. In a combination of American ingenuity, German and Swedish immigrants some of the finest and most accurate rifles in the world were produced at this time in America.

The American Rifle that evolved was lighter, better balanced and had smaller calibers: .36 to .45 were fabricated. They were called rifles because the barrels were produced with groves inside the barrel that made a gradual rotation from the chamber to the muzzle. Riffling is a helical grove pattern that spirals down the length of the barrel that is machined into the internal surface of the gun's barrel. This rifling exerts torque on the ball producing a spin on the projectile such that it would travel further and straighter, like the spin on a football. There were a couple of drawbacks to the American Rifle though, it took longer to load and did not have a bayonet lug or a bayonet. It did, however, have front and rear sights. Powder was carried in a powder horn and a measured amount was poured down the barrel; with experience you just knew how much to pour down the barrel. Next, a small piece of cloth, paper or leather was placed over the end of the barrel then the ball was forced into the barrel and run home with the ramrod. The wrapping on the bullet made it fit very snuggly in the barrel so that on discharge the bullet was in contact with the rifling groves. The tight fit also allowed for the powder to burn much more efficiently, producing more foot pounds of pressure and more velocity on the bullet. Ramming the tight-fitting ball down the barrel took more time than just dropping a ball down a smoothbore. Bullet velocity and accuracy were also increased by the smaller, lighter caliber bullets. A smoothbore would propel the musket ball at 1,000 feet per second (fps), about 680 miles per hour (mph). The rifled bullet had a muzzle velocity of 1600 fps or about 1,100 mph. A smaller, faster bullet with a spin on it produced long–range accuracy out to 300 and 400 yards. The American rifle did not have a bayonet. Most riflemen carried a tomahawk. Aside from a vastly superior weapon, Americans had a different mindset. As soon as a child was able to handle a five to six-foot weapon, they began to practice shooting. Americans loved their rifles. There were: turkey shoots, beef shoots, competition shooting, shooting fests and shooting just for sport. There were even contests where you had to drive a nail into a tree with your rifle's projectile. American marksmanship was legendary in the colonies.

On June 16, 1775, the day before the Continental Congress appointed George Washington Commander-in-Chief, congress approved the creation of ten rifle companies. John Adams said, "These are said to be all expert riflemen and by means of excellence of their firelocks, as well as their skill in the use of them, to send sure destruction at great distances." To qualify as a member of a rifle company a marksman had to put ten consecutive shots on a ten-inch target at 200 yards. The first rifle company was formed under the command of Daniel Morgan. Daniel Morgan is loosely portrayed by Mel Gibson in the movie "The Patriot." Daniel Morgan was the son of Welsh immigrants. During the French and Indian War Morgan, along with his cousin Daniel Boone, were teamsters on the military excursion of General Braddock at the Battle of

Monongahela. Morgan was recruited as a Lieutenant for Pontiac's Rebellion and again returned to battle for Dunmore's War against the Shawnee. Because of his reputation as a crack shot, he was again recruited in 1775, during the siege of Boston and told to raise a company of militia riflemen. He raised ninety-six sharpshooters in ten days. Morgan participated in the raid on Quebec with Benedict Arnold and General Montgomery. Montgomery was killed in the action and Arnold was wounded. Morgan was captured and taken prisoner. Upon his release, as part of a prisoner exchange, he was promoted to Colonel for taking command of the American forces after Montgomery's death and Arnold being wounded.

Morgan as Colonel was given command of a 500-man Provisional Rifle Corps. He and his sharpshooters were charged with gathering supplies and harassing and demoralizing Howe's men by the use of sniping and guerilla tactics. In August of 1777, Morgan and his sharpshooters were ordered north of Albany to join the forces of General Horatio Gates for his impending battle with General John Burgoyne. For the British soldier the American rifleman came to have almost a supernatural mystique about him. Lt. Colonel George Hanger of the Hessian Jaegers said, "I never in my life saw better rifles, or men who shot better, than those Americans." Hanger was considered one of the finest marksmen in all of Europe. British troops, when they were not on a campaign, stayed in cities and towns. In the countryside they were ravaged by the marksmen, often shot at such distances no one knew where the shots were coming from. The American Rifle had devastating consequences for the British during the Revolutionary War, especially at the battles of Bunker Hill, Québec, Saratoga, Cowpens, King's Mountain, and Freeman's Farm. This new weapon and skillful marksman transformed how wars would be fought from the Revolutionary War forward and around the world through guerilla tactics, ambushes, hit–and–run, skirmishes and sniping. This is how a collection of minutemen and citizen militia defeated the greatest army and navy in the world at the time. American exceptionalism and innovation inspired by divine providence, intervention and marksmanship.

Secular Historians and the entertainment industry like to have you believe soldiers fight for their comrades in arms; they are fighting for each other. So, what happens when your friend is killed, what if they all are killed, as was my experience?[19] This is a nice romantic sentiment; but it is not enough to get you through the true reality of war. The thing that gets you up every day, the thing that allows you to endure hardships, the thing that appeases the death of your fellow warriors in arms is that you are fighting for something very important; something beyond yourself. You are fighting for justice against evil and oppression. Fighting to ensure God's unalienable rights and freedom are there for all. Another extremely important factor in the performance and tenacity of the infantry soldier is their confidence in their leader. George Washington was a man of deep religious convictions, a man of honor, bravery and exceptional character, who relied heavily on the providence of God His decisions in battle were competent, often brilliant and showed a daring confidence in his men that inspired them all. He did not take liberties of other officers, he slept where his men slept and ate what they ate and endured what they endured. His men respected and admired him and were willing to go the distance with him and for him.

Some of the Founding Fathers, Washington, Adams and Jefferson were well known for their belief that a republic is only sustainable by a religious and moral people. The Founding Fathers understood, as Franklin pointed out; "we have studied all of the governments of the world, and it is all inadequate for what we are trying to accomplish here." A government based on God's law, governed by the consent of the people, the governed. Our Founding Fathers understood man's proclivity for corruptibility and his fallen nature: hence, we must rely on the precepts, statutes and commandments of God. As Scripture reads, men without God are beasts.[20] Religion is needed as the only means of administering the necessity of man's inability to restrain himself; not only from evil, but from greed, a lust for power, wealth and influence. If you wanted to run for any political office in the original thirteen colonies you had to sign an oath that stated you believed that God is watching, that you will be held accountable, and that there will be a day of judgment where good will be rewarded and evil will be punished. These are the values that kept the soldiers of the Continental Army in dedicated duty to the defense of a new nation, wholly unlike anything else promulgated by mankind.

In General George Washington's address to his troops he said, "The General most earnestly requires, and expects, a due observance of the articles of war, established for the government of the army which forbid

---

[19] Just War: A Soldier's Revelation by Tom Newman
[20] Ecclesiastes 3:18

profane cursing, swearing and drunkenness; and in like manner requires and expects, of all officers, and soldiers, not engaged on actual duty, a punctual attendance on divine service, to implore the blessings of heaven upon the means used for our safety and defense."

General Washington held his men to a high standard which improves discipline and moral and gave his men a sense of self-worth. Because of General Washington's profound faith, his integrity of character and his exemplary leadership, his men respected and admired him.

General Eisenhower, the Supreme Commander of all Allied Forces during WWII famously said; "There are no atheists in foxholes." This means that when you are in the midst of battle there is not a soldier that does not have an intimate relationship with Christ. In combat people are dying every day, and as far as you are concerned you may be next. That reality puts you in a very close relationship with Christ.

Thomas Paine, who traveled from Britain to the colonies in 1774, had a significant impact on Americans by encapsulating their cause in his many writings. When Paine wrote "The Crises", George Washington had him read it to the troops at the winter camp before they crossed the Delaware River to defeat the Hessians at Trenton. It reads in part,

"THESE are the times that try men's souls. The summer soldier and the sunshine patriot will, in this crisis, shrink from the service of their country; but he that stands by it now, deserves the love and thanks of man and woman. Tyranny, like hell, is not easily conquered; yet we have this consolation with us, that the harder the conflict, the more glorious the triumph. What we obtain too cheap, we esteem too lightly: it is dearness only that gives everything its value. Heaven knows how to put a proper price upon its goods; and it would be strange indeed if so celestial an article as FREEDOM should not be highly rated. Britain, with an army to enforce her tyranny, has declared that she has a right (not only to TAX) but 'to BIND us in ALL CASES WHATSOEVER' and if being bound in that manner, is not slavery, then is there not such a thing as slavery upon earth. Even the expression is impious; for so unlimited a power can belong only to God… I have as little superstition in me as any man living, but my secret opinion has ever been, and still is, that God Almighty will not give up a people to military destruction, or leave them unsupported to perish, who have so earnestly and so repeatedly sought to avoid the calamities of war, by every decent method which wisdom could invent. Neither have I so much of the infidel in me, as to suppose that He has relinquished the government of the world, and given us up to the care of devils; and as I do not, I cannot see on what grounds the king of Britain can look up to heaven for help against us: a common murderer, a highwayman, or a house-breaker, has as good a pretense as he... Howe, in my little opinion, committed a great error in generalship in not throwing a body of forces off from Staten Island through Amboy, by which means he might have seized all our stores at Brunswick, and intercepted our march into Pennsylvania; but if we believe the power of hell to be limited, we must likewise believe that their agents are under some providential control... General Washington... God hath blessed him with uninterrupted health, and given him a mind that can even flourish upon care... I am as confident, as I am that God governs the world, that America will never be happy till she gets clear of foreign dominion. Wars, without ceasing, will break out till that period arrives, and the continent must in the end be conqueror; for though the flame of liberty may sometimes cease to shine, the coal can never expire... There are cases which cannot be overdone by language, and this is one. There are persons, too, who see not the full extent of the evil which threatens them; they solace themselves with hopes that the enemy, if he succeeds, will be merciful. It is the madness of folly, to expect mercy from those who have refused to do justice; and even mercy, where conquest is the object, is only a trick of war; the cunning of the fox is as murderous as the violence of the wolf, and we ought to guard equally against both."

FAITH OF OUR FATHERS

Historical revisionists consistently portray the founding fathers as deist. This is so far from an accurate portrayal that it is actually a lie. In England a deist included anti-Christians, non-Christians and those that thought God was the Creator but does not interfere with His creation. They further assert that God can be known by reason and by observing His creation and not through anything supernatural or by miracles, which is more assumptive language; if you buy the term or the phrase you buy into the underlying philosophy. If you have not looked up the term or researched the Founders, then you think of the Founders as deist, which is to say they were not Christians. We do not see things as they are, we see things as we are. If you are a deist then you see the Founding Fathers as deists. The argument the revisionists like to seize upon is that the Founding Fathers had a disdain for religion. Religious intolerance is what drove them to the New World—organized religion consisting of the church of England and the institution of the Catholic Church. If you are a Christian then you understand they were Christians, and our nation was founded wholly on Christian principles. Most recent writings on the history of America's founding either omit our Christian origin or distort the reality of the character of our Founders. Those who cannot distort the message attack the character and integrity of the messenger. There are very few sources or textbooks since 1950 that give an accurate portrayal of our true Christian heritage. Revisionists also maintain that most of the Founders were criminals, when this is a matter of worldviews. Those in England, in that the Founders were planning a revolution, considered them traitors, and as such criminals. Those that are not of that opinion see them as men seeking freedom from tyrannical rule and therefore courageous and honorable men. The Protestants that journeyed to America were weary of institutional religion, as was Christ with the Sadducees and Pharisees, because of the history of the Catholic Church and the Church of England, "Teaching as doctrine the precepts of men. Neglecting the commandments of God, you hold to the traditions of men."[21]

The Reformation caused drastic cultural, economic, moral, religious and political changes across the world. It was these ideas and changes from the Reformation which the Protestants brought to America, a virgin land not corrupted by European politics or religious practices like theocracies or the divine rights of a king or a pope. "All men are created equal." And each person was to read the Bible and establish a personal relationship with Jesus Christ, God and the Holy Spirit, according to his/her own conscience. One does not need a priest, pastor, minister, or an institution to be a person of faith. The idea of a republican government came from Exodus 18:21 "Furthermore, you shall select out of all the people able men who fear God, men of truth, those who hate dishonest gain, and you shall place these over them as leaders of thousands, of hundreds, of fifties and of tens." The idea of liberty is also from Scripture; 2 Corinthians 3:17 "Now the Lord is the Spirit, and where the Spirit of the Lord is, there is liberty."

Other contributors to our formation as a country were people like John Locke, Samuel Rutherford, John Calvin, Adam Smith and Martin Luther. Chief among the influential personalities in the formation of a Christian America were the early preachers. The preachers and pulpits of America were the media of the day. Sermons from Jesus Christ to the evils of tyranny and the blessings of God ordained liberty. Many of the preachers were among the most influential men in a settlement, a town or a city. For the most part they were responsible for organizing the local militia. Peter von Muhlenberg, a minister in Virginia, was one of many preachers who received a letter from George Washington urging them to form a regiment of militia. The following Sunday he preached a sermon from Ecclesiastes 3:1-8, ending with an appeal to the men in his congregation. "There is a time for war, and there is a time for peace, there is a time to pray and there is a time to fight." Then he, while still in the pulpit, legendarily pulled off his clergy robe, displaying his dress in the uniform of a colonel in the Continental Army. He got his regiment and served for eight years in the Continental Army during the Revolutionary

---

[21] Mark 7:7-8

War. Other early men of faith worth researching are; Jonathon Edwards, George Whitfield, Charles Finney, John and Charles Wesley's, James Caldwell, Francis Asbury, Samuel Kirkland, Josiah Smith, David Zeisberger and John Gano, who baptized George Washington.

As to the claims that our Founding Fathers were deists, that God is not involved in His creation, George Washington, at his first inaugural address, said; "No people can be bound to acknowledge and adore the invisible hand, which conducts the Affairs of men more than the People of the United States. Every step, by which they have advanced to the character of an independent nation, seems to have been distinguished by some token of providential agency."

Benjamin Franklin addressed the congress; "Mr. President, the small progress we have made after 4-or five-weeks close attendance & continual reasonings with each other-our different sentiments on almost every question, several of the last producing as many noes as ays, is methinks a melancholy proof of the imperfection of the Human Understanding. We indeed seem to feel our own want of political wisdom, since we have been running about in search of it. We have gone back to ancient history for models of Government, and examined the different forms of those Republics which having been formed with the seeds of their own dissolution now no longer exist. And we have viewed Modern States all round Europe, but find none of their Constitutions suitable to our circumstances. In this situation of this Assembly, groping as it were in the dark to find political truth, and scarce able to distinguish it when presented to us, how has it happened, Sir, that we have not hitherto once thought of humbly applying to the Father of lights to illuminate our understandings? In the beginning of the Contest with G. Britain, when we were sensible of danger, we had daily prayer in this room for the divine protection. - Our prayers, Sir, were heard, & they were graciously answered. All of us who were engaged in the struggle must have observed frequent instances of a superintending providence in our favor. To that kind providence we owe this happy opportunity of consulting in peace on the means of establishing our future national felicity. And have we now forgotten that powerful friend? or do we imagine that we no longer need his assistance? I have lived, Sir, a long time, and the longer I live, the more convincing proofs I see of this truth – that God governs in the affairs of men. And if a sparrow cannot fall to the ground without His notice, is it probable that an empire can rise without His aid? I firmly believe this; and I also believe that without his concurring aid we shall succeed in this political building no better, than the

Builders of Babel: We shall be divided by our little partial local interests; our projects will be confounded, and we ourselves shall become a reproach and bye word down to future ages. And what is worse, mankind may hereafter from this unfortunate instance, despair of establishing Governments by Human wisdom and leave it to chance, war and conquest. I therefore beg leave to move-that henceforth prayers imploring the assistance of Heaven, and its blessings on our deliberations, be held in this Assembly every morning before we proceed to business, and that one or more of the Clergy of this City be requested to officiate in that Service-"

Mr. Sharman seconded the motion.

When the Founding Fathers wrote in the Declaration of Independence; "With a firm reliance on the protection of Divine Providence, we mutually pledge to each other our lives, our fortunes, and our sacred honor," they were declaring to the world that they were making a declaration of their dependence upon God and not some earthly power. John Adams wrote his wife when the Declaration was passed: "I am well aware of the toil, and blood, and treasure, that it will cost to maintain this declaration, and support and defend these states; yet through all the gloom I can see the rays of light and glory. I can see that the end is worth more than all the means." The "end" being a constitutional republic with individual liberty, elected representatives and limited government. A government with powers checked and balanced by five separate entities to keep each other in check. Three branches of government-the Executive, the Legislative, and the Judicial. After God, the individual came first. Only by the consent of the governed could the government govern and only then to protect every citizens life, liberty, property and happiness, making the citizenry the fourth check on the government. The Declaration professed that all men are created equal, which demonstrated there was no superior authority granted to anyone, popes and kings included. It was understood that men of liberty must be under self-restraint. The new republic was to be governed by the sovereignty of God and His law, as corruptible man could never be his own lawgiver and judge. The Declaration makes a declaration of unalienable rights. These are natural rights, granted to all people by God and cannot be denied or restricted by any government or individual; they include that all men are created equal with the rights of life, liberty, property and happiness, as outlined by Thomas Jefferson. In return, citizens were expected to follow the legal laws enacted by the government. These were ideas expressed by John Locke as well. The laws of man were

173

written by man. The laws of God and our unalienable rights were revealed. The government, for its part, was to protect the unalienable rights of its citizenry. If it failed to do so, ("a long train of abuses,") the people have a right to change or remove the government for one that will. This is why the Founding Fathers drafted the second amendment. If the people are unarmed, then the only people with guns will be the military. The experience of the Revolutionary War is that an unarmed citizenry has very little chance of removing a corrupt or tyrannical government. Legal rights, on the other hand, are rights granted by governments or legal systems. One should be mindful of the difference. America would be One Nation Under God, with the unalienable right of self-defense.

George Washington stated, "Let us with caution indulge the supposition that morality can be maintained without religion. Reason and experience both forbid us to expect that national morality can prevail in exclusion of religious principle."

The Founding Fathers, by professing that the originator of these unalienable rights is the Creator are stating that He works in and governs the affairs of men, establishing absolute standards to which men are held accountable, attested to by the fifty-six signors of the Declaration, absolutely, not deists. The Ten Commandments, although they are found in Scripture, are not religious, they are behavioral guidelines, laws of God, for us to be held accountable to, along with six-hundred and thirteen other laws found in the Torah. In the Hebrew religion the Torah, or the books of Moses, are the first five books of the Old Testament. The six-hundred and thirteen laws are dispersed in Genesis, Exodus, Numbers, Leviticus and Deuteronomy. Within the six-hundred and thirteen there are 365 do nots and 248 dos. They include things like "do not move your neighbor's boundary marker" and "do not drink wine if you are with child" and "whoever spills man's blood his blood shall be spilt by man" and "establish a holy people."

This is essentially what Christian theism is, that man is accountable to God, all men equally are under the law. Noah Webster said, "The moral principles and precepts contained in the Scripture ought to form the basis of all our civil constitutions and laws. All the miseries and evils which men suffer from vice, crime, ambition, injustice, oppression, slavery, and war, proceed from their despising or neglecting the precepts contained in the Bible."

The wisdom of Scripture also gave us the golden rule; "In everything, therefore, treat people the same way you want them to treat you. "And "Treat others the same way you want them to treat you."[22]

Thomas Jefferson is often portrayed as non-religious. Revisionists often cite his cutting up the Bible so that his version would just state what he thought was true. In a letter to Dr. Benjamin Rush, Jefferson wrote, "My views...are the result of a life of inquiry and reflection, and very different from the anti-Christian system imputed to me by those who know nothing of my opinions. To the corruptions of Christianity, I am, indeed, opposed; but not to the genuine precepts of Jesus himself. I am a Christian in the only sense in which He wished any one to be; sincerely attached to his doctrines in preference to all others'."

In actuality, The Jefferson Bible was all of the teachings of Jesus Christ. Jefferson's intent was to produce a Bible for others to use in evangelizing to the Indians. He removed anything that he thought would foster any justification for violence and presented just the morality and the wisdom of Christ.

Jefferson, in his second inaugural address stated: "I shall need, too, the favor of that Being in whose hands we are, who led our fathers, as Israel of old, from their native land and planted them in a country flowing with all the necessities and comforts of life."

Again, this is confirmation that God deals in the affairs of men. Jefferson supported the Virginia Bible Society which provided Bibles to any family that could not afford one.

Jefferson wrote to a friend, Charles Thomson: "I too have made a wee little book, from the same materials, which I call the Philosophy of Jesus. it is a paradigm of his doctrines, made by cutting the texts out of the book, and arranging them on the pages of a blank book, in a certain order of time or subject. a more beautiful or precious morsel of ethics I have never seen. it is a document in proof that I am a real Christian, that is to say, a disciple of the doctrines of Jesus, very different from the Platonists, who call me infidel, and themselves Christians and preachers of the gospel, while they draw all their characteristic dogmas from what it's Author never said nor saw."

Written in the front of his personal Bible, Jefferson wrote, "I am a real Christian, that is to say, a disciple of the doctrines of Jesus. I have little doubt that our whole country will soon be rallied to the unity of our   creator."

---

[22] Matthew 7:12, Luke 6:31

THE REVOLUTIONARY WAR

After the battles of Lexington and Concord the British forces returned to Boston. The militia followed them along the way. When they reached Boston, the militia were joined by minutemen from the surrounding communities, as the prearranged ringing of the church bells had alerted the minutemen. Throughout the colonies, local leaders begin to prepare for military resistance and develop new political institutions to replace British authority.

The militia had existed in the colonies ever since there had been confrontations with the Indians during the early settlements. They were organized by community. Every male between the ages of sixteen and sixty was expected to be part of the local militia. From this information the revisionists surmise that the Continental Army was made up of kids and the very old.

The militia was encouraged by England, as they did not have the resources or personnel to provide a police force for the colonies. In addition, to the militia, communities had minutemen, who were part of the militia, however, they were much more serious about soldiering and spent a lot of time training. The notion was to be ready for military action with a minute's notice from those with a warrior's heart.

The militia surrounded Boston in what would become the Siege of Boston—lasting from April 19, 1775, until the British retreat on March 17, 1776. A company of 96 riflemen under the command of Daniel Morgan arrived at Cambridge and reported to Major General Artemas Ward. Artemas immediately dispatched Morgan's sharpshooters around the perimeter to snipe the visible British soldiers. The sharpshooters were so effective that the British soldiers refused to walk their guard posts; instead they took a position behind cover and very cautiously kept watch. The sharpshooters then moved onto artillerymen and any officer, with their bright gold shoulder braids, became fair game. The snipers had a profound effect of lowering the morale of all the garrison troops. One major is to have said, "The redcoats are so amazingly terrified by our riflemen that they will not stir beyond their lines." The colonial sniper took on mythical proportions amongst the British.

General Gage requested reinforcements, stating that he was severely outnumbered. Boston sits on a peninsula in Boston Harbor, opposite of Charleston, which is also on a peninsula in Boston Harbor. The sharpshooters kept the British from using the necks of the peninsula as a passageway to the countryside to procure food, wood and other provisions. General Ward had his soldiers remove all the livestock and burned the hay on the surrounding islands in an effort to starve out the British. Gage sent one of his ships to fire on the colonists and collect livestock and hay for the horses. The ship ran aground and could not get free. The colonists stormed the vessel, allowing the sailors' escape to a second ship. They then set the ship ablaze. This encounter became known as the "Battle of Chelsea Creek." This was the first naval victory for the Continental Army.

Colonial privateers began raiding British ships for supplies, weapons and gun powder. Some privateers, under the command of John Paul Jones, raided a British fort in the Bahamas, securing the fort and all of the supplies and equipment. John Paul Jones had an accompaniment of 200 marines with him. When they went ashore to secure the fort, this action constituted the first amphibians landing by an American military force.

British ships from Nova Scotia began raiding coastal towns for provisions to take to the troops besieged at Boston, but these efforts were met with heavy resistance from the local militia. In the small coastal town of Machias about forty militia captured a small British sloop and its provisions. A sloop is a small sailing vessel with one main sail and one mast, with fore and aft rigging. If a sailing vessel has more than one mast it is called a cutter. This was the second naval victory of the war for the colonists. This action, of course, severally embarrassed Admiral Graves. In retaliation he ordered the destruction of several coastal towns. Lieutenant Henry Mowatt was dispatched to carry out the orders. Because of bad weather, Mowatt was only able to attack one town, the town of Falmouth, which was burned to the ground. The act so outraged the colonists that the Second Continental Congress authorized the creation of a navy, but with no money this was not going to happen. General Washington stepped up his efforts to recruit privateers.

By the beginning of May of 1775, the colonial militia was occupying all of the land and high ground surrounding Boston Harbor. General Gage pulled his troops off the Charleston Peninsula, not wanting to have his army divided in case the colonists should attack. He was also waiting on his reinforcements to arrive from England. On May 25th, Major General William Howe, General Henry Clinton, and General John Burgoune arrived from England with 120 ships and 6,000 reinforcements.

Now, with Gage's army reinforced to 11,000 soldiers, he informed the newly arrived generals of his plan to lift the siege of Boston and crush the rebellion. Howe would take a third of the army across the harbor to Charleston, work his way north over the Charleston neck, then move west to converge on Cambridge, where the rebel army garrisoned. General Burgoune would take a second third of the army down the neck of the Boston peninsula and circle west and north to meet Howe at Cambridge in a pincer move.

The American Revolution probably had more spies than any other war in history, and this cannot be taken lightly. There were about 45 percent of the population that wanted independence from Britain. About 20 percent were considered Loyalists and wanted to maintain ties to England as English subjects, and there were some who were uncertain. Loyalists remained loyal to Britain because they did not believe that a free society was possible if it had to rely on people's ability for self-restraint. Loyalists would report Continental movements and troop locations to the British. There were Patriots that would report British locations, movement, and plans to the Continental Army. And there were those on both sides that would feign support for one side while giving false information to the other side. In short, it was a field intelligence nightmare.

In any event, word got to Prescot of the British plans to converge on Cambridge. As long as Charleston had been evacuated of British troops, Prescott moved his 1,500 soldiers down the Charleston neck to build a fortification on Bunker Hill. Upon their arrival, Breed's Hill looked to be a better location, closer to Boston, and strategically easier to defend. The Continental Army began construction of a redoubt on Breed's Hill.

Charleston was on the west side of the peninsula; Breed's Hill in the middle. Prescot had Captain Thomas Knowlton construct a defense position to the east of Breed's Hill at a location called Rails Fence. The Continental soldiers worked all night to construct their defenses. In the morning, General Gage and Howe saw the defenses and had to cancel their plans for the attack on Cambridge. They decided instead to mount an offensive against the colonial position on Breed's Hill. They sent a landing force of 500 to Charleston, directly south of the redoubt and southwest of Rail Fence. British forces landed at Charleston and began advancing towards the redoubt; however, they were so inundated with sniper fire, they had to withdraw to the beach. They asked for replacements to replace the soldiers killed and wounded by snipers before they could continue their attack.

At Rail Fence Captain Knowlton had been reinforced by two rifle companies lead by John Stack and James Reed. The British attacked the redoubt and Rail Fence with 2,000 – 2,500 Regulars. The British main thrust was against Rail Fence, as they assumed it would be the weakest defense and they could then flank the center-positioned redoubt. The British attack was repulsed by the deadly accuracy of the American rifle. The strategy of line-on-line fighting is that, when a brightly dressed, highly disciplined troop formation advances on a position, it is supposed to instill fear into the opposing side and make them doubt their confidence. However, the accuracy of the riflemen was so devastating that the British troops broke ranks and ran. General Howe requested reinforcements, and when they arrived, he launched a second attack, with the same results: repelled by the onslaught of accurate rifle fire. Howe requested more reinforcements, and cannon support from the Admiral, they arrived at 5:00 PM. The cannons on the ship could not be elevated high enough to fire over Howe's men and onto Breed's Hill. The ships retreated. Howe tried one more attack before dark. The outcome of the third attack was totally unexpected. Prescot, because they were low on ammunition, had his men hold their fire until "you can see the whites of their eyes." The British advanced again, and again were cut down by intense accurate rifle fire. As the British prepared for their bayonet attack, and under the heavy Continental barrage, they withdrew. The Continental Army was low on ammunition, and few of the riflemen had bayonets for the ensuing hand-to-hand combat. The Continentals, with smoothbores–and, therefore, bayonets–were vastly outnumbered by the thousands of British regulars, however, they held the line as the rest of the force retreated. The riflemen began a retreat and took up positions to cover the retreat of the rest of the army.

The Continentals withdrew to the other side of the neck and formed a line that the British would be unable to penetrate. If Howe had pursued, he could have, if victorious, wiped out the Continental Army; however, he chose not to pursue. It may be that Howe was so devastated by the unbelievable number of losses among his soldiers that he chose not to pursue, it could also have been divine intervention. Or, maybe Howe was unsure how to address this new element of warfare, how were they able to kill his soldiers from so far away? His frontal attack left 1,000 of his men dead or dying. He would have to devise a new strategy for engaging the colonists. The British had never before come up against such accurate rifle fire that could be delivered at such great distances. Howe had lost a third of his men. Britain had never suffered such atrocious losses in a battle. As Howe surveyed the battlefield he commented, "This is not a rebellion, this is a war."

General Gage was relieved of his command and re-called to England to give an accounting of his horrendous defeat, yet historians call this a British victory because the Americans abandoned the battlefield. The colonists lost 411 soldiers, most of whom fell in the bayonet charge. Howe lost 1,054 of his soldiers. Up to this point in time, with line formations opposing another line formation and firing volleys of musket balls at each other, followed by a bayonet charge, victory was determined by who held the battlefield after the engagement.

The American Revolution completely changed the nature of warfare and military tactics. This was the introduction of guerrilla warfare. The colonist's settlers, trappers, backwoodsmen and soldiers in the French and Indian War learned the guerilla tactics from the American Indians. The guerilla tactics, along with their supremely accurate rifles, would completely change the nature of warfare. The militia would snipe, fire on the British from unheard-of distances, and engage from concealed positions. The Americans would not meet the British in line formation but from behind breastworks, cover and concealment. Because the nature of warfare had dramatically changed, the definition of victory also changed with guerrilla warfare. In guerrilla warfare the enemy is engaged, suddenly, usually from ambush. The guerillas inflict as much damage as they can and retreat before the enemy can organize a counterattack. The victor is determined by body-count, who has inflicted the most casualties.

I take issue with historians calling this a British victory. The Continentals were low on ammunition, did not posses' bayonets for the hand-to-hand combat, which were obstacles they would have to overcome. However, they had delivered a decisive blow to the British army. They not only won the engagement; they contained the enemy on the peninsula so that they could not carry out their plans to encircle the American forces. The British were still under siege in Boston, they had not improved their position. In modern warfare, you engage the enemy, deliver as much damage as possible, and retreat to fight another day. It is clear to me this was an American victory. So much for non-combatants pontificating on the victors of war.

After the battle, General Clinton wrote in his diary: "A few more such victories would have shortly put an end to British dominion in America."

General Washington really had no choice, almost out of ammo and facing bayonet charges, he would have lost a lot of soldiers. However, the genius, or providence, in all of this, by withdrawing to the neck, the British troops were completely cut off. It did not matter how many troops Howe had; Washington held the bottleneck–not only a victory but a terrific strategic maneuver. Guerilla warfare and the rifle drastically changed warfare just as the smoothbore musket had earlier. The American militia for the most part had smoothbore muskets unless they had purchased a rifle on their own. Minutemen, frontiersmen and backwoodsmen all had rifles, which they bought as personal weapons. The soldiers in the Continental Army were equipped with smoothbore muskets and bayonet, however, they were usually a smaller part of the fighting force. The smoothbore musket was standard issue for most armies they were inexpensive and readily available.

The Indians involved in the French and Indian War were impacted by the Revolutionary War as well. As with the earlier war, many Indians were divided over who they should support. This was never an issue of who they supported as much as it was who offered the best chance of maintaining their sovereignty. Most tribes saw the Americans as the bigger threat; however, others did not trust the British, as they had repeatedly violated the Proclamation of 1763. The Iroquois Confederacy could not come to an agreement about who to support. The Seneca, Onondaga and the Cayuga sided with the British. The Mohawk nation split and fought on both sides. The Tuscarora and Oneida sided with the colonists. About 13,000 Indians from the Iroquois Confederacy participated in the northern campaign of the Revolutionary War. The split among the tribes devastated their Confederacy. The Cherokee allied with the British in the southern campaign in the western frontier areas of North Carolina. The Cherokee and the British were defeated in the western frontier. The defeat splintered the Cherokee Nation. The Chickamauga broke away and remained bitter enemies of the colonists, continuing to fight with them for decades.

The Battle of Bunker Hill and the Siege of Boston took place in June of 1775. In May of 1775, Colonel Ethan Allen had been commissioned by the citizens of Connecticut to capture Fort Ticonderoga to prevent the British from using it if hostilities continued. Allen assembled his "Green Mountain Men" and set out for the fort. Benedict Arnold was also charged with taking Fort Ticonderoga by the Massachusetts Safety Committee. He was to assemble a company of men as he traveled to the fort; however, he was unable to recruit any volunteers en route. He met with Allen and the Green Mountain Men just a few miles from the fort. General Arnold assumed he would take command; however, the Green Mountain Men said they would only fight under Allen. Arnold just accompanied the force. There were only fifty Redcoats stationed at the fort and were immediately disarmed by Allen's forces. Allen approached the commander's quarters, knocked on the door, and told the commander to surrender the fort. The commander asked Allen under what authority he was demanding that he surrender the fort. Allen replied, "By the great Jehovah and the Continental Congress." The fort was taken without a shot being fired.

This was the first offensive action taken by the colonists and it put the Continental Congress in a quandary. They figured there was no turning back now and decided to form a unified army of the colonies, The Continental Army. They appointed and voted to make George Washington the commander-in-chief of the army. General Washington took command of the army in Cambridge after the Battle of Bunker Hill and during the initial stages of the Siege of Boston. General Washington inspected the troops upon his arrival. One thing he noticed was the superb work done on the fortifications which had been designed by Colonel Knox. They developed a relationship, and Washington held a high opinion of Knox's tactical knowledge. He made Knox a part of his general staff.

General Washington wanted to storm Boston and put a blocking force on the Charleston Peninsula; however, his generals disagreed. Colonel Knox proposed that he proceed to Fort Ticonderoga and bring the cannons back to break the siege of Boston. General Washington immediately approved the plan. Knox initially had a hard time finding volunteers in the sparsely populated region around the fort but eventually put together enough men, sleds, and wagons to make the return trip. General Washington, like Alexander the Great, listened to all of his generals; then, when a course of action was decided on, he demanded 100 percent support of the plan. It took Knox 58 days to move 59 cannons and mortars 300 miles down Lake George and the Hudson River to Albany, then on to Boston in the dead of winter.

General Washington immediately put his men to work cutting trees for fortifications and laying straw to quiet the movement of cannons. When all preparations were ready, Washington, at dark, had his men fortify Dorchester Heights and moved his cannons into place, overlooking Boston and the Harbor where the British ships were in anchor.

Cannons during the Revolutionary War fired solid iron balls; these were primarily designed for siege warfare and to knock down barricades and the walls of forts. There were also iron balls filled with explosives, designed to detonate when fired at troops. Some of the iron balls were cut in half and then chained together. These were designed to destroy rigging on ships. The most lethal were called "grape shot." The grape shot held three or six pounds of musket balls, rocks, glass, or anything else that could impart tissue damage. It was called grape shot because the projectile looked like a cluster of grapes when the shrapnel was bound up, usually in cloth, and fired at infantry, with devastating results. The canons used in infantry battles were three and six pounders; anything larger than that was too hard to navigate over terrain. A three-pound cannon would fire a three-pound cannon ball, six pounders; would fire a six pound-cannon ball, and so on.

Boston woke under the guns of the Continental Army. It is recorded that General Howe looked to the Heights and said, "Good Lord, they have done more in one night then my men could do in a month."

The British Admiral informed Howe that his ships were in harm's way, and he was sailing north. Howe sent a letter to Washington stating he wanted to evacuate, and if he or the ships were fired upon, he would burn Boston to the ground. On March 4th, 1776, Washington let Howe's army and about 2,000 Loyalists depart Boston on the British ships. Howe left over 200 cannons behind; they tried to sabotage them, but most were repairable and added to Washington's inventory.

General Howe set sail for Halifax, Nova Scotia to resupply, rest, and await reinforcements. General Washington speculated that, when Howe returned, he would try to take New York—the second largest port in the northern colonies. If the British controlled New York, they would also control the Hudson River, isolating the northern-most colonies of New York State, Pennsylvania, and Virginia from the southern colonies. He began moving his army of 10,000 to New York in April 1776. By June, Howe returned and anchored off Staten Island. On July 4th, the audacious Americans declared their Independence to the world, a nation under the providence of God

THE DECLARATION OF INDEPENDENCE

T he Articles of Confederation created a weak national government; the states had much more power than Congress as the national government. Under the Articles, no provisions were made for an executive branch to enforce the laws nor for a national court system to interpret them. The Declaration of Independence was adopted by the Second Continental Congress on July 4, 1776. The Declaration proclaimed that the thirteen colonies, then at war with Great Britain for 16 months, regarded themselves as thirteen independent sovereign states and no longer under British rule. The Declaration justified the independence of the United States by listing colonial grievances against King George III and by asserting certain natural and legal rights, including a right of revolution.

From Noah Webster's 1828 Dictionary: "Law, …The laws which enjoin the duties of piety and morality, are prescribed by God and found in Scriptures…Moral law, a law which prescribes to men their religious and social duties, in other words, their duties to God and to each other. The moral law is summarily contained in the decalogue or ten commandments, written by the finger of God on two tablets of stone, and delivered to Moses on mount Sinai."

THE DECLARATION OF INDEPENDENCE

IN CONGRESS, July 4, 1776, The unanimous Declaration of the thirteen United States of America

When in the Course of human events, it becomes necessary for one people to dissolve the political bands which have connected them with another, and to assume among the powers of the earth, the separate and equal station to which the Laws of Nature and of Nature's God entitle them, a decent respect to the opinions of mankind requires that they should declare the causes which impel them to the separation.

We hold these truths to be self-evident, that all men are created equal, that they are endowed by their Creator with certain unalienable Rights, that among these are Life, Liberty and the pursuit of Happiness.-- That to secure these rights, Governments are instituted among Men, deriving their just powers from the consent of the governed, --That whenever any Form of Government becomes destructive of these ends, it is the Right of the People to alter or to abolish it, and to institute new Government, laying its foundation on such principles and organizing its powers in such form, as to them shall seem most likely to affect their Safety and Happiness. Prudence, indeed, will dictate that Governments long established should not be changed for light and transient causes; and accordingly, all experience hath shewn, that mankind are more disposed to suffer, while evils are sufferable, than to right themselves by abolishing the forms to which they are accustomed. But when a long train of abuses and usurpations, pursuing invariably the same Object evinces a design to reduce them under absolute Despotism, it is their right, it is their duty, to throw off such Government, and to provide new Guards for their future security.--Such has been the patient sufferance of these Colonies; and such is now the necessity which constrains them to alter their former Systems of Government. The history of the present King of Great Britain is a history of repeated injuries and usurpations, all having in direct object the establishment of an absolute Tyranny over these States. To prove this, let Facts be submitted to a candid world.

He has refused his Assent to Laws, the most wholesome and necessary for the public good.

He has forbidden his Governors to pass Laws of immediate and pressing importance, unless suspended in their operation till his Assent should be obtained; and when so suspended, he has utterly neglected to attend to them.

He has refused to pass other Laws for the accommodation of large districts of people, unless those people would relinquish the right of Representation in the Legislature, a right inestimable to them and formidable to tyrants only.

He has called together legislative bodies at places unusual, uncomfortable, and distant from the depository of their public Records, for the sole purpose of fatiguing them into compliance with his measures.

He has dissolved Representative Houses repeatedly, for opposing with manly firmness his invasions on the rights of the people.

He has refused for a long time, after such dissolutions, to cause others to be elected; whereby the Legislative powers, incapable of Annihilation, have returned to the People at large for their exercise; the State remaining in the mean time exposed to all the dangers of invasion from without, and convulsions within.

He has endeavoured to prevent the population of these States; for that purpose obstructing the Laws for Naturalization of Foreigners; refusing to pass others to encourage their migrations hither, and raising the conditions of new Appropriations of Lands.

He has obstructed the Administration of Justice, by refusing his Assent to Laws for establishing Judiciary powers.

He has made Judges dependent on his Will alone, for the tenure of their offices, and the amount and payment of their salaries.

He has erected a multitude of New Offices, and sent hither swarms of Officers to harrass our people, and eat out their substance.

He has kept among us, in times of peace, Standing Armies without the Consent of our legislatures.

He has affected to render the Military independent of and superior to the Civil power.

He has combined with others to subject us to a jurisdiction foreign to our constitution, and unacknowledged by our laws; giving his Assent to their Acts of pretended Legislation:

For Quartering large bodies of armed troops among us:

For protecting them, by a mock Trial, from punishment for any Murders which they should commit on the Inhabitants of these States:

For cutting off our Trade with all parts of the world:

For imposing Taxes on us without our Consent:

For depriving us in many cases, of the benefits of Trial by Jury:

For transporting us beyond Seas to be tried for pretended offences

For abolishing the free System of English Laws in a neighbouring Province, establishing therein an Arbitrary government, and enlarging its Boundaries so as to render it at once an example and fit instrument for introducing the same absolute rule into these Colonies:

For taking away our Charters, abolishing our most valuable Laws, and altering fundamentally the Forms of our Governments:

For suspending our own Legislatures, and declaring themselves invested with power to legislate for us in all cases whatsoever.

He has abdicated Government here, by declaring us out of his Protection and waging War against us.

He has plundered our seas, ravaged our Coasts, burnt our towns, and destroyed the lives of our people.

He is at this time transporting large Armies of foreign Mercenaries to compleat the works of death, desolation and tyranny, already begun with circumstances of Cruelty & perfidy scarcely paralleled in the most barbarous ages, and totally unworthy the Head of a civilized nation.

He has constrained our fellow Citizens taken Captive on the high Seas to bear Arms against their Country, to become the executioners of their friends and Brethren, or to fall themselves by their Hands.

He has excited domestic insurrections amongst us, and has endeavoured to bring on the inhabitants of our frontiers, the merciless Indian Savages, whose known rule of warfare, is an undistinguished destruction of all ages, sexes and conditions.

In every stage of these Oppressions We have Petitioned for Redress in the most humble terms: Our repeated Petitions have been answered only by repeated injury. A Prince whose character is thus marked by every act which may define a Tyrant, is unfit to be the ruler of a free people.

Nor have We been wanting in attentions to our British brethren. We have warned them from time to time of attempts by their legislature to extend an unwarrantable jurisdiction over us. We have reminded them of the circumstances of our emigration and settlement here. We have appealed to their native justice and magnanimity, and we have conjured them by the ties of our common kindred to disavow these usurpations, which would inevitably interrupt our connections and correspondence. They too have been deaf to the voice of justice and of consanguinity. We must, therefore, acquiesce in the necessity, which denounces our Separation, and hold them, as we hold the rest of mankind, Enemies in War, in Peace Friends.

We, therefore, the Representatives of the united States of America, in General Congress, Assembled, appealing to the Supreme Judge of the world for the rectitude of our intentions, do, in the Name, and by Authority of the good People of these Colonies, solemnly publish and declare, That these United Colonies are, and of Right ought to be Free and Independent States; that they are Absolved from all Allegiance to the British Crown, and that all political connection between them and the State of Great Britain, is and ought to be totally dissolved; and that as Free and Independent States, they have full Power to levy War, conclude Peace, contract Alliances, establish Commerce, and to do all other Acts and Things which Independent States may of right do. And for the support of this Declaration, with a firm reliance on the protection of divine Providence, we mutually pledge to each other our Lives, our Fortunes and our sacred Honor."

The declaration of Independence states; "Laws of Nature and of Nature's God entitle them…" "these truths are self-evident, that all men are created equal…endowed by their Creator with certain unalienable Rights, that among these are Life, Liberty, and the pursuit of Happiness." The connotation of happiness has changed over the years. Benjamin Franklin defined happiness as; "Without virtue, man can have no happiness in this world. Let me add that only a virtuous people are capable of freedom. As nations become corrupt and vicious, they have more need of masters"

The last paragraph of the Declaration reads; "We, therefore…appealing to the Supreme Judge of the world…" 'And for the support of this Declaration, with a firm reliance on the protection of Divine Providence, we mutually pledge…"

Thomas Jefferson, who composed the original draft of the Declaration said, "Believe me, dear Sir: there is not in the British Empire a man who more cordially loves a union with Great Britain than I do. But, by the God that made me, I will cease to exist before I yield to a connection on such terms as the British Parliament propose; and in this, I think I speak the sentiments of America." In the first draft of the Declaration, Jefferson had listed as one of the offenses that Britain had forced slavery upon the colonies.

When Thomas Jefferson submitted his Declaration of Independence to the second Continental Congress, there was considerable debate amongst the delegates. Many of the colonists wanted to be independent from British rule; however, not everyone wanted to go to war with the Crown. The Congress made several deletions from the

Declaration. One of these was the portion Jefferson had included regarding his disdain for slavery, and that the Crown had forced slavery upon the colonies. Jefferson included the passage on slavery, ever mindful that his declaration stated that "all men are created equal and endowed by their Creator with certain unalienable rights." Many of the members of congress thought the passage on slavery was too inflammatory and would only serve to provoke King George to even more punitive measures. The passage was stricken from the Declaration, leaving the issue of slavery for another day. Believing their Declaration would be perceived by George and Parliament as paramount to an act of treason, which, in and of itself, would bring retaliation from the world's mightiest military power; some members thought that the deleted passage may alienate members of parliament that were sympathetic to the Colonists cause.

The stricken passage reads as follows: "He has waged cruel war against human nature itself, violating its most sacred rights of life and liberty in the persons of a distant people who never offended him, captivating & carrying them into slavery in another hemisphere or to incur miserable death in their transportation thither. This piratical warfare, the opprobrium of infidel powers, is the warfare of the Christian King of Great Britain. Determined to keep open a market where Men should be bought & sold, he has prostituted his negative for suppressing every legislative attempt to prohibit or restrain this execrable commerce. And that this assemblage of horrors might want no fact of distinguished die, he is now exciting those very people to rise in arms among us, and to purchase that liberty of which he has deprived them, by murdering the people on whom he has obtruded them: thus paying off former crimes committed again the Liberties of one people, with crimes which he urges them to commit against the lives of another."

At the time of the signing, slaves could gain freedom by, military service, working off their indebtedness as an indentured servant, purchasing their freedom, or by manumission, which was repayment for service to the community or other good deeds. Many slaveowners did pay their slaves, although it was usually a meager sum, and the amount varied by slaveowner. Major cultural and economic changes within a society do not happen overnight; all of the slaves in the northern states were freed by 1804.

The Declaration of Independence was not without those who objected to it. Pennsylvania and South Carolina voted against declaring independence. The New York delegation abstained, lacking permission to vote. After much debate, the resolution of independence was adopted with twelve affirmative votes and one abstention. On July 2nd, the colonies had officially severed political ties with Great Britain. After voting in favor of the Declaration of Independence, Congress turned its attention to drafting a final document. Few changes were made in the wording of the document; however, almost a fourth of the original document had been deleted. On July 4th, 1776, the final wording was approved; fifty-six delegates affixed their signatures and the document was sent to the printer for publication.

By August, the largest armada ever put to sea was outside of Staten Island, including 300 supply ships, 100 ships-of-the-line with 1,200 cannons, and 32,000 soldiers, 8,000 of whom were Hessians and 10,000 sailors. General Washington, not sure where Howe would attack, split his army between Long Island and Manhattan. General Washington had his men build breastworks with sharpened pikes stuck in the breastwork facing the enemy. Washington's most capable man, General Green fell ill and had to be replaced by General Stirling. Stirling built his fortification on the high ground of the western edge of Long Island. General Sullivan, whom General Washington, had put in charge of the of the second half, built his fortifications on the high ground in the center known as Guana Heights.

On August 22nd, Howe landed 11,000 British troops and 4,000 Hessians on the southern end of Long Island. General Washington wrote out his general orders for the upcoming engagement and had the officers read it to the troops:

"The time is now near at hand, which must probably determine whether Americans are to be freemen or slaves; whether they are to have any property they can call their own; whether their homes and farms are to be pillaged and destroyed. The fate of unborn millions will now depend, under God, on the conduct and courage of this army . . .. We have therefore to resolve to conquer or die..."

As Howe's men were advancing on the fortifications, a Loyalist told Howe that the Americans were vulnerable to the east of their fortifications. Howe took 10,000 soldiers in a night march around the flank of the American positions. Howe reasoned that an attack on the American flank would avert another deadly frontal attack. Traveling in unknown territory, Howe and his men got lost in the dark and would be delayed in their attack on the flank of the American position.

On the morning of August 27th, the Hessians and British Regulars assaulted the American positions. In a repeat of Breed's Hill, the sharpshooters began firing when the enemy was 300 yards out. They continued to advance but had to retreat because of heavy losses; the second attack was repulsed as well. As they mounted their third advance, Howe's men began firing and advancing on the right flank. There was a militia unit from Maryland, known as the Marylanders, that had earned a reputation as being very courageous, tenacious and very good shots. General William Alexander asked the 400-man company if they would stay and hold off the attack to cover the retreat of the rest of the army. The Marylanders valiantly stalled the British and held off six attacks until 267 of them had been killed or wounded, then they retreated to Brooklyn Heights with the rest of the army. There was a small bridge used to traverse a marsh; the Marylanders took a stand at the bridge. After repeated attempts, Howe called his men back. Brooklyn Heights was a small peninsula jutting into the East River. General Washington and his army had nowhere to go. Once again, Howe declined to pursue Washington; if he had, he could have destroyed Washington's army and ended the war. When I read of Howe's refusal to pursue General Washington after Breed's Hill and again on Long Island, I am reminded of the passages from Scripture when God tells Moses and Joshua: "This day I will begin to put the dread and fear of you upon them..."[23] Howe had 15,000 troops to Washington's 9,000. General Washington knew there may by Loyalists in his ranks so, as a means of disguising his intention, he told his officers to tell the men reinforcements were on the way.

General Washington called on Colonel John Glover to collect as many boats as he could find and ferry the army across the one-mile wide East River to Manhattan during the night. John's father died when he was four years old. Like many who have a humble beginning in life, he strove to be successful. He was first a sailor in the fishing industry, then acquired his own boat, a schooner, and eventually he had a fleet of six boats. During the siege of Boston, General Washington charged Glover with being his navy, to attack British ships of supply and to collect provisions for his army. One of the first British ships captured was the ordinance brig, the H.M.S. Nancy, with a cargo of 2,000 Brown Bess muskets, 100,000 flints, 30,000 rounds of cannon ammunition, 30 tons of musket ammunition, and a 13" brass mortar. When the siege of Boston was over, Glover joined Washington's army as one of his trusted advisors. Acting on General Washington's orders, Glover and his men, all of whom were sailors and fishermen, collected as many boats as possible and, at dark, began

---

[23]23 Deuteronomy 2:25, 11:25, Joshua 10:8

ferrying the 9,000 men to Manhattan. General Washington ordered those waiting for their escape to keep the campfires burning and to continue with building the breastwork so as to not arouse the British suspicions of their departure. Glover and his men ferried troops all night, as it was getting near dawn, half of Washington's army was still on Brooklyn Heights. Just before dawn, providentially, a heavy fog rolled in and obscured the troop movement across the river. Glover and his men continued to ferry the rest of the army to Manhattan under the cover of the fog. When the last boat reached Manhattan, the fog lifted, and the British found the Continental's camp empty.

General Washington and his army pushed north up Manhattan to the northern plateau by Fort Washington. By September 15, 1776, Howe reached Manhattan. He had his naval guns fire on the Virginia militia that had set up a breastwork at Kip's Bay. The militia retreated under heavy fire to General Washington's location on the plateau. After the militia retreated, Howe began moving his army off the ships and onto Kip's Bay. There were a few skirmishes, but, for the most part, Howe remained at Kip's Bay while the rest of his army would go ashore further north. Howe moved the ships and more transports further north, and on October 12th, tried another landing at Throg's Neck. This attempt failed; without good maps, Howe was unsure of the countryside topography. The British first encountered an impassable marsh, and with the only alternative being a well defended road through the marsh, Howe retreated. Determined not to let the American army escape he tried a third landing at Pell's Point on October 18th. To defend this avenue of entry, General Washington had sent Colonel John Glover to stop the British expeditionary force. On the morning of October 18th, Glover noticed hundreds of sails on the horizon off the point. He considered his position: there was only one way onto the Point–a gravel road leading into a small meadow, lined with small stone walls. Glover had 750 men. He set a company behind each wall with instructions that they were to lay down, concealing themselves behind the walls. When the British came onto the meadow, the men behind the first wall, and only the first wall, would rise up, fire off a volley, then retreat. The rest were to follow this same pattern. As the British emerged from the tree line on the road, the first company got up and fired a volley with their rifles. The deadly accurate rifles sent many British to the ground dead or wounded. The militia then turned and ran. Thinking it was a rout, the British fixed bayonets and charged after the fleeing militia, only to be met by the second round of sharpshooters as they rose up from behind the second wall and fired a volley; then the second company took off in retreat. Some of the British continued the bayonet charge and some were confused about what to do next, but that did not matter; they were still within range of the sharpshooters. The third company rose and fired off a volley, and they too retreated. The fourth company rose and fired a volley at the retreating British. The British had lost more men today than at the entire battle of Long Island. The Continental's delaying actions on the British on Manhattan gave General Washington and his army time to retreat to White Plains, where General Washington chose to make his stand.

Before we go on, I want to address the American rifle. The first, long gun, firearm was the Japanese matchbox musket, which made the longbow obsolete. The matchbox gave way to the smoothbore flintlock, which was more reliable as it used a flint striking on steel, to create a spark, which ignites the powder, rather than a "slow match," which was like a wick, used on the matchbox musket. The smoothbore flintlock musket, used by the British and the Hessians, and by most of the armies of the world, could fire a musket ball about 100 yards. However, it was only effective out to 40 yards; meaning at 40 yards you could probably hit what you were aiming at. Before infantry used in-line formation, they used to fight in a box configuration. Infantry would be in a square–usually 8 soldiers across and 8 deep, armed with muskets. Using a universal command, left face or right face the cube could advance in any direction, in unison. There would be a square of pickets; these were soldiers with long sharpened poles used to stab the enemy. The musket ball made the armored knight obsolete. The introduction of the bayonet made the squares and pickets obsolete. The tactic now was a line of highly disciplined soldiers, arrayed in a colorful uniform, moving forward in unison, which was designed to intimidate the enemy.

American militia proficient with the rifle were called sharpshooters, or marksman. They could effectively hit a target out to 300 yards. In the in-line combat the real fighting would begin when the lines were within 100 yards of each other. The American Revolutionary War introduced two very significant innovations in warfare. First was the American grooved rifle and shooting in-line soldiers at 300 yards. The second, was the American use of guerrilla warfare; striking fast and hard from cover and concealment; strike and retreat. When confronted with an in-line formation with the potential of a bayonet charge; the Americans would engage the enemy at 300 yards, to which the British had no defense. When the remaining British were close enough to engage the Americans with bayonets, the American marksmen would simply, retreat and set up defensive positions and wait for the British to approach; then they would eliminate them one by one from distances at which the British could not return fire; for the most part the British did not pursue. Revisionists often write that American soldiers would often break and run when confronted by British Regulars or Hessians. There is a difference between breaking and running, which implies cowardice and a strategic retreat to continue to engage the enemy on your terms not theirs.

The American rifle was first produced in Pennsylvania by Pennsylvania Dutch gunsmiths who were not Dutch but German. Dutch comes from the German word Deutsch, meaning German. People unfamiliar with this thought when people said Deutsch it meant Dutch. The clients of the Deutsch gunsmiths, American frontiersmen, wanted a firearm that could take down game: deer, moose, bear, and turkeys with one shot from great distances. The Germans made the finest rifles in Europe, and the German immigrants to America, comprising about a third of the population of Pennsylvania, in turn produced the finest firearms in America. To meet the requirements of the American market, rifling was added to the barrel to put a spin on the bullet, which stabilized the flight providing more accuracy. Rifles had front and rear sights to align the barrel with the target. The barrel was lengthened to ensure that all of the powder would burn providing more velocity. The size of the caliber was reduced for a number of reasons. A smaller projectile would travel further and have a flatter trajectory. Lead and powder were in short supply in the frontier and the smaller caliber required less lead and powder to fire a round. The second most innovative battlefield tactic introduced by the Americans in the Revolutionary War was a type of guerilla warfare learned from the American Indians, primarily during the French and Indian War. However, these tactics were also modified and advanced by Americans as American Indians and American settlers, backwoodsmen and frontiersman were in a constant state of war. The very nature of war is such that the victory goes to whomever has the edge in tactics delivered by a technological advantage. The defeated mimic the tactics and technology of the victor, which creates a need for newer tactics and technologies and thus nations are in a constant state of warfare evolutionary innovations. Americans also produced American rifles in many gunsmithing companies that opened before the war and in state arsenals. This gave birth to the U.S. Springfield Armory which is said to have produced the finest rifles in the world.

Historians love to tell America the Continental Army was manned by inexperienced, undisciplined, underfed, uninspired soldiers of misfortune, ready to abandon the cause as soon as their enlistment was up. That certainly may be true for some; however, with the way historians portray the Revolutionary soldier you have to wonder how this disheveled band of misfits were able to defeat the mightiest army and navy in the world. There are patriots, and there are civilians. Historians are describing civilians. The patriots are men of courage, stamina, understand war is not easy, and will take on the hardships of war and the carnage of battle for the ideals that began the war in the first place: independence, freedom, justice and liberty. They know if they are defeated so are these ideals. These are stronger motivations for war than what motivated the British: duty, in a far-away land. The British had such a hard time filling their ranks they had to hire German mercenaries, offer freedom to black Americans, bribe the Indians, rely on Loyalists and exchange prison time for military service. Historians love to call Americans nothing but volunteers, farmers and tradesmen, discounting that they were unique Americans, quick to join the fight, only to return home after the battle; yet, being ever ready for the next call to arms. There were also the eager fighting backwoodsmen from Virginia, Pennsylvania, Carolinians and New York State. When congress called for the formation of ten rifle companies, the ranks filled so rapidly two more companies were formed, then a thirteenth. A new weapon of war, the rifle, a new kind of soldier and completely new battlefield tactics. Small bands of men that would attack by ambush or by sniping from cover and concealment firing two or three rounds then relocating; leaving dead and dying solders behind, holding the field be dammed. American Soldiers also knew that if you kill a soldier, he is dead, if you wound a soldier he is just as out of commission and it will take one or two soldiers to tend to each wounded, this was a burden to light and fast moving tactics. Americans were fighting for the ideals that made America great, nowhere else in the world was there an opportunity to start a country from scratch; a country of the People, governed by the People; and for the people, that is a lot worth fighting for, for men with a warrior's heart.

The real taste of the American soldier is best portrayed by eyewitnesses. A letter dated August 1775, from a correspondent in Frederick Maryland to a contemporary in Philadelphia, reads: "I have had the happiness of seeing Captain Michael Cresap marching at the head of a formidable company of perhaps one hundred and thirty men, from the mountains and backwoodsmen, painted like Indians, armed with tomahawks and rifles, dressed in hunting shirts and moccasins, and though some of them had traveled near 800 hundred miles from the banks of the Ohio, they seemed to walk light and easy, and not with less spirit than at the first hour of the march. Health and vigor, after what they have undergone, declared them to be intimate with hardship, and familiar with danger..."

A Loyalists from Philadelphia wrote to a friend in London. The letter appeared in the London Chronicle on August 17, 1775 and read in part: "This providence has raised 1,000 riflemen, the worst of whom will put a ball in a man's head at a distance of 150 or 200 yards, therefore advise your officers who shall hereafter come to America to settle their affairs in England before their departure."

Captain Henry Beaufoy, a British veteran of several wars remarked, "these Americans...with their widow-makers...went out on a sort of predatory warfare conducting incessant attacks...their opponents could never be prepared; as the first knowledge of a patrol in the neighborhood was generally given by a volley of well-directed fire, that perhaps killed or wounded the greater part." Beaufoy later noted, "It has been radially confessed...by old soldiers, that when they understood they were opposed by riflemen, they felt a degree of terror never inspired by general action, from the idea that a rifleman always singled out an individual, who was almost certain to be killed or wounded."

One of the most celebrated riflemen of the Revolutionary war was Timothy Murphy. He was born in Pennsylvania in 1751 to Thomas and Mary, who had recently arrived from Ireland. The family moved to the cutting edge of the frontier, where land was cheap but so was life. Indian raids were frequent and could bring death, or worse, capture. Frontier families had to learn to adapt or be annihilated. By the time Tim was in his mid-teens he already had a reputation among both whites and the Indians as an extraordinary marksman and skilled warrior. In June of 1775, Tim and his brother enlisted in Captain John Lowdon's Company of Northumberland County Riflemen. In order to qualify as a rifleman for Lowdon, a shooter had to be able to fire at and repeatedly hit a seven-inch target at 250 yards. Tim fought in the Siege of Boston, Long Island, and Westchester. By 1776 he was a sergeant in the 12th Regiment of the Pennsylvania Line and fought at Trenton, Princeton and New Brunswick. In July of 1777, Tim was transferred to Morgan's Rifle Corps, still led by Morgan himself, who had received 100 lashes for punching a British officer during the French and Indian War. Colonel Morgan and his corps were ordered to join the American forces opposing General John Burgoyne and his force of 10,000 marching from Canada into New York. The British were trying to divide the colonies along the Hudson River, with Burgoyne coming from the north. He was to meet Howe coming from the south. As part of Burgoyne's plan Lieutenant Colonel Barry St. Leger was to capture Fort Stanwix, then push east and rendezvous with Burgoyne and Howe. Morgan joined the cause and dedicated himself to his duty. This is the American soldier of the American Revolution.

General Washington moved his army up the western side of Manhattan, while Howe was advancing on the East. General Washington was reluctant to give up New York and thought he would make a stand at White Plains. As they advanced, General Washington sent a company of his rangers under the command of Lieutenant Colonel Thomas Knowlton to scout on the movement and position of Howe's army. Knowlton commanded the fighting at the Rail Fence on Breed's Hill. Knowlton was promoted to Major after Breed's Hill, as his men had beaten back every British attack because of the accuracy of his sharpshooters and only losing three men. The extensive use of Knowlton by General Washington to gather field intelligence earned him a reputation as the first of army intelligence officers. As the rangers moved towards the British lines, they encountered a company of the famed Scots regiment of Highlanders known as the Black Watch. No one knows for sure how the fighting started, but, seeing that Knowlton at the age of fifteen fought in the French and Indian War, this may have been too big of an opportunity to pass up. The rangers took position from concealment and began firing at the Highlanders. They fired seven volleys before the Highlanders were close enough to return fire. British regulars heard the shooting and moved to support the Highlanders. At the sight of the British reinforcements, Knowlton pulled his rangers back. As they retreated, the British bugler played the "Fox Horn." The fox horn was a signal to the other hunters that the fox had given up and was ready to fight. After the battle of Long Island, Howe had been pursuing General Washington up Manhattan, forcing him out of New York. General Washington was not about to have his men ridiculed; he ordered regiments to flank both sides of the Highlanders and sent 150 men up the center to draw them out. The feint worked and the Highlanders advanced. The rangers took up a position and began shooting at the Highlanders while they were still 300 yards off. The flanking movements were discovered, and the British turned and ran, leaving 400 dead and wounded on the battlefield verses American's less than 100 casualties. Unfortunately, one of the wounded, was Colonel Thomas

Knowlton, who died of his wounds the next day. General Washington chose not to pursue; he wanted to make a stand at White Plains where he could dig in and have the high ground.

At the urging of the Continental Congress, General Washington was instructed to not leave New York to the British. They told him to reinforce Fort Lee and Fort Washington to protect New York and the Hudson River. General Washington left 2,800 troops under the command of Colonel Robert Magaw to occupy Fort Washington. He also dispatched 3,500 troops under Major General Nathanael Greene to Fort Lee. Nathanael's family were Quakers; he was shunned by his family and the Quakers in that he took it upon himself to become educated and join the militia as a private. Quakers were staunch passivists and frowned on formal education and military service. Greene participated in the siege of Boston and because of the contributions of his leadership displayed in the eleven-month siege, he was promoted to Brigadier General. Greene became one of General Washington's most trusted advisors. When General Washington arrived at White Plains, he dispersed his army along a defensive line anchored by high ground between Purdy Hill and Hatfield Hill between the Bronx River and the River Cotton. To the far-right General Washington's men set up defenses on Chatterson's Hill. Howe delayed in engaging General Washington until reinforcements arrived. The delay gave General Washington's troops the time needed to develop their breastworks and set their artillery in place. When Howe was reinforced by 8,000 Hessians, he felt confident enough to move against General Washington. On October 27, the British advance guard arrived at Chatterson's Hill, which was interlaced with small stone walls. Howe moved his men into the open and halted about a half a mile from the American line. He dispatched 4,000 British regulars and Hessians to take Chatterson's Hill. Howe commanded his artillery to pound the American position on Chatterson's Hill. The artillery barrage stopped as the troops approached the hill, only to run into directed fire from the hilltop and from behind some of the small stone walls along the top of the hill. After suffering heavy casualties, the British were forced to retreat. They regrouped and tried a second time, but, were repelled again. After suffering heavy losses, Howe decided to make a third attempt, but not until he had his Hessians in place for a flanking move on the left. The British began moving up the hill and the Hessians on horseback conducted a cavalry charged on the flank. This was the first cavalry charge of the American Revolution.

The Americans fled across the Bronx River and joined General Washington's forces. Howe moved two columns against General Washington's front line and sent two more regiments around General Washington's flank to attack from the rear. The frontal attack was met with artillery fire and well directed rifle fire. After sustaining heavy casualties, they withdrew. The attack from the rear met the same fate as the frontal attack. Howe moved his army to Chatterson's Hill and made camp for the night. His intention was to mount a full-scale attack on General Washington's flank on the next day. That night providentially, a very heavy rain started to fall, and continued through the whole next day, postponing any plans of attack Howe had. As the rain started General Washington decided this was a perfect opportunity to slip away. He mobilized his army and moved north and into New Jersey. Howe once again decided not to pursue General Washington and retreated to New York City.

We must understand some of the significant precedent in the beginning of the Revolutionary War– precedents that I do not find in any of my research. In the first battle of the war at Lexington eight militia and one British Regular lay dead or dying. The British then marched on Concord, burned the armories, and began a march of 700 regulars back to Boston. Having heard the church bells, which summoned the minutemen, they sniped at the British from cover and concealment, all the way back to Boston, engaging the enemy, unseen, from distances they could not respond to. If the British sent a squad into the woods after them, they would be ambushed. If they sent a larger force, the minutemen would simply vanish into the woods. They had to continue their march and watch their comrades fall, one by one, all the way back, 267 of them, very demoralizing. Next, we had the Siege of Boston, and because of the sharpshooters, the British had to remain out of sight or risk being picked off one by one. The next event to consider is the British attack on Breed's Hill. Britain fought the way they usually fought and suffered a tragic loss of men that resulted in the Commander of Forces in America, General Gage, being recalled and disgraced. There were 1,054 British casualties to American losses of 411, most of whom were killed during the bayonet charge. General Washington learned to avoid bayonet charges in the future; surrendering the battlefield was of little consequence compared to the number of soldiers killed in battle. If General Washington lost his army the revolution would be over. Howe learned that he could not pursue the American army without significant losses. Washington's strategy became, "kill so many of them they no longer want to fight us," stealth, surprise attacks, and fighting from cover and concealment, a strategy he learned from the French and Indian War, became his mode of operation. Each side was responsible for reporting their own war dead. We can have a good deal of confidence in the war dead reported by Americans, because there were plenty of witnesses. Howe and Clinton reported their loses to London–Parliament and King George. Britain had never suffered such significant war casualties in battles as they experienced in America. So, how did they cover the actual number of war casualties? General Howe and General Clinton reported to London that their army was plagued with desertions, and disease. Granted, some did desert as the Continental Congress offered 40 acres to any soldier that deserted. (Land was a very effective inducement, as, in Europe, most of the land was owned by the aristocrats or the Catholic Church, who was the largest landowner in Europe. The opportunity to have your own land in Europe was extremely remote). That being said, hard and fast numbers have been very hard to come by; some numbers I have seen are that 45,000 British and 9,000 Hessians deserted. Britain had to make a lump–sum payment to Germany for every Hessian soldier killed in battle. Claiming a soldier deserted would alleviate Britain from making the payment. Many of these deserters could actually have been killed in battle and the British commanders were unwilling to provide accurate battle casualties and receive the same fate as General Gage–humiliated and drummed out of the service. There were other ways to hide body counts as well: number taken prisoner or died of disease. Of the 32,000 American POW's taken prisoner in New York, and those held on prison ships, 18,000 died of disease. The battle deaths and the effects of a new style of warfare listed in the above three examples give an accurate portrayal of the war. After this realization, reporting battlefield casualties became very unreliable.

As Howe retreated back to New York, he knew his army outnumbered the troops at Fort Washington 2,800 to 8,000. Fort Washington was the last American military presence on New York. Howe thought it could be an easy victory. He planned his attack for November 16th, 1776. His plan called for the fort to be attacked on all sides, to eliminate the men in the redoubt, then to storm the fort. 2,000 Hessians approached from the south and into Lieutenant Colonel Moses Rawlings Rifle Regiment of 250 sharpshooters. The sharpshooters inflicted heavy casualties on the Hessians, preventing them from advancing on the fort for several hours; however, after several hours of gunfire, the rifles needed cleaning and were staring to jam and would not fire, Moses had his men retreat to the fort. Brigadier General Mathew was moving his troops across the Harlem River on flatboats. As they were navigating the passage, sharpshooters from the walls of the fort killed eighty of his men before they could reach land. Howe had the HMS Pearl, with 32 guns, bombard the fort from the river, eventually knocking out the cannons in the fort. In the redoubt on the west, cannon fire was slowing the advance of the British. John Corbin, who was manning a cannon at the top of a small ridge was struck and killed. Margaret Corbin, a nurse, was with her husband on the battlefield. When John was killed, Margaret manned the cannon and continued firing until she was wounded. She was the first American female wounded in a combat role. By late afternoon, most of the men in the redoubts had retreated into the fort, the fort was completely surrounded. Colonel Robert McGaw, realizing his calamitous situation, surrendered the fort to avoid a bloodbath. The Americans had lost 59 killed, 90 wounded; British and Hessian losses were 450. At the surrender, 2,838 Americans were taken prisoner. Only 800 would survive their captivity in the British prison ships and were released 18 months later in a prisoner exchange.

General Washington gave orders for General Greene to abandoned Fort Lee and join him. General Washington moved his army through New Jersey and crossed the Delaware River into Pennsylvania, northwest of Trenton, to New Brunswick, New Jersey. General Washington wanted to spare his 3,200 soldiers and General Green. It was becoming increasingly difficult to accept battlefield orders from congress when they had no firsthand knowledge of the ever changing strategies and tactics being deployed by both sides. A lot of battlefield decisions are impromptu and made rapidly after a quick battlefield assessment

As General Washington deliberated his next move, he no doubt contemplated that the bulk of his successes were from new battle tactics employed by his sharpshooters in stealth, secrecy, surprise engagements, and engaging the enemy from cover and concealment. With these new tactics, and "the hand of Providence," could provide the advantage a militia army could use to defeat the most powerful army in the world. William Prescott, Commander of the militia at Bunker Hill told his men, "We consider that we are all embarked in, the same boat, and must sink or swim together....Let us all be of one heart, and stand fast in the liberty wherewith Christ has made us free. And may He, of His infinite mercy, grant us deliverance of all our troubles."

Ten Days That Changed the World

General Washington sent some rangers to reconnoiter the Hessian garrison at Trenton, the closest target of opportunity. The rangers reported that the garrison had minimal security in force, perhaps in light of some time of relaxation for Christmas the following day. Washington was also informed that the Hessians had not constructed any fortifications. When Colonel Rahl's, the German Commander of the Hessians, engineers had recommended building fortifications, Rahl said, "we have seen them fight. If they come, we will give them our bayonets." Rahl, first encounter with the Americans had been at the battle of Fort Washington, he had not been impressed.

General Washington held a war council and the decision was made; the army would cross the Delaware River under the cover of dark and launch a surprise raid on the garrison. General Washington again called on Glover to secure river transports. He then deployed the rangers across the river to silence any lookouts or listening posts the garrison may have. The operation did not get under way until 11:00 PM. General Washington was concerned that he may not reach Trenton before dawn and was further concerned the element of surprise may be compromised. The Delaware River was partly covered in ice and as they commenced operations a snowstorm set in with near blizzard conditions.

Colonel Rahl had been warned by spies that an attack on Trenton would occur that night. At about 9:00 PM, some minutemen providentially attacked the outer perimeter of the Trenton garrison, firing at any Hessian in the open. The firing only lasted a short time, inflicting six casualties, before they withdrew. Rahl may have thought this was the impending attack. Although it was Christmas and some of the Hessians were celebrating, we can rest assured these were very professional, well-disciplined soldiers who would have maintained wartime vigilance. Because of the severe weather, Rahl did not send out any mounted patrols that evening. He was having dinner, that evening, in a local tavern; a loyalist slipped him a note, warning him that Washington was crossing the Delaware River. The note was found in Rahl's pocket the next day after he died. The note was written in English, which Rahl could not read.

General Washington had planned a 9-mile march to Trenton, dividing his forces upon arrival for a three-pronged attack. On the march, General Washington encountered Adam Stephen and fifty-armed militia; they had attacked the garrison outposts the night before and wanted to join in the fight. As the night wore on, the weather worsened and the third division, under General Cadwallader, that was to attack from the south, never made the crossing.

General Washington split his forces and attacked from two sides. The Hessians were caught off guard and completely surprised; they scrambled to get their weapons and form up; however, the Americans were already attacking. General Knox and Captain Alexander Hamilton (yep) manned the cannons and fired on the Hessians. The sharpshooters occupied second– story windows and picked off the Hessian gun crews, preventing them from returning fire. The pincer movement crippled the three Hessian regiments and they were unable to form into a cohesive fighting force. One regiment broke, ran and escaped across Assumpink Creek, the route Cadwallader was to defend and from whence to launch his attack. The Hessians fell back and tried to regroup in an apple orchard. Colonel Rahl was shot off his horse and mortally wounded. The Hessians tried to re-enter Trenton but were met by, not only General Washington's forces, and sharpshooters, but also townspeople that had taken up arms. They again retreated and headed for Assumpink Creek, only to find it now guarded by Americans.

The Hessians, without their leader, and with no means of escape, turned and surrendered. Hessian losses were six officers and twenty enlisted men, along with 100 wounded and 918 captured. American losses were two killed; however, they were not killed in battle, they froze to death on the road to Trenton. Four Americans were wounded, including James Monroe, who would later become the fifth president of the United States. Also, in the battel, aside from Hamilton, was James Madison, forth president, Aaron Burr, third vice-president, and John Marshall, who would later become the chief justice of the Supreme Court. I wonder, exactly, what historians mean when they say General Washington's soldiers were a bunch of rag-tag misfits.

British officers, as most of the officers in Europe, bought their rank from within their family of influence. Some would become exceptional officers, but most were very inexperienced. Their inexperience in battle caused a lack of confidence amongst the soldiers. Enlisted men ate rations, officer's ate chef prepared meals on china, even on the battlefield. There was very little commonality between the officer elite and the enlisted men, the distinction between the have and the have nots. American officers achieved their rank and promotions by their successes and the soldiers could have confidence, at the outset, by their established reputation. American officers obtained rank by experience in the army, they earned their rank by their achievements. Exceptional performance in battle weighted heavily within the order of qualifications for promotion. Most soldiers in the American system attempted to advance their rank by exemplary performance, when the opportunity arose American soldiers displayed what has become to be known as field expedience. Which is using whatever resources are available to turn a negative battlefield situation into one of opportunity for your side. When American officers were killed or wounded in battle, command was passed to the next junior officer, down to the rank of even an enlisted man. This was a large part in the idea of the spirt of American exceptionalism. Americans would take whatever initiative was necessary to achieve success. European enlisted ranks fell apart when their officers were taken out of action, they needed orders. American enlisted ranks improvised. Settlers had to improvise from the first settlement through the war, nothing preexisted, everything had to be created or built, and that takes ingenuity.

After the battle of Trenton, the American army took position of six cannons, forty horses, 1,000 muskets, bayonets, powder, ammunition, boots, clothing and other military equipment and supplies. General Washington wanted to press on and take Princeton as well; however, because half of his army had not crossed the Delaware River he returned to Pennsylvania. At the end of the year, many of the soldier's enlistments would be ending. The victory at Trenton was great for the morale of the nation, congress was invigorated, enlistments went up, and people began to think we could win this war.

After the battle of Trenton, General Washington and his army crossed back across the Delaware River to Pennsylvania, only to find out that General Cadwallader had crossed when the weather moderated. Not wanting his army divided, and expecting a counterattack from Howe, General Washington crossed the river back into New Jersey on December 30th. General Washington's two armies were to rendezvous at Trenton. As General Washington rode into Trenton the Loyalists hastily removed the red cloth rages on their doorposts identifying the residents of this house were loyal to king George III.

Most of the Continental Army's soldier's enlistments were due to expire on December 31st. General Washington gave an impassioned plea to his soldiers: "My brave fellows, you have done all I asked you to do, and more than could be reasonably expected; but your country is at stake, your wives, your houses and all that you hold dear. You have worn yourselves out with fatigues and hardships, but we know not how to spare you. If you will consent to stay only one month longer, you will render that service to the cause of liberty and to your country which you probably never can do under any other circumstances." First, one soldier stepped forth; "I might as well stay and fight!" Soon, others stepped forward. Most of the soldiers remained with General Washington. General Cadwallader and his militia of 1,800 arrived at Trenton and joined forces with the Continentals.

General Washington had his men establish a fortification south of town on the south bank of the Assumpink Creek. Spies had informed General Washington on December 31st, that Lord Cornwallis was assembling an army of 8,000 at Princeton 11 miles away. General Washington ordered Colonel Edward Hand, who was commanding Fermoy's Regiment of Pennsylvania rifleman halfway up the Trenton Road, to intercept Cornwallis and impede his march to Trenton.

Colonel Hand positioned his men, alternating between a platoon, that would fire two rounds and then redeploy 100 to 150 yards back, and a smaller unit that would provide covering fire as they regrouped. The British did not know how to respond to these "shoot and scoot" tactics. If the British sent a squad into the woods to hunt them down, they would be ambushed. If the British sent in a platoon, the riflemen would fade into the woods and could not be found. With the first volley, Cornwallis's men formed into a line, only to present themselves as targets. Cornwallis's Regulars were taking heavy casualties and were instructed to slow their pace and to be ever watchful for snipers. This change in the cadence only made better targets. It also served to slow their advance. Colonel Hand had accomplished his mission. Cornwallis and his troops were delayed and did not arrive into Trenton until 4:00 PM.

Cornwallis assembled his troops in Trenton and sent a company to charge the bridge over Assunpink Creek. General Washington's sharpshooters repelled the attack, inflicting heavy casualties. The second and third attacks had the same result. Exasperated, Cornwallis pulled his men back to an orchard just outside of town to set up camp for the night. He was fully determined to overwhelm the Continentals with his superior numbers of 5,500 British to 3,040 Continental and militia in the morning with a full-scale frontal attack, "to bag that old fox."

General Washington held a war council; the British stood in the way of retreating across the river. They knew they were heavily outnumbered and where unsure of where the rest of Cornwallis 8,000 troops were. it was supposed that they were garrisoned at Princeton, or, as usual for the

British, they were conducting a flanking move on General Washington's position. It was decided they would leave several hundred troops behind to stock the campfires and make digging sounds so that Cornwallis would think, first, they were still there, and second, they were increasing their fortifications for battle. General Washington would move his army west far enough to flank any flanking move and then north to Princeton, in case they were not flanking and then they would take the garrison at Princeton. The temperature dropped below freezing that night, freezing the muddy roads, making them easy to traverse, even with cannons.

General Nathanael Greene was leading an advance party of 276 Continentals up Quaker Road north to Princeton. A mile and a half from town they encounter 800 British troops heading south commanded by Colonel Mawhood. The British troops formed up, and Greene's troops took a defensive position behind a fence. The firing commenced. Mawhood knew that he had the superior force and ordered a bayonet charge just as American General Mercer arrived with 120 troops. Mercer tried to rally the troops, but there was a lot of chaos and confusion. In the middle of this melee, General Cadwallader arrived with 1,000 troops and joined in the fray. The British 55th Regiment heard the battle and rushed to the scene of the engagement. Both sides were in disarray; Mawhood was trying to form up his men into a line for a bayonet charge as most of the Continentals did not have bayonets; some of them began a retreat. At this point, General Washington arrived with the Virginia Continentals and Colonel Edward Hand's riflemen. General Washington rode up between the two sides and shouted to his troops, "Parade with us my brave fellows! There is but a handful of the enemy and we shall have them directly!" General Washington was between both armies. American Colonel Fitzgerald pulled his hat over his eyes so he would not see when General Washington is shot. ("the particular favorite of Heaven, and who can never die in battle"). When the smoke from all the musket, rifle and cannon fire clears, General Washington is seen on his horse and the British broke and ran. General Washington shouts," Come, it's a fine fox hunt boys." When a soldier in battle survives situations, which should have cost him his life, yet he survived, one can only think of Divine intervention. In Hebrews we read; "Are there not ministering spirits sent out to service those who will inherit salvation.'24 After these situations a soldier realizes his end will come at God's decree not at anything he has or has not done. That understanding

---

24 Hebrews 1:14

causes a soldier to become a little less cautious, not careless, just less cautions.[25] General Washington exceptional courage and bravery came from experiencing the many times God's providential hand had intervened in the affairs of conducting the war, and for him personally.

Some of the British broke towards Trenton; the others retreated to Princeton. With the Continentals in pursuit of those running to Princeton, some kept running right past Princeton, others, 197, took shelter in a brick building. Alexander Hamilton wheeled up his cannon and fired a round at the building. The cannon ball bounced off the wall. The second cannon ball pierced the wall and all of the inhabitants came out under a white flag. General Washington's army suffered 25 killed and 40 wounded in Trenton, and 23 killed and 20 wounded at Princeton. General Mercer was killed in the melee. When he was knocked from his horse he was asked to surrender; instead, he drew his sword. The British thought they had General Washington. They beat him severely and bayoneted him seven times. Cornwallis lost 365 killed in Trenton and 100 wounded. Losses in Princeton for the British were 95 killed and 70 wounded with 323 taken prisoner. General Washington's men collected what muskets, bayonets, ammunition, powder, cannons, and equipment they could and locked the captured in the brick building.

General Washington and his army departed for Morristown to set up a winter camp. A British historian said of the 10 days from December 26th to January 3rd, 1777, "It may be doubted whether so small a number of men ever employed so short a space of time with greater and more lasting effects upon the history of the world."

The Battle of Saratoga

I'll only briefly mention the Battle of Oriskany, also know, as the "Battle of Bloody Creek," because all of the participants were from North America. The battle took place in what is known, today as Rome, New York. Fort Stanwix was under siege from British and Iroquois Indians. The local militia leader, Brigadier General Nicholas Herkimer, rallied his militia to go to the aid of the besieged fort. Local Loyalists were aware that General Herkimer was assembling his militia. Some of the Loyalists went to Chief Joseph

---

[25] I served with the 101st Airborne in 1968 in I Corp of Vietnam our company sustained 97% casualties and fatalities

Brand to make him aware of the Herkimer's activity. They decided to set up an ambush. General Herkimer assembled 800 militia and 100 Oneida Indians and began their march to Fort Stanwix. Along their route was a ravine that dipped about 50 feet; it is here the Iroquois, numbering 400, and the 100 Loyalists set their ambush. As Herkimer's column entered the ravine, the ambush was sprung. Herkimer's leg was hit by a musket ball and shattered. The rear of the column panicked and ran off. However, the Indians ran many of them down and they were killed. In the aftermath, 385 militia were killed, 50 wounded. Herkimer would have to have his leg amputated; however, the surgery did not go well, and he died eleven days later. Joseph Brand and the Loyalists lost 158 killed and 50 wounded. The siege of Fort Stanwix can actually be considered part of the Saratoga Campaign.

As General Burgoyne was moving south from Canada expecting to rendezvous with General Howe and his army at Albany, New York. His army stopped to retake Fort Ticonderoga. 2,000 Continentals manned the fort. Burgoyne had his artillery placed on the high ground at Mount Hope and Sugar Loaf and was positioned with 7,800 soldiers, including Hessians and Indians. Major General Arthur St. Clair realizing the futility of trying to hold the fort, ordered a night retreat and abandoned the fort. The fort was given up without a fight which greatly upset General Washington and the congress. St. Clair was removed from command and did not receive another command for the rest of the war.

During the siege of Fort Stanwix General Benedict Arnold was sent to relieve the siege. With the use of spies, he had the size of his force greatly exaggerated in the reports going to St. Leger. Many of St. Leger's Indian allies abandoned him with the word of reinforcements. St. Leger abandoned his siege and led his troops to Fort Ticonderoga. This diversion would prevent St. Leger from his rendezvous with General Burgoyne.

Burgoyne was concerned that his supplies were running low and that he would not be getting the horses he was planning on for his dragoons. He received intelligence that Bennington was lightly guarded. On August 16th, 1777, he sent a foraging party, 800 regulars, mostly Hessians,100 Loyalists and 100 allied Indians, commanded by Lieutenant Colonel Fredrick Baum, to the supply depot in Bennington, Vermont. This would become known as the "Battle of Bennington," a part of the campaign of Saratoga. The battle actually took place in Walloomsac, New York.

Burgoyne was unaware that the citizens of Vermont and New Hampshire had petitioned Massachusetts and New Hampshire Safety

Committees for protection from the advancing army now that Fort Ticonderoga had fallen to the British. New Hampshire responded by authorizing militia Major General John Stack to raise a militia for the defense of the people. Stark had served as an officer in the British army during the French and Indian War, and was well familiar with the British tactics, and strategies. In six days, John had a militia force of 1,500 men. It is interesting to note that this number represents about 10 percent of the male population of New Hampshire. When America needs an army about 10 percent are ready to answer the call; 12 percent for WWII and 9.6 percent for Vietnam, 10 percent for the Civil War and overall participation rate for the Revolutionary War was 10 percent.

Baum forces marched off to the supply depot; there were a few skirmishes, on the way. Loyalists came out to join Baum, informing him of the sizeable force at the supply depot. Baum requested reinforcements from Burgoyne and took a position on high ground and had his men establish a defensive position. The Indians and Loyalists set up in a secondary position. Baum was going to wait until reinforcements arrived. It started to rain, which postponed battle plans for either side; however, Stark deployed some of his sharpshooters with instructions to focus on the Indians. Stark wanted to demoralize the Indians, hoping they would abandon Burgoyne, depriving him of the Indians he used as guides in the unfamiliar territory and for reconnaissance. The sharpshooters killed thirty Indians.

Stark sent two formations out to flank the defensive position. The Loyalists would put a white piece of paper in their hat band to identify them as friendlies to the British and the Hessians, most of whom could not speak English, the militia did the same thing when fighting Hessians.

That night, Parson Thomas Allen arrived with his 500 militia. He insisted on being able to join in the battle, threatening that if they could not participate Stark should never call on him again, to which Stark replied, " If the Lord gives us sunshine to-morrow and I do not give you fighting enough, I will never call on you again." In the afternoon of the following day, the rain stopped. The process of loading a flintlock gives too many opportunities for the powder to get wet and the muskets or rifles would not fire if the powder was wet.

Stark led a frontal attack and simultaneously the flanks charged. The position held by the Loyalists and the Indians was immediately overrun, the Loyalist surrendered, and the Indians ran off. The Hessians, being picked off one by one by the sharpshooters, led a saber charge that went dreadfully wrong. Baum was mortally wounded; some of the Hessians surrendered and others made a break for the woods. Thinking some may have a chance to get away while the Americans were reloading, however, they were still targets out to 400 yards. Just then, the Hessian reinforcements arrived and immediately engaged the militia. As Stark was trying to rally his troops, Colonel Seth Warner arrived with his Green Mountain Men. The battle went on until dark and both sides disengaged. Under the cover of darkness, the British and Hessians retreated to Burgoyne. Baum's forces had failed to get the supplies and horses, and Burgoyne had lost 1,000 of his soldiers; killed or captured. The Americans had lost 30 killed and 40 wounded. The Parson said it was a good fight and he and his militia could be called on anytime.

As Burgoyne continued his march south, the Green Mountain Men felled trees on the road and took out bridges to impede their progress. The entire column would stop at the felled trees because of the wagons. The Green Mountain Men took advantage of the halted process and used the opportunity to snipe at the British soldiers. They first targeted the Indians until enough of them had been killed; the rest quit and went back to Canada, leaving Burgoyne with no guides. They then targeted the officers.

In the European theaters of war, when a country's capital was captured, that was usually synonymous with the defeat of the country. General Howe thought, rather than meet General Burgoyne in Albany, he would capture the rebel capital in Philadelphia and declare Britain victorious; however, America's government and political infrastructure was not that developed yet. The Continental Congress had just packed up and moved to Baltimore. As long as General Washington's army was intact and continued the fight, the war for independence would go on.

General Washington, after his victories in Trenton and Princeton chose Morristown for his winter quarters as a precautionary measure to protect Philadelphia and be close enough to Howe's army should the need or opportunity arise to engage him. General Washington kept his rangers on the move, collecting field intelligence and harassing the British.

On July 8th, Howe began loading his army onto 260 ships at Sandy Point, New Jersey. The rangers estimated the size of Howe's army at 16,000. Howe wanted to sail up Delaware Bay and as far up the Delaware river as he could to get to Philadelphia; however, Howe was informed by double agent patriots that the river had been seeded with submerged, iron tipped poles imbedded in rocks to pierce the hulls of his ships. Howe decided to use the Chesapeake Bay, sail up as far as he could, and then march to Philadelphia. The excursion was fraught with disaster; there were ship collisions and delays by storms and rough seas that slowed progress and put a strain on supplies. Horses without fodder had to be pushed overboard to ease their suffering. By August 22nd, the British fleet was entering the northeast portion of the Chesapeake Bay. By now, Howe's plan was obvious to General Washington and he could begin to strategize.

The Battle of Brandywine Creek

On August 25th, Howe's army began to disembark at Turkey Point, eight miles south of Elk, Maryland, after twenty-eight days on board. On September 3rd, with Howe's troops rested, he began marching to Philadelphia in two divisions: one commanded by General Knyphausen, the other commanded by Major General Charles Cornwallis. From where Howe's army was located, General Washington surmised, they would take the Nottingham Road as the most direct route to Philadelphia. Along the road they would have to cross Brandywine Creek. The road crossed directly at Chadds Ford. General Washington would set his main force there. The rest of the army was spread out over six miles with heavy fortifications at two other fords: Pyle's and Buffington's. Four other fords were within observations range. General Washington was told the other ford upriver, Jefferies; was deep, and probably too deep for an army with equipment to cross. General Washington kept General Greene with a battalion in reserve so he could deploy wherever the attack was strongest or wherever additional troops may gain an advantage over the British. General Washington deployed General Maxwell with a rifle company across the creek with instructions to harass, slow and demoralize the advancing army.

An important figure makes his first appearance on the battlefield at Brandywine; nineteen-year-old Brigadier General Marquis de Lafayette. From a long line of warriors, knights in the crusades, to his father being killed by the British in the Seven Years War, at thirteen he was a member of the King's Black Musketeers; (from which the stories of the 3 Musketeers evolved) he pressed the king for a commission. Lafayette was from a very wealthy family in France and was awarded a commission as a Brigadier General; however, the king told him not to go to America. Lafayette immediately set sail for America. Upon arrival, he petitioned congress for a commission in the Continental Army, a request which was rebuffed by congress; however, Lafayette had important friends in high places–well one at least, Benjamin Franklin. Franklin spent most of the war years in France as America's representative, primarily entreating them for money, rifles, ammunition, supplies, troops, and of course ships. During his stay, he had the opportunity to make the acquaintance of young Lafayette. Franklin wrote to congress and told them they had better take this young man seriously if they were desirous of having France intervene in the war effort on behalf of America, as he does have a genuine commitment to our war effort and simply has nothing else to gain. On July 31, 1777, an act of congress commissioned Major General Marquis de Lafayette. Lafayette rode out to join General Washington's forces at Brandywine.

At 4:00 AM, General Howe with half of the army, set out on a seventeen-mile flanking march in order to conduct a surprise attack on General Washington's positions. By 5:45 AM, Howe's army had cleared the camp and General Knyphausen set out with the rest of the army for the seven-mile march down the Nottingham Road to Chadds Ford. Four miles from the ford, the British encountered the widow-makers. One British soldier wrote in his diary, "We fell in vert early with large bodies of the Enemy who form'd upon ever advantageous Posts & behind fences fired on the troops as they advanced – this galling fire was sustained the whole way..." Maxwell's riflemen killed three hundred British and Loyalist soldiers on their march. The Americans did not lose a soldier; however, there were a few wounded–one wounded rifleman, John Marshall, would later become Chief Justice of the US Supreme Court.

Patrick Ferguson, of the British Army, was the inventor of the Ferguson rifle, the first breech loading rifle used in combat. As a rifle, it was very accurate and, being a breechloader, it was able to be loaded much faster than American rifles. Also, as a breechloader it was the only rifle that could effectively be fired from a prone position. If mass produced the British and the Americans would have been on an equal footing in terms of rifle range and accuracy. Providentially, Ferguson was wounded during the battle and his 100 rifles were shipped off to a warehouse awaiting his recovery and return. Upon his return he was killed in his next engagement, the Ferguson rifle died with him. I find it curious the British did not respond to the American Rifle by producing a rifle of their own and when Ferguson did, it was not seen as important. The effectiveness of the American Rifle and sharpshooters must have been obvious to the British after every battle.

Early on, General Washington had become suspicious about the size of the force deployed on the west side of the creek; it certainly was not Howe's entire army. Early in the morning, and throughout the morning, General Washington was getting conflicting reports about Howe's army. Spies and double spies no doubt, who's information could be trusted? At the creek, both sides were exchanging artillery, rifle and musket fire; however, the British were not being very aggressive–there were no bayonet charges. Remembering the roust on Long Island, General Washington re-deployed two brigades onto the high ground to the left of his position on the creek. Then, he moved his cannons onto the hill tops, in case this was only half of Howe's army on the east side of the creek. General Washington made a bold move–he ordered his army to attack across the creek. If General Washington was going to be attacked on two fronts, he wanted to inflict as much damage as he could on the part of the army he could engage. He launched a frontal attack on the British at the ford before Howe showed up on his flank. At several points along the British lines, soldiers broke and ran. The Americans inflicted heavy casualties and then were called back by General Washington. General Greene stayed in reserve. Under his command was Brigadier General Peter Muhlenberg, the Lutheran minister. At 2:00 PM, Howe's army could be seen on Osborne Hill, about a mile away to the right and rear of General Washington's army. Understanding Howe's army had just completed a 17-mile march in eleven hours, his troops probably needed a rest before the battle. However, Howe halted his men on the hilltop for two hours for rest, lunch and tea. In these two hours, General Washington completed his defenses facing Howe.

At 3:30 PM, the artillery bombardments started from both sides and lasted until 4:00 PM, when Howe's forces began advancing up the hill. This will prove to be the longest day of continual fighting and the only times armies of this size will engage in battle in the Revolutionary War. The battle, some of it hand-to-hand raged until dark. The hill was traded back and forth five times, with the Americans being pushed back, then, in renewed attack, with General Greene and his battalion, the Americans pushed the British back. On one of the turnovers of the hill, the retreating soldiers looked to be in a panic. Although General Washington had not given Lafayette a command in the battle, when the troops broke, Lafayette rode out into the battle and rallied the troops. If there is to be a retreat, it is very important that it is orderly so that an organized unit can respond cohesively to a new threat. A disorganized route leaves every man for himself and little or no chance for a defensive or counter move. Lafayette was shot in the leg but did not leave the battlefield until the retreat was reorganized and they were ready to retake the hill. When General Washington heard that Lafayette had been wounded, he rode over to the army's surgeon and told him, "Take care of him as if he were my son."

The fighting went on until dark, at which time General Washington again began a nighttime retreat. Historians call this a British victory because they held the battlefield; however, American casualties were 700 and British losses were 1,974. General Howe reported to king George that he had lost 90 killed and 450 wounded. Jacob Hitzheimer, a local resident of Brandywine, who recorded the battle of Brandywine in his journal, wrote that the British losses were 1,976. Howe's army remained around Chadds ford while he sent out foraging parties to look for food, horses and supplies.

General Washington's position was between Howe and Philadelphia, as he was intending to take whatever opportunity presented itself, or that he could devise to impede Howe's march to the capital. There was a brief skirmish at present–day Malvern, Pennsylvania, known as the Battle of the Clouds; but heavy rains broke off the engagement. Howe learned that General Washington had separated some of his army along the route to Philadelphia. In case Howe tried another flanking movement, they could engage Howe until reinforcements arrived.

American General Wayne had a small force of 1,500 near Paoli Tavern, which Loyalists reported to Howe on September 20, 1777. Howe assembled a small force to attack Wayne's position from the nearby woods, at night, when most would be asleep, and to use only their bayonets in the attack. The attack caught the Americans completely by surprise. They were overwhelmed, as 5,000 British forces rushed out of the woods without firing a shot. Fifty-one Americans were bayoneted and seventy-one were taken prisoner. This action became known as the "Paoli Massacre." Wayne was court-martialed but exonerated of any wrongdoing during the trial.

General Washington sent Colonel Alexander Hamilton and a small detachment to remove or destroy the supplies being held at Valley Forge to prevent them from being secured by the British. Soon after arriving, a much larger British force arrived, and Hamilton and his men had to leave before accomplishing their mission. The British removed the supplies and destroyed the buildings.

By September 26, 1777, Howe had reached Philadelphia. Patriots fled the city; the Continental Congress had already packed up and fled to York, Pennsylvania. Howe left 3,462 soldiers in Philadelphia and moved the majority of his army; 9,728 soldiers to Germantown, an outlying community five miles from the city. General Washington, upon learning that Howe had separated his army, decided on a last attack before winter weather set in.

General Washington planned a four-pronged attack, with four columns from different directions, to create a double envelopment. At dusk, on October 3rd, the American army began their 16-mile march to Germantown. The attack was to occur at dawn. The sky was cloudy, so it was very dark, and, as they marched, a heavy fog began to form over a large area. The vanguard, led by General Sullivan, encountered a British picket as they approached town. The two sides engaged each other, and the overwhelmed British withdrew and took a defensive position in a brick stone mansion. Sullivan's troops attacked and took heavy casualties. General Knox brought up a 3-pound cannon; the shot had very little effect on the sturdy stone structure. The element of surprise was blown. General Washington called a war council. Some of his generals wanted to by-pass the building and continue with the attack; however, General Knox thought it was not a good strategy to proceed and leave a garrison behind that could attack the forward advance from the rear or pose a challenge to a retreat.

General Greene's column made it into town and engaged the British in a fierce firefight that drove the British back further into town. A brigade of Greene's column, under the command of General Stephen, took a wrong turn in the fog and ran into General Wayne's column–wrong place, wrong time. The two American forces engaged each other with musket fire, friendly fire. In the dense fog, neither side realized how large the other force was, so both sides broke off the engagement.

On the north side of town, General McDougall confronted the Troy Loyalists and some British reserves. There was a heavy exchange of fire from both sides during the firefight, inflicting heavy casualties on both sides. As the battle raged and troops on both sides began to reposition, it became apparent to all that further firing was going to lead to friendly fire incidents. Almost as if on que, both sides disengaged. The Continental Army retreated; American casualties were 652, while the British lost 519. Howe ordered a pursuit of the American's; however, heavy fire from concealed positions by the Americans as they made a fighting retreat;

soon dissuaded the British from the pursuit. The soldiers reported that Stephen had been drunk, for which he was court-martialed and dishonorably discharged from the army.

Burgoyne Must Go it Alone

General John Burgoyne had presented his plans for splitting the rebellious northern colonies from the loyalist's southern colonies along Lake Champlain and the Hudson River to British Ministry Lord Germain, who approved the plan. The plan called for Burgoyne to march his army south from Canada to Albany. General Howe's was to march his army north to meet Burgoyne in Albany. St Legers was to approach from the west in a flanking move; all three elements converging on Albany. St Leger had a force of 800 regulars and 1,000 Indians.

Howe had also submitted a plan to Lord Germain to take the rebel capital of Philadelphia which was also approved. Germain thought Howe could take Philadelphia and still have time to meet with the others in Albany. After losing his Indian allies, British General Barry St. Leger retreated from Fort Stanwix and led his men to Fort Ticonderoga. Because the siege at Stanwix had taken much longer than expected, the loss of his Indian allies and regulars lost in the battle for the fort. General St. Leger decided to stay at Fort Ticonderoga, not thinking his now dwindled force of 600 would be of much aid to Burgoyne. General Burgoyne continued his march towards Albany, and it is painstakingly slow. The columns are continually harassed by sniper fire from an unseen adversary; huge trees are felled on the road and bridges are burned.

The Battle of Freeman's Farm

In a moment of desperation Burgoyne posts a proclamation;
"I have given stretch to the Indian forces under my direction, of which there are thousands, to overtake the hardened enemies of Great Britain wherever they may lurk."

Soon after the proclamation is published, two braves capture a young woman, Jane McCrae, and scalped her. When the scalp is presented to Burgoyne, one of the loyalists' present recognized it as the scalp of his fiancée. He deserted the camp, grief stricken, he went back to

Vermont. The story was printed in the papers and militia began streaming into General Horatio Gate's camp; his army swelled to over 10,000. Four miles from Saratoga, Burgoyne sent a scouting party of 1,500 to reconnoiter the terrain and the town of Saratoga. As the vanguard advanced, they came across a note nailed to a tree. The note quoted a verse from the Book of Job 38:11,

"Thus far you shall come, but no further."

After a morning march, the vanguard stopped to rest and consider the warning. They are at a place called Freeman's Farm, which will be the site of the first battle of Saratoga. General Washington has dispatched Daniel Morgan and his rifle corps to Saratoga. Daniel Morgan and his men are ready. The vanguard approached a clearing. In the first volley, all but one officer is either killed or wounded. The British, not wanting to be in the open, take to the woods to find the sharpshooters. Morgan's sharpshooters continue to thin the British ranks; when they think they have done enough damage, they withdraw, leaving 600 British soldiers dead or dying. Morgan's men, to communicate with each other in the woods, mimic the sound of a turkey gobble. The comment of the rangers is; "today was a good turkey shoot."

Burgoyne continued his march to Saratoga; however, none of his men want to walk in the vanguard–it is suicide. The sharpshooters continue to drop the men at the head of the column. Burgoyne must dispense with the vanguard altogether and rotate, by platoon, the men at the front of the column. As the British continue their march, the sharpshooters focus on their next target; those manning the artillery pieces. Burgoyne's army reached Saratoga and they took up a defensive position. He received word that Howe will not be able to reinforce him.

The Battle of Bemis Heights

Burgoyne calls a war council with his officers; without the aid of Howe's army, they recommend retreating to Fort Ticonderoga. Burgoyne tells his officers, "we have lost over 2,000 men since Bennington, we are short on supplies, we will not survive a march to Ticonderoga, we will be picked off one by one all the way there. We will make a stand here."

Burgoyne plans to attack the Americans on a small hill called Bemis Heights. In the morning, Burgoyne sent a reconnaissance force of 1,500 to Bemis Heights. Daniel Morgan dispatched his corps in the woods to await the British. General Benedict Arnold, who had been relieved by Gates, in defiance, leads a charge of 1,500 troops against the British. Morgan spots British General Simon Fraser leading the British advance; he signals, and three of his sharpshooters come to his side. He orders the general taken out. The first to fire misses; the second misses as well; the shot is over 300 yards. The third sharpshooter fires his rifle and General Fazer falls from his horse the victim of Timothy Murphy; he is dead before he hits the ground.

With the general dead, the British fall back to two redoubts. Burgoyne sent reinforcements forward, as did Gates. The sheer number of Americans overwhelmed the British and they retreated. American losses were 30 killed and 100 wounded. British casualties were 450 killed and 470 wounded. Burgoyne retreated with his army back to their defensive position at Saratoga. Gates advanced to Saratoga and, in order of several days, set his camp of his 10,000 soldiers encircling Burgoyne's camp. On October 17th, Burgoyne asked for terms of surrender for himself and his 5,234 men. Gates told him his army could keep their colors, and, if they would not return to fight in America, he would let the army depart for Britain. However, upon arrival at Albany, the Continental Congress did not agree with these terms and had them all locked up.

With the victory at Saratoga, confidence in America and in other nations for America began to grow. Just maybe these religious dissidents, these Americans, can defeat the most powerful army and navy in the world, after all. On Feb 6, 1778, Benjamin Franklin was able to sign a treaty of alliance with France. France pledges full support and recognizes the United Sates as an independent country. Spain and the Dutch Republic also pledged their support for America.

Valley Forge

General Washington took his army into winter quarters at Valley Forge. While Lafayette was recovering from his wound, he inundated King Louis XVI and the rest of the French government with letters of appeal for arms, ammunition, uniforms, and supplies for this very worthy cause in America. King Louis XVI was reluctant he had lost everything to the British in the French and Indian War, however, if he could help America defeat, humiliate and otherwise undermine Britain's world domination, he could be convinced to support the Americans. The Marquis de Lafayette rejoined

General Washington at Valley Forge. General Washington sent Lafayette to France to influence the government in support of the war effort. When Lafayette arrived in France, his first act was to secure muskets, ammunition, powder and bayonets for General Washington. His procurement and shipping of the supplies to Valley Forge was completely covert, without the French government's knowledge. Lafayette, from his experience at Brandywine, knew the Continental Army was at a real disadvantage by not having bayonets for the closing charges of a battle. Lafayette, not able to procure a ship to transport the supplies to America, bought a ship and sent the supplies.

Much has been written and there is a lot of videos on Valley Forge, I will be brief and only comment on a few essentials. Firstly, any winter war campaign a is extremely hazardous and dismal understaking. General Washington picked the site himself, as the location was eighteen miles from Philadelphia. The distance was close enough to the British Army to be able to dampen any attempts for foraging, and far enough away to prevent any surprise attacks; it was a very defensible position. Congress made a couple of important decisions regarding Valley Forge and the army in the winter camp. There are accounts of going for four days without food and people boiling their shoes for something to eat. Even in today's army, in theaters of operations, there are occasions when troops cannot be resupplied.

There were several times in Vietnam where we could not be reached with supplies and we went for four days without food and water. We did not boil our boots; we toughed it out–after the second day you are not really very hungry anyway.

When food was in short supply it was supplemented by wild game. There is much written about the soldiers having to eat fire cakes, which is flour mixed with water to make a kind of a paste. The Continental Congress deployed Baker General Christopher Ludwig to Valley Forge. Ludwig said for every one hundred pounds of flour he could make 125 loaves of bread. Ludwig baked bread every day for the troops, and he stayed with General Washington until the end of the war. When the Continental Army first arrived at Valley Forge in six weeks, the soldiers built 1,000 log cabins for themselves and the camp followers. Soldiers said that they were warm and comfortable. Disease was gaining a foothold in the camp and General Washington ordered inoculations for all of his troops, which dramatically reduced the spread of disease. While the troops were at Valley Forge, Lafayette's pleas paid off; France began sending the much-needed supplies to the Americans. Congress also commissioned, on the recommendation of Ben Franklin, Baron Friedrich Wilhelm von Steuben, from the Prussian Army's General Staff, to help train the troops at Valley Forge. Von Steuben, along with General Greene and Alexander Hamilton, began training the army. Von Steuben, Greene and Hamilton trained all of the Continental Sergeants, who, in turn, trained their men. The troops of the Continental Army were trained but not trained uniformly to fight as a cohesive unit up until now. The various militia units were all trained differently by their respecting officers. Together, Von Steuben, Greene and Hamilton wrote the first US Military Training Manual. The soldiers were taught the tactics of European fighting and how to defensively fight against them. With the newly arrived muskets and bayonets from France, the sergeants were taught how to fight with bayonets, how to parry a bayonet, deliver a vertical butt strokes of the rifle in close hand-to-hand combat. The general tactics of guerilla warfare were taught uniformly among all the troops. Although the French muskets were smoothbore, they were equipped with bayonets; the Continental Army was at least on an equal footing when it came to bayonet charges. The sharpshooters had made a significant difference in many of the battles. After the battle of Saratoga, Morgan re-joined General Washington at Valley Forge. He began training soldiers in marksmanship and formed new rifle companies. General Greene had become so proficient at securing livestock and supplies he was made the first Quarter Master General. Whereas the British just took whatever they needed from local farmers, at least General Greene left them with an IOU from the Continental Congress. Von Steuben had been so effective he was made the first Inspector General.

After the surrender of Burgoyne at Saratoga, General Clinton pulled his forces back to Philadelphia. General Washington knew the new treaty with France would affect the British position in North America, but he was unsure how Britain would respond. General Washington sent Lafayette with 500 troops to look for any indication of the British plans. Lafayette recruited 100 French speaking Oneida Indians to accompany him. As evening closed, Lafayette was near Barren Hill and decided to make camp for the evening. The camp site was on high elevation with the steep bank of the Delaware River to their back. General Clinton though Loyalists spies learned of Lafayette's position and sent 8,000 regulars to collect "the boy." Indian scouts informed Lafayette of the British troops' movements to encircle the camp. Lafayette set small groups of men, with three men in each group, to fire on the enemy, then quickly change position to give the impression of a much larger force; he also instructed his Indian allies to do the same. Lafayette then lead his men down a well–concealed road to the river. Instructing his men that once the main force was at the river, they too should take the road to the river. Once Lafayette and his men were at Matson's Ford, the rest of his men joined the main body. His troops and the Indians had continued firing on the British until the British flank was closing in and they too departed. The stationary British troops had been returning fire on Lafayette's troops, unaware that they had retreated. They continued to fire into the woods. When the flank came around, they were in line of the British firing, so they returned fire. By the time the British troops realized they were firing at each other, Lafayette's troops had reached the opposite riverbank.

After the surrender of Burgoyne at Saratoga, General Howe was recalled to London to give an accounting. General Sir Henry Clinton was named as Commander in Chief of British forces in America. Along with his new assignment came orders from Lord North to send soldiers to Florida and the West Indies to counter any new threat that may be poised by the French. He was also told to abandon his reduced garrison in Philadelphia, as his position could be compromised should the French choose to blockade the Delaware River. With France entering the war against Britain, they also challenged British positions in the West Indies, India, Africa and Asia; Britain could no longer just focus on the rebellion in America.

Patriots brought word to General Washington that General Clinton was preparing to march his 11,500 army to New York, as no ships were available to move his men. Clinton's soldiers, wagon train, and camp followers stretched out for twelve miles. General Washington thought this procession presented an opportunity to good to pass up. He immediately sent out advance parties to fell trees across the road, snipe at the soldiers, and burn bridges. Clinton was only able to travel forty miles in the first week and suffered 400 sharpshooter casualties.

General Washington called a war council and wanted to conduct a full-scale attack with his army of 10,000 on Clinton's army. Some of the Generals thought something should be done but not a full-scale attack. Greene and Lafayette were most supportive of some type of action; General Lee was adamant against any attack. General Washington proposed a force of 4,000 to attack the rear guard. He, with the rest of the army, would be in reserve in case it developed into a major battle. They would attack on the road leading to Monmouth Court House. Lee, as senior general, should have led the attack, but he refused, saying they could not defeat the British. General Washington gave command to Lafayette. The following morning Lee insisted it was his right to lead the charge; Washington relented.

The Battle of Monmouth Court House

At 9:00 AM, it was already 96 degrees and would be over 100 by the time the Battle of Monmouth Court House would begin. When Lee's forces approached the British column, Lee held back and did not engage but sent out small units to attack portions of the British line. With his men spread out, he lost control of the battle and told his men to retreat. Lafayette, frustrated with Lee's incompetence, rode back to General Washington to inform him of the situation. Washington rode ahead and came across Lee's men in retreat. He confronted Lee with; "what in the hell are you doing?" and without a satisfactory response, he dismissed him from the field. Stories say this was the first time General Washington's troops heard him swear.

General Washington began forming up his men along a hedgerow on a small rise in the terrain. He told Lafayette to rally Lee's men behind his. The British were starting across an open field towards the hedgerow. General Washington also instructed Alexander Hamilton to take 4 cannons from Knox and set them on Combs Hill, which would provide an enfilade, where Hamilton would be able to fire along the long axis of the British lines, providing sustained fire. Once again, the sharpshooters began dropping British soldiers 300 yards away. All twelve cannons opened fire; the British took heavy casualties and withdrew. Clinton sent in his cavalry; they were knocked from their horses by the sharpshooters before they could effectively mount a charge against the hedgerow. Von Steuben's training had paid off; the Continentals, with smoothbores, held their ground and fought as a cohesive unit. Towards late evening, the British infantry made one more attack with the same results. Clinton did not set camp but continued his march into the night. General Washington did not pursue; it had been a long, hot day and his men were exhausted. Washington had lost 37 troops to heatstroke; Clinton had 59 soldiers succumb to the heat. Battlefield losses were 500 killed or wounded Americans and 1,100 British killed or wounded. Clinton left his wounded on the battlefield.

General Washington moved his army to the fort at West Point. General Lee, who had raised a campaign against General Washington after the loss of Fort Lee, complained to congress that General Washington was unfit for command and the army should be turned over to him. After the loss of forts, Lee and Washington, General Washington had told Lee to join him; however, Lee delayed in moving his army. As Lee's army was camped, he went to a local tavern for dinner and a room. While there, he was captured by the British. A year later, he was returned in a prisoner exchange championed by General Washington. Congress had made Lee General Washington's second in command because of his experience as a British officer during the French and Indian War and after the war as an officer in the Prussian army. Unable to find a role in the British army, he came to America and offered his service to congress. I have read that, as a prisoner of war, Lee received special treatment–was not treated as other prisoners and even dined with British officers. General Washington had Lee tried in court martial for his negligence; he was found guilty of disobedience and willful neglect of duty, which was upheld by congress. He was dismissed from the army for one year; he refused to accept the verdict and was dishonorably discharged. It is even thought he may have advised the British about fighting the war in the south, where support for the crown was much stronger than in the north. Lee may have been a greater traitor than Benedict Arnold.

In the battle of Quebec Arnold was wounded, his performance was inconsequential. However, his wound would leave him with a limp. In the capture of Fort Ticonderoga Arnold was humiliated by the Green Mountain Men deferring the command under a general to one of a colonel. In the battle of Saratoga General Gates relieved Arnold of his command. However, as the battle unfolded Arnold saw an opportunity and rallied his men to engage the British. This action had a significant impact on the positive outcome of the battle, however, in his report Gates made no mention of the heroics of Arnold or Morgan. It is recorded that people thought Arnold was a fine figure of a man. We cannot be certain of his motives all we do know is that he sold the blueprints to Fort West Point, for 20,000 dollars and a commission in the British army. The spy Arnold was working with was stopped by a routine patrol and the blueprints for the fort were discovered in his boot. Arnold made his way to safety with the British.

With the British Northern Campaign in a stalemate, Lord North and his military advisors decided on a southern campaign. London's largest trading partner in the colonies was Charleston South Carolina, the fourth largest city in the colonies and the busiest port. They would also offer the slaves freedom and land if they fought on the side of the British. They had tried this in the northern colonies but with limited success, as General Washington had promised the northern slaves' freedom and land if they fought with him. General Washington had heard that the slaves fought bravely at Bunker Hill, so he actively recruited them. During the Battle of Brandywine, Edward Hector, a black private from Pennsylvania, heroically saved two wagons of ammunition and rifles during the retreat. One in seven Northern Continental soldiers were black. Congress could not make this a congressional mandate, as the southern states refused to arm their slaves. Congress thought that if they forced the issue the south would align themselves with the crown and not with the newly forming America. The slaves and Loyalists made up a much larger percentage of the population in the south than in the northern colonies. Lord North was under increasing pressure because of the war debt, now at about 160 million pounds.

Parliament was demanding to know why this rebellion had not been put down yet. There was a great deal of concern about how France entering the war was going to affect not only the war in America but all of Britain's trading interests elsewhere in the world. Lord North needed a drastic change from the stalemate in the north and ordered Clinton to take his army south and subdue the rebels in North and South Carolinians as well as in Georgia. Clinton decided to switch to what London called the Southern Campaign. London thought that, because of the extensive trading between the south and England, his troops would find much more support among southern Loyalists than was achieved in the north; the south had an economic stake in the war's outcome. About 45 percent of Americans were in favor of separating from the crown; 20 percent were still loyal to the crown, the rest were trying to remain neutral in the whole affair, especially the frontiersmen in the backcountry. London thought the combination of slaves and southern Loyalists would join in with the British troops to defeat the Continental Army.

On December 26th, 1779, General Clinton was ordered south. He departed for Charleston, South Carolina with 100 ships and 8,700 British Regulars. He was also ordered to send 5,000 troops to Florida and the Caribbean to protect British interests. Three months earlier, Major General Benjamin Lincoln was ordered south by General Washington with 2,400 Continentals to defend Charleston. Charleston is on a peninsula with the Asley River to its south, the Cooper River to its north, the deep-water

Chesapeake Harbor to its east, and is adjacent to James Island. On January 10th, reports came to Lincoln that the British Navy was heading to the harbor. Lincoln asked the South Carolina Governor for his state's militia to defend the city; his request was denied. He then asked for the slaves to be armed and reinforce his position; again, his request was declined. Desperate, Lincoln made a request to Congress and he was told they would raise 3,000 troops from Virginia and North Carolina and dispatch them immediately. Lincoln also wrote to General Washington to inform him of his desperate situation. General Washington's army was enduring one of the worst winters on record in Morristown, New Jersey and was unable to march his army south the 800 miles. General Washington was not sure how many men he would lose on the march; two soldiers froze to death on the nine-mile winter march to Trenton. He was also unsure if he could arrive in time, moving wagons and artillery pieces over the snow-covered roads. It had taken General Howe fifty-six days to travel from Fort Ticonderoga to Boston, 300 miles, with the fort's artillery. The risk of losing many soldiers on the way and perhaps not even arriving in time was too much to ask of his men.

The Battle for Charleston

General Lincoln decided to make his stand in Charleston rather than abandon his post. The reinforcements promised from congress arrived; not 3,000 but 750. Clinton arrived and his army commenced with digging parallel trenches in concentric circles 800 yards from the fort. Clinton would lay siege to Charleston; he did not want to alienate the citizenry with an all-out attack. The soldiers continued digging the trenches, moving closer and closer to the city. The long and the short of it is the British continued moving closer. When Lincoln refused to surrender, Clinton ordered the shelling to begin, using hot shot. They began bombarding the city with artillery, and on day forty-one Lincoln surrendered his post. The British lost 76, killed and 182 wounded. The Americans 92 killed, 148 wounded and 4,650 captured. This is the largest American surrender of the war. The prisoners of war would-be put-on prison ships in the harbor to suffer the ravages of starvation and disease. American prisoners of war were horribly neglected. The British did not see them as regular prisoners but as traitors.

After the surrender, General Clinton sailed back to New York, leaving General Lord Charles Cornwallis in charge with orders to subdue Georgia, North and South Carolina. Cornwallis had fought in the Seven Year's War in Europe. In 1776, he was dispatched to America with a force of 2,500 men from Ireland. In America he was assigned to Major General Henry Clinton. Together, they conducted a failed attempt to take Charleston, South Carolina by sea in 1776. They then sailed north to join General Howe for the battle of Long Island. Cornwallis was defeated by General Washington at the Battle of Princeton. Cornwallis was also at the battles of Brandywine, Germantown, and Monmouth Court House. After the surrender at Charleston, Cornwallis left a residual force to protect the city and moved his remaining forces into the back country with the objective of subduing the rebel forces and enlisting the help of the Loyalists' militia. During the siege of Charleston, Clinton had offered freedom and land to any slave that would join the ranks of the British Army, many of whom fled their plantations to enlist. The southern colonists had protested vigorously with congress about arming the slaves, and this action set many locals against the British. From the beginning of the colonial settlements in North America, every settlement and community had a militia. There was always a need for protection against Indian attacks on the settlements and farms. Slaves and blacks, as indentured servants, had always been a part of the militia. Some enlisted for military service in exchange for freedom, and those already free served out of a patriotic duty. When the Continental Army was forming, most states sent part of their militia, (whoever was in the militia could be recruited into the army), blacks included.

It is unfortunate that Hollywood characteristically has to resort to extremes to sell their stories. A majority of slaves were owned by small southern farmers. A family would have one slave, and the slaves and owners worked alongside each other tending the family's homestead. They were paid a modest amount depending on the success of the family's endeavor. Once they had earned enough to buy their freedom they could; however, most stayed on until they earned an extra 30 dollars so they could buy land of their own. Thirty dollars would buy 150 acres in the back country. The slaves would live with the family in their dwelling and often took the family name as their own. Freed slaves also bought other slaves, often to wed. Slave ownership was more prevalent in the south, which was primarily agricultural. The economy in the north was more industrial in nature, where you would have a job and not as much need for a slave. There were very large plantations in the south, where the owner might

227

have hundreds of slaves; it is easy to imagine, that in some instances, extreme measures may have been employed by some to keep control of the slaves. Unfortunately, these wealthy slave owners also had the most clout with congress and other elected representatives–unfair then, unfair now. We can read a lot about George Washington having slaves–he did. He inherited them from his brother with his estate. Virginia had a law making it illegal to free slaves; however, in Washington's will he freed all of his slaves and paid those over sixty a pension. Some of the slaves chose to stay on with Martha. Shock value sells, and, unfortunately, that is what Hollywood and the news media rely on for sales. In colonial America 98 percent of the residents were Protestant, 2 percent were Catholic and there were about 200,000 of Jewish heritage. I believe a good portion of the slaves were well treated by people that believed; God is watching, and I will be held accountable. I do not think we should rely on Hollywood, historical revisionists or the news to understand history.

Clinton, also before he left, issued a proclamation stating that if a colonist was not in support of the crown, they were criminals and traitors. There were a lot of issues in the south that were not present in the north. There was animosity to the British and Loyalists for freeing slaves and for arming them. Loyalists and Patriots never got along very well; however, it did not get out of control until the armed conflict broke out. Clinton's proclamation did not help, either. Some Loyalists had been run off their property and now it was time for revenge. There were 113 skirmishes fought in South Carolina alone between Loyalists and Patriots, none of them involving soldiers. The armed conflict in the back-country set off a local civil war. This is the hot bed Cornwallis is going to ride into and try to subdue and seek compatriots for his effort.

The Battle of Waxhaws

Six days after the surrender of Charleston, Cornwallis and 2,500 men went into the backcountry. As Cornwallis began his backcountry operation, he was approached by a Loyalist that told him the Governor of South Carolina, John Rutledge, was being escorted out of South Carolina to seek refuge in North Carolina. His escort was Colonel Abraham Buford with 420 men on foot, the remnants of Lincoln's Charleston Army. Cornwallis sent Lieutenant Colonel Banastre Tarleton, the man who had captured General Lee, and his cavalry to capture the governor. Tarleton and his cavalry rode almost 100 miles in 54 hours to catch Rutledge. On May 28th they caught up with Buford six miles from the border near a place called Waxhaws. Warned of Tarleton's pursuit, Buford sent Rutledge with a small detachment ahead while he formed his men on high ground. Buford deployed his men in a single line across the top of the hill and told his men to wait for his command to fire. Facing mounted cavalry, he should have deployed his men in a circular perimeter, two or three deep, behind cover. Tarleton, with 270 men, divided his force in three: a right flank, left flank, and a frontal charge. Tarleton's men came within 300 yards and the cavalry charged. Buford waited too long to give the command to fire and his men only got off one volley before the cavalry was in their midst. There were far too few rounds fired at the flanking cavalry to have any effect. Buford raised a white flag and surrendered; however, the cavalry did not stop and continued to cut down men with their sabers. This engagement would become known as the "Waxhaws Massacre," and Tarleton would become known as "Bloody Ban." 113 militia were killed, 150 were wounded and 53 captured. Tarleton's losses were 5 killed and 12 wounded. Tarleton's strategy was to terrify the backcountry folk into submission by establishing a reputation for ruthlessness; however, this had the opposite effect on the Presbyterian Scots and Irish that primarily made up the population in the communities around Waxhaws. The ranks of the local militia swelled once word was out that the flag of surrender was ignored, and men were summarily executed.

Huck's Defeat

There was one small skirmish in the backcountry of South Carolina that played an integral part in future battles in the war of the backcountry. Patriot Colonel William Bratton and Captain John McClure commanded a militia force of 140 men. After the capture of Charleston, Cornwallis took to the backcountry and sent Lieutenant Colonel George Turnbull to establish a base of operations at Rocky Mount, South Carolina. In early July, Turnbull sent Captain Christian Huck to find and destroy the militia under Bratton. On July 11, Huck visited the home of John McClure. John was not home, so Huck took his younger brother into custody and sentenced him to be hung the next morning. He terrorized John's wife and set fire to their home. Huck and his men moved on to Bratton's plantation. One of the Loyalists' militia threatened Bratton's wife, Martha, with a reaping hook, but she would not reveal the whereabouts of her husband. Finding neither of the men at home, Huck moved his men to a nearby Loyalists' home who had a large field of oats the men could use to feed their horses. Martha Bratton sent their slave, Watt Bratton, with a note giving Huck's location, to be given to her husband at the militia camp.

Bratton's militia moved at night and took up positions from cover around Huck's encampment. At first light, Bratton's militia commenced placing well-placed shots into the encampment of the Loyalists and Dragoons. Unable to mount a defense, they left their horses and scattered into the woods. Huck got on a horse, attempting to flee; a militiaman, John Carroll, loaded two balls, took careful aim, and fired; Captain Huck, killed instantly, fell from his horse. Along with Huck, 35 of his men were killed, 30 wounded and 30 taken prisoner. Amongst Bratton's troops, one was killed, and one was wounded. The victory was a great moral boost for the Scot and Irish Presbyterians of Chester and York counties and for the south as well, after the American defeat at Charleston and Waxhaws. Frontier militia had defeated the feared British Army. Patriot militia swelled the militia ranks of General Thomas Sumter. This was the first of thirty-five battles fought around Chester and York counties; all but five of which would be won by the Patriot militia.

The Battle of Camden

After the battle of Waxhaws, the Continental Army had almost no presence in the south. General Washington and Congress decided that a contingency of the Continental Army must be sent into the south to prevent the British from gaining outright control of the south. General Washington recommended General Greene for the command position of the army in the south. Congress overrode his recommendation and appointed General Horatio Gates, the hero of Saratoga, to command the army. General Washington was extremely upset by the choice; he considered Gates to be completely incompetent as a leader. He also knew that the heroes of Saratoga were Daniel Morgan and General Benedict Arnold, and that Gates, in his reporting, merely stole the credit from the real heroes of the battle.

Gates was organizing his army at Charlotte, North Carolina, consisting of 1,500 Continental soldiers from Maryland and Delaware, and about 2,000 local militia. Once formed, and against the council of his other officers, he decided to attack the garrison at Camden manned by 1,000 British Regulars. Cornwallis had established his outpost and supply depot in Camden and was intending to use it as his base of operations for subduing South Carolina. Camden was an ideal location, logistically, at the crossroads of Wateree River and the Catawba Indian Trail. Gates wanted to attack Camden before reinforcements could be sent. General Cornwallis, through Loyalists, learned of Gates' troop movements and set off with his army of 5,000 to intercept him. The two armies ran into each other during the night of August 15th, 1780. Neither army wanting an engagement in the dark, they took up defensive positions where they were. Gates moved his men onto a small ridge, positioning his militia on the right and his regular troops in the center and on the left. The British always put their best soldiers on the right, as the right is considered the position of honor. Gates, having been a British officer, should have known this. He put his militia, who had never fought in a line formation, and without bayonets, to face off against the best of the British. At first light, both sides opened up with cannon fire. Cornwallis formed up his right side for two volleys, then a bayonet charge against the militia. As the bayonet charge was to commence, Cornwallis had Bannister Tarleton and his Legion, with sabers drawn, attack the militia line from the flank. The militia, backwoodsmen with rifles, of course, had no bayonets, so they broke and ran. The North Carolina Militia held its ground against the onslaught. Not only did the militia break and run, Gates got on his horse and rode off the battlefield. Not only off the battlefield, he rode his horse 60 miles to Charlotte, North Carolina before he stopped. This, of course, ended his military career. The remaining Continental Regulars were flanked where the militia had left a void and the battle was a complete roust. Many of the American troops surrendered. Some of the Americans took off running; Tarleton and his dragoons rode after them for miles, hacking them with their sabers. In the Battle of Camden, the Americans lost 300 killed in action, 600 wounded, and 1,000 captured. British loses were sixty-eight killed and 245 wounded.

There are soldiers that are called to duty and fill out their enlistment with honor and bravery, and there are soldiers that run the entire gamut from exceptional bravery to reluctant participants. A soldier to be exceptional must have a strong moral fiber, such that no matter the circumstances they do not cross the line and commit brutalities. Some soldiers cannot mitigate the carnage of battle and there are those with a warrior's heart, who do everything in their power to win, and sometimes out of their power. There are also some like Bannister Tarleton who have a bloodlust, an eagerness to shed blood, they do not fight with honor and do not belong in any professional army.

After the Battle of Camden, Cornwallis knew the American southern army would have to be reinforced and resupplied from the north. He devised a three-prong attack to go into North Carolina and then into Virginia. Cornwallis knew Lord Germain and General Clinton were convinced that if they took the war to the south and abandoned the deadlocked struggle in the north, they could fill their ranks with Loyalist Militia. The north had proven to be too much of a hotbed because of the extraordinary number of rebels and their extreme hostility to the British. The rebellion had started in the northern colonies, and the southern colonies, for the most part, stayed out of the rebellion. The south depended heavily on trade with England, and Germain and Clinton thought the south would produce a lot of Loyalists that would not want to see their livelihood ruined by war with England. Secondarily, Britain was fighting on a world stage and Germain told Clinton he was going to have to fill his ranks with Loyalists because England could not spare any more soldiers for the colonial rebellion. Cornwallis was leery of enlisting Loyalists; he thought he may be allowing rebels into his ranks that could turn on him in battle. Over the objections of Cornwallis, Clinton enlisted Major Patrick Ferguson to form an army of strictly southern Loyalists. Cornwallis, in his three-pronged attack, told Tarleton to take his army up the coast to Wilmington. He would take the center route to Charlotte. Cornwallis told Ferguson to travel west, recruiting his militia on the way, and serve as the left flank into North Carolina. Ferguson was quite successful in his recruiting endeavors and had enlisted several thousand militia. However, he would only take the best of the recruits. For reasons of logistics and supplies, he wanted to keep his force at 1,000 militia.

The Skirmish at Musgrove Mill

On August 18th, some Loyalists were camping near a ford on the Enorge River, en route to Fort Ninety-Six. The local militia thought to set up an ambush. The Patriot Militia took up a position down river from the ford where the Loyalists were camped at the next ford near the Musgrove Grist Mill. They sent a small detachment of Patriots down river to fire on the loyalists to try to lure them upriver to their position. The detachment of

Patriot Militia fired their rifles, across the river, killing several of the Loyalists, they worked their way up the shoreline staying in sight. As the Loyalists approached the next ford, they decided to cross the river and engage the Patriots, as they had them outnumbered by at least ten to one. As the Loyalists started across, the Patriots turned into a clearing in the woods and began up a small gradual embankment. As the Loyalists progressed to halfway up the incline, the Patriots split in two and broke off into the woods to serve as the flank, should any of the Loyalists seek cover. Just as the Patriots broke off, the Loyalists came under intense rifle fire from the Patriots in hiding. The Loyalists, after firing their one shot, were in panic as soldiers kept falling. They turned and ran for the river; however, the Patriots continued to fire. The Loyalists lost 63 killed and 90 wounded. The Patriots lost 4 killed and 8 wounded.

Major Patrick Ferguson continued north, recruiting militia. He was in Gilbertson in September when he heard of the skirmish at Musgrove Mill. He issued a proclamation that the Patriot Militia had better stay out of the war in the Carolinas or "he would ride over the Blue Ridge Mountains and hang all the leaders and lay waste the land with sword and fire." After hearing the threat, Colonel John Sevier told Colonel Benjamin Cleveland, a North Carolinian Presbyterian Scot, that he thought Colonel Isaac Shelby may martial the militia against this threat and, if the Scot-Irish Militia was interested, they could rendezvous with Shelby at the Sycamore Shoals of the Watauga River. Cleveland said the whole of the Scot-Irish Community had been looking for an opportunity to teach the British a lesson since the horrendous slaughter at Waxhaw, and he could count on them being there. Sevier rode the forty miles back to the Wataugan Settlement.

The Wataugan Settlement had been established after the Battle of Alamance, which was actually the first battle in the War for Independence with Great Britain. Orange County, part of the backcountry was populated before western boundaries had been established between Virginia, Tennessee, Kentucky, and North Carolina. Orange county was administered by a Royal Governor. The Governor William Tryon established courts, sheriffs, judges, attorneys, and a tax system to cover the costs. The sheriff would ride out into the deep backcountry to collect taxes. Most of the frontiersmen used a barter system comprised of furs, game, crops, and tobacco leaves, which were often used in lieu of cash, which they had very little of. When the sheriff showed up to collect taxes, the frontiersmen had no money to part with so the sheriff would fine them. Sometimes property was confiscated for lack of payment. The fines were often excessive and used by the sheriff, judges, and lawyers to enrich themselves. Tensions increased and the Governor called out the militia. The frontiersmen took up arms, and there was a skirmish. The militia won, and some of the leaders of the rebellion were hung. This action set in motion a group of, mostly, Baptists–people to pack up and move over the Appalachian Mountains to establish a new settlement, because they refused to take an oath of loyalty to the crown. It is said the Baptist community in Orange county went from 900 families to 13. The first thing the 1,500 new residents did was to build a house of worship, The Sinking Creek Baptist Church, then developed the settlement. The church housed the women and children. The men camped outside while building the settlement. The settlement was called the Wataugan Settlement. The next order of business was to write the charter of the Wataugan Settlement Association, which declared the settlement was independent and free of British rule. The settlement was in violation of the 1763 Proclamation that forbid any land purchases of settlements west of the Appalachian Mountains. The determined and fiercely independent frontiersmen, to get around the proclamation, did not buy the land, they leased it from the Cherokee Indians. John Sevier was one of the first administrators of the Association and would also be the first governor of Tennessee. When Sevier told Colonel Isaac Shelby, who would later become the first governor of Kentucky, of the threat, he organized the militia of the Overmountian Men and they rode across the Blue Ridge Mountains. They joined up with the Scot-Irish from the back country of the Carolinians. Now 900 strong, they set out to find Ferguson.

The Battle of King's Mountain

Loyalist spies informed Ferguson that the Overmountain Men, on horseback, were on his trail. Half of Ferguson's militia were on foot and he had seventeen wagons in tow; he would have to make a stand. The Loyalists within his ranks who were very familiar with the terrain told him the top of Kings Mountain would give them a good vantage point and the steep, craggy slopes would be hard to climb. The Loyalist Militia moved to the plateau on top of the hill. It was sixty feet above the surrounding terrain, and the plateau was 600 yards long and 70 feet wide at one end and 120 at the other. Ferguson spread his wagons around the perimeter and stationed his 1,100 militia around the perimeter. As these were British

Loyalist Militia, they were supplied by the British and they carried the Brown Bess muskets and bayonets. Ferguson had all of his men fix their bayonets immediately.

On Saturday, October 7, 1780, the Overmountain Men and the Scot-Irish Militia arrived at the base of Kings Mountain. They dismounted their horses and dispersed around the foot of the hill in a horseshoe; the back side of the hill was too steep to scale. Ferguson told his men that God Almighty could not remove him from this hill. The soldiers in the Battle of Kings Mountain, aside from Major Patrick Ferguson, were all Americans–Patriots against Loyalists. The Patriots, going from cover to cover, slowly worked their way up the hillside, firing as they moved. The Loyalists, firing the Brown Bess, found that, firing downhill, most of their shots were going high–over the target. The American rifle had no challenges. With deadly accuracy each time a Loyalist exposed himself to fire his weapon, it would be his last. The fire fight only lasted an hour, and the remaining Loyalists tried to surrender; Ferguson tore down their white flag and, in exposing himself, was shot seven times. The white flags went back up and the Patriots massed over the crest. There were yells of, "Tarleton's Quarters" and, remember Buford, (from Waxhaws). Some of the Loyalists were killed under the white flag until the colonels were able to gain order amongst their troops.

A detachment was formed to escort the prisoners to Hillsboro. The rest of the Scot-Irish and the Overmountain Men went back home to take care of business and protect family and communities from Indian attacks, until the next call. The British had recommitted their efforts to instigate Indians to attack any settlements. Once at Hillsboro, the Patriots put thirty-nine of the Loyalists on trial for crimes against Patriots in the fighting that had been raging between Loyalists and Patriots– crimes for burning homes, stealing livestock and murder. All thirty-nine were sentenced to be hanged. Nine of them were hanged before the colonels, again exerted their authority and put an end to the hangings.

It is said that when Cornwallis heard about Ferguson, he leaned on his sword so hard that the blade snapped. Cornwallis continued his pursuit of Greene towards Virginia. In order to catch Greene, Cornwallis ordered all unnecessary supplies and all of their wagons burned, so that they may travel as light and as fast as Greene. In a very unconventional move, Greene split his army. He sent Daniel Morgan west while he continued north. Cornwallis followed the decoy; however, he soon realized that

Greene had split his army. He sent Tarleton after Morgan while he resumed his march on Greene.

The Battle of Cowpens

Morgan was heading for the ford on the Broad River. Once across, he would link up with Greene. Local Patriots warned Morgan that Tarleton was in pursuit of his regiment. When Morgan arrived at the Broad River, providentially, it was over–flowing its banks. Morgan thought he would take his men back the short distance to the Cowpens Pasture they had just crossed and make a stance there. Otherwise he may be caught with half of his men on the far side of the river and the other half on this side when Tarleton caught up with them. Morgan thought he had 600 Continental Soldiers and 600 militia, and he thought the militia could not stand to a bayonet charge. Whenever the battle got close enough, the militia without bayonets had no realistic option but to break their line and regroup. The British knew better than to chase the militia after the line broke; their bayonets were of no use on militia when they were free to return fire at the British from several hundred yards away. Morgan set a first line of 150 sharpshooters and told them to fire two rounds a piece, then retire to the second line, reloading on the run. In the second line, Morgan put his remaining 450 riflemen with the same instructions. When they retreated, they were to go over and behind a small hill crest, then break left and right and serve as the flanks. He also ordered a platoon on each side to work their way down the wood line to a position behind the battle lines where the road entered the clearing.

Cowpens was a pasture where most of the locals grazed their cattle. It was about a mile long and a half a mile wide and surrounded by trees on all sides, with one road coming onto the pasture. The Continentals behind the crest were out of sight from the road coming onto the pasture. Tarleton marched his men all night. As he approached Morgan's lookouts told him they would be there at dawn. Morgan formed his lines and when Tarleton saw only militia, he immediately ordered his infantry forward. At about 200 to 250 yards the first line fired 2 rounds apiece–300 rounds. The sharpshooters had to be able to hit a 10-inch square ten times consecutively at 200 yards. Even if half of them missed it would still be 150 killed or wounded. They retired back to the second line. The British kept moving forward, again at 200 yards, 900 rounds would have been fired.

This has to represent hundreds of soldiers killed and wounded. I am very skeptical of the battlefield casualties reported by the British, the numbers are way too low. The British field commanders did not want London to know how bad things really were, Britain was out of money, the populace wanted the war over, there were no more troops to send to America. I think the number killed were buried in reports of lost to disease, desertions, captured and wounded. When a soldier walks out of a firefight, it is usually for two reasons, they missed, and you did not.

The militia turned and disappeared behind the crest. The British fixed bayonets and advanced on the hill. When they got to the top, they saw the 600 Continental Soldiers who fired their volley and charged with bayonets. The British that were not shot laid down their weapons. The right flank began firing well-placed shots at the dragoons in reserve. As they began falling off their horses, the rest of the dragoons turned and fled down the road. When Tarleton saw his dragoons abandon the field and his men laying down their weapons, he rode off the battlefield. At the Battle of Cowpens, Morgan lost 25 soldiers killed, and 124 wounded. Tarleton lost three hundred killed and as many wounded, with 500 to 600 captured.

Cornwallis caught up with Greene; however, because of the delay, Greene had succeeded in getting all of his men across the Dan River before Cornwallis arrived. All of the boats were on the opposite side of the river from Cornwallis. He decided to camp there the night, as it was almost dusk, and retrieve the boats and cross in the morning. Again, providentially, it stormed that night, washed the boats away, and flooded the river. Cornwallis waited a few days. No Loyalists came out to fill his ranks. They had become very intimidated by the Continental and militia wins, along with the acts of retribution for not joining the cause for America. Loyalists told Cornwallis that Major General Lafayette was on his way to Greene with 2,000 replacements.

Morgan arrived at Greene's camp and told him of his effective use of the militia and sharpshooters against British Regulars. Leading with sharpshooters to reduce the number of combatants and leaving the Continentals to hold at the bayonet charge. The sharpshooters were then sent to the flanks to provide continual coverage during the bayonet attack. Lafayette was very excited. He told Greene the way to beat the British was to be unconventional in all battle strategies. He told Greene and Morgan about his unconventional winter attacks and his attacks on encampments at night. Morgan, however, asked to be relieved of his command, as the pain from his sciatic nerve had become unbearable, he would need a buggy for his return trip home.

The Battle of Guilford Court House

General Greene now resupplied and reinforced with militia from Virginia, and Lafayette and his 2,000 soldiers decided to go after Cornwallis; the hunted now became the hunter. Greene moved in pursuit of Cornwallis and came very near to him and his army on the night of March 14th. Cornwallis informed of the close proximity of Greene, decided to go on the offensive. Greene, being informed of Cornwallis' movement towards his location, positioned his men in the same manner as Morgan had done at Cowpens–in three lines. Cornwallis had his men advance on the first line, and the sharpshooters dropped many of the regulars. One of the officers of the Highlanders said the first volley dropped a full half of his men. The first line fell back, and the British moved on the second line; again, the firing was accurate and many British fell. 1,500 rifles and muskets poured out fire from the second line; the second line fell back. Cornwallis regrouped his men as they started to retreat. He re-formed the line and told them to charge with their bayonets, expecting the line to break. The British rushed to Greene's line of Continentals, armed with bayonets, and they held. It quickly turned into hand-to-hand combat. Cornwallis was so rattled and fearful of losing the battle he ordered two of his artillery men to fire grape shot into the battle. Two rounds were fired and as many British fell as Continentals. Greene, seeing this madness, ordered an immediate retreat. His men fell back, loading as they went. Cornwallis, shaken and not wanting to lose any more of his men, ordered them to stand down; he had lost 27 percent of his army.

The Battle of Yorktown

The French fleet landed 5,200 soldiers at Rhode Island and marched south to connect with General Washington. Clinton was convinced that General Washington and his new allies were going to try and take back New York. He did not want his army split in the face of this new threat. Clinton dispatched orders to Cornwallis to find a secure deep-water port and garrison there while he sent ships to pick him and his army up and bring him to New York. Cornwallis was to inform Clinton when he was secure in his new garrison. Cornwallis had lost half of his army at Kings Mountain, Cowpens, Guilford Courthouse, and the Battle of Eutaw Springs. The Loyalist support that was supposed to rally to Cornwallis in the south never materialized. The Loyalists on the coast focused on their trade and they were very upset with the British for Lord Dunmore's emancipation proclamation telling any slaves that joined the British cause would be given their freedom. The southern plantation owners had vigorously fought Cornwallis and the American Congress against arming slaves, for fear of a revolt. The Loyalists in the back country, initially seemed to be focused on their civil war with the Patriots, which were set off by Clinton's proclamation of no neutrality and all were to swear allegiance to the crown. After significant Patriot victories in the south and the hangings of Loyalists charged with murder, few Loyalists were willing to join the British cause. The Loyalists were further angered by the British recruitment of Indians to attack settlements, as the Indians did not differentiate between Loyalists and Patriots; settlers were settlers.

The English Parliament was divided over the war in the colonies. William Pitt, who had been the prime minister of England during the French and Indian War, sided with the colonists and their quest for independence. He told the Parliament, "If I were an American...while a foreign troop was landed in my country, I would never lay down my arms, never, never, never,"

Cornwallis was determined to move into Virginia, as he thought a resounding victory there could bring about the end of the war. However, Loyalists informed Cornwallis that General Lafayette was headed to Charlotte with a force of 2,000 Continentals to join forces with General Greene. In light of Ferguson's defeat, and with word that Lafayette was heading to his destination, Cornwallis decided to obey Clinton's orders and on June 20th, he marched his men for Yorktown. Cornwallis had intended to rendezvous with General Philips and his 3,500-man army in Virginia; instead, he sent word for Philips to meet him at Yorktown. Cornwallis had selected Yorktown as it was a good seaport, and it would save him the time of marching all the way back to South Carolina. He also sent word to the remaining garrisons at Wilmington, Charleston, Savana, Hanging Rock, Rocky Mount, Camden and Ninety-six, to leave a residual force and march the rest of the troops to Yorktown.

Clinton often complained to King George III that Germain was undercutting his ability to wage war by sending orders without understanding that he must adapt to hourly changes in circumstances. The real challenge with the Southern Strategy was that Cornwallis was given an army of 4,870 men to cover 141,000 square miles and 507,000 people; he also had to man eight outposts. Clinton, in the north, had an army of 16,000, although he did have to dispatch troops to Florida and the West Indies after France entered the war. The whole Southern Strategy originating in London relied too heavily on support from Loyalists; and London served to undermine their own strategy by initiating policies that alienated the Loyalists.

The French Army, under the command of Lieutenant General Baptiste de Rochambeau, marched south from Rhode Island and joined forces with General Washington at White Plains on July 6th. General Washington wanted to attack Clinton at New York. Rochambeau cautioned General Washington that their combined forces were 12,000 up against Clintons 14,500. Clintons' force of 1,800 in Novia Scotia would not be able to arrive in time. Rochambeau also thought it unlikely that the French fleet under the command of Admiral Francois Joseph Paul Comte de Grasse would be likely to bring his fleet to New York. Admiral de Grasse had left France and sailed to the Caribbean. If all went well, he would return to France via America, sailing up the coast looking for a target of opportunity. Rochambeau told General Washington a target of opportunity would not be New York where the English fleet was anchored. Rochambeau told General Washington that he had dispatches from Lafayette and that he and General Greene had chased Cornwallis to the town of Yorktown. They had 4,000 troops and estimated Cornwallis had 7 to 8,000 and was beginning to build fortifications. Rochambeau postulated to Washington that their combined forces, with Greene, totaling 16,000 should be able to easily defeat Cornwallis and score a significant victory. General Washington cautioned that they would have to wage an all-out frontal attack, which would have a heavy cost in loss of life to his troops. General Washington continued that if they tried to take Yorktown by siege that would give Clinton time to send his ships to Cornwallis for an escape by sea.

On August 19th, General Washington and Rochambeau began to move their troops to Yorktown. They had no way of communicating the new developments to Admiral de Grasse, who was somewhere between America and the Caribbean. Washington sent out dispatches and other routes of false information to give the appearances of an attack on New

York. He left some of his troops behind to make it look like preparations were being made for an attack on Clinton. Lafayette and Greene stationed their sharpshooters around the perimeter of Yorktown and the snipers would snipe at the troops working on the fortifications and on the redoubts. This made the work progress at a very slow pace as the casualties continued to climb. By the end of August, it was obvious to Clinton that General Washington was not going to attack New York but was in fact heading to Yorktown. Clinton dispatched Rear Admiral Sir Thomas Graves with troop transports and ships-of-the line to evacuate Cornwallis from Yorktown.

As Admiral de Grasse sailed up the American coastline, he providentially sailed into the Chesapeake Bay. There was really no reason for this move, as Yorktown had never been a British port. De Grasse sent a reconnaissance team ashore and they were met by Lafayette, who informed them of the situation. The reconnaissance team returned to the ship and de Grasse sent his 3,500 marines to join Lafayette. De Grasse then made ready to meet the anticipated arrival of British transports. On September 5th, the British fleet under Rear Admiral Graves arrived at the Chesapeake Bay with the intension of collecting Cornwallis and his army for transport back to New York. The two fleets began forming online, and the cannonade began. After four hours, even before all of the ships of the line were in position, twenty-four French and nineteen British, were able to line up, the British fleet retreated and sailed back to New York. Both fleets had been heavily damaged in the engagement.

With the escape route by the sea cut off, General Washington and the French forces formed a 2,000-yard line from the Chesapeake Bay to the James River, completely sealing the Yorktown peninsula. Both French and Americans began digging their parallels on October 10th; General Washington took his pickaxe and made the first strike where the trench would be dug. British cannons fired at the French and American soldiers as they worked on the trench. The Americans returned fire by employing sharpshooters to eliminate the artillery crews. By October 10th, the first parallel was complete with artillery in place; General Washington fired the first cannon at the British defenses.

By October 11th, the second parallel was completed four-hundred yards closer; the next day the new line was occupied. By October 14th, General Washington's army was within 150 yards of the defensive redoubts. Cornwallis had abandoned all but redoubts number nine and ten. That evening, General Washington charged Lafayette and four-hundred troopers to take out redoubt number nine. He also instructed Alexander Hamilton, with four-hundred light infantry, to neutralize redoubt number ten. The raids took place at night. They had to first ax their way through the abatis–no shots were fired–bayonets only. After the redoubts had been taken and the 120 men either killed or run off, the Americans and French turned the redoubt cannons on Yorktown and commenced firing into the British positions. Just before dawn on the morning of October 19th, 1781, the sole beat of a single drum could be heard–the sound of the British request for terms of surrender. Drums and fifes were used during many conflicts during this era, as voice commands could seldom be heard in battle, or for miles if it was a large compliment of soldiers. The drums and fifes translated the orders from the commanders. Cornwallis was not at the surrender ceremony; his second in command said that he was ill. He tried to present the sword of capitulation to French General Rochambeau, as a slight to General Washington. The general of a rebellion, not of a nation, he refused, and deferred to General Washington. When the sword was offered to General Washington, he refused and deferred to General Lincoln, the American General who had surrendered to the British at Charleston.

The Aftermath

After the war, all three of the major players: America, Britain and France had tremendous war debts; the consequences of their respective debts played out differently for all three. France experienced its own revolution. Britain, while France was occupied with its revolution, focused on building trade in the West Indies, Africa and India. Britain also retained Canada, and consequently built what would be called the "Second British Empire." America had to create a government, and with that new government find a way to protect its interests and pay its war debt.

In 1770, fifteen-year-old Louis and fourteen-year-old Marie-Anionite of Austria were married in a political union. Louis XVI's father died of smallpox and he was propelled to the throne when he was twenty years old. France was still dealing with its war debt from the French and Indian War and past wars with Britain. Louis XVI added to its war debt by helping the Americans in the Revolutionary War. He looked for ways to ease the nation's debt by introducing some radical reforms that were not popular, especially with the commoners. In 1789, he called for a General Address of the Three Estates: the clergy, the nobles, and the commoners; however, the assembly did not go as Louis XVI had hoped. The Third Estate declared itself the National Assembly and set out to draft a constitution. The lesson learned by the French from the American Revolution was that people can change an unjust government. Louis called out the army. The National Assembly responded by forming a National Guard, a militia of sorts. The years of 1786 and 1787, were years of very poor harvests, and 1788, was the worst winter in ninety years. The price of bread soared; bread was a mainstay of the French diet. The French consumed about two pounds of bread per day per person. People began to starve. In October, before the next winter, 20,000 women from Paris marched the twelve miles to Versailles where the king and queen had their residence. By morning the crowd had grown to 60,000 and in the morning the palace was stormed. The guard's heads were cut off and put on spikes and Louis and Marie were escorted to Paris–in effect, they were prisoners. The National Guard raided the Paris armory, took 28,000 muskets, then raided the Bastille. They took the gunpowder and razed the building. They made a new flag–red and blue stripes–the colors for Paris separated by a white stripe, the color of the Louis's House of Bourbon. A Declaration of the Rights of Man was written and did away with class distinctions, promoted equality, declared the sovereignty of the people and recognized the National Assemble. They demanded a Constitutional Monarchy, with equal rights for all men, equal justice for all men under reasonable law, and freedom of the press. Louis XVI and Marie tried to flee to Austria but were caught and arrested. Marie's royal family mobilized its army and invaded France. In April of 1792, France declared war on Austria, although France, in such a state of chaos, was in no position to conduct a war of any scale. Prussia joined Austria against France. In August, 27,000 armed citizens tried to enter the palace; 800 guards were killed, as well as 800 citizens. The rest of the guards were marched to the guillotine. The guillotine was a new means of execution that was said to be quick, humane and painless. Louis XVI was stripped of his title and the French Republic was born. On January 20th, King Louis XVI went on trial for treason, was found guilty, and the next day he was beheaded. Nine months later, on October 15th, Marie was put on trial for salacious charges, incest and other crimes. She was also found guilty and brought to the guillotine. Martial law was declared because of all of the traitors and conspirators; the constitution was suspended; it was neighbor against neighbor. A twelve-man Committee of Public Safety was put in place to rule during martial law. God was replaced by a cult of the supreme being to create a society of virtue, and virtue was obtained by terror. 800 people were sent to the guillotine every month. By the end of the revolution, 100,000 people had been killed. France begins to see some victories in the war with Austria from a new commander named Napoleon Bonaparte; who would become France's first emperor.

The surrender at Yorktown took place on October 19th, 1781. The treaty was not signed until September 3rd, 1783. King George III was so despondent after losing the war he eventually had a nervous breakdown. The breakdown bordered on insanity. A new prime minister was put in place–William Pitt, the younger, who governed during George's period of incapacity. Parliament finally passed the Regency Act, which gave regency to George III's son Prince George, who co-ruled until his father's death in 1820. Prince George had to navigate his father's erratic behavior and, by 1803 Britain was at war again with France, as Napoleon began his quest for dominance of Europe.

America had gained her independence; however, the challenges for the new nation were far from over. America was also laden with debt, and there were no immediate solutions to service that debt. Congress could not tax, but only appeal to the states for financial assistance. Spain still occupied Florida, southern Alabama, Mississippi and Louisiana. Britain still occupied Canada and their forts in the Great Lakes region. Britain was also encouraging settlements along the Mississippi River. Great Britain was selling land to new English settlers and keeping the money for the crown's war debt, not giving it to the Indians, which was in violation of their own treaty with the Indians. American settlers and frontier families still had to contend with Indian raids, encouraged by the British. Britain was enforcing trade embargos against America in an attempt to restrict trade with America and traffic trade through England enriching itself with tariffs. Britain also tried to bar America from trading with the West Indies. Additionally, Britain put tariffs on American goods but would not allow America to charge tariffs. There was also going to have to be reconciliation between the Loyalists and the Patriots

A style of government was going to have to be invented. The Founding Fathers were in agreement that America would not be ruled by a king or a monarch. America as thirteen colonies could not present a united front to other nations. Each state was establishing trade independently of the other states; which in effect had the state competing with one another. If a state wanted to charge a tariff, Britain would merely trade with a state that did not, rather than lose the trade, the states would acquiesce on their tariffs. All of Britain's interference on American trade made it increasingly difficult for America to retire its war debt. Tariffs were Americas only immediate source of income.

Slavery was also an important issue in America. The Declaration of Independence contained a clause eliminating slavery; however, as slavery in the colonies had been instituted by England, the verbiage on slavery was though to inflammatory, so it was removed. America at the time was still hoping to reconcile with Britain and thought the slavery issue would lessen their chance for reconciliation. Slavery was also an issue during the formation of the Articles of Confederation, which southern states would not ratify if it contained verbiage eliminating or discouraging slave ownership.

The American Indians had been devastated by the French and Indian War, internal civil wars, land encroachment and the Revolutionary War. Civil wars resulted over differences as to who the various tribes should support in wars between France, Britain and America. France and Britain always had a policy, because of the limited number of soldiers their respective governments could spare, that encouraged Indians to raid settlements and war against the colonial settlers. Britain continually violated the treaties they had established with the Indians; however, because of the Indians need for weapons, gunpowder, ammunition and other metal goods, they continually made concessions to the British. Although disease was rampant in the world until the advent of vaccinations the Indians' were hit particularly hard because of the lack of antibodies for many of the diseases brought to America, from: Spain, England and Africa.

Slavery had its origins in the Bible; initially slavery was work. There were not many jobs', hence, people would become beggars or slaves in order to have some income. After numerous rebellions, slaves began receiving monetary compensation; however, there was so little work and so many slaves that the pay was very minimum.

In the colonies, workers were imported as slaves. This was a policy of England and many other countries. Because there was not a central government in America, the states would establish their own state charters for governing their state. The state charters in some states forbid slavery such as: Massachusetts, Maine, and Vermont.

We know we cannot trust Hollywood for an accurate portrayal of early American history, as their goal is an emotional response from the audience, with globalists messaging. I am sure there were instances of abuse with some of the slaves, and the Indians were notorious for torturing their captives, which I am sure at times was savagely revenged; however, I think the history that is untold is that the behavior of most Christians was that of compassion and a desire for peace. The Christians of the colonial era were very different than most Christians of today. The Christians believed God was watching them and that they would be held accountable for their behavior in a day of judgement. They were all schooled in reading Scripture, and when you read Scripture every day you begin to incorporate Biblical principles into your thinking, and that is reflected in your behavior. Your definition of right and wrong, good and evil comes from Scripture, not yourself. Unlike today where we have a predisposition to rationalize just about any behavior we want to. Our current population cannot imagine what it was like to live in a country where just about everyone believed in God and behaved accordingly.

The Formation of a More Perfect Union

The Articles of Confederation, passed by the Second Continental Congress on November 15, 1777, served as our first constitution; however, it failed in its intended objective for a number of reasons. The Articles did not provide for an executive to enforce the laws nor did it provide for a judicial branch to interpret the law. The only provision was for a Congress. Under the Articles, Congress could not levy taxes–that power resided with the states, making the government dependent on the states. The Continental Congress had borrowed money to fight the Revolutionary war and could not repay its debts. The Articles also withheld from Congress the power to regulate trade and collect tariffs. What it did allow for was Congress to raise armies and declare war with no means of financing either. Congress was also allowed to sign treaties. A central challenge to the weak national government is that other nations did not recognize the United States; they viewed each state as a separate entity. There was no universal law of the land and no specific protection for individual rights. The Articles had created a government that could not tax, it authorized a national army, with no means to pay for it, hence, a government with no ability to enforce a foreign policy. Britain still restricted Americas' ability to trade freely, and the West Indies were off limits to American ships. Spain demanded that America relinquish its navigational rights on the Mississippi and made claims to western lands. In 1786, Daniel Shays, who was a veteran of Bunker Hill and Saratoga, led a rebellion in Massachusetts of farmers who were suffering from debt as a result of the state's high taxes; many of whom were going broke. James Madison, the author of the Constitution and Alexander Hamilton decided something needed to be done and called for a Constitutional Convention to remedy the deficiencies of the Articles to, "decide forever the fate of republican government." Madison addressed the convention with the task at hand, not as we the states, but, "We The People

WE THE PEOPLE

A Constitutional Convention was convened in 1787. The intent was to strengthen the Articles of Confederation; however, it was soon realized that an entirely new document was required. Two opposing sides quickly developed: The Federalists and the anti-Federalists. The proposed new Constitution would provide a legislature to write the laws of the Republic, a president or an executive branch to enforce the laws, and a judicial branch to interpret the laws. The idea for a government consisting of three separate branches came from the book of Isaiah chapter 33 verses 22; "For the Lord is our Judge (a judicial branch), The Lord is our lawgiver (a legislative branch), the Lord is our king (an executive branch); He will save us," All three branches under the authority of God. Provisions were also proposed for a standing army, and to give the federal government the power to tax and levee tariffs.

The anti-federalists, among whom were Samuel Adams, Patrick Henry, and James Monroe, were apprehensive that the new government would use its power to minimize the role of the states in managing their own destiny. They also felt the federal government would be too far removed from "We the People" to adequately represent the average citizen, which could threaten liberties and would fail to protect individual rights. In order to convince "We the People," that a federal government was needed, Alexander Hamilton, James Madison and John Jay published the Federalists Papers to which the anti-Federalists responded with the anti-Federalists Papers.

The Federalists Papers supported and urged American citizens to accept the idea of a federal government–that the three separate branches of government with separate authority and responsibilities would keep one another in check. Presidential appointees would have to be approved by the senate. They also maintained that further restraints would be provided

248

by the states and, in that the representatives were elected by "We the People" they could remove from office anyone if their performance was contrary to the interests of "We the People."

The lower house was to have short, two-year terms to keep them accountable to their constituents, the number of which would be determined by the population of each state. The upper house would have two representatives from each state serving a six-year term; each senator having one vote. The federal government would keep the states in check and the states would keep the federal government in check.

The anti-Federalists thought self-government was impossible because it had failed everywhere else it had been tried because of man's passions, emotions and greed for power, influence and money. Acquiescing to that line of reasoning, the Federalists maintained that the government must be built on man's ability to self-govern and can only occur if man is accountable to his Creator. The United States of America was not built on the constitution alone; it is built on a firm belief in the providential hand of God and the teachings of Jesus Christ. The Federalists believed that a government built on morality and religion was the surest safeguard against men acting in their own self-interest, as each person is accountable to God for their actions and there is a judgment day for rewards or punishment. Three branches of government operating under natural law, God's Law as revealed in Scripture, being held accountable, not only to God but, "We The People."

The Federalists gleaned much of their governing philosophies from the ancient Israelites under the law of Moses, and the lessons from the fall of the Greek and Roman Republics. Israel's decentralized form of government allowed for maximum individual liberty. The Founding Fathers had a model to follow. God freed the Hebrews from a tyrannical ruler and demonstrated liberty and self–rule, guided by the providential hand of God and His requirements for human behavior. Everyone was expected to obey the law and make sure his neighbor was doing the same. There was no need of a police force with the Hebrews living in compliance to the law. There was no need of a standing army as every man twenty and older was expected to come to the aid of the nation or any tribe in danger. Under Moses, there was no king, no monarchy, they were a people governed by law. In like manner America was established as a Republic, with three branches of government; the legislature to make the laws, the executive branch to enforce the law and the judicial branch to interpret the law. Three branches of government to provide for a separation of powers, incorporating by design checks and balances, and a distribution of power. The justification for abandoning The Articles of Confederation was; "In order to provide a more perfect union."

"The highest glory of the American Revolution was this that it connected in one indissoluble bond the principles of civil government with the principles of Christianity."   President John Quincy Adams

A government with orchestrated separation of powers was a very unprecedented concept. The world was familiar with kings, oligarchies, czars, dictators, juntas and failed republics. In ancient Israel, each of the twelve tribes elected their own leaders and all the people were treated as equals. Judges were appointed by Moses for the tribes and any decision too complicated for the judge to resolve was referred back to Moses.[26] God warned Israel on several occasions to follow his commandments and statues and He would continue to bless them; if they became disobedient, they would experience His wrath.

We read in Deuteronomy, "See, I have set before you today life and prosperity, and death and adversity; in that I command you this day to love the Lord your God, to walk in His ways and to keep His commandments and His statues and His judgement, that you may live and multiply, and that the Lord your God may bless you in the land where you are entering to possess it. But if your heart turns away and you will not obey but are drawn away and worship other gods and serve them, I declare to you today that you shall surely perish. You will not prolong your days in the land where you are crossing the Jordan to enter and possess it."[27] A religion that teaches personal responsibility to God is the very foundation of morality. The Hebrews and the Founding Fathers knew the ultimate check on human depravity is our own moral conscience, and an omniscient, omnipresent Creator, to whom we are accountable, as the only effective restraint on human behavior.

"For His eyes are upon the ways of men, and He sees all his steps."[28]

Not only is the Creator all-knowing, He will hold us accountable for our deeds. "...and the dead were judged from the things which were written in the books, according to their deeds."[29] Within the Christian faith, if a person commits a sin, they are to ask for forgiveness and are not repeat the sin. That is inherent in the definition of repentance–a turning away from

---

[26] Deuteronomy 1:8-18
[27] Deuteronomy 30:15-16 NASB
[28] Psalm 34:21
[29] Revelation 20:12, 22:12

the behavior that caused the sin, however, not all deeds are sinful. Some actions are just wrong, and for those all will be judged, as we will all stand before the throne in the day of judgment.

Not only is there a day of reckoning, there is also a day of rewards and punishment.[30] God has also given us the Ten Commandments which define our relationship with Him and our relationship to one another. They are part of God's moral law, written by the finger of God, and they will never change.

I AM Jehovah your God, who brought you out of Egypt, from the house of bondage. You shall not have any other gods besides Me.

You shall not make a graven image for yourself, of any likeness which is in the heavens above or which is in the earth beneath, or which is in the waters under the earth; you shall not bow to them, and you shall not serve them; for I am Jehovah your God, a jealous God.

You shall not take the name of Jehovah your God in vain; for Jehovah will not leave unpunished the one who takes His name in vain.

Remember the Sabbath day, to keep it holy, six days you shall labor and do all your work; and the seventh day is a Sabbath to Jehovah your God; you shall not do any work, you, and your son, and your daughter, your male slave and your slave girl, and your livestock, and your stranger which is in your gates. For in six days Jehovah made the heavens and the earth, and the sea, and all, which is in them, and He rested on the seventh day; on account of this, Jehovah blessed the Sabbath day and sanctified it.

Honor your father and your mother, so that your days may be long on the land which Jehovah your God is giving to you.

You shall not murder.

You shall not commit adultery.

You shall not steal.

You shall not testify a witness of falsehood against your neighbor.

---

[30] Revelation 22:12

You shall not covet your neighbor's house; you shall not covet your   neighbor's wife, or his male slave, or his slave girl, or his ox, or his ass, or anything which belongs to your neighbor.
(Exod. 20:2–17 Interlinear Hebrew Old Testament)[31]

John Adams, the second president of the United States, said, "Suppose a nation in some distant region should take the Bible for their only law book, and every member should regulate his conduct by the precepts there exhibited! Every member would be obligated in conscience, to temperance, frugality, and industry; to justice, kindness, and charity towards his fellow men; and to piety, love, and reverence toward Almighty God...What a Eutopia, what a paradise would this region be."

Samuel Adams, the father of the revolution said, "The rights of the colonists as Christians...may be best understood by reading and carefully studying the institution of the great Law Giver and Head of the Christian Church, which are to be found clearly written and promulgated in the New Testament."

George Washington said, 'Of all the dispositions and habits which lead to political prosperity, religion and morality are indispensable supports. In vain would that man claim the tribute of patriotism, who should labor to subvert these great pillars of human happiness..." The   govern-ment had to protect the rights of the people and still maintain a civil society. The people, in like manner, had to control the government. At the end of the day, the role of government is to ensure the safety of its citizenry and to ensure justice for all. The best means of accomplishing this equality is for the people and the government to exhibit proper restraint to do good, as guided by their accountability to their Creator and His expectations.

It was the states' jealous desire to keep religion under their jurisdictions that motivated them to insist that a First Amendment be added to the U.S. Constitution to prohibit the federal government from inter-meddling with religion or defining a national religion. Lessons learned from the Catholic Church and the Church of England. Virginia was the most populated state and the other states had apprehensions that the Anglican Church of Virginia would become the denomination of America.

When all state representatives agreed to the verbiage of the first

---

[31] Hendrickson's Interlinear Hebrew Old Testament

amendment, George Washington called for a day of thanksgiving with prayer and fasting, saying that; "it was an act of divine intervention that such a diverse group of men could be so uniformity in their thoughts of expression."

The Constitution declared the origins of the natural rights and instituted a form of government where our divinely granted rights could not be compromised by mortal power. The Constitution attempted to insulate the rights of the people by restricting human nature's proclivity toward greed for power, wealth and influence. The Fathers understood that law must be divinely inspired to protect our unalienable rights. Political law is often capricious and arbitrary; natural law is not written, it already exists; it is revealed ("these truths are self-evident," "we are endowed by our Creator.") Our birth right is from God and as such it is beyond the reach of man. States began to state their own independence in their state constitutions. Many were leery of Virginia being the most populated state; they did not want to see themselves being forced to be a member of another state church, much as the Catholic Church in Rome had become the preeminent source of the Catholic faith. The individual states expressed their beliefs in their respective state constitutions.

Delaware, the first state to ratify the U.S. Constitution, stated in its 1776, state Constitution: "Every person ... appointed to any office ... shall ... subscribe ... 'I ... profess faith in God the Father, and in Jesus Christ His only Son, and in the Holy Ghost, one God, blessed for evermore; and I do acknowledge the Holy Scriptures of the Old and New Testament to be given by Divine inspiration.'"

Pennsylvania, the second state to ratify the U.S. Constitution, stated in its 1776, state Constitution, signed by Ben Franklin: "Each member, before he takes his seat, shall ... subscribe ... 'I do believe in one God, the Creator and Governor of the Universe, the Rewarder of the good and the Punisher of the wicked. And I do acknowledge the Scriptures of the Old and New Testament to be given by Divine Inspiration.'"

New Jersey, the third state to ratify the U.S. Constitution, stated in its 1776, state Constitution: "All persons, professing a belief in the faith of any Prostestant sect, who shall demean themselves peaceably under the government ... shall be capable of being elected."

Georgia, the fourth state to ratify the U.S. Constitution, stated in its 1777, state Constitution: "Representatives shall be chosen out of the residents in each county ... and they shall be of the Prostestant religion."

Connecticut, the fifth state to ratify the U.S. Constitution, retained its 1662, Colonial Constitution, which was established Prostestant Congregational, till 1818: "By the Providence of God ... having from their ancestors derived a free and excellent Constitution ... whereby the legislature depends on the free and annual election. ... The free fruition of such liberties and privileges as humanity, civility and Christianity call for."

Massachusetts, the sixth state to ratify the U.S. Constitution, stated in its 1780, state Constitution, written by John Adams: "Any person ... before he ... execute the duties of his ... office ... [shall] subscribe ... 'I ... declare, that I believe the Christian religion, and have a firm persuasion of its truth.' ... The legislature shall ... authorize the support and maintenance of public Prostestant teachers of piety, religion and morality."

Maryland, the seventh state to ratify the U.S. Constitution, stated in its 1776, state Constitution: "No other test ... ought to be required, on admission to any office ... than such oath of support and fidelity to this State ... and a declaration of a belief in the Christian religion."

South Caroline, the eighth state to ratify the U.S. Constitution, stated in its 1778, state Constitution: "No person shall be eligible to a seat ... unless he be of the Prostestant religion ... The Christian Prostestant religion shall be deemed ... the established religion of this state."

New Hampshire, the ninth state to ratify the U.S. Constitution, stated in its 1784, state Constitution: "No person shall be capable of being elected ... who is not of the Prostestant religion."

Virginia, the 10th state to ratify the U.S. Constitution, stated in its 1776, state Constitution, Bill of Rights, written with the help of James Madison and George Mason: "It is the mutual duty of all to practice Christian forbearance, love, and charity towards each other."

New York, the 11th state to ratify the U.S. Constitution, stated in its 1777, state Constitution: "The United American States ... declare ... 'Laws of nature and of Nature's God ... All men are created equal; that they are endowed by their Creator with certain unalienable rights ... Appealing to the Supreme Judge of the world ... A firm reliance on the protection of Divine Providence.' ... People of this state, ordain ... the free exercise and enjoyment of religious profession and worship, without discrimination ... Provided, That the liberty of conscience, hereby granted, shall not be so construed as to excuse acts of licentiousness (sexuality immorality)."

North Carolina, the 12th state to ratify the U.S. Constitution, stated in its 1776, state Constitution: "No person, who shall deny the being of God or the truth of the Prostestant religion, or the Divine authority either of the Old or New Testaments, or who shall hold religious principles incompatible with the freedom and safety of the State, shall be capable of holding ... office."

Rhode Island, the 13th state to ratify the U.S. Constitution, retained its 1663 Colonial Constitution till 1843, which stated: "By the blessing of God ... a full liberty in religious concernements ... rightly grounded upon Gospel principles, will give the best and greatest security ... in the true Christian faith and worship of God. ... They may ... defend themselves, in their just rights and liberties against all the enemies of the Christian faith."

The colonists having just won a war of independence were determined to establish a government that not only would prevent the creation of a monarchy but would not be patterned on the British form of government. The constitution was designed to prevent the accession of an autocrat as was the case in much of Europe. The solution was in the election of a president, and vice president, by "We The People," with executive authority, held in check by the judicial and legislative branches of the government. And as was stated in the Declaration of Independence; "deriving their just powers from the consent of the governed," and proclaiming to the world, "with a firm reliance on the protection of divine Providence." An entirely new form of government, never seen before in the history of mankind was being created, a government based on God's law.

THE CONSTITUTION OF THE UNITED STATES

If it has been a while since you read our Founding documents, it would be prudent to do so now as they probably have never made more sense than in the context of *"What The Hell Went Wrong.* "

The spelling and punctuation are as they appear in the original document.

We the People of the United States, in Order to form a more perfect Union, establish Justice, insure domestic Tranquility, provide for the common defense, promote the general Welfare, and secure the Blessings of Liberty to ourselves and our Posterity, do ordain and establish this Constitution for the United States of America.

Article. I

Section. 1.

All legislative Powers herein granted shall be vested in a Congress of the United States, which shall consist of a Senate and House of Representatives.

Section. 2.

The House of Representatives shall be composed of Members chosen every second Year by the People of the several States, and the Electors in each State shall have the Qualifications requisite for Electors of the most numerous Branch of the State Legislature.

No Person shall be a Representative who shall not have attained to the Age of twenty-five Years and been seven Years a Citizen of the United States, and who shall not, when elected, be an Inhabitant of that State in which he shall be chosen.

Representatives and direct Taxes shall be apportioned among the several States which may be included within this Union, according to their respective Numbers, which shall be determined by adding to the whole Number of free Persons, including those bound to Service for a Term of Years, and excluding Indians not taxed, three fifths of all other Persons. The actual Enumeration shall be made within three Years after the first Meeting of the Congress of the United States, and within every subsequent Term of ten Years, in such Manner as they shall by Law direct. The Number of Representatives shall not exceed one for every thirty Thousand, but each State shall have at Least one Representative; and until such enumeration shall be made, the State of New Hampshire shall be entitled to chuse three, Massachusetts eight, Rhode-Island and Providence Plantations one, Connecticut five, New-York six, New Jersey four, Pennsylvania eight, Delaware one, Maryland six, Virginia ten, North Carolina five, South Carolina five, and Georgia three.

When vacancies happen in the Representation from any State, the Executive Authority thereof shall issue Writs of Election to fill such Vacancies.

The House of Representatives shall chuse their Speaker and other Officers; and shall have the sole Power of Impeachment.

Section. 3.

The Senate of the United States shall be composed of two Senators from each State, chosen by the Legislature thereof, for six Years; and each Senator shall have one Vote. Immediately after they shall be assembled in Consequence of the first Election, they shall be divided as equally as may be into three Classes. The Seats of the Senators of the first Class shall be vacated at the Expiration of the second Year, of the second Class at the Expiration of the fourth Year, and of the third Class at the Expiration of the sixth Year, so that one third may be chosen every second Year; and if Vacancies happen by Resignation, or otherwise, during the Recess of the Legislature of any State, the Executive thereof may make temporary Appointments until the next Meeting of the Legislature, which shall then fill such Vacancies.

No Person shall be a Senator who shall not have attained to the Age of thirty Years, and been nine Years a Citizen of the United States, and who shall not, when elected, be an Inhabitant of that State for which he shall be chosen.

The Vice President of the United States shall be President of the Senate, but shall have no Vote, unless they be equally divided.

The Senate shall chuse their other Officers, and also a President pro tempore, in the Absence of the Vice President, or when he shall exercise the Office of President of the United States.

The Senate shall have the sole Power to try all Impeachments. When sitting for that Purpose, they shall be on Oath or Affirmation. When the President of the United States is tried, the Chief Justice shall preside: And no Person shall be convicted without the Concurrence of two thirds of the Members present.

Judgment in Cases of Impeachment shall not extend further than to removal from Office, and disqualification to hold and enjoy any Office of honor, Trust or Profit under the United States: but the Party convicted shall nevertheless be liable and subject to Indictment, Trial, Judgment and Punishment, according to Law.

Section. 4.

The Times, Places and Manner of holding Elections for Senators and Representatives, shall be prescribed in each State by the Legislature thereof; but the Congress may at any time by Law make or alter such Regulations, except as to the Places of chusing Senators.

The Congress shall assemble at least once in every Year, and such Meeting shall be on the first Monday in December, unless they shall by Law appoint a different Day.

Section. 5.

Each House shall be the Judge of the Elections, Returns and Qualifications of its own Members, and a Majority of each shall constitute a Quorum to do Business; but a smaller Number may adjourn from day to day, and may be authorized to compel the Attendance of absent Members, in such Manner, and under such Penalties as each House may provide.

Each House may determine the Rules of its Proceedings, punish its Members for disorderly Behaviour, and, with the Concurrence of two thirds, expel a Member.

Each House shall keep a Journal of its Proceedings, and from time to time publish the same, excepting such Parts as may in their Judgment require Secrecy; and the Yeas and Nays of the Members of either House on any question shall, at the Desire of one fifth of those Present, be entered on the Journal.

Neither House, during the Session of Congress, shall, without the Consent of the other, adjourn for more than three days, nor to any other Place than that in which the two Houses shall be sitting.

Section. 6.

The Senators and Representatives shall receive a Compensation for their Services, to be ascertained by Law, and paid out of the Treasury of the United States. They shall in all Cases, except Treason, Felony and Breach of the Peace, be privileged from Arrest during their Attendance at the Session of their respective Houses, and in going to and returning from the same; and for any Speech or Debate in either House, they shall not be questioned in any other Place.

No Senator or Representative shall, during the Time for which he was elected, be appointed to any civil Office under the Authority of the United States, which shall have been created, or the Emoluments whereof shall have been encreased during such time; and no Person holding any Office under the United States, shall be a Member of either House during his Continuance in Office.

Section. 7.

All Bills for raising Revenue shall originate in the House of Representatives; but the Senate may propose or concur with Amendments as on other Bills.

Every Bill which shall have passed the House of Representatives and the Senate, shall, before it become a Law, be presented to the President of the United States; If he approve he shall sign it, but if not he shall return it, with his Objections to that House in which it shall have originated, who shall enter the Objections at large on their Journal, and proceed to reconsider it. If after such Reconsideration two thirds of that House shall agree to pass the Bill, it shall be sent, together with the Objections, to the other House, by which it shall likewise be reconsidered, and if approved by two thirds of that House, it shall become a Law. But in all such Cases the Votes of both Houses shall be determined by yeas and Nays, and the Names of the Persons voting for and against the Bill shall be entered on the Journal of each House respectively. If any Bill shall not be returned by the President within ten Days (Sundays excepted) after it shall have been presented to him, the Same shall be a Law, in like Manner as if he had signed it, unless the Congress by their Adjournment prevent its Return, in which Case it shall not be a Law.

Every Order, Resolution, or Vote to which the Concurrence of the Senate and House of Representatives may be necessary (except on a question of Adjournment) shall be presented to the President of the United States; and before the Same shall take Effect, shall be approved by him, or being disapproved by him, shall be repassed by two thirds of the Senate and House of Representatives, according to the Rules and Limitations prescribed in the Case of a Bill.

Section. 8.

The Congress shall have Power To lay and collect Taxes, Duties, Imposts and Excises, to pay the Debts and provide for the common Defence and general Welfare of the United States; but all Duties, Imposts and Excises shall be uniform throughout the United States;

To borrow Money on the credit of the United States;

To regulate Commerce with foreign Nations, and among the several States, and with the Indian Tribes;

To establish an uniform Rule of Naturalization, and uniform Laws on the subject of Bankruptcies throughout the United States;

To coin Money, regulate the Value thereof, and of foreign Coin, and fix the Standard of Weights and Measures;

To provide for the Punishment of counterfeiting the Securities and current Coin of the United States;

To establish Post Offices and post Roads;

To promote the Progress of Science and useful Arts, by securing for limited Times to Authors and Inventors the exclusive Right to their respective Writings and Discoveries;

To constitute Tribunals inferior to the supreme Court;

To define and punish Piracies and Felonies committed on the high Seas, and Offences against the Law of Nations;

To declare War, grant Letters of Marque and Reprisal, and make Rules concerning Captures on Land and Water;

To raise and support Armies, but no Appropriation of Money to that Use shall be for a longer Term than two Years;

To provide and maintain a Navy;

To make Rules for the Government and Regulation of the land and naval Forces;

To provide for calling forth the Militia to execute the Laws of the Union, suppress Insurrections and repel Invasions;

To provide for organizing, arming, and disciplining, the Militia, and for governing such Part of them as may be employed in the Service of the United States, reserving to the States respectively, the Appointment of the Officers, and the Authority of training the Militia according to the discipline prescribed by Congress;

To exercise exclusive Legislation in all Cases whatsoever, over such District (not exceeding ten Miles square) as may, by Cession of particular States, and the Acceptance of Congress, become the Seat of the Government of the United States, and to exercise like Authority over all Places purchased by the Consent of the Legislature of the State in which the Same shall be, for the Erection of Forts, Magazines, Arsenals, dock-Yards, and other needful Buildings;—And

To make all Laws which shall be necessary and proper for carrying into Execution the foregoing Powers, and all other Powers vested by this Constitution in the Government of the United States, or in any Department or Officer thereof.

Section. 9.

The Migration or Importation of such Persons as any of the States now existing shall think proper to admit, shall not be prohibited by the Congress prior to the Year one thousand eight hundred and eight, but a Tax or duty may be imposed on such Importation, not exceeding ten dollars for each Person.

The Privilege of the Writ of Habeas Corpus shall not be suspended, unless when in Cases of Rebellion or Invasion the public Safety may require it.

No Bill of Attainder or ex post facto Law shall be passed.

No Capitation, or other direct, Tax shall be laid, unless in Proportion to the Census or enumeration herein before directed to be taken.

No Tax or Duty shall be laid on Articles exported from any State.

No Preference shall be given by any Regulation of Commerce or Revenue to the Ports of one State over those of another: nor shall Vessels bound to, or from, one State, be obliged to enter, clear, or pay Duties in another.

No Money shall be drawn from the Treasury, but in Consequence of Appropriations made by Law; and a regular Statement and Account of the

Receipts and Expenditures of all public Money shall be published from time to time.

No Title of Nobility shall be granted by the United States: And no Person holding any Office of Profit or Trust under them, shall, without the Consent of the Congress, accept of any present, Emolument, Office, or Title, of any kind whatever, from any King, Prince, or foreign State.

Section. 10.

No State shall enter into any Treaty, Alliance, or Confederation; grant Letters of Marque and Reprisal; coin Money; emit Bills of Credit; make any Thing but gold and silver Coin a Tender in Payment of Debts; pass any Bill of Attainder, ex post facto Law, or Law impairing the Obligation of Contracts, or grant any Title of Nobility.

No State shall, without the Consent of the Congress, lay any Imposts or Duties on Imports or Exports, except what may be absolutely necessary for executing it's inspection Laws: and the net Produce of all Duties and Imposts, laid by any State on Imports or Exports, shall be for the Use of the Treasury of the United States; and all such Laws shall be subject to the Revision and Controul of the Congress.

No State shall, without the Consent of Congress, lay any Duty of Tonnage, keep Troops, or Ships of War in time of Peace, enter into any Agreement or Compact with another State, or with a foreign Power, or engage in War, unless actually invaded, or in such imminent Danger as will not admit of delay.

Article. II.

Section. 1.

The executive Power shall be vested in a President of the United States of America. He shall hold his Office during the Term of four Years, and, together with the Vice President, chosen for the same Term, be elected, as follows

Each State shall appoint, in such Manner as the Legislature thereof may direct, a Number of Electors, equal to the whole Number of Senators and Representatives to which the State may be entitled in the Congress: but no Senator or Representative, or Person holding an Office of Trust or Profit under the United States, shall be appointed an Elector.

The Electors shall meet in their respective States, and vote by Ballot for two Persons, of whom one at least shall not be an Inhabitant of the same State with themselves. And they shall make a List of all the Persons voted for, and of the Number of Votes for each; which List they shall sign and certify, and transmit sealed to the Seat of the Government of the United

States, directed to the President of the Senate. The President of the Senate shall, in the Presence of the Senate and House of Representatives, open all the Certificates, and the Votes shall then be counted. The Person having the greatest Number of Votes shall be the President, if such Number be a Majority of the whole Number of Electors appointed; and if there be more than one who have such Majority, and have an equal Number of Votes, then the House of Representatives shall immediately chuse by Ballot one of them for President; and if no Person have a Majority, then from the five highest on the List the said House shall in like Manner chuse the President. But in chusing the President, the Votes shall be taken by States, the Representation from each State having one Vote; A quorum for this Purpose shall consist of a Member or Members from two thirds of the States, and a Majority of all the States shall be necessary to a Choice. In every Case, after the Choice of the President, the Person having the greatest Number of Votes of the Electors shall be the Vice President. But if there should remain two or more who have equal Votes, the Senate shall chuse from them by Ballot the Vice President.

The Congress may determine the Time of chusing the Electors, and the Day on which they shall give their Votes; which Day shall be the same throughout the United States.

No Person except a natural born Citizen, or a Citizen of the United States, at the time of the Adoption of this Constitution, shall be eligible to the Office of President; neither shall any Person be eligible to that Office who shall not have attained to the Age of thirty five Years, and been fourteen Years a Resident within the United States.

In Case of the Removal of the President from Office, or of his Death, Resignation, or Inability to discharge the Powers and Duties of the said Office, the Same shall devolve on the Vice President, and the Congress may by Law provide for the Case of Removal, Death, Resignation or Inability, both of the President and Vice President, declaring what Officer shall then act as President, and such Officer shall act accordingly, until the Disability be removed, or a President shall be elected.

The President shall, at stated Times, receive for his Services, a Compensation, which shall neither be encreased nor diminished during the Period for which he shall have been elected, and he shall not receive within that Period any other Emolument from the United States, or any of them.

Before he enter on the Execution of his Office, he shall take the following Oath or Affirmation:—"I do solemnly swear (or affirm) that I will faithfully execute the Office of President of the United States, and will to the best of my Ability, preserve, protect and defend the Constitution of the United States."

Section. 2.

The President shall be Commander in Chief of the Army and Navy of the United States, and of the Militia of the several States, when called into the actual Service of the United States; he may require the Opinion, in writing, of the principal Officer in each of the executive Departments, upon any Subject relating to the Duties of their respective Offices, and he shall have Power to grant Reprieves and Pardons for Offences against the United States, except in Cases of Impeachment.

He shall have Power, by and with the Advice and Consent of the Senate, to make Treaties, provided two thirds of the Senators present concur; and he shall nominate, and by and with the Advice and Consent of the Senate, shall appoint Ambassadors, other public Ministers and Consuls, Judges of the supreme Court, and all other Officers of the United States, whose Appointments are not herein otherwise provided for, and which shall be established by Law: but the Congress may by Law vest the Appointment of such inferior Officers, as they think proper, in the President alone, in the Courts of Law, or in the Heads of Departments.

The President shall have Power to fill up all Vacancies that may happen during the Recess of the Senate, by granting Commissions which shall expire at the End of their next Session.

Section. 3.

He shall from time to time give to the Congress Information of the State of the Union, and recommend to their Consideration such Measures as he shall judge necessary and expedient; he may, on extraordinary Occasions, convene both Houses, or either of them, and in Case of Disagreement between them, with Respect to the Time of Adjournment, he may adjourn them to such Time as he shall think proper; he shall receive Ambassadors and other public Ministers; he shall take Care that the Laws be faithfully executed, and shall Commission all the Officers of the United States.

Section. 4.

The President, Vice President and all civil Officers of the United States, shall be removed from Office on Impeachment for, and Conviction of, Treason, Bribery, or other high Crimes and Misdemeanors.

Article. III.

Section. 1.

The judicial Power of the United States, shall be vested in one supreme Court, and in such inferior Courts as the Congress may from time to time ordain and establish. The Judges, both of the supreme and inferior Courts, shall hold their Offices during good Behaviour, and shall, at stated Times, receive for their Services, a Compensation, which shall not be diminished during their Continuance in Office.

Section. 2.

The judicial Power shall extend to all Cases, in Law and Equity, arising under this Constitution, the Laws of the United States, and Treaties made, or which shall be made, under their Authority;—to all Cases affecting Ambassadors, other public Ministers and Consuls;—to all Cases of admiralty and maritime Jurisdiction;—to Controversies to which the United States shall be a Party;—to Controversies between two or more States;— between a State and Citizens of another State,—between Citizens of different States,—between Citizens of the same State claiming Lands under Grants of different States, and between a State, or the Citizens thereof, and foreign States, Citizens or Subjects.

In all Cases affecting Ambassadors, other public Ministers and Consuls, and those in which a State shall be Party, the supreme Court shall have original Jurisdiction. In all the other Cases before mentioned, the supreme Court shall have appellate Jurisdiction, both as to Law and Fact, with such Exceptions, and under such Regulations as the Congress shall make.

The Trial of all Crimes, except in Cases of Impeachment, shall be by Jury; and such Trial shall be held in the State where the said Crimes shall have been committed; but when not committed within any State, the Trial shall be at such Place or Places as the Congress may by Law have directed.

Section. 3.

Treason against the United States, shall consist only in levying War against them, or in adhering to their Enemies, giving them Aid and Comfort. No Person shall be convicted of Treason unless on the Testimony of two Witnesses to the same overt Act, or on Confession in open Court.

The Congress shall have Power to declare the Punishment of Treason, but no Attainder of Treason shall work Corruption of Blood, or Forfeiture except during the Life of the Person attainted.

Article. IV.

Section. 1.

Full Faith and Credit shall be given in each State to the public Acts, Records, and judicial Proceedings of every other State. And the Congress may by general Laws prescribe the Manner in which such Acts, Records and Proceedings shall be proved, and the Effect thereof.

Section. 2.

The Citizens of each State shall be entitled to all Privileges and Immunities of Citizens in the several States.

A Person charged in any State with Treason, Felony, or other Crime, who shall flee from Justice, and be found in another State, shall on Demand of the executive Authority of the State from which he fled, be delivered up, to be removed to the State having Jurisdiction of the Crime.

No Person held to Service or Labour in one State, under the Laws thereof, escaping into another, shall, in Consequence of any Law or Regulation therein, be discharged from such Service or Labour, but shall be delivered up on Claim of the Party to whom such Service or Labour may be due.

Section. 3.

New States may be admitted by the Congress into this Union; but no new State shall be formed or erected within the Jurisdiction of any other State; nor any State be formed by the Junction of two or more States, or Parts of States, without the Consent of the Legislatures of the States concerned as well as of the Congress.

The Congress shall have Power to dispose of and make all needful Rules and Regulations respecting the Territory or other Property belonging to the United States; and nothing in this Constitution shall be so construed as to Prejudice any Claims of the United States, or of any particular State.

Section. 4.

The United States shall guarantee to every State in this Union a Republican Form of Government, and shall protect each of them against Invasion; and on Application of the Legislature, or of the Executive (when the Legislature cannot be convened), against domestic Violence.

Article. V.

The Congress, whenever two thirds of both Houses shall deem it necessary, shall propose Amendments to this Constitution, or, on the Application of the Legislatures of two thirds of the several States, shall call a Convention for proposing Amendments, which, in either Case, shall be valid to all Intents and Purposes, as Part of this Constitution, when ratified by the Legislatures of three fourths of the several States, or by Conventions in three fourths thereof, as the one or the other Mode of Ratification may be proposed by the Congress; Provided that no Amendment which may be made prior to the Year One thousand eight hundred and eight shall in any Manner affect the first and fourth Clauses in the Ninth Section of the first Article; and that no State, without its Consent, shall be deprived of its equal Suffrage in the Senate.

Article. VI.

All Debts contracted and Engagements entered into, before the Adoption of this Constitution, shall be as valid against the United States under this Constitution, as under the Confederation.

This Constitution, and the Laws of the United States which shall be made in Pursuance thereof; and all Treaties made, or which shall be made, under the Authority of the United States, shall be the supreme Law of the Land; and the Judges in every State shall be bound thereby, any Thing in the Constitution or Laws of any State to the Contrary notwithstanding.

The Senators and Representatives before mentioned, and the Members of the several State Legislatures, and all executive and judicial Officers, both of the United States and of the several States, shall be bound by Oath or Affirmation, to support this Constitution; but no religious Test shall ever be required as a Qualification to any Office or public Trust under the United States.

Article. VII.

The Ratification of the Conventions of nine States, shall be sufficient for the Establishment of this Constitution between the States so ratifying the Same.

Attest William Jackson Secretary

In Convention by the Unanimous Consent of the States present the Seventeenth Day of September in the Year of our Lord one thousand seven hundred and Eighty-seven and of the Independence of the United States of America the Twelfth In witness whereof We have hereunto subscribed our Names,

The federalists and anti-federalists finally came to terms and the Constitution in its final form was signed by the members of congress. The document was printed and sent to the states for ratification. However, when, "We the People," read and understood the document, concerns arose.

The colonists had come to America as British citizens however, the way they were treated, being taxes without representation, illegal search and seizure, confiscation of firearms and gun powder and all of the grievances listed in the Declaration of Independence felt they had been stripped of their rights. They understood how the government was to be formed and they understood the checks and balances that were in place. However, not wanting to see a recurrence by the new government of what had just occurred with Britain they wanted to know what protected their rights; the rights of, "We The People."

The population at this time was ninety-eight percent Protestant, two percent Catholic and there were about 200,000 Jews. Each state had its own preferred religious denomination and its one state preferred religion. Virginia was the most populated state and carried the most weight. The state church of Virginia was the Anglican church. Some of the states would not ratify the Constitution until, "We the People," were assured their rights were protected.

James Madison who wrote the Constitution developed a list if nineteen rights for the individual citizen. Nine of the new additions to the Constitution were removed. The Congress finally agreed on a list of ten, termed the Bill of Rights and they were added to the Constitution.

THE BILL OF RIGHTS

Amendment I

Congress shall make no law respecting an establishment of religion or prohibiting the free exercise thereof; or abridging the freedom of speech, or of the press; or the right of the people peaceably to assemble, and to petition the government for a redress of grievances.

Amendment II

A well regulated militia, being necessary to the security of a free state, the right of the people to keep and bear arms, shall not be infringed.

Amendment III

No soldier shall, in time of peace be quartered in any house, without the consent of the owner, nor in time of war, but in a manner to be prescribed by law.

Amendment IV

The right of the people to be secure in their persons, houses, papers, and effects, against unreasonable searches and seizures, shall not be violated, and no warrants shall issue, but upon probable cause, supported by oath or affirmation, and particularly describing the place to be searched, and the persons or things to be seized.

Amendment V

No person shall be held to answer for a capital, or otherwise infamous crime, unless on a presentment or indictment of a grand jury, except in cases arising in the land or naval forces, or in the militia, when in actual service in time of war or public danger; nor shall any person be subject for the same offense to be twice put in jeopardy of life or limb; nor shall be compelled in any criminal case to be a witness against himself, nor be deprived of life, liberty, or property, without due process of law; nor shall private property be taken for public use, without just compensation.

Amendment VI

In all criminal prosecutions, the accused shall enjoy the right to a speedy and public trial, by an impartial jury of the state and district wherein the crime shall have been committed, which district shall have been previously ascertained by law, and to be informed of the nature and cause of the accusation; to be confronted with the witnesses against him; to have compulsory process for obtaining witnesses in his favor, and to have the assistance of counsel for his defense.

Amendment VII

In suits at common law, where the value in controversy shall exceed twenty dollars, the right of trial by jury shall be preserved, and no fact tried by a jury, shall be otherwise reexamined in any court of the United States, than according to the rules of the common law.

Amendment VIII

Excessive bail shall not be required, nor excessive fines imposed, nor cruel and unusual punishments inflicted.

Amendment IX

The enumeration in the Constitution, of certain rights, shall not be construed to deny or disparage others retained by the people.

Amendment X

The powers not delegated to the United States by the Constitution, nor prohibited by it to the states, are reserved to the states respectively, or to the people.

In an October 13, 1789, address to the military, John Adams said: "We have no government armed with power capable of contending with human passions unbridled by morality and religion. Avarice, ambition, revenge, or gallantry would break the strongest cords of our Constitution as a whale goes through a net. *Our Constitution was made only for a moral and religious people. It is wholly inadequate to the government of any other."*

In a letter to Thomas Jefferson dated June 28, 1813, Adams wrote: "The general principles on which the fathers achieved independence were the general principles of Christianity"

On September 3, 1783, Britain recognized American independence with the signing of the Treaty of Paris. By November 25, the British evacuated New York City. On December 23, 1783, General George Washington retired his commission as commander of the Continental Army and retired to his home at Mount Vernon.

In 1787, James Madison, prevailed upon George Washington to come out of retirement to attend the Constitutional Convention to be held in Philadelphia starting on May 25th. George Washington obliged Madison and upon arrival was voted to preside over the proceedings. The convention concluded with the signing of the US Constitution on September 17, 1787; the Constitution was adopted by the states in 1788.

THE FORMATION OF A NATION

The convention delegates decided they would elect the first president and establish a voting process during the first term. The delegates were confident that George Washington would be elected because of the leadership he had demonstrated during the Revolutionary War and bringing them victory against seemingly impossible odds. They were very prayerful he would be elected as what the new government would look like had yet to be defined. Washington had formed an army and a quasi-navy, defeated the major world power through his vision and leadership. He had also guided the Constitutional Convention to a successful conclusion in producing the document forming a national government.

On February 4, 1789, the delegates to the convention cast votes for the first president of the United States. George Washington, uncertain of the outcome departed for Mount Vernon. George Washington looked forward to retirement at Mount Vernon after over a decade of public service, without pay, and being away from his home with only infrequently visits to see his wife Martha. A quorum of the delegates was finally reached on April 5th and the votes were counted. George Washington was the clear winner; John Adams had the second highest vote count and became vice-president. Word was sent to Washington at Mount Vernon; he was reluctant to accept the presidency. However, as he was concerned about the partisan differences forming in the senate and thought, without resolution, they may undermine republicanism, or deliberations could result in a monarchal government. Weighing the possibility of either of these undesirable outcomes George Washington accept the result of the delegate voting and traveled to Philadelphia to accept the presidency.

George Washington was inaugurated as the first president of the United States of America on April 30, 1789. He ended his oath of office with the unscripted; "So help me God," his first precedent. Washington knew one of his primary responsibilities would be defining the character of the office of the first constitutional republic; in his words; "I walk on untrodden ground." In his first remarks to the Senate, at their first session, President Washington remarked; "that Almighty being who rules over the universe, who presides in the council of nations, and whose providential aids can supply every human defect, consecrate the liberties and happiness of the people of the United States."

The Supreme Court would convene for the first time the following year; with one Chief Justice and five associate justices.

The Senate suggested Washington's title should be, "His Highness the President of the United States and the Protector of Liberties." Washington wrote to James Madison: "As the first of everything in our situation will serve to establish a precedent, it is devoutly wished on my part that these proceedings be fixed on true principles." To that end that Mr. President should suffice.

The Senate also voted to create cabinet offices; Secretary of State, whom Washington appointed John Jay. However, Jay vacated the post to become the first chief justice of the Supreme Court and was replaced by Thomas Jefferson. Washington appointed Henry Knox as Secretary of War and Alexander Hamilton as the Secretary of the Treasury. President Washington appointed Edmund Randolph as Attorney General and Samuel Osgood as Postmaster General. The cabinet became a consulting and advisory board, not mandated by the Constitution, but authorized by Congress. In 1790, the first census was taking showing America's population at three million, nine hundred thousand. In 1791, the Bill of Rights would be added to the Constitution.

Alexander Hamilton favored a national bank, with the authority to print money, raise taxes, and to make loans. He also favored a strong federal government. Thomas Jefferson favored strong state governments and opposed the national bank. These two diametrically opposed ideologies would bring about a two-party system, which Washington opposed. The two parties that emerged were the Hamilton Federalists and the Jeffersonian Republicans.

President Washington was coming into office of a new country fledging to define its character. America had a large war debt with no means or plans to repay it. President Washington did not have the power to tax and the nations paper money was worthless. Britain had left the east coast, however, they refused to give up their occupation and forts in the American west. Britain was still restricting American trade abroad. When America tried to circumvent British trade restrictions by trading with southern Europe through the trade routes of the Mediterranean Sea our merchant vessels were attacked by the Muslim Barbary Pirates, America was defenseless without a navy; and now as an independent nation they no longer had British protection of their merchant vessels.

The Muslim Barbary Pirates

The Barbary Pirates were from the four Muslim Barbary States of the Ottoman Empire located in North Africa: Tripoli, Algeria, Morocco and Tunis. The Muslim pirates would raid merchant ships from around the world that entered the Mediterranean Sea, steal the cargo and imprison the sailors and bribe nations for safe passage; the bribes were paid but safe passage was a rare exception. The sailors were held for ransom; if payment was not forthcoming the captured sailors were enslaved at hard labor. The Muslim Barbary States funded their governments from: tributes collected from other countries, ransom for captured sailors and stolen cargo. The Muslim pirates also raided the coastal villages as far as Europe and Iceland to capture slaves to be sold in the Ottoman slave markets in Africa.

Britain, Spain, France, Portugal and the Dutch paid the bribes to the Muslim Barbary Pirates, called tribute, because their merchant ships would be protected by their own navies, and the nations that could not afford the tributes avoided the Mediterranean, thereby limiting the competition for trade.

Without an army or a navy in 1784, America paid $80,000.00 to the Muslim Barbary Pirates for safe passage. Thomas Jefferson, John Adams and Benjamin Franklin sailed to England to meet with the ambassador from Tripoli. Thomas Jefferson asked the ambassador what gave the pirates the right to attack American merchant shipping. To which he replied; "It was written in their Qú ran, that all nations which had not acknowledged the Prophet were sinners, whom it was the right and duty of the faithful to plunder and enslave; and that every mussulman who was slain in this warfare was sure to go to paradise." The $80,000.00 America paid the Muslims freed Americans being held prisoner but did not stop the raids on American merchant ships. On their return from London Jefferson urged President Washington to build a navy and take a stand against the Muslims. John Adams disagreed and said; "We ought not fight them at all, unless we determine to fight them forever."

As a time, reference, because we have already covered the French Revolution which began in 1789, while George Washington was president.

America's First Presidents

President Washington was elected to a second term in 1793. America did not immediately act on the Muslim Pirates until in 1794, when payments to the Muslims reached 20 percent of Americas GDP. That year President Washington authorized the building of six frigates with a compliment of fighting men, reinstituting the US marines. The frigates were heavily outnumbered and saw limited success, a bigger navy was needed. However, President Washington did send a statement to the world: America will not be taken advantage of; we will stand up for our rights and if that means armed conflict, so be it.

President Washington, in his second term, sought to resolve some of the issues that were still unresolved by the 1873, Treaty of Paris, signed with Britain ending the American Revolutionary War. Britain had agreed to abandon the forts in US territory, they had not. Britain continued trade restrictions on the US including banning trade with the West Indies. The British navy continued to seize American ships and "impress" US sailors. President Washington sent John Jay to London to resolve these unresolved issues. The result was the Jay's Treaty of 1794. None of the intended issues were resolved; all that was accomplished was ten years of peace with Great Britain while America was able to build an economy based primarily on agriculture, ship building and fishing. The treaty received a lot of criticism from the American people; especially in that nothing had changed regarding American ships being seized, sailors being impressed, and Britain remained on U.S. soil in the Ohio River Valley. Thomas Jefferson demanded congress declare war on Britain, which fell on deaf ears.

In 1796, President Washington informed the nation; he would not serve a third term as president. He was an advocate of limited time in office as a means of keeping elected officials accountable to "We The People." King George III said President Washington was the greatest leader on earth because he willingly gave up his power. Every other leader: fights, schemes, threatens and bribes to stay in power. Truly it was a government of the people. By President Washington declining to run for a third term he demonstrated to the world that America was like no other country or government on earth. When leaving office President warned congress and America that the United States should not borrow money from other nations, thereby, becoming indebted to them; and we should not form alliances with other nations which would only embroil us in affairs of other nations and would force us to take sides. He also thought that America had too many domestic issues, too small of an army, virtually no navy, and therefore to vulnerable to engage in any strident foreign policy.

President Washington was adamantly opposed to the idea of political parties that would divide the nation; and he saw them forming in his own cabinet.

John Adams was elected as the second president of the United States in 1797, receiving the second most votes, Thomas Jefferson was his vice-president. In 1798, Britain declared war on France. President Adams continued the determination of President Washington to remain a country of neutrality in the affairs of other nations. However, the agreement between Britain and America, Jay's Treaty, upset French officials as they saw the treaty as America siding with Britain and in violation of the alliance they had signed with America during the Revolutionary War. President Adams, to try and calm the waters, sent a delegation led by John Marshall to France. The three French representatives that met with the American delegation stated that in order to have a meeting with Frances Foreign Minister, Charles de Talleyrand, they would first agree to three conditions; guarantee a low interest loan to France, make a payment of $250,000.00 to Talleyrand and the U.S. had to reimburse France and its merchants for damage to any French vessel. The American delegation immediately departed for the United States and reported to President Adams.

President Adams reported the disastrous diplomatic effort to congress by stating; "I will never send another minister to France without assurances that he will be received, respected, and honored as a representative of a great, free, powerful, and independent nation." In a report President Adams prepared for congress he replaced the names of the French delegation's names with the letters; X, Y and Z. This became known as the X,Y, Z affair. France, in response, began what became known as the "Quasi War," although no war was declared France began aggressively attacking American merchant vessels. American merchant ships were still being attacked by the Muslims in the Mediterranean; which had become even more vital for American trade as United States merchant vessels were now being attack by France, and Britain. President Adams realized the great peril to the American economy caused by the decreasing ability of America to engage in trade with other nations. Adams ordered the construction of ships of war to build a U.S. Navy. However, it would take time to build a navy. President Adams because of his inability to protect American merchant shipping from Britain, France and the Barbary Pirates, remove Britain from the Ohio Valley or stop impressment of U.S. sailors was perceived as a weak president and lost his bid for reelection to Thomas Jefferson.

Thomas Jefferson running as a Democrat-Republican ran against fellow party member Aaron Burr, both received 73 votes and Adams received 63. The House of Representatives broke the tie and voted Thomas Jefferson as the third president of the United States. Because of the tie Congress proposed the twelfth Amendment to the Constitution; requiring separate voting for the president and vice-president. The Amendment was ratified in 1804.

John Adams was of the Federalists Party, with his defeat the peaceful transition of one party to another was a landmark transfer of power not seen anywhere else in the world.

Just before President Jefferson's inauguration congress passed naval legislation that provided for six frigates that; "shall be officered and manned as the President of the United States may direct..."

The development of America's industries was driven by resources and climate. The south was well suited for agriculture because of the long growing season, favorable temperatures and precipitation. Crops of tobacco, sugar cane, cotton and rice met the demands of the European markets. A fishing industry grew out of the preternatural cod population from Maine to Newfoundland. Shipbuilding grew out of a need for fishing boats, then merchant vessels for trade and finally ships for the U.S. Navy.

A 150-ton ship would require 200 workers. Shipbuilding requires carpenters, painters, sail makers, blacksmiths, coppers; as the ship's hulls were coated with corrosion resistant copper. Shipbuilding also required iron, which birthed the coal industry, and foundries. There grew a tremendous need for rope for ship rigging. The wood for the ships were in abundant supply and this necessitated logging and lumber mills. There also was the creation of an infrastructure and a transportation industry to haul the wood from the lumber mills to the port cities where the shipyards were located. The very hard American oak was well suited for ship building. American ships were soon the best built ships in the world. Because of the abundance of labor and American Oak the ships were also very competitively priced. An American ship could be built for $36.00 per ton, whereas ships from England, France and Holland cost $55.00 per ton. American ships of oak were very rugged, inexpensively built and in large demand by other countries, which became an industry in itself. In the War of 1812, the USS Constitution was given the name "old iron sides" because the cannon balls from the British warships bounced off her oak sides. The USS Constitution was named by President George Washington and was one of the first six frigates commissioned by congress in the Naval Act of 1794. By 1750 America had 125 shipyards in: Massachusetts, Virginia, Maryland, Delaware, Maine, New Hampshire, Connecticut, Rhode Island and Vermont. During the 1700's American ship builders produced over 1,000 ships.

Upon President Jefferson's inauguration in 1801 Muslim Barbary Pirates demanded $225,000.00, plus an annual tribute of $25,000.00 of the new president. The $225,000.00 represents 3.4 million dollars in today's money when U.S. annual revenues were 10 million dollars. When President Jefferson refused, the Pasha of Tripoli, declared war on the United States, the first declared war on the newly established nation. In his first annual message to congress on December 8, 1801, Jefferson told congress: "Tripoli, the least considerable of the Barbary States, had come forward with demands unfounded either in right or in compact, and had permitted itself to declare war on our failure to comply before a given day. The style of the demand admitted but one answer. I sent a small squadron of frigates into the Mediterranean, with assurances to that power of our sincere desire to remain in peace, but with orders to protect our commerce against the threatened attack." Although the Muslim Barbary Pirates had been raiding merchant ships for centuries; American merchant ships had been under the protection of the Royal Navy until we gained our independence. Without that protection American merchant ships now fell prey.

The USS Frigates were sent to the Mediterranean to blockade the port of Tripoli, however, there were too few ships for an effective blockage. Sweden had been at war with the Muslim Pirates since 1800, because of the U.S. small navy they joined forces to combat the Muslims. The USS Philadelphia ran aground on an uncharted reef and was captured by Muslim Barbary Pirates her officers and crew were taken as prisoners. On the night of February 16, 1804, Lieutenant Stephen Decatur led a force of seventy-five sailors in a captured fishing boat alongside the USS Philadelphia. Within ten minutes they overpowered the crew, killing some but, most dove overboard. They set fire to fuses leading to the barrels of gunpowder in the ship's magazine. As they rowed away from the Philadelphia there was a tremendous explosion, the ship burst into flames, the sky lit up and the escaping vessel was illuminated against the black sky and the dark waters. The 150 cannons from the walled city opened fire as did the twenty-four pirate ships at anchor. Miraculously, not a single cannon ball hit the escaping vessel.

The turning point in the war was the Battle of Derna (April–May 1805). Ex-consul William Eaton, a former Army captain and US Marine Corps 1st Lieutenant Presley O'Bannon, with eight marines, located the Pasha's brother, Hamet, in Egypt. Yusuf killed his older brother so that he could be Pasha, and Hamet went into exile. Eaton convinced Hamet to recruit an army of mercenaries and they would take Tripoli and make him Pasha. The ad hoc army marched 500 miles across the Sahara Desert to Derna, a neighboring town to Tripoli. Three US navy vessels bombarded the city and the marines and mercenaries stormed they city, capturing it with ease. This was the first time the United States flag was raised in victory on foreign soil, thus in the marine hymn, "the shores of Tripoli." Pasha Yusuf capitulated and signed a peace treaty with the United States, thus ending the U.S. war with the Muslim Barbary Pirates. Eaton was bitterly disappointed that he had promised Hamet the throne and was unable to deliver on his promise. This was also the first joint operation between American land and sea forces.

During the drafting of the Declaration of Independence, Thomas Jefferson had included language that condemned Britain for forcing slavery on the colonies. The language was removed as some thought the language was inflammatory and may turn those in parliament in favor of American Independence to the opposing position. Among King George's grievances Thomas Jefferson wrote;

""he has waged cruel war against human nature itself, violating its most sacred rights of life and liberty in the persons of a distant people who never offended him, captivating & carrying them into slavery in another hemisphere, or to incur miserable death in their transportation thither."

Jefferson, in London at the drafting of the Constitution, sent recommendations, although they arrived after the Constitution was signed. He later in 1783 proposed them for the State Constitution for Virginia;

279

"The General assembly shall not have to power to ...permit the introduction of any more slaves to reside in this state, or the continuance of slavery beyond the generation which shall be living on the 31st day of December 1800; all persons born after that day being hereby declared free."

Jefferson had also proposed Constitution restrictions that would prevent politicians from running for reelection and would have defined rights for native Americans.

At this early date Georgia and the Carolinas threatened to succeed from the union if the issue of emancipation was pursued by the government.

By 1804, there were no slaves in the northern colonies and in 1805, President Jefferson sent U.S. Frigates to capture Barbary slave ships, return them to their port of origin, and release the slaves.

President Jefferson was in a dilemma, his desires was to end slavery, but he feared a civil war would destroy America before it had a chance to become fully established and stable enough to endure such a cataclysmic event. He wasn't alone, President Washington denounced slavery as repugnant, although he had inherited slaves, Virginia law made it illegal to free slaves. He would however, free all of his slaves in the last will and testimony. James Mason condemned slavery as "evil." Jefferson, himself called slavery, "a hideous blot" on America.

President Jefferson realized his opportunity with the Louisiana Purchase. France had surrendered its North American possessions at the end of the French and Indian War. New Orleans and Louisiana west of the Mississippi River were transferred to Spain in 1762. French territories east of the Mississippi River, including Canada were ceded to Britain in 1763. Napoleon Bonaparte seized power in France in 1799. By 1800 rumors of war between England and France were again putting Europe on edge. Spain would align itself with France and unsure of its ability to hold its territory in North America, King Charles IV transferred its holdings to France in October of 1802, and revoked America's access to the port city of New Orleans and its warehouses. President Jefferson sent James Monroe to Paris with plans drawn up by James Madison to offer Napoleon 10 million dollars for New Orleans and lands east to and including Florida. If that could not be arranged, then he was to offer 10 million for just New Orleans and if that failed renegotiate shipping rights to the Mississippi and the port city.

By the time Monroe arrived in Paris a completely different offer was on the table. Napoleon had sent his forces to quell a slave rebellion in Haiti, Frances riches colony, only to see his forces wiped out by yellow fever. Napoleon's war council had advised him that if war did break out with Britain, which Napoleon knew was inevitable as he was soon to begin his conquest of Europe, Britain with troops in Canada could occupy the land forcing Napoleon to fight on two continents. They advised Napoleon to sell his holdings in America to help finance a war and limit the engagement to Europe, Napoleon agreed. In 1803, Britain again declared war on France. Napoleon stopped the Qazi-War with the United States to conserve his resources, especially his navy.

Monroe entered negotiations with the French Foreign Minister Talleyrand, they agreed on 15 million dollars for the entire area held by France. Monroe authorized to spend 10 million, exceeded his authority by agreeing to the 15-million-dollar purchase price. The Louisiana Purchase doubled the size of America; adding 828,000 square miles at about .03 ¢ per acre: from the Mississippi River, to the Rocky Mountains and from the Gulf of Mexico to Canada. Up until this point in time most Americans lived within fifty miles of the Atlantic Coast. President Jefferson commissioned Lewis and Clark to explore and map the new territory. The land would be developed into 15 states and parts of two Canadian providences.

President Jefferson made the announcement to the American people on July 4th, 1803, and the senate ratified the purchase on October 20th.

As America grew boundaries were being established as land was being developed. During President Washington's administration Vermont, Kentucky, Tennessee, North Carolina and Rhode Island were added to the union. Under President Jefferson Ohio was added. President Thomas Jefferson had a plan to end slavery without a civil war. While Jefferson was part of the Virginia Legislature, the boundaries of Virginia were established north, east and south. The west was as of yet undefined. The area west of Virginia, everything west, was called the Northwest Territory and included: Ohio, Indiana, Illinois, Michigan and Wisconsin. Jefferson persuaded the legislature to cede the Northwest Territory to the general government of America for future development. Jefferson saw the colonies as old world, he saw the future of America's preeminence in the future growth and development of America's people, industry and resources in the newly acquired lands. He often referred to the west as; "the mystery of the west." Jefferson made a condition of the deed of the Northwest Territory that slavery would be prohibited in the new lands. President Jefferson maintained that the prohibition of slavery was preexistent in the Northwest Territory and would therefore apply to all of the Louisiana Purchase. Jefferson thought that with a majority of the population and a majority of the states living in free states slavery would just collapse under the consent of the majority and he would have his; "that all men are created equal, that they are endowed by their creator with certain unalienable rights, that among these are life, liberty and the pursuit of happiness."

President Jefferson, following the precedent set by President Washington, refused a third terms as president.

James Madison, the architect of the constitution, was elected the fourth president of the United States in 1809. Each successive presidency was establishing precedents that were defining America. President Madison had inherited some very important issues that had gone unresolved by previous administrations. Ignoring the Treaty of Paris, the British Parliament intensified its efforts to eliminate American trade competition. Britain had been limiting U.S. trade by blocking trade with the West Indies and the Mediterranean. Re-invoking the colonial–era Navigation Act of 1756, Parliament required that all goods transported to, from and between England and its possessions must be carried on British ships. Britain also, insisted that its treaty allies, Spain, and Portugal, embargo American trade and forbid U.S. trade with any of their colonies. In 1807, Britain began issuing decrees that further hampered U.S. trade. Britain wanted to cut off supplies to Napoleon's army, they decreed any U.S. ship sailing to France had to first stop in Britain. The cargo would be inspected for war material, which would be confiscated, and a duty would be assessed for any and all other goods. Britain seized hundreds of U.S. ships trying to avoid the port call in Britain. When the British would seize a U.S. ship if they thought any member of the crew was of English heritage they would be "impressed" (forced), into service in the Royal Navy. Britain had 120,000 sailors and were losing about 10,000 per year as war casualties, disease and desertions. If they could not maintain their navy, they would lose the war against Napoleon. The British impressed 9,600 sailors thought to be British, however, 1,600 of them were natural born Americans. Britain also challenged America's neutrality in the war, they decreed that they were at war with France and if the U.S. was trading with France, we were no longer neutral. The Treaty of Paris signed in 1783, brought an end to the Revolutionary War. One of the stipulations of the treaty was for Britain to cede control of the Northwest Territory to the U.S. Britain did not leave the Northwest Territory and continued to occupy their forts in the region and continued land sales of Indian property. Britain also controlled the Great Lakes. They also aggressively supported continued Indian raids on U.S. settlements. Britain promised the Indians their own nation east of the Mississippi River which they would help protect and defend. British traders continued to supply Indians with muskets, powder and ammunition. It was in the best interest of Britain to suppress American expansion and they had not totally given up on the idea that the colonies may be reclaimed.

President Washington sent two expeditions into the Northwest Territory in 1790, and 1791, in an attempt to enforce the Treaty of Paris. Both expeditions ended in defeat for the Americans fighting against the British and their Indian allies. In 1794, President Washington sent General Anthony Wayne to the Northwest Territory. He won a decisive victory against a confederation of Indians at the Battle of Fallen Timbers. The Treaty of Greenville signed after the battle ceded much of the Indian land in the Ohio Valley to America.

A prominent Indian at the time was a Shawnee named Tecumseh and his brother Tenskwatawa, known as the prophet. Tecumseh had earned a reputation as a great warrior in the 1780's, conducting raids on settlements in Tennessee and Kentucky. Tecumseh had organized a tribal confederacy capable of fielding 10,000 warriors. Tecumseh refused to sign the Greenville Treaty. The British encouraged Tecumseh to form a confederation of all of the tribes east of the Mississippi. Promising him muskets and whatever war material the confederation would need to wage war against the colonists. Tenskwatawa had a vision of a great victory, and together they began to build a confederation.

Tecumseh traveled to the south recruiting tribes for his confederacy, not all tribes were willing to join. The Creek Nation split over the idea, with the Red Sticks favoring the confederation and removing the settlers from their land. The White Sticks preferred to integrate with the settler's cultural. White Sticks worked with the settlers, some lived together, and they intermarried.

Indiana Governor William Henry Harrison mustard a force of 1,000 men to confront the Indians at their base in Prophetstown. Tecumseh was away so, leadership fell to Tenskwatawa. Tenskwatawa learned of Harrison's force and decided to attack them in their camp. At 4:30 AM, a surprise attack was launched against Harrison's encampment, however, the first and second attack were beaten back, and the Indians retreated to Prophetstown. This engagement is known as the "Battle of Tippecanoe," on the Tippecanoe River. The Shawnee warriors berated Tenskwatawa for his weak medicine and he departed for Canada in disgrace. This defeat weakened the confederation. The next day Harrison's army marched on Prophetstown only to find it deserted. They found a very large cache of newly made British muskets, gun powder and musket balls. They burned Prophetstown to the ground. The discovery of the weapons cache only strengthen President Madison's resolve.

THE WAR OF 1812

In June of 1812, President Madison laid out America's grievances against Britain to congress and told them they may want to consider a course of action. After two weeks of debate in the senate, America declared war on Britain.

America was not in a position to declare war on Britain. Britain had the largest navy in the world. Britain's navy had 600 vessels, 85 of which were in American waters. Britain's army numbered 250,000 and was the only army in Europe that had not suffered a defeat in battle against Napoleonic France. America's army numbered 7,000 soldiers and the navy had 17 ships. The officers and enlisted men of the army had no combat experience, aside from a few of the aging veterans from the Revolutionary War, which had ended thirty-one years previously. President Madison in 1811, had allowed congress to vote Alexander Hamilton's Bank of the United States out of business, as a result America was now broke. Britain had only 6,000 troops in Canada and Lieutenant General Sir George Prevost, commander of British forces in Canada, was told to fight a defensive war. However, a very relevant consideration was that Britain was in a death struggle with Napoleon's conquest of Europe and would not have an appetite, or resources, for a second war.

President Madison, his cabinet and many in congress thought Americans would be welcomed as liberators in Canada. Canada was unofficially divided into two parts, Upper and Lower Canada. Lower Canada along the St Lawrence Seaway was populated by French Canadians, who had no love for Britain and Britain and France were at war. Upper Canada was comprised of the Loyalists that had fled America during and after the Revolutionary War and pioneers from Europe. This was a miscalculation on the part of America. The Canadians knew what they had with British rule, they were left alone, and there was no pressure to change their language, culture or Catholic religion. The Canadians were not sure what American rule would be like and they were well aware that almost all of America was Protestant. The battles and skirmishes America would fight with the Canadians along America's northern border were primarily French Canadians. They saw the invasion of their homeland as an intrusion on their freedom and liberty, they were not fighting for the British. Canada celebrates the anniversary of the War of 1812, as we celebrate the 4th of July. Canada won their independence from England on July 1st, 1867.

The first year of the war did not go well for America. Canadians in the Northwest Territory learned about the declaration of war before the Americans did. The Canadians and British surrounded Fort Mackinac and after firing one shot from a cannon, Lieutenant Porter Hanks, surrenders American forces and the fort. General Hull surrendered Detroit without a fight. British and Canadian forces defeated the Americans at the Battle of Queenston Heights, Ontario. On the seas, however, the USS Constitution defeated the HMS Guerriere and the HMS Jave, earning the nickname "Old Ironsides." The USS Constitution was made from American oak and layered three planks thick. The British cannon balls bounced off the sides of the ship.

In January of 1813, Britain declared war on America. By spring British ships put in force a blockade of American shipping. The Blockade extended from Delaware to Florida, which virtually closed down American shipping. Congress and President Madison began to aggressively recruit privateers to attack the British ships in the blockade. Hundreds of sailors armed their ships and commenced a sea war against British ships. Britain responds by shelling coastal towns setting several of them ablaze. There is virtually no American response, aside from the privateers, as most of the military was engaged in the north with the Canadians and the British on the Canadian border.

America's strategy was to take control of the waterways, as they were the key routes for trade and transportation, and at the same time denying their use to the British and Canadians. American forces easily took the ship-building port of York (present day Toronto) and the lightly defended Fort York. However, as the British forces retreated, they set their abandon supplies on fire, the fire reached their magazine containing their gun powder, there was a devastating explosion. Americans that were in or near the fort were either killed by the explosion or debris from exploding buildings. More than 250 Americans were killed, among the dead was

General Zebulon Pike. In retaliation the Americans set the government buildings in York on fire.

The U.S. Indian Agent in the south was Benjamin Hawkins, he learned the Spanish from Pensacola and the British were supplying muskets and munitions to the Red Sticks Indians. Hawkins recruited the 150 regular U.S. soldiers from Fort Mims to intercept the supply train. The U.S. Soldiers ambushed Chief Peter McQueen and some of his Red Stick warriors transporting the munitions provided by the Spanish and paid for by the British. Peter McQueen was the son of a Scottish trader and a Creek mother. The ambush would come to be known as the "Battle of Burnt Corn," and ended with the Red Sticks running off the militia. On August 30th, 1813, the Red Stick Indians attacked the White Stick Indians at Fort Mims, Alabama, in retaliation for the ambush. The Red Sticks were part of Tecumseh's confederation. All 550 inhabitants of the fort were killed, men, women and children. The force of 150 militia were no match for the 700 Indian attackers. Many of the people inside the fort took refuge in the home of Mr. Mims, the Red Sticks set fire to the home. Rescuers to arrive on the scene said it was impossible to count or identify the bodies of those burned alive in the house.

In September 1813, Captain Oliver Hazard Perry defeated the British on Lake Erie giving the US control of Lake Erie, Fort Malden and partial control of the Ohio Valley. This victory also allowed the Americans to recover Detroit and was pivotal in the U.S. victory at the "Battle of Thames." Perry sent a dispatch to William Henry Harrison, saying, "We have met the enemy and they are ours. Two ships, two brigs, one schooner, one sloop.

The first battle on the Great Lakes was building ships to gain the upper hand in upcoming engagements. The Americans had taken York and the British decided to attack the American shipyard at Sackets Harbor on Lake Ontario. Anticipating a reprisal Harrison sent reinforcements to Sackets Harbor. General Prevost was unaware of the reinforcements that had arrived at Sacket's. As the engagement began, he realized that he was outnumbered. The winds were not favorable, and his ships were unable to give him any cannon support. With a victory doubtful Prevost retreated.

By early 1814, American forces finally had competent leadership in Major Generals Jacob Brown and Winfield Scott. The generals set about to find new recruits, began extensive training, and instilling discipline within the ranks. The new leadership and well-trained troops drastically improved

America's fighting ability.

After the defeat of Napoleon Britain began pouring resources into Canada for the war against America. In September 1814, the American Navy battled the British for control of Lake Champlain. Prevost with an army of now 15,000 was heavily dependent on Lake Champlain to keep his forces supplied with food and other supplies for his invasion of America. An army this large would need tons of stores delivered every day, an impossible endeavor to be accomplished by ox cart on land. Once again, the first order of battle was to build ships big enough for victory instead of a dueling match between sloops. In charge of American forced was Lt. Thomas Macdonough. Thomas was the Lieutenant that co-led the raid to set the captured Philadelphia on fire in Tripoli. He had also been impressed by the British to serve in the Royal Navy. His guard fell asleep, and Thomas knocked him out, stole his clothes and commandeered a rowboat to affect an escape. He has been quoted as saying, "If I live, I'll make England remember the day she impressed an American soldier."

When Thomas arrived at Lake Champlain his charge consisted of six sloops and two gunboats. He sent two of his vessels north to block the entrance of Lake Champlain at the Richelieu River, to prevent British ships from entering the lake. Disobeying orders they crossed into British waters and were captured, the vessels were then put under the British Flag, and the crew imprisoned. In July of 1813, the British began attacking American villages along the lake, looting personal belongings and setting fire to homes. The two navies had a brief encounter that was indecisive.

Thomas sailed to Vergennes, Vermont to winter. There he received orders to construct ships with the ability to defeat the British. Sloops were desirable for the lake because of their shallow draft. Thomas was also promoted to Master Commandant, although, there was no such official rank, it gave him the authority to commandeer all that was needed for the construction of two ships. The two ships he had constructed; Saratoga and the Eagle, were 26-gun, 20-gun, respectively, vessels, larger than a sloop but, by no means a ship of the line. The British Captain George Downie had as his flagship the largest ship that ever sailed on Lake Champlain, the 37-gun HMS Confiance, was completed 10-days after the USS Eagle.

On September 11th, Thomas positioned his ships off Cumberland Head in such a position that when the British ships rounded Cumberland Head they would have to tack into the north wind. Captain George Downie tried desperately to line up his ships. Rodney Macdonough, quotes from his grandfather's ship minutes, "There was now a hushed, expectant moment like the stillness that precedes the storm. Macdonough, whose manly courage was supported by a childlike faith, knelt on the deck of his flagship with his officers around him and repeated the following prayer: "Stir up Thy strength, O Lord, and come and help us, for Thou givest not always the battle to the strong, but can save many of few...through Jesus Christ, our Lord." Thomas laid anchor both fore and aft and waited for the British. Downie was unable to come abreast of the Saratoga, he dropped anchor and fired all guns. Two of Downies' smaller ships were dispatched by two American smaller boats. The main confrontation was between the 37- gun HMS Confiance, and the 16-gun HMS Linnet. The 26-gun USS Saratoga and the 20-gun USS Eagle. Both the Saratoga and the HMS Confiance were badly damaged, when Thomas cut his front anchor line, his ship came about with the undamaged side of the ship now bringing all cannons to bear against the badly damaged Confiance. The USS Eagle deployed the same tactic. Under withering fire and unable to return sustainable fire, the HMS Confiance lowered her colors, Downie lie dead on the deck. Fifteen minutes later the HMS Linnet surrendered as well. Hearing of the British defeat on Lake Champlain and the loss of his supply line, Prevost turned his 15,000 man army around and headed back to Canada, the great invasion of America was over. The Battle for Lake Champlain was a decisive victory and a turning point in the war. It saved America from conquest, and substantially weakened Britain's position of strength in the peace negotiations.

After the massacre at Fort Mims Secretary of War, John Armstrong notified General Thomas Pinckney that the U.S. was prepared to take action against the Creek Nation. He also told Pinckney if the Spanish are indeed supporting the Creeks he could move on Pensacola. Pinckney chose the General commanding the Tennessee militia for the task, Andrew Jackson. Jackson, his Tennessee militia and scout, Davy Crockett, traveled to Alabama and recruited some of the White Stick and Cherokee Indians in search for the Red Sticks. The Red Sticks had built a camp–of–war on a peninsula on the Tallapoosa River. The entire width of the peninsula was fortified by an earthen redoubt seven feet high. Jackson split his forces, sending several hundred to the opposite bank at the tip of the peninsula to prevent any Indians from escaping. Jackson had his cannons blast the redoubt, after several hours there was a breach in the wall. Sam Houston led the charge, in what would become known at the "Engagement at Horseshoe Bend," of militia and Indians through the breach, he was wounded twice in the attack. Sam Houston would become

Governor of Tennessee and later the general who defended Texas against Santa Anna's Mexican forces in 1836. After the war he became the president of the Lone Star Republic. Jackson's men were able to overwhelm the Red Sticks inside the redoubt. Jackson gave orders that women and children were to be sparred. In the aftermath; Jackson lost 49 killed and 154 wounded. The Indian allies of Jackson lost 75. Estimates are that between 550 and 800 Red Sticks were killed and wounded, about 200 escaped. There were 250 women and children taken prisoner. Jackson went into Florida and captured Pensacola.

With the loss of Lake Erie supply lines for the British and Canadians were cut off. General Provost decided to retreat to Canada. Harrison's regular army and Major General Isaac Shelby with his Kentucky volunteers caught the fleeing British near Moraviantown, Ontario. The British and their Indian allies were quickly overrun in fighting that lasted about 10 minutes, before the British broke and ran. Tecumseh and his warriors did not retreat but chose instead to make a stand. This was the "Battle of the Thames." Tecumseh was killed during the fighting. Overall, casualties were very light. After Tecumseh's death his confederation slowly dissolved.

Washington is set to the Torch

On April 4th, 1814, Napoleon abdicated and was exiled to Elba off the coast of Tuscany. Great Britain turned ifs focus on the conflict in North America. Vice Admiral Alexander Cochrane ordered Major General Robert Ross with 4,500 British Regulars to America to seize the port city of Baltimore. He was to join forces with Rear Admiral George Cockburn and his 19 war ships. Cockburn had been terrorizing the coastal cities along the eastern seaboard, but without an army was unable to do more than fire on American cities. Cochrane called Baltimore, "a nest of vipers," as most of the privateers operated out of Baltimore, the third largest city in America. His further orders stipulated, "to destroy and lay waste such towns and districts upon the coast as you may fine assailable." The British, during the war with Napoleon, developed a new cannon shot filled with a flammable liquid that wreaked havoc on American towns along the coast, setting many towns ablaze. Ross and his men were experienced and battled hardened having spent the last four years in the Napoleonic war. Ross's soldiers were known as, "Wellington's Invincible," as they were the soldiers facing Napoleon in his last battle. The original plan was to land British Regulars on the eastern side of Baltimore while the navy attacked Fort McHenry, allowing for naval support of the Regulars when they advanced on and attacked the city's defenders. Cockburn suggested to Cochrane that the capture of D.C. would be greatly demoralizing to America and it would give them a favorable position in the peace negotiations, Cochrane agreed. President Madison sent a peace delegation to meet British counterparts in Ghent, Belgium, however, nothing had been accomplished in seven months. Cockburn ordered a detour from sailing to Baltimore and on August 19th, 1814, Ross and Cockburn with 4,500 British Regulars landed at Benedict, Maryland.

Secretary of War John Armstrong convinced President Madison that Washington was safe and that the British target was the city and port of Baltimore. As the third largest city in America and a major seaport; the British could use Baltimore as a base of operations. From which they could land troops and supplies, as well as be within striking distance of New York and Philadelphia. Armstrong ordered Continental Soldiers to Baltimore, 500 remained to guard the capital. Washington D.C. was largely undeveloped; President Washington had picked the site for the new capital. Both Virginia and Maryland ceded property for the development of the nation's capital in the non-state, District of Columbia.

Ross set camp outside of Benedict and word soon traveled to Washington that the British were on American soil. Brigadier General William Winder was in charge of the defenses of Washington and Baltimore, known as the tenth district, he sent out word for assistance from other local militia. Although he was the commander of the Militia, he had no military experience other than being captured and held prisoner in June of 1813. He marshaled his 2,000 militia on the west side of the Anacostia River. Brigadier General Tobias Stansbury, commander of the Maryland militia arrived and formed his militia with Winders. Brigadier General Walter Smith commander of the militia of the District of Columbia set his troops online a mile behind Winder's formation, not bothering to tell Winder of his arrival. Winder met with President Madison, Armstrong, Secretary of State, James Monroe and the cabinet to decide on a strategy. President Madison was advised to leave Washington D.C., Monroe rode out to Winder's position giving field commands to the troops, weakening their overall position.

At noon the British made their first contact with the American line, the first attack was repulsed with rifle and artillery fire. On the second attack the British forged the river and made it to the west bank. Winder had his men fall back and reform. The British attacked the left of the line and Winder sent reinforcements, which checked the British advance. Then all hell broke loose. I have mentioned victory is often achieved in battle by improvements in technology or in strategies. With the British line being checked twice they brought forth their newest warfare technology, developed during the war with Napoleon, Congreve Rockets. The rockets were fired from long tubes, each projectile weighing 32 pounds. The projectiles were either; explosive, incendiary or contained shrapnel, they were as much of a psychological weapon as they were tactical. The Americans at Bladensburg had never seen a rocket before, unsure of what they were and what damage they could cause the milia broke formation and ran when the rocket barrage was unleashed. Winder had not given orders for an orderly retreat or established a secondary staging location; he gave no orders for appropriate conduct should there be a breach in one of the lines. It is said the militia ran in such a fashion the retreat was called the "Bladensburg Races." President Madison borrowing a couple of pistols from a member of his cabinet rode out to watch the battle, members of the cabinet accompanied him. Upon witnessing the rout of American militia Madison said, "I could never have believed that so great a difference existed between regular troops and a militia force, if I had not witnessed the scenes of this day."

The British marched on to Washington D.C.Dolly Madison's guards had deserted her, she remained behind securing national treasures that she did not want to fall into British hands. Most notably she had the full-length portrait of George Washington cut from the frame, it hangs in the White House today. It is reported that at one-point Dolly exclaimed, "if I but had a cannon in every window." She departed the White House as the British entered Washington. The British sustained 64 killed in action and 185 wounded. The Americans had 26 killed, 51 wounded and 100 taken prisoner.

The British found Washington nearly deserted. A sniper from a house on the road into Washington, engaged the British, they set the house on fire. Upon entering Washington, the British set fire to every public building; the Library of Congress, House of Representatives, Treasury, the War Office, Arsenal, the shipyards, and of course, the White House. The only building sparred was the U.S. Patent Office. With Washington ablaze, the British marched back to their encampment at Benedict. As they marched a hurricane swarmed in off the ocean and doused all of the flames in Washington. The British out in the open hastily set up camp. There have been seven tornadoes in Washington D.C. in the last 200 years, one of them was this night and it swept through the British camp. One of the British officers said to a female resident of the capital, "Great God, Madam! Is this the kind of storm to which you are accustomed in this infernal country?" To which she replied, "No, Sir, this is a special interposition of Providence to drive our enemies from our city." The British lost more soldiers to the storm than they had lost in the battle. When the weather cleared the British boarded their ships for the journey to take Baltimore. Admiral Cochrane planned a two-pronged strategy to take Baltimore. He would put Ross, 4,000 soldiers and marines ashore at North Point to advance overland to Baltimore. He would sail up the bay and with his cannons take out Fort McHenry, which guarded the entrance to Baltimore, they would then converge on the city.

President Madison fired John Armstrong and replaced him with James Monroe. Revolutionary War veteran Major General Samuel Smith, called out of retirement, was put in charge of Baltimore's defenses. General Smith enlisted all able-bodied citizens to participate in constructing the city's defenses, a major earthwork on the outside of the city. Needing more time Smith dispatched Major General John Stricker, 3,200 troops and 6 cannons to delay the British advance. Stricker arrayed his men across Long Log Lane, the narrowest part of the peninsula. As the British began their march to what would become known as the, "Battle of North Point," Ross had said, "Tonight I'll eat dinner in Baltimore, or in hell." An advance reconnaissance force sent by Stricker, under orders from Smith, were to attack the British advance guard. A brief skirmish took place in which Ross was shot in the arm and chest and died. Command was passed onto the poor leadership of Colonel Arthur Brooke. As Brooke advanced, they ran into Stricker's line. For an hour both sides exchanged rifle, musket and cannon fire. A poorly conceived British attempt to flank the Americans on the left was repulsed. At 4:00 PM, Stricker pulled his men back and reformed his line at Bread and Cheese Creek. At the late hour Stricker was anticipating the British would not attack again as the fighting could go into dark. Brooke, deciding not to pursue and told his men to set up camp. Having lost 300 men Brooke was reluctant to pursue Stricker. As the storm clouds formed, the impending rain dispelled any chance of a reengagement that day. The next day Stricker surmising he had accomplished his mission of delaying the British pulled his men back to the Baltimore fortifications. Brooke made several attempts to engage the fortifications, finding them very well constructed and well manned, pulled his men back to await the outcome of the bombardment of Fort McHenry.

General Smith convinced some of the privateers to sink their boats in the harbor, restricting British ships from sailing up the bay to Baltimore and restricting the size of the ships that could progress. Major General George Armistead, with 1,000 men, was in charge of artillery at Fort McHenry. Fort McHenry, a star shaped configuration, is located (state park today) on the end of the Baltimore peninsula. Support for Fort McHenry was provided by Forts Covington and Babcock to the west in the city of Baltimore. Fort Babcock was a 6-gun earthwork, semi-circle redoubt. Fort Covington was a V-shaped, 10-gun brick fort.

Cochrane's attack force consisted of; 10 warships, the rocket vessel HMS Erebus, and 5 Bomb-Ketches. The Bomb-Ketches were another technological advancement, each vessel was equipped with two mortars. Typically ships would fire their cannons at the walls of a fort until there was a breach, through which the infantry could attack. Hence, the walls on forts became wider and wider. A Mortar represents the uttermost refinement of naval gunnery. The mortar projectile has a very high arch, over the walls, so the ball can be shot into the fort, laying waste to the occupants. Cannons on a ship cannot attain that degree of elevation. Cochrane had his ships anchor just out of reach of the fort's artillery. For the next 25 hours the fort was bombarded with; cannon fire, mortar fire and rockets. Armistead had a flag made; 32 feet by 42 feet and had it hoisted over the fort. In sight of Francis Scott Key, inspiring him to write the Star-Spangled- Banner. One of the 186-pound mortar rounds landed in the fort's magazine, containing 1,000 pounds of gun powder, and providentially the mortar round did not detonate. If it had, it would have destroyed half of the fort and killed many of the occupants. During the night Cochrane sent men in small boats to flank Fort McHenry. The cannons from Fort Babcock and Covington inflicted heavy casualties forcing the men to retreat. By the next morning, the fort had sustained no visible damage. Cochrane sent several of his ships in for closer ranging, however the ships received such heavy fire from the fort's artillery they were forced to withdraw. Cochrane contemplated firing 1,800 cannon balls, mortar rounds and rockets, to no avail.

A new strategy was needed. The New Strategy; Cochrane with the infantry would take New Orleans and move north. He was to be reinforced with 6,500 British Regulars that had beaten Napoleon into submission and were assembling in Jamaica. General Prevost, from Canada, with his veteran British reinforcements of 15,000 regulars would march south to Albany supported by the navy on Lake Champlain. His army's presence in Albany would give confidence to the New Englanders threat to succeed from the colonies over the economic disaster the war had brought to their economy. This being accomplished he would proceed to rendezvous with Cockburn along the Mississippi. They would take control of the navigation on the Mississippi and the millions of dollars' worth of shipping of cotton, tobacco and grain heading to New Orleans for export. Once again, the plan was to split America in half and take control of all parts west. Each side was trying to secure a major victory so that they would be negotiating in Ghent from a position of strength. The inability of Cockburn to capture Baltimore was a significant failure of the British war effort. This was August of 1814; Cockburn would soon learn that in September of 1814 Lake Champlain was lost to America in Lieutenant Thomas Macdonough victory over the British fleet and that Prevost had retreated to Canada.

Major General Andrew Jackson

After Andrew Jackson's victory over the Creek Indians, he was promoted to Major General and put in charge of the 7th Military District. This commission included: Tennessee, Louisiana, and the Mississippi Territory. His immediate orders were to negotiate a treaty between the Creek Nation and America. The treaty designated areas of land as American and as Indian; the intent was to place the Creek Nation in an area where it could more easily be patrolled.

While in Pensacola the sails of the vanguard of the British fleet were seen in the Gulf of Mexico. General Jackson ordered a force march to Mobile Alabama. Once in Mobile Jackson reinforced the defensive at Fort Bowyer and added 130 soldiers to its defenses. Jackson reasoned that if the British were going to attack, they would take Mobile, march to Baton Rouge and then capture New Orleans in an attack from the north; this was in fact Cochrane's plan. Jackson sent an urgent message to his Tennessee Militia to come to New Orleans at once. Cochrane, probably overconfident as Britain had just defeated Napoleon and the militia his men had met at Bladensburg had been no contest. He ordered only a four-ship squadron and a company of Royal Marines, commanded by

Lieutenant Colonel Edward Nicholls to Pensacola in neutral Spanish Florida. Once in Florida the British, again, began recruiting and arming the Seminole Indians. On September 12th, Nicholls and his marines attacked Fort Bowyer. To the surprise of the British the attack was repelled and a frigate that was to offer cannon support was sunk by the fort's cannons. Nicholls, his marines and Indian allies retreated to Pensacola.

Jackson mustered the Mississippi Territory Dragoons and with his 700 Regular Army troops, on November 7th, attacked the British Fort San Carlos in Pensacola. Jackson's surprise was complete the camp was attacked by the troops and the Dragoons rode straight into the camp. The fighting was so vicious and brutal the British survivors burned the fort and fled to their ships. The Spanish and Seminole Indians abandoned the British and fled into Florida. Jackson, leaving two regiments in Pensacola, led the rest of his men back to Mobile where he was greeted by frantic pleas from William Claiborne, Governor of Louisiana, to come immediately to New Orleans.

Jean Lafitte was the pirate ruler of the islands of Grand Terre and Grand Isle on the southern end of Barataria Bay at the end of the Mississippi Delta. Lafitte sent a letter to Governor Claiborne telling him the British were trying to recruit him to join them in their attack on New Orleans. Lafitte's proviso was that if he and his men were given complete amnesty they would join with America against the British.

Major General Andrew Jackson arrived in New Orleans and immediately began shoring up its defenses. He reinforced Fort Saint Philip, 50 miles south of New Orleans to obstruct the British from sailing up the Mississippi. He also placed an additional battery at English Turn on the Mississippi River, 14 miles south of New Orleans. English Turn presented the opportunity to fire on ships sailing up to the turn in the river, the battery could then fire on the ships as they slowed for the turn, in uncertain waters, and again as they sailed up the river towards New Orleans. Jackson employed axmen to cut down trees and block the bayous feeding off the Mississippi that an amphibious enemy may use to mount an attack. He also began to recruit men for his defense, he had half of the 700 Regular Army, the other half he left in Pensacola. It is said he gave an electrifying speech, "I will push them into the sea, or perish in the effort," many came forward to volunteer, including; local businessmen, 200 Creoles, and 200 free blacks from Haiti, most however, were without weapons. He also recruited local Choctaw Indians. Orders would have to be given in five languages: English, Spanish, French, Creole, and Choctaw. Jackson was reluctant to recruit Jean Lafitte, a notorious pirate, but Lafitte had what Jackson needed: cannons, powder, flints, and 500 muskets, for his volunteers, in exchange for amnesty.

When Napoleon abdicated his rule, Britain sent 10,000 regulars to Canada, Cochrane and Ross to Baltimore and sent word for the 6,585 British Regulars reforming in Jamaica, under the command of Major General John Keane, to rendezvous with Cochrane off the Florida coast at Pensacola. Cochrane anchored his 60 ships and 10,000 Napoleon eight-year combat veterans through the Mississippi Sound and at the mouth of Lake Borgne. Aboard his flagship HMS Tonnant Cochrane studied maps and listened to local Creole spies. He decided on Lake Borgne, this shallow arm of the Gulf came within six miles of New Orleans, just above English Turn. It also provided a route to Lake Pontchartrain from which his army could launch an attack on New Orleans from the north. Cochrane ordered Commander Lockyer to lower 42 armed longboats to remove the New Orleans defense of 5 gunboats and two sloops. 36-hours later the small American navy was destroyed.

The Battle That Made America, America

To Jackson, Cochrane's route was now clear, he would advance through Lake Borgne. He immediately sent word to General Coffee, whom he had stationed in Baton Rouge, "You must not sleep, until you reach me." With the defeat of the small navy the New Orleans legislature was in a panic, discussing surrendering rather than have the city ravaged by war. By-passing the inept Governor Claiborne, Jackson walked into the legislature and declared martial law, he told the legislature to adjourn and he assumed command of the city.

Based on information from Creole spies Bayou Bienvenue a waterway leading from Borgne towards the town of Chalmette, which the Creoles were supposed to block, remined open. Cochrane ordered Major General John Keane to take 2,100 men ashore via the bayou and establish a beachhead. Keane advanced to the Villeré Plantation, home of the local militia commander, neutralized the guards and established a camp. Major General Gabriel Villeré escaped and gave Jackson the news. Jackson was enraged, how could the British be on American soil, eight miles south of New Orleans without a shot being fired, he exclaimed, "They will not sleep on American soil." Jackson assembled his men and instructed the USS Carolina, a 14-gun schooner to sail opposite the camp and open fire with grapeshot. Jackson assembled his force on three sides of the camp, as soon as the USS Carolina had fired its battery, Jackson's forces charged the camp, rifle fire, then hand to hand. General Keane surprised by the fierce fighting exclaimed, "What kind of fighting is this?" Jackson told his men to withdraw, a captured Britain had told Jackson 6,000 British Regulars were on their way down the Bienvenue. Jackson was sure the fight was on, and he needed to fortify a defensive position, not wanting a lose a man, he called off the engagement. However, Jackson instructed the USS Carolina to resume the grapeshot and keep them up all night.

The nighttime raid rattled the British, Keane had his men dug in rather than marching on New Orleans as had been the plan. Keane thought they had drastically underestimated the size of Jackson's army, Jackson would not have attacked at night unless he had a large force, he would wait for the rest of the British army before moving on New Orleans. When Major General Edward Packenham, overall commander of ground operations arrived, he was furious with Keane and wanted to know why he had not pressed into New Orleans.

Jackson took his que from the British, fell back two miles to the Rodrigues Canal which was directly in their path to New Orleans and had his men construct a fortification. The Rodrigues Canal ran from the Mississippi River down to a Cyprus swamp 1,000 yards away. The canal was twenty feet wide and four feet deep. Jackson had his men, working through the night, construct a rampart behind the canal. As the work progressed 2,000 riflemen from Tennessee and Kentucky joined Jacksons ranks, with them 1,100 rifles and muskets, taken from an order Jackson had placed but was taking too long to arrive.

On Christmas Day the two sides exchanged artillery. The British artillery had little effect on Jackson's rampart which caused Pakenham a great deal on concern, he had an eighty-mile supply line from ship to his position, he could not hold very long. On December 28th, Pakenham sent two attack forces to test the defenses of the flanks. The force on the left parallel to the Mississippi was cut to pieces by rifle fire and grapeshot. The right had better success and were to the point of breaking through when the Choctaw warriors intervened and turned the course of the fighting. Half of the Choctaw's had bow and arrows, a skilled warrior could fire ten arrows in the time it took to reload a musket. Both British attack forces retreated in defeat.

On January 1st, there was another artillery duel, which lasted until the British ran out of ammunition. While resupplies were coming Packenham devised his strategy. On January 8th, he would send Colonel William Thornton with 1,100 men across the Mississippi to take the artillery on the west bank, then turn the guns on the American rampart. General Gibbs would attack the line on the right, Gen Keane would attack the left and Gen Lambert would be in reserve in the center of the field, to reinforce wherever necessary. The plan was to be executed in the predawn, they would advance under the cover of the morning fog, leaving American riflemen and artillery without a target as they advanced, and could conduct a bayonet charge.

Jackson had positioned his men with muskets on the flanks of the Rodriguez Canal, in defense of Laffite's artillery. If the British attempted to storm the artillery batteries, fighting most certainly would be hand to hand and bayonet to bayonet. Jackson positioned his marksmen in the center. Their fields of fire were the plains of Chalmette, directly in front of the "Jackson Line." He also placed a battery on the west bank of the Mississippi, again with muskets and bayonets, off the battlefield, in hopes they would be isolated and free from attack. On the main line Jackson positioned his Tennessee and Kentucky riflemen, three feet apart and four deep. The lead marksman would fire his rifle, go to the rear of the four-man column, and would have reloaded by the time he was again the first man. This would present a steady stream of fire superiority with deadly accuracy out to 300 yards.

Father d'hubert in New Orleans issued a mandate, "for all to unite under the wing of religion to implore Divine protection for the arms of our defenders," and called for three days of prayer. The Ursuline Nuns held an all-night prayer vigil on January 7th with a mass of Thanksgiving on Jan 8th. Many local citizens joining in the three days of prayer and the overnight vigil.

In the predawn hours of January 8th Packenham moved his men towards the Jackson Line, shrouded in the early morning fog. Colonel Thornton's men immediately ran into difficulty, the current was stronger than anticipated, when they finally got to the west bank there were 1,000 yards south of where they were supposed to land. General Packenham was waiting to hear the sounds of engagement from Thornton, as a diversion, and a dividing of defenses, before he launched his attack. As Packenham waited, he was concerned dawn may break and the fog would lift. He ordered rockets fired to signal all forces to advance on the Jackson line. The British forces began to press forward, suddenly the fog lifted, it lifted so suddenly there were those who said it was an act of God. The British forces exposed; Laffite's cannons opened fire with grape shot ripping into the ranks. As they reached firing range the Kentucky and Tennessee marksmen opened fire with withering accuracy, the lethal volley sent soldiers to the ground by the hundreds. Jackson's Brigadier General John Adaiz, pointed to Gibbs, told one of his best marksmen, "Snuff his candle," the bullet pierced Gibb's temple, he fell from his horse. General Keane was severely wounded and carried off the battlefield. General Packenham was wounded in the arm, and his horse shot dead. He mounted another horse and was shot in the spine, his last order was, "tell Lambert to attack." On the left 868 of the 1,000 highlanders were either killed or wounded. Gibb's attack force of 900 lost 650. Lambert seeing the absolute carnage, refused to commit his men into the bloodbath. Without leadership, the men turned and ran in a roust. General Lambert conferred with Vice Admiral Cochrane, who told him to mount an offensive. Lambert returned to the battlefield and asked General Jackson for a cease-fire so he could bury his dead and collect his wounded. 828 British soldiers lie dead and 2,468 were wounded from a battle that had lasted 25 minutes. Most of the wounded would die. There were very few medical staff, an eighty-mile trek back to the ship for treatment then the voyage home. There were no anesthetics, the antidote of the day was amputation. In the early wars of America 65 percent of the wounded died, either delayed care, infection, shock or not surviving the amputation procedure.

Jacksons men suffered 8 killed and 14 wounded. After Jackson surmised the battle was truly over, he sent his men out to help bury the dead and tend to the wounded.

Word of the victory was sent to New Orleans, a messenger burst into the Ursuline Chapel just as communion was being administered. A mass of Thanksgiving is still held today on the anniversary date of the victory of the Battle of New Orleans. After the battle Jackson went to the Ursuline Chapel to personally thank the Nuns for their prayers. He told them, "By the blessings of Heaven, directing the valor of the troops under my command, one of the most brilliant victories in the annuls of war was obtained."

It would take a week for the British to ferry the wounded and survivors onto waiting ships. In the meantime, Admiral Cochrane sent some of his ships to attack Fort Saint Philip. Then bombarded the fort until fuses for the fort's mortars arrived on January 15th and they were able to fend off the attack. Two of the fort's soldiers had been killed during the bombardment.

As Admiral Cochrane's navy sailed along the coast, they attacked and captured Fort Bowyer near Mobile. Recovering from his wounds Major General Keane and Cochrane thought they easily took Fort Bowyer, next Mobile and with the remaining 5,500 soldiers they could fall back on their original plan. Take Mobile, march to Baton Rouge and attack New Orleans from the north. The following day a British frigate arrived with news that America and Britain had signed a peace treaty in Ghent on December 24th. The treaty called for a cessation of hostilities, and all boundaries would be as they were before the war. The American congress would ratify the treaty in February.

Jackson was later asked by a congressman if there had been any point in the battle, as a treaty had already been signed, to which he replied, "If General Pakenham and his 10,000 matchless veterans could have annihilated my little army... he would have captured New Orleans and sentried all of the contiguous territory, though technically the war was over...Great Britain would have immediately abrogated the Treaty of Ghent and would have ignored Jefferson's transaction with Napoleon."

Jackson left Louisiana with a contingent of his Kentucky and Tennessee volunteers and headed to Florida to run the Spanish out and claim Florida for America. On his person was a letter from President Madison establishing Jackson as the Governor of Florida. Jackson would become the 7th President of the United States of America. After the Federalists had threated to secede from the Union during the War of 1812, they were considered traitors, which ended the Federalists as a political party. Jackson would form the Democratic Party and become its first president.

As much as Jackson was an American hero, as president he pushed for slavery in the to be added western states. He also aggressively and unsympathetically pushed the Indians west; he was responsible for the "Trails of Tears." The forced relocation of Indians from the Southeastern United States to designated Indian territories in the west.

By many accounts the American victory in the War of 1812 was a miracle, the uneven, even unrealistic comparisons of the size of the respective armies and navies at the outset of the war to the Battle of New Orleans. Jackson's force of 4,000 men, relatively untrained militia, could hand a British army of 10,000 well-trained veterans such a devastating defeat has long thought to be a military miracle. It set the stage for America, One Nation Under God and established our national identity as a free and independent nation. In 1819, the Adams-Onis Treaty led to the American purchase of Florida from Spain, encouraged by Jackson's presence. In 1823, the Monroe Doctrine told European powers that the Western Hemisphere was off limits to European expansion. It also helped put the United States on a course of internal expansion. By stating out of European affairs the United States expected, and demanded, the same treatment in kind. The people of the United States stopped thinking of themselves as; Virginians, or New Yorkers and started seeing themselves as Americans. The War of 1812 also convinced the U.S. Government and most of the people that if America was to stay free and independent, they needed a standing army, a world class navy and an always ready militia. And Britain began to develop rifles for all of their armed forces.

THE FEDERAL GOVERNMENT

"From the day of the Declaration...they (the American People) were bound by the laws of God, which they all, and by laws of the gospel, which they nearly all acknowledge as the rules of their conduct." John Quincy Adams, Secretary of State, speaking at the July 4th, 1821, celebration.

As the founders began to grapple with establishing a new government under the Constitution. Aside from the structure of government how would they shape the nation's economy to deal with their excessive war debt and provide a viable economy for enterprise in commerce. The prevalent economic policy of most nations at the time was mercantilism where a nation attempts to maximize its trade exports and accumulate as much gold and silver as it possible can. America did not have any gold or silver at the time, but it did have the ability to produce and export. The question how does one to turn that into a national economic system. Providentially in 1776, a Scottish Economists, Adam Smith, published his five-volume work called "The Wealth of Nations." American exceptionalism can be traced to the first nation structured under natural law and the first nation to fully engage in a free-market concept as the bases of their economy. The concepts entailed in Smith's free-market economy were adopted by the Founders as the basic premise of conducting business in America. The concepts were simple and straight forward. The initial concept of "Laissez-faire" had been tried in France, however there was always some type of Government involvement. The Founders committed to letting the market be free of government intervention, no government production or interference with pricing and wages, however, the government would provide checks against monopolies. A free market lets

303

the people decide what products they want. Producers, to attract customers will have to produce the best product in the marketplace to create demand and gear production to meet that demand, supply and demand. Competition will drive the best quality and a fair price. Profit is viewed as the means of expanding production, new locations and providing jobs.

What the Hell Went Wrong? Several things, all in direct opposition to the original design created by our Founders. Government intervention, rules and regulations. Twenty-five percent of the cost of a new home is the result of compliance to governmental regulations. The government is involved with setting the minimum wage, subsidizing some business and establishing consumer protection. Some of the regulations exerted by the government was brought on by poor business practice of some employers. All to prevalent, however, are government agencies that set up rules and regulations that consume time and money and are stumbling blocks to business. These agencies also extract money from businesses with fees and fines, which represent taxing without representation. Where there is a disregard for the environment or pollution, again the government gets involved, with more rules and regulations. As systems and policies go unchecked, they become more and more extreme to the point of a rational being based on distortions and deception, such as global warming. Global warming's GCF (Global Climate Fund) collects 100 billion a year for the world's nations. Where does the money go? Who is accumulating the wealth? 30,000 scientists, and one of the experts, John Coleman, founder of the Weather Channel, have declared climate change a hoax. In July of 2019, a team of researchers from the Turku University in Finland, found no evidence for man-made climate change in studying global temperatures over the last 100 years. The answer as continually stated by our Founders; the only guarantee of our success is, "a morally and religious people," all the more so in political offices. Moral and religious people will not advance and promulgate scientific hoaxes to perpetuate a system of lies to the determinant of a society.

The monetary system established by the Constitution was considered radical by the other nations of the world. The Constitution gave congress the right to "coin" money out of precious metals, obtained through trade. It did not authorize printing of paper money. Gold was first discovered in North Carolina in 1799. Later mines were opened in South Carolina, Virginia and Georgia. These mines provided much of the metal for coining until the gold rush of California in 1849. This system of real value in the coins that were used produced tremendous economic prosperity. However, this unique and radical system all came to an end in 1934, when President Franklin Roosevelt made it illegal for Americans to own gold.

Americans were told to turn in their gold coins to the federal government of face felony convictions. Federal bills were made the official currency of the United States and were not redeemable in gold or silver. Now Roosevelt's administration could print money to meet every need, or every dream. This is in effect what the Federal Reserve is all about, created in 1913. The goal was for Roosevelt to have the Fed's expand the money supply to accommodate the ever-increasing expenditures and debt that would be needed to support his welfare state. Here's the lie. The Federal Reserve through tragic and inept mismanagement brought about the crash of 1929. Roosevelt then used the crash to outlaw gold and transition into a fiat money system, that would pay for his welfare state. This is the closest America ever came to becoming a socialist country, unless the democrats win in 2020. Roosevelt to rally support for his actions blamed the 1929, crash on the free-market enterprise and that his actions were necessary to save free enterprise. If the free-market caused the 1929 crash, why would Roosevelt want to save it, camouflage and subterfuge, never addressing the real issues. This drastic change in American government should have never occurred without an amendment to the Constitution. The end result of these changes is inflationary debasement of our currency, out-of-control federal spending and excessive borrowing to fund the ever-increasing expenditures of the welfare state. Only being made worse by the funding and costs of illegal aliens. The Federal Reserve must be abolished, and America needs to return to the original idea of a free market based economy based on the gold standard.

"A democracy cannot exist as a permanent form of government it can only exist until the voters discover that they can vote themselves a largesse from the treasury. From that moment on, the majority will always vote for the candidates promising the most benefits from the public treasury. With the result the democracy always collapses over loose fiscal policy." Professor Alexander Tyler 1787.

The challenge for the Founding Fathers in establishing a new government was to avoid the historic pitfalls of other nations throughout history. Kings, monarchies, emperors, czars, and dictators (equally) all solved their nations problems by issuing more laws, violent enforcement, establishing more bureaucracy with more regulations and charging people for services by increasing the tax burden, fees and fines. Monarchs claimed that God gave kings the right to govern, and the king would grant or rescind rights, and often in a very capricious manner. Because rights did not inherently belong to an individual English culture accepted many inequities with no means of redress.

The Founding Fathers proclamation was:

"We hold these truths to be self-evident, that all men are created equal...are endowed by their Creator with certain unalienable Rights, that among these are Life, Liberty and the pursuit of Happiness."

"That to secure these rights, Governments are instituted among Men, deriving their just powers from the consent of the governed."

The desire of the Founding Fathers was to establish a government under the control of the people, with enough checks and balances so that no agency of government would hold unchecked power. The government should be sovereign enough to maintain security, justice, civil order and provide an environment for individual prosperity but not enough power to abuse people's rights. The specific role of American government was to secure these unalienable rights for the governed and insure they were never abridged. That each person possesses inherent dignity, value, and freedoms which the government ought to protect.

There were several historical figures and legacy ideologies that helped shape the ideas that would become the foundational principles of the American Republic. One was Marcus Tullius Cicero, a Roman senator and lawyer, who is also quoted extensively in "The Federalist Papers." Cicero dreamed of, "some future society based on Natural Law."

Another prominent figure in the formation of America's government was William Blackstone, a British jurist, who wrote a four-volume work entitled, "Commentaries on the Laws of England." His writings became the foundation of America's jurisprudence. Blackstone believed that God's laws are, "those superior Laws." He stated,

"Upon these two foundations, the law of nature and the law of revelation (God's written laws), depend all human laws; that is to say, no human law should be suffered to contradict these."

Blackstone was talking about God's written law as found in the Bible. He went on to say,

"As man depends upon his Maker for everything, it is necessary that he should in all points conform to His Maker's will. This will of His Maker is called the Law of Nature. These laws laid down by God are the eternal, immutable laws of good and evil to which the Creator Himself conforms in all dispensations. This Law of Nature, being co-equal with mankind and dictated by God Himself is, of course, superior to any other law. It is binding over all the globe, in all countries, and at all times: no human laws are of any validity if contrary to this; and such of them that are valid derive all their force and all their authority, mediately of immediately, from this original. The doctrines thus delivered we call the revealed or divine law, and they are found only in the Holy Scripture."

James Wilson, one of the signers of The Declaration of Independence, explained to legislatures, "As promulgated by reason and the moral sense, it has been called natural; as promulgated by the Holy Scripture, it has been called revealed law. As addressed to men, it has been dominated the law of nature; as addressed to political societies, it has been denominated the law of nations. But it should always be remembered, that this law, whether natural or revealed, made for men or for nations; flows from the same divine source: it is the law of God."

The law of God is the objective standard for people to know when their government is making immoral, unjust laws or if laws are contrary to The Constitution. The role of government is to protect and defend the unalienable rights granted to all persons from their Creator. In that these unalienable truths were revealed by God, as is anything revealed by God, they embody absolute truth. The Founding Fathers were creating a new form of government that would establish God given rights as a practical reality for a nation. In so doing they created the greatest charter of liberty the world had ever seen; recognizing and protecting God given individual rights. The Declaration of Independence lists; life, liberty and the pursuit of happiness as unalienable rights, these are listed as examples as there are many unalienable rights, in the Bill of Rights and those found in Scripture. Some of the others are:

> That all men are created equal
> Fair and just laws
> A right to representation in the government
> To act in self-defense, right to safety
> Protection from foreign dangers of invasion from without and
> convulsions within
> To own and carry a weapon, protection of self, family, innocent, the
> nation.
> To own, develop and control property.
> To earn a living and keep the fruits of your labor
> Taxing without consent

The right of self-government
The right to petition
The right to assemble
The right to elect leaders
The right to vote in elections
The right to run for public office
The right to worship, or not to worship
To express and idea through, print, speech, or other media
To be secure in one's home, person, papers against unlawful
      search and seizure
The right to privacy
The right to contract
The right of free association
To be advised of charges if arrested
The right of Habeas Corpus (unlawful detention or imprisonment)
The right of due process, and a fair trial
The right of a jury trial
The right to face one's accusers
To suffer no cruel or unusual punishment
To establish, monitor, control and petition government to help
      secure these rights
To abolish government when it becomes negligent in protecting
      these rights
To institute a new government

President John Kennedy said, "The right of the individual against the State has ever been one of our most cherished political principles. The American Constitution has set down for all men to see the essentially Christian and American principle that there are certain rights held by every man which no government and no majority, however powerful, can deny. Conceived in Grecian thought, strengthened by Christian morality, and stamped indelibly into the American political philosophy, the right of the individual against the State is the keystone of our Constitution. Each man is free."

Blackstone describes Natural Law as;

"For as God,…when He created man, and endued (provided) him with free-will to conduct himself in all parts of life, He laid down certain immutable laws of human nature, whereby that free-will is in some degree regulated and restrained, and gave him also the faculty of reason to discover the purport of those laws."

This idea of Natural Law restraining and regulating one's behavior drives right to the point the Founding Father's made about the Republic under the rule of law and the Constitution is only for a religious and moral people. People must be able to restrain their behavior and that only happens when people know they are accountable to God for their actions.

John Locke, "Human Laws are measures in respect of Men, whose actions they must direct, howbeit such measures they are as have also their higher rules to be measured by, which rules are two, the Law of God, and the Law of Nature; so that laws human must be made according to the general Laws of Nature, and without contradiction to any positive Law of Scripture, otherwise they are ill made."

American citizens along with possessing unalienable rights also have duties and responsibilities to their government and fellow citizens:

> The duty to protect and honor the Constitution
> The duty to defend the country if called upon
> The duty of obey state and federal laws
> The duty to support law and order and to keep the peace
> The duty to be informed of issues the effect your country and community
> The duty not to harm or take the life of another
> The duty to pay taxes
> The duty to make wages to pay for the cost of living, self-sufficient
> The duty to act morally responsible
> The duty to respect the rights of others
> The duty not to steal or destroy private property
> The duty of parents to provide for and educate their children, not in school alone
> The duty to participate in the democratic process, including voting
> The duty to honorably and fairly conduct business
> The duty to have just weights and measures
> The duty to register for selective service
> The duty to serve in the armed forces if called
> The duty to engage in armed conflicts if so deemed necessary by the commander-in-chief
> The duty to serve on a jury, when called
> The duty to as far as possible provide for the poor and needy
> The duty to honorable perform contracts to God and fellow citizens
> The duty to maintain the integrity of the family unit

The duty not to participate in crime or break the law
The duty not to aid or abet criminals
The duty not to take a bribe

The participants of government also have specific duties in addition to those listed above. I will not spend too much time on specific duties as they are detailed in the Constitution, aside from addressing "What The Hell Went Wrong." The legislative branch of government makes the laws of the nation. Members of the House of Representatives and the Senate are elected to their position by their constituents for their district or state. In a representative form of government, as in our American Republic, representatives are to represent the views of their constituents, not their own. The Founders envisioned that a citizen after he had conducted a successful career would devote himself to a term in office at the completion of his work, as a public service. The Founders thought it important that representatives should represent all walks of life. In a nation ruled by law it was probably inevitable that we would have a preponderance of lawyers, seeking political office. The Founders never envisioned that representatives would yield their responsibility to their constituents to lobbyists and special interest groups for financial gain. By so doing they completely destroy the workings of a representative government. Instead, members of Congress should send out questionnaires to their constituents ever 90-days identifying pending issues, asking for their input. In 2011 Peter Schweizer published: Throw Them All Out," a detailed examination of political corruption as it is actually practiced in the halls of Congress. In his investigation, Schweizer found one single member of Congress against whom no allegations could be made – one person who had never taken a dime, had never cut any backroom deals, had never, played the Game. The single member of Congress was Senator Jeff Sessions. President Harry Truman said; "The only way to get rich in politics, is to be a crook." Some people insist that the Constitution is outdated and should be replaced. However, that is not the case, if any adjustments are needed it is the workings of the checks and balances. First would be to reestablish the most profound of our original check and balance, "The Constitution and our republic are for a religious and moral people, it is wholly inadequate for anyone else." It is obvious we need a new set of checks and balances for Congress. Representatives in the house elected for two-year terms should be audited every year. Members of the senate elected for six-year terms should be audited every other year. The financial audits should be conducted by the IRS, or better still the audits should be by the FBI, so those seeking financial gain can arrested on the spot. How do representatives making $174,000 per year become millionaires, as 50 percent of them are? 248 representatives became millionaires after being elected.[32] The laws that are revealed by God should be looked at as sacred and not subject to change by human legislative bodies. New laws should not contradict the provisions of Divine Law. The United States Constitution can never become outdated, because it is built on the absolute truths of God's Law; and designed to control that which never changes, human nature.

The executive branch consists of the President, Vice-President and the fifteen-member cabinet. The president serves as the Head of State and as Commander-in-Chief of the armed forces. He enforces the law and the judicial branch interprets the law. The President has veto power over legislation passed by the legislature. He is responsible for appointing heads of all executive agencies, federal commissions and supreme court justices, subject to senate approval. The President is also responsible for international diplomacy, signing treaties and issuing executive orders. He also, annually, present a State of the Union message to congress, which outlines the current state of affairs for the nation and his intended agenda. The President may be impeached from office by the House of Representatives and a two-thirds majority vote of the senate for Treason, Bribery, High Crimes and Misdemeanors.

The Supreme Court is the highest court in the land and its decisions are not subject to review by any other court. A schism has developed in our judicial system that is causing irreparable damage not only to our Republic as a nation of laws but there are dramatic implications for our culture. As the court has evolved it has split into two separate ideologies. The first challenge is that the court is to be politically neutral, where the jurist's sole responsibility is interpreting the law, however this is far from the reality, and part of what has gone wrong. There are in fact liberal and conservative justices. The liberals tending to be Democratic and appointed by Democratic Presidents and the conservative justices are appointed by Republican Presidents. Jurists, to their discredit, tend to make decisions in favor of the political agenda of the party that appointed them. Liberal justices subscribe to an ideology that sees the Constitution as a living document which means the meanings of the words evolve as

---

[32] Care2Petitions

our society evolves. Conservatives subscribe to one of two theories: original intent or original meaning. In original intent, jurists interpret the Constitution as those who drafted it intended it to be understood. Original meaning jurists interpret the Constitution as the people living at the time of its adoption would have understood the meaning of the text. As for checks and balances, a justice for the Supreme Court must be approved by the majority of the Senate. Secondly, if congress is unhappy with a Supreme Court decision they can adjust or amend the relevant law, or they can pass an amendment to the Constitution. Thirdly, the court can also overrule itself if it is obvious an error was made arriving at a decision.

The Supreme Court is not the body designated for making laws, yet that is what they have done in several instances. As they have legislated that the death penalty is cruel and unusual punishment, yet the punishment for murder, according to Scripture is; "whoever sheds man's blood, by man his blood shall be shed." A ruling, made by man, in direct contradiction to Natural Law. The Supreme Court has also determined that if a person injures a pregnant woman that results in the death of her child, he can be tried for murder; yet, the court has sanctioned abortion. The decision favoring abortion was based on the mother's liberty yet denying the fetuses' unalienable right to life. Justice Antonin Scalia, probably the greatest legal mind in our day, said of the abortion ruling, "the best the court can do to explain how it is that the word "liberty" must be thought to include the right to destroy human fetuses is to rattle off a collection of adjectives that simply decorate a value judgement and conceal a political choice," camouflage and subterfuge. These rulings that result in the courts legislating should be deferred back to the legislature. Issues of major cultural significance should be put on a ballot for the people to decide, even if that requires annual trips to the ballot box, every November.

Justice Scalia understood that over time a secular ideology has formed in America and to preserve the original intent of the Constitution he says, "We seek a return to the oldest and most commonsensical interpretative principle: In their full context, words mean what they conveyed to reasonable people at the time they were written." The ultimate check and balance for the U.S. Constitution and its government is we are a nation of laws, God's Law, and we risk Divine wrath should we abandon or disregard His law. The meanings of words change over time and that is why Noah Webster felt compelled by the Spirit to write a dictionary. His dictionary standardized spelling, pronunciation and the meaning of words in his day. According to Noah Webster's 1829 Dictionary the word amusing meant something was thought-provoking, awful meant something was awe-inspiring and artificial meant that something is highly artistic. Judges that subscribe to textualism and originalism think the Constitution should be interpreted by the meaning of the text, the word, had at the time it was written. As judges and legislators have become more Godless, they want to change the meaning of the Constitution based on God's law to one based on man's law.

Causes to "What in the Hell Went Wrong?" was our failure to implement the most stringent requirements of our Founding Fathers.

John Adams, "We have no government armed in power capable of contending in human passions unbridled by morality and religion...Our Constitution was made only for a religious and moral people. It is wholly inadequate to the government of any other."

Noah Webster, "...the moral principles and precepts contained in the Scripture ought to form the basis of all our civil constitutions and laws...All of the miseries and evils which men suffer from vice, crime, ambition, injustice, oppression, slavery, and war, procced from their despising or neglecting the precepts contained in the Bible."

Benjamin Franklin, "...only a virtuous people are capable of freedom. As nations become corrupt and vicious, they have more need of masters."

Patrick Henry, "The great pillars of all government and social life; virtue, morality and religion. This is the armor...and this alone that renders us invincible."

Samuel Adams, "Religion and good morals are the only solid foundations of public liberty and happiness."

Charles Carroll, signer of the Declaration, "Without morals, a republic cannot subsist any length of time; they therefore who are decrying the Christian religion...are undermining the solid foundation of morals, the best security for the duration of free governments."

Benjamin Rush, "The only foundation for...a republic is to be laid in religion. Without this there can be no virtue, and without virtue there can be no liberty, and liberty is the object of life and all republican governments."

John Adams, "Statesmen, my dear Sir, may plan and speculate for liberty, but it is Religion and Morality alone, which can establish the Principles upon which Freedom can securely stand."

George Washington, Farewell Address, "Of all the dispositions and habits which lead to political prosperity, religion and morality are indispensable supports... In vain would that man claim the tribute of patriotism who should labor to subvert these great pillars of human happiness, these firmest props in the duties of men and citizens…"

Noah Webster, "In my view, the Christian religion is the most important and one of the first things in which all children, under a free government, ought to be instructed…no truth is more evident to my mind than that the Christian religion must be the basis of any government intended to secure the rights and privileges of a free people."

Gouverneur Morris, signor of the Articles of Confederation and the Constitution, "Religion is the only solid basis of good morals; therefore, education should teach these precepts of religion, and the duties of man towards God."

Daniel Webster, "To preserve the government we must also preserve morals. Morality rests on religion; if you destroy the foundation, the superstructure must fall. When the public mind becomes vitiated (depraved) and corrupt, laws are a nullity and constitutions are wastepaper."

Sir Edward Coke (1552-1634), "The law of nature is that which God at the time of creation of the nature of man infused into his heart, for his preservation and direction…the moral law, called also the law of nature."

America was well on its way to becoming the most powerful nation on earth. Built on the premise of God's Providence and His direct involvement in the affairs of man. America was established on the bases of God's revealed law; God law is truth and has remained unchanged since it was written. The founders in their wisdom and guided by the Hand of God established man's law based on God's Law and the profound wisdom that man has a proclivity for evil and that man can only check those evil tendencies through self-restraint, effective by man's accountability to his Creator; morality and religion. America's next major battle was more foundational in its strivings.

CELL THEORY

O nce we understand the origin of things in and of life, things that exist in both provisional (3-D reality, our everyday touch and feel reality) and foundational reality (metaphysical, supernatural, God and His celestial realm) we can explain these things in one of two ways. That is, there are two fundamental explanations we can look at, or two worldviews: evolution and creationism. Both of these belief systems attempt to explain how we got from nothing to everything. The reason this is so profoundly important is because the worldview you prescribe to will determine how you interpret information, how you see reality, and, ultimately, how that will influence your behavior. We do not see things as they are, we see things as we are.

Evolution and natural selection were first hypothesized in the early 1800's by British naturalist Alfred Wallace. Charles Darwin built upon Wallace's work several years later. However, at the time very little was known about the mechanics of physiology, biology and the basic underpinnings of life. Natural selection is or was a hypothesis that all species of organisms develop through natural selection, which means that as organisms reproduce small variations occur in their development. These small variations over time increase the adaptability of some organisms over others. Those organisms with heritable traits better suited to the environment will survive. This is where the survival of the fittest hypothesis originates. Survival of the fittest is directly contradictory to the behavioral repertoire of most well-adjusted people, who for the most part exhibit compassion, are helpful and display altruistic motives. Current revisions of the hypothesis of natural selection indicate that these small variations are transmitted genetically. Evolution maintains that life began with a single cell organism and over millions of years evolved into man. In contrast to the Second Law of Thermodynamics which describe the

315

relationships between thermal energy, or heat, and other forms of energy, and how energy affects matter. The Second Law of Thermodynamics is about the *quality* of energy. It states that as energy is transferred or transformed, more and more of it is wasted. The Second Law also states that there is a natural tendency of any isolated system to degenerate into a more disordered state. In short everything is in a constant state of entropy, lack of order or predictability. Over time there is a gradual decline into disorder.

In science an idea begins with a hypothesis, which is an educated guess based on observation. A hypothesis becomes a theory when it summarizes a hypothesis or group of hypotheses that have been supported and confirmed with repeated testing and observation. A theory is valid as long as there is no evidence to dispute it. Therefore, theories may be disproven. This is why evolution has remained a theory and has not earned the right to be considered a law of science. A scientific law generalizes a body of observations. At the time it is made, if no exceptions have been found, it becomes a scientific law; i.e. the Law of Gravity. Scientific laws tell us what happens. Theories explain how and why something might happen. Evolution cannot and has not been observed, rather, it assumes a process of continual development contrary to existing Laws of Thermodynamics. Evolution cannot become a law. There is no evidence to support the theory becoming more than just a theory, that is why many evolutionists refer to aspects of evolution as fact, which they are not. The theory of evolution is unproven and unprovable.

The challenge with the current hypothesis of evolution is that as science has learned more and more about human physiology and genetics over the years and with increasingly advanced technologies the new information has to be used to evaluate older concepts. Evolutionists do not apply the new information in a critical thinking manner, but instead rationalize the new information to justify the old theory. The interpretation you have of the information will depend on your worldview. Everyone thinks, and we do so because it is part of our very nature. However, there are different types of thinking. Thinking can be biased, distorted, partial, prejudiced, we would hope that our thinking style is objective, subjective, fair, analytical and above all truthful. Critical thinking is analytical, assessing, self-directed, disciplined and a search for objective truth without any preconceived notions or intent. All too often our thinking is influenced by our worldview; critical thinking is a deliberate effort that must be systematically cultivated to overcome our inherent biases. However, the new information should serve as a litmus test for an old theory, "Okay, now that we know this, does the old theory still hold up?"

In 1859, the year Darwin published "Origins of the Species," which was considered the doctrine of evolution, very little was understood about the origins of and the nature of living organisms. A concept active in the scientific community at this time was spontaneous generation. Spontaneous generation hypothesized that life can spring from non-living matter. An example of this was the observance that maggots just suddenly appeared on meat. At the time people were unaware that flies laid eggs and the eggs hatched as maggots. It's important to understand that in Darwin's time this was the level of understanding in the scientific community. Louis Pasteur, with the discovery of the microscope, proved in 1862 that microscopic contaminates are responsible for what was considered spontaneous generation.

Born in 1822, Pasteur became a professor of chemistry at the University of Strasbourg where he met and married Marie Laurent. Tragically, three of their five children died of typhoid fever. With a worldview based on, "The more I study nature, the more I stand amazed at the work of the Creator." As a man of faith, rather than being destroyed by the loss of his children, he went on to research and found the means of curing and preventing diseases. Pasteur developed the process of heating liquids to kill most bacteria and molds, which became known as "pasteurization." He was also one of the first scientists to reject the evolutionary theory of spontaneous generation; "Microscopic beings must come into the world from parents similar to themselves...There is something in the depths of our souls which tells us that the world may be more than a mere combination of events." Pasteur was also responsible for convincing Doctors to wash their hands and sterilize their medical equipment after demonstrating that when the doctors did not wash their hands, after performing autopsies, their next surgical patient would die from whatever it was that had killed the person of his last autopsy.

Pasteur performed several experiments to disprove spontaneous generation. He placed boiled liquid in a flask and let hot air enter the flask. Then he closed the flask, and no organisms grew in it. In another experiment, when he opened flasks containing boiled liquid and left them uncovered, dust entered the flasks, causing organisms to grow.

In 1839, Matthias Schleiden and Theodor Schwann, two German scientists, advanced the cell theory. With the discovery of cells three important tenets were confirmed.

All living organisms are composed of one or more cells.

The cell is the basic unit of structure and organization in organisms.

Cells arise from pre-existing cells.

Charles Darwin's book, The *Origins of Species* stated; "If it could be demonstrated that any complex organism existed, which could not possibly have been formed by numerous successive," slight modification, my theory would absolutely breakdown. But I can find no such case."

Since its early conception, cell theory has advanced to include what is now called the "modern cell theory," which adds to the previous assumptions;

The activity of an organism depends on the total activity of independent cells.

Energy flow (metabolism and biochemistry) occurs with cells.

Cells contain DNA which is found specifically in the chromosome and RNA found in the cell's nucleus and cytoplasm.

All cells are basically the same in chemical composition in organisms of similar species.

Heredity information (DNA) is passed on from cell to cell.

In Darwin's time the cell was thought to be a small unit of protoplasm. Scientists at the time had no idea that there was anything inside the cell and if there was it was not of any importance.

In light of new scientific understanding the theory of spontaneous generation was quietly abandoned. Whenever a scientific proof of evolution is disproven, the proof is just quietly ignored, it is never reported. Science continued to advance with the development of stronger microscopes, and the electronic microscope. Scientist began to see within the cell. They discovered there are all kinds of activity within a cell with many small machines performing a variety of functions. It wasn't until 1952, that the human genome was mapped, and its segments identified.

IRREDUCIBLE COMPLEXITY

Darwin's concern with a complex organism is that if it cannot have been formed by numerous successive slight modifications, then his theory would break down. Every time this complexity is demonstrated, as it is with every step of our increasing understanding of life, the excuse of the evolutionists is; "if there is enough time, the complexity could have evolved." That is why evolutionists always talk of millions or billions of years ago, so that any degree of complexity can be explained if given enough time.

Human DNA consists of four elements, which are sugar and phosphate molecules they are; A (adenine), T (thymine), C (cytosine), and G (guanine). This sequence is different for every one of us except identical twins. Each one of our 100 trillion cells have a nucleus, except red blood cells, and each nucleus contains a double helix of DNA. The inability of red blood cells, without a nucleus, to carry out protein synthesis means that no virus can evolve to target mammalian red blood cells, (God's quarantine). Keep in mind the afore mentioned numerous successive slight modifications. Within the human genome are three billion pairs in 23 pairs of chromosomes in the nucleus of each cell. Each chromosome carries hundreds to thousands of genes, which carry the instructions for making protein and cell self-replication. There are 20 amino acids in the human body that produce the 100,000 different types of protein the body needs. This is the information, in the DNA, needed for the cell to function as it was designed, for self-replicating, elemental interactions within the cell, repair and maintenance instructions. One teaspoon of DNA could hold all of the information in the world today. We used to think of existence in terms of matter and energy. It appears we need to expand that understanding to include information as well. This may have implications for the Laws of Thermodynamics. The additional considerations of information to the Laws of Thermodynamics would not change the relationship of matter and energy; it may, however, enrich our understanding of the basic elements of life.

Gregor Mendel (1822-1884), scientist and Augustinian friar and abbot of St Thomas' Abbey began his study of genetics in 1865. Almost nothing was known about the biological properties of heredity until he began his experimentation and study of genetics. In 1924, Henri Dutrochet, established the first tenet, "the cell is the fundamental element of an organism."

The problem with evolution is the theory of irreducible complexity. How does something evolve into something else, when the parts that have not evolved yet are missing but needed for the next stage of development? Given enough time…

There are many examples of irreducible complexity. There is one example I understand so I'll use that one. I am not a molecular biologist; I only took biology as a secondary in college. However, you can use your search engine, or go to YouTube to look up irreducible complexity.

To get a general understanding of irreducible complexity let's look at our circulatory system. I'm using this as an example because the process is absolutely fascinating. First some facts, so we can understand all the mechanisms involved with our circulatory system.

The human heart will beat about 3 billion times in the average life span.

That's 4,800 times per hour or 115,200 times per day.

8 million red blood cells die every second and the same numbers are born.

In a droplet of blood there are 5 million red blood cells.

It takes 20 seconds for a red blood cell to circulate the whole body.

Red blood cells make approximately 250,00 round trips of the body before returning to the bone marrow, where they were born, to die.

Red blood cells live about 4 months circulating throughout the body, feeding the 100 trillion other cells of the body.

There are 60,000 miles of arteries, veins and capillaries in our circulatory system.

To put this into perspective, the earth is 25,000 miles in diameter.

Capillaries make up 80 percent of the circulatory system.

Capillaries are about a tenth of the diameter of a human hair and reach every cell in the body.

Red blood cells are about the same size as the capillaries, so they must travel single file in the capillaries.

With each beat of the heart, blood is pushed under high pressure away from the heart along the main artery, the aorta. From the aorta, blood flows, at about 4 miles per hour, into the arteries, arterioles and ultimately, to the capillary beds. When the blood leaves the heart, it is filled with nutrients and oxygen. When the red blood cells reach the capillaries, they exchange oxygen for carbon dioxide and nutrients for waste product. The blood then circulates back to the left side of the heart where it is pumped into the lungs to exchange the carbon dioxide for new oxygen, then pumped back into the right side of the heart to begin the journey again. Nutrients enter the bloodstream through fingerlike projections called villi that are along the inner wall of the small intestines. Our bodies absorb most of the nutrients during the process of moving the food from the stomach to the small intestine. Waste products are deposited in the large intestine. At this point we would have to examine an entirely different, but integrated system; the digestive system.

Scripture says: "For the life of the flesh is in the blood, and I have given it to you on the alter to make atonement for your souls; for it is by reason of the life that makes atonement. For as for the life of all flesh, its blood is identified with its life...for the life of all flesh is its blood..." Leviticus 17:11

Your blood must flow continuously throughout your body for your entire lifetime but shut off quickly to prevent loss when you get a cut or are injured. The process begins whenever flowing blood comes in contact with something called a tissue factor. Tissue factors are called collagen and are a structural protein that exists everywhere inside the body except in the circulatory system. In your blood are tiny blood cells called platelets. Any contact with collagen triggers them into action. If collagen is present, there has been a breach in the vessel wall. There are enzymes in your blood system that inhibit the platelets from doing any clotting activity until the platelets are turned on by collagen. Otherwise, your blood would be continually clotting everywhere in your circulatory system. The platelets immediately stick to the walls in the area of the damage, changing shape to form a plug that fills in the broken part to stop the blood from leaking out. When platelets become active, they initiate a chain reaction. The platelets release chemicals to attract more platelets and other cells. A complex known as a prothrombin activator is produced by a long sequence of chemical reactions. The prothrombin activator converts a blood protein called prothrombin into another protein called thrombin. Thrombin converts a soluble blood protein called fibrinogen into an insoluble protein called fibrin. Fibrin then transforms into long strands that get tangled up with the platelets in the plug to create a net that traps even more platelets and cells. The clot becomes much tougher and more durable. Fibrinogen is actually fibrin with, let's say, a shield on it to prevent the fibrin from sticking to other fibrin in the blood vessel. Once activated, the shield falls off, turning fibrinogen into fibrin, but only where collagen is present. The fibrin then joins with other fibrin to form the long strands to create the net. Other proteins in this chain reaction offset extra clotting factor proteins so the clot doesn't spread farther than it needs to. As the damaged tissue heals, which is a whole separate system that works in conjunction with the circulatory system called the immune system, which is also activated by the clotting process, you no longer need the clot. The fibrin strands dissolve, and your blood takes back the platelets and cells of the clot.

If the wound is serious, more than just a cut, the circulatory system employs techniques to reduce the loss of blood. If the hemorrhage is severe, there is a reduction in blood pressure. The severed vessel narrows and the inner lining sticks to itself to try and seal off the tear. Other blood vessels near the surface of the body become constricted, thus conserving an adequate supply of blood for direction to vital organs such as the heart and the brain. Contraction of the spleen may add up to a pint or more of blood to the general circulation to compensate for the amount lost. Also, since it is not immediately vital to replace red blood cells, the blood vessels borrow fluid from tissue to restore volume to the circulation and bring blood pressure back to normal. In this way, with a natural "transfusion" of blood from the spleen and tissue fluid, a human being can survive the loss of up to a quarter of its blood.

In order for there to be life in the flesh, the flesh must have oxygen and nutrients, all of which is supplied by the blood, all of which God told us over 3,000 years ago.

"Intelligent design" alludes to a Supreme Creator; it is the most reasonable explanation for the vast amount of information contained in our DNA. The information in the DNA are the instructions for life, how cells self-replicate, and how and which amino acids are to build what proteins. The information determines where and how the proteins will be built, in what order, and what their function is based on that development. Intelligence can only come from intelligence it cannot come from randomness. You cannot build complex structures or organisms gradually, in small incremental steps over time, when there is no functioning until you have all the parts in place. How can a system, a cell, an organism be assembled without the assembly instructions contained in the DNA?

A well-constructed, ordered grouping of letters create information.

Jrvmdnjfle fmddlfkmt edlvmekrle fdmotw[dvmsdl = randomness

Evolutionists cling to evolution because the alternative is to acknowledge the intelligence behind the design, if there is intelligence behind the design there must be a plan or a purpose, which means accountability to that plan or purpose, and even to the designer, which means it is no longer all about you. No, you cannot do whatever you please. It is not one thing morphing into something else. It is the trillion cells in our body functioning and constructing and self-replicating, all in conjunction and in synthesis with all of the other cells.

Darwin's Theory of Evolution by Natural Selection maintains that more individuals are produced each generation than can survive. Phenotypic variation exists among individuals and the variation is genetically transmitted. A phenotypic expression of a gene is something that can be seen, such as eye or hair color. Those individuals with heritable traits better suited to the environment will survive. Remember Darwin's statement; "If it could be demonstrated that any complex organ existed, which could not possibly have been formed by numerous successive, slight modification, my theory would absolutely breakdown." Natural selection selects out aspects that do not serve adaptation to the environment and promotes aspects that will. The circulatory system could not have evolved by numerous successive modifications.

Every element in the process of the blood clotting sequence has to be present for the process to work. You cannot take an element out of a chain reaction and expect the rest of it to work. How would the platelet inhibitor come into being if there weren't any platelets? And the platelets without an inhibitor would have clotted all of the blood in the body. It is a system of irreducible complexity; if you remove any protein or interrupt any part of the chain reaction in the circulatory system, what remains will not sustain life. There are twenty-five different agents and processes involved in the chain reaction that produces a blood clot. In that the modifications are random it cannot be assumed that the next slight variation will be linked to the previous one, nor can it be assumed that the next variation will be beneficial. It is more probable that the next randomly occurring independent event of a slight variation will be detrimental rather than beneficial to the next modification. For the most part mutations represent a loss of something and would therefore be destructive. If two compatible agents develop at the same time, that is not randomness, that is design.

In the 2nd century, Galen of Pergamon came up with a model of the circulatory system that was believed until the 1600's. His model said; "The circulatory system consists of two one-way systems of blood distribution, and the liver produces venous blood that the body consumes." He also thought the heart was a sucking organ, rather than a pump. With the advent of more sophisticated equipment his theory was thrown out, as Darwin's should be.

However, evolutionists have held tightly to their belief that, even complex systems can evolve given enough time. This is why they profess billions of years of time so that everything can eventually evolve into its end state, despite the evidence of a young earth.

Evolutionists also profess that the first living thing on earth was a single-celled micro-organism, called a prokaryote, an organism that lacks a nucleus. If the prokaryotes lack a nucleus it would not contain any DNA, which is needed for traits to be passed on and the information needed to build proteins that our bodies need to function and reproduce. Evolutionists maintain the prokaryotes first appeared on earth almost four billion years ago, just a few hundred million years after the formation of the earth. Evolution attempts to explain the brain's development, but it cannot explain thought or consciousness. Evolution attempts to explain the body and its systems, but it cannot explain the soul. Evolution is silent on the nature of the spirit; how can a natural process explain the existence of something supernatural? 1 Corinthians 15:44 "it is sown a natural body; it is raised a spiritual body. If there is a natural body, there is also a spiritual body." The only place where numerous successive, slight modifications actually exist is in the world of germs, pathogens, bacteria, and viruses. When there is a modification in the DNA material it is called a mutation. A mutation occurs when there is a loss of genetic information, never the addition of information.

Evolutionists say earth came into being during the "Big Bang", however even that is now in doubt. Evolutionists also cannot explain how the first prokaryotes came to be a living organism, so they think it must have come from another planet. This is not an answer to the question; "how did life originate?" This solution just kicks the can further down the road. There was a big bang and it is called the first day of God's creation.

Francis Crick, a Nobel Prize winner and an evolutionist said, "An honest man, armed with all the knowledge available to us now, could only state that in some sense, the origin of life appears at the moment to be almost a miracle, so many are the conditions which would have had to have been satisfied to get it going. "

Albert Einstein said; "There are only two ways to live your life. One is as though nothing is a miracle. The other is as though everything is a miracle." Two different worldviews.

Michael Behe a biochemist and an advocate of intelligent design writes in his book *Darwin's Black Box: The Biochemical Challenge to Evolution.*

"By *irreducibly complex* I mean a single system composed of several well-matched, interacting parts that contribute to the basic function, wherein the removal of any one of the parts causes the system to effectively cease functioning. An irreducibly complex system cannot be produced directly (that is, by continuously improving the initial function, which continues to work by the same mechanism) by slight, successive modifications of a precursor system, because any precursor to an irreducibly complex system that is missing a part is by definition nonfunctional.

THE FOSSIL RECORD

The second problem with evolution, aside from irreducible complexity, is the "fossil record;" which is often referred to as "Darwin's Dilemma," in his own words. (*Words in italics are the authors.*) Quoting Darwin, "There is another and allied difficulty, which is much more serious. I allude to the manner in which many species in several of the main divisions of the animal kingdom suddenly appear in the lowest known fossiliferous rock. (*This means there are advanced species, which did not go through an evolutionary process, that are in the bottom layers of the fossil record*) Most of the arguments which have convinced me that all the existing species of the same group are descended from a single progenitor, apply with nearly equal force to the earliest known species. For instance, it cannot be doubted that all the Silurian (*443-416 million years ago*) trilobites (*crustaceans)* are descended from someone crustacean, which must have lived long before the Silurian age, and which probably differed greatly from any known animal. Some of the most ancient Silurian animals, such as the Nautilu,(*a small marine mollusc, ie squid*) Lingula,(*shelled invertebrate*) etc, do not differ much from living species; and it cannot on our theory be supposed, that these old species were the progenitors of all the species belonging to the same groups which have subsequently appeared, for they are not in any degree intermediate in character *(they look the same today as they did then*). Consequently, if the theory be true, it is indisputable that, before the lowest Silurian or Cambrian (*541 – 485 million years ago*) stratum was deposited long periods elapsed, as long as, or probably for longer then, the whole interval from the Cambrian age to the present day; and that during these vast periods the world swarmed with living creatures…To the question why do we not find rich fossiliferous deposits belonging to these assumed earliest periods, I can give no satisfactory answer...the difficulty of assigning any good reason for the absence beneath the Upper Cambrian formations of vast piles of strata rich in fossils is very great. It does not seem probable that the most ancient beds have been quite worn away by denudation, or that their fossils have been wholly obliterated by metamorphic action, for if this had been the case we should have found only small remnants of the formations next succeeding them in age, and these would always have existed in a partially metamorphosed condition. But the descriptions which we possess of the Silurian deposits over immense territories in Russia and in North America, do not support the view that the older a formation is, the more it has invariably suffered extreme denudation and metamorphism. The case at present must remain inexplicable; and may be truly urged as a valid argument against the views here entertained. (*The problem Darwin has is that there are no fossils before the Cambrian strata, when he assumes the earth would have been teeming with life. He further reasons that, whatever fossils were there, no matter what happened to them, there would be some trace of their existence, but there is none. The older fossils could not have just disappeared from the fossil record; there would be some residual trace of their existence.*)

The problem Darwin was having is that the stratum, or the layers of rock referred to as the Cambrian era has fossils of fully developed species. His rationalization is that the Cambrian era must have occurred much later than they thought. The problem with that is that there are virtually no fossils in the rock layers below the Cambrian layers. In fact, this era, the Cambrian era, is referred to as the Cambrian explosion, because so many different kinds of species appear all at once, in the layers of rock assumed to be from the Cambrian era. There are also no fossils after the strata that contain the fossil record. Darwin said his current problem was that there were not many fossils in 1859, and that, with time and more fossils, his theory would be vindicated. However, we now have over 250,000 fossils and nowhere is there a fossil showing any transitional signs of one species evolving into another. No fossils have been found outside of what is considered the fossil record. There is one fossil record, and only one. The many layers of strata were not formed over many millions of years, they were all formed by the sedimentary layering of the earth's material as the waters of Noah's flood receded. The fossil record does not support any of Darwin's claims, in fact the record contradicts his basic assumptions.

327

THE
HYDROPLATE
THEORY

Dr. Walt Brown has developed what he calls the Hydroplate Theory[33]. The premise of the Hydroplate theory is that Noah's Flood actually did happen; however, it was much more cataclysmic and violent than anyone realizes. In Genesis 1:6 Scripture reads; "And God said, Let an expanse be in the midst of the waters, and let it divide between the waters and the waters. And God made the expanse, and He separated between the waters which were under the expanse and the waters which were above the expanse.

Psalm 33:7 The waters of the sea were gathered like a heap, setting the depths in storehouses.

Psalm 24:1 The earth is Jehovah's and the fullness of it the world, and those who live in it. For He has founded it on the seas and established it on the rivers.

Psalm 136:6 to Him who spread the earth on the waters; for His mercy endures forever.

Psalm 75:3 ...I set firm its pillars.

To envision what Dr. Brown is theorizing, imagine that water is on the earth, (oceans, seas, lakes and rivers) and under the earth, in subterranean chambers between the earth's crust and the mantle supported by pillars, naturally forming rock supports.

Scripture says very specifically in Genesis chapter 7:11, "In the six

---

[33] Dr Walt Brown Hydroplate Theory; Text, *In the Beginning,* there is also a YouTube video under Hydroplate Theory

hundredth year of Noah's life, in the second month, in the seventeenth day of the month, in this day all the fountains of the great deep were risen, and the windows of the heavens were opened up. And the rain was on the earth forty days and forty nights."

According to Dr. Brown's theory, the waters of the great deep were the waters that were under the earth's crust in the subterranean chambers and exploded out under tremendous pressure. Imagine, since the creation of the earth, the water under the crust would be continually absorbing increasing amounts of energy from a lunar pumping action. The water under the crust would be affected just as the tides above the crust; however, there would be no release mechanism for the gathering energy, until the pressure became so great it forced a crack in the crust. The water carrying all of the rocks and debris from under the crust, and the erosion from the sides of the crack, are blasted along with the water, high into the atmosphere. This is why the surface of the moon has impact craters on the earth side and is relatively smooth on the back side. It also explains why chemicals on the moon are the same as those found on earth. The crack spread around the earth spewing water and debris into the troposphere, through the stratosphere and into the mesosphere. It took less than two hours for the crack to circumnavigate the entire earth.

This explosion also contained all of the material needed to form the strata of the fossil record. This rupture that encircled the earth can be seen now as the mid-Atlantic ridge - the longest mountain range in the world that runs for 46,000 miles under the surface of the ocean. The water was released with such force that it rose to tremendous heights, froze and returned to earth as super cooled hail and froze much of the earth, causing the ice age. Along with the hail was the flood waters themselves that covered the entire earth, killing and burying everything that "breathes air through its nostrils"[34]. The Biblical account of the flood reads; "And the rain was on the earth forty days and forty nights...And the waters were strong, exceedingly violent on the earth...and the waters were strong on the earth a hundred and fifty days...And the fountains of the deep and the windows of the heavens were stopped...and the waters diminished at the end of a hundred and fifty days"[35] The rains fell for forty days and the waters continued to rise as the "waters did not diminish for one hundred and fifty days." Once the earth was sufficiently covered in water the upward force of the water was quelled, however, the water continued to pour out of the subterranean chambers. It's like a leaky pipe once the water is deep enough and covers the pipe you no longer see the water spray, but the water level continues to rise. Some of the fossils remains are found with food still in their mouth and stomach. The vegetation in these preserved mammals are from a sub-tropical climate, although they are found within the arctic circle. This was our one and only ice age and the slow recovery has been termed "global warming."

The flood was so cataclysmic that the earth shifted off its axis by as much as 40 degrees. Some of the mammoths that have been found in the northern most part of the globe have been found with other animal fossils that burrow into the ground which could not occur in areas with permafrost. Dr Brown theorizes that the earth at creation was one large continent surrounded by water. This subterranean eruption spilt the land mass into today's continents, as is evidenced by the fact that the earth's mountain ranges parallel the mid-Atlantic ridge. As the continents drifted apart, they came into contact with the mid-Atlantic ridge, the earth buckled and crumbled forming the current mountain ranges and huge land basins. This occurred before the water drained out of the pliable granite on the newly laid sediment which eventually hardened with the loss of the water trapped in the granite.

---

[34] Genesis 6:17
[35] The Interlinear Bible; Genesis 7:12,19,24, Ch 8:2,3

Mountain range British Columbia

There is considerable evidence in Dr Brown's book; *In the Beginning*, also view his short 10-minute video on YouTube. There is also a two-and-a-half-hour version of the Hydroplate Theory by Bryan Nickel, on YouTube, that goes into considerable detail of the Hydroplate Theory.

https://www.youtube.com/watch?v=sD9ZGt9UA-U Dr Walt Brown

https://www.youtube.com/watch?v=4hhE6tzJR_c   Bryan   Nickel extended explanation.

The most significant part of Dr. Brown's theory for our discussion are the mechanics of the flood and what it means for understanding of evolution and creationism.

The Hydroplate Theory demonstrates that the fossil record is the result of the flood. There are no fossils before or after the flood. We have fossils because during the flood all of the life on the earth, "with breath in its nostrils," suffocated, drowned, and were buried under all of the hail and sediment created by the flood, thereby preserving the fossils. This explains Darwin's dilemma of advanced species being at the bottom of the layers of fossils in the strata. In a process called liquefaction everything was sorted by weight, size and shape, and formed into layers as the material settled out of the flood waters.

Most of this theory, like evolution, cannot be observed, which makes it difficult to ascertain with certainty what actually happened. That is until the eruption of Mount St. Helens in 1980. Two years after the eruption the crater on Mount St. Helens was filling with rain and snow run off until it breached the edge of the crater. All of the contents spilled over the side, widening the opening, and the contents spilled out at 90 miles per hour and rushed down the side of the mountain. The mud flow carved a canyon into the terrain below, ranging in depth from 150 to 650 feet deep. The mud flow revealed a twenty-five-foot-thick layer of layered rock that had been formed from the initial eruption.[36]

https://www.youtube.com/watch?v=mcm9YgrvJlE   Mt.   St.   Helens eruption

Dr. Brown spent a year on the Colorado Plateau and discovered what he maintains is a large basin that was filled with water; two great lakes; - Grand Lake and Hopi Lake. As the flood waters receded, all of the great basins on all of the continents and low-lying areas were filled with water. As time passed and rain continued to fall, and with the snow run off, the lakes breached their boundaries and flooded out of the basin, just like at Mount St Helens. This immense amount of water rushing in one direction cut the Grand Canyon in a matter of weeks, not millions of years. Rivers may broaden their width, but they do not dig a deeper river bottom. Where are the canyons for the Mississippi, the Nile, the Amazon, the Tigris or the Euphrates rivers?

Dr. Brown also maintains the debris and water that blasted out of the bursting of the fountain of the deep spread much of the debris and water into the stratosphere forming the meteors, asteroids and comets that fill the skies today. That is why when these celestial objects are examined, they are found to contain water, salt, dormant bacteria and other elements

---

[36] Origins- Mount St. Helens - Explosive Evidence For Creation with Dr. Steve Austin - YouTube

common to earth.

The pictures we are rarely shown by evolutionists are tree trunks that span many layers of the strata. We are hard pressed to think that a tree can live for millions of years. Use your search engine to find, "trees in strata" under images.

The fossil record was formed by Noah's flood. It is at the same depth all across the earth. Over 250 cultures have a history of a massive flood, in which only eight people were spared. We do not have any fossils since the flood, outside the fossil record, because when creatures die, they are eaten by scavenger species, decompose and are eaten by various insects. We have one fossil record, and only one, formed by the rapid burials of all land dwellers during the time of Noah's flood. This is also why there are so few human fossils. When a human drowns, the lungs fill with water and the body sinks. After a couple of days, depending on the temperature of the water, the bacteria in the gut and chest cavity produce enough gas— methane, hydrogen sulfide, and carbon dioxide—to float it to the surface like a balloon. The floating bodies were food for all of the sea creatures to consume. As the sea creatures do not have breath in their nostrils, they were not killed by the flood. The skeletal remains would be scattered all over on the ocean floor.

The worldwide flood also explains all of the fossil fuel deposits, as vegetation was buried compressed and superheated, creating the coal, oil and natural gas deposits we find today. Additionally, before the waters completely receded there were land bridges between many of the continents which allowed for the dispersal of the earth's growing population of both man and animals.

In March 2009, scientists released the results of their research on deep-sea (depths of ~300 to 3,000 m) corals throughout the world. They discovered specimens of _Leiopathes glaberrima_ to be among the oldest living organisms on the planet: around 4,265 years old. They show that the "radial growth rates are as low as 4 to 35 micrometers per year and that individual colony longevities are on the order of thousands of years" They know how much the reef grows in a year, so they can calculate the age of the reef. If the flood occurred approximately 1400 years after creation, this would put the age of the earth at about 6,000 years. The idea of millions or billions of years of the earth's existence is a myth.

https://www.youtube.com/watch?v=SOtGb8hKyWE Dr Berlinski

Dr. Mary Schweitzer, a paleontologist, discovered pliable soft tissue and red blood cells in the thigh bone of a Tyrannosaurus Rex. The tissue and red blood cells could not have survived millions of years but suggested instead thousands of years. Dr Schweitzer was ridiculed, and attempts were made to discredit her work. She quotes in an article in Discover Magazine, April 2006, "I had one reviewer tell me that he didn't care what the data said, he knew that what I was finding wasn't possible, "says Schweitzer. "I wrote back and said, "Well, what data would convince you?" And he said. "None." No matter what the evidence says it has to be repudiated, evolution must be protected. Not for the sake of science but because, if we rule out evolution, all that remains is intelligent design, - God. And that means accountability and a judgment day of rewards and punishment. From the book of Job, chapter 21; 14 "And they say to God, Depart from us, for we do not desire the knowledge of Your ways – 15 What is the Almighty, that we should serve Him? And what do we profit if we entreat Him...30 For the wicked is kept for the day of calamity – they shall be brought to the day of wrath."

Professor Sören Löutrup from the University of Sweden is quoted as saying; "I suppose that nobody will deny that it is a great misfortune if an entire branch of science becomes addicted to a false theory. But this is what has happened in biology: I believe that one day the Darwinian myth will be ranked the greatest deceit in the history of science. When this happens, many people will pose the question; How did this ever happen?"

Before we leave this subject matter completely, I want to address the references to dinosaurs in Scripture and some things to ponder that I came across in my research. God tells Job, in the book of Job, which incidentally is believed to be the oldest book in the Bible, but nobody really knows when it was written. However, there is speculation that Moses wrote Job when he was in exile after fleeing from Egypt. In exile he lived for forty years in Midian which is believed to be a neighboring community of Job's residence in Uz. Quoting from Job, "Now behold Behemoth, (behold, which means see or observe, as in look at Behemoth) which I made along with you; he eats grass like an ox; see, now, his strength is in his loins, and his force in the muscle of his belly he hangs his tail like a cedar...his bones are like tubes of bronze, his bones like bars of iron."[37] And in the next chapter; "Can you draw out the leviathan with a hook, or hold down his tongue with a cord...Put your hand on him; remember the battle; you will not do it again!" "His sneezing flash forth light, and his eyes are as the eyelids of the dawn. Out of his mouth go burning torches, and sparks of fire leap out. Smoke goes out of his nostrils, like a boiling pot fired by reeds. His breath kindles coals; and the flame goes out from his mouth...There is nothing like him on earth, one made without fear."[38]

The word dinosaur was first used in 1842. Prior to that, these various creatures were referred to as dragons. Webster's 1828 dictionary defines dragon as follows; "Dragon; drag is fire, dragon is a leader, chief or sovereign reign. In Welsh, draig is rendered by Owen a procreator or generating principle, "a fiery serpent, a dragon. Hence, I infer that the word originally signified a shooting meteor in the atmosphere, a fiery meteor, and hence a fiery or flying serpent. A kind of winged serpent."

In Scripture, dragon seems sometimes to signify a large marine fish or serpent;" Isa 27:1 "In that day the Lord will punish Leviathan the fleeing serpent, With His fierce and great and mighty sword, Even, Leviathan the twisted serpent; And He will kill the dragon who lives in the sea." "Sometimes it seems to signify a venomous land serpent. Ps xci (Psalm 91). The dragon shalt thou trample underfoot. It is often used for the devil, who is called the old serpent." Rev. 20: 2.

Almost all of the dinosaur fossils are found in North America, Europe and Argentina, areas that were not populated until after the flood. Fossils in the Mid-east are very rare and the one found there was an herbivore. It is conceivable that man and dinosaurs coexisted at one time. I think Dr. Walt Brown's theory is correct and as such man and dinosaurs would have lived at the same time. You may remember that reptiles continue to grow until they die. The early earth people lived for a very long time. The oldest recorded person was Methuselah who lived to be 969 years old. Methuselah's death was followed by the flood, and his name means "when he is dead it shall be sent." If dinosaurs exist today, they would not be very big. There are marshes and swamps in Africa and South America as big as states that no one has ever explored. Marco Polo, St

---

[37] Job 40:15-18
[38] Job 41: 1, 8, 18-21, 33

George and Alexander the Great all wrote of dragons in their memoirs. Alexander the Great wrote that his men were terrified of the dragons that lived in the caves. Many cultures have representations of dinosaurs, the fire breathing dragons of the Orient, and the cave and pottery hieroglyphics of dinosaurs found in many cultures. How could they so accurately portray dinosaurs if they weren't observed? To think about a fire breathing dragon reminds me of the bombardier beetle. The beetle when threatened emits a chemical mixture at 212 degrees through a nozzle at the end of its shell. The chemicals are stored in two separate chambers within the beetle. When a threat is present the chemicals are released and just as the chemicals exit the body an enzyme is releases which in effect acts as a spark plug and ignites the chemicals. Those strange protrusions on the foreheads of some dinosaurs could serve the same function, ergo fire breathing dragons.

There are many stories of Mokele Mbembe from the Congo[39] and South America which is purported to be a brontosaurus the size of an elephant. An expedition into the Congo showed drawings of animals to local tribes and they were unable to identify a bear or a deer, but they did recognize a drawing of a Sauropod, a member of the Brontosaurus family, whom they called Mokele Mbembe. They added the caution that you do not go in the river when Mokele Mbembe is there. The tribe is near a 55,000 square mile jungle area that has never been explored.[40]

Then there is the controversy over the Biloxi Footprints. At an excavation site in Biloxi Mississippi, creationists maintain human footprint impressions in the rock are found on the same strata layer as dinosaur footprints. Some of the footprints overlap each other. The research is called Biloxi Footprints. Evolutionists disagree and say they were made by a previously unknown dinosaur. Your worldview with or without God determines how you interpret reality. Where are the fossils for this unknown dinosaur?

---

[39] YouTube – In search of the Congo Dinosaur
[40] YouTube video 9:58 min – Tribal people of Republic of Congo: There are dinosaur like creature is in jungle

WE WILL NOT
HAVE THIS MAN
TO RULE OVER US
Luke 19:14

The word oligarchy means "few." It is a form of government that is, in essence, a power structure in which power rests with a small number of people, who are virtually unaccountable to anyone else. Historically, these "few" have been nobility, those who gained wealth and position through family ties, or positions of corporate, religious, and military control. Throughout history, oligarchies have often been tyrannical, relying on public obedience or oppression in order to exist. They often use their military to enforce their decrees when citizens offer resistance or protest, which is why so many governments do not want their citizens to bear arms.

Most governments devolve into an oligarchy. Our Founding Fathers anticipated this, and there was much debate, without resolution regarding term limits. However, they did establish as a check the president, vice president and legislators must be elected by the people. President Washington and President Jefferson set the president of leaving office after two four-year terms. This president held until President Franklin Roosevelt was elected president to four terms. After which congress passed the 22nd Amendment limiting the president to 2, 4-year terms. To avoid an oligarchy the Founding Fathers constructed a government with checks and balances. It is also why the Founding Fathers wrote the Constitution and the Bill of Rights as a means of checking governmental power, against eventual abuses and protecting the rights of Americans. "Congress shall make no law..." The Founders vision was of a hierarchy consisting of: God, "We The People", three branches of government, overseen by checks and balances.

Legislative Branch Checks on the Executive Office and the Judiciary

Checks on the Executive

Impeachment power (House)

Trial of impeachments (Senate)

Selection of the President (House) and Vice President (Senate) in the case of no majority of electoral votes

May override Presidential vetoes with a 2/3 majority vote

Senate approves departmental appointments

Senate approves treaties and ambassadors

Approval of replacement Vice President

Power to declare war

Power to enact taxes and allocate funds

President must, from time-to-time, deliver a State of the Union address

Checks on the Judiciary

Senate approves federal judges

Impeachment power (House)

Trial of impeachments (Senate)

Power to initiate constitutional amendments

Power to set courts inferior to the Supreme Court

Power to set jurisdiction of courts

Power to alter the size of the Supreme Court

Checks on the Legislature - because it is bicameral, the Legislative branch has a degree of self-checking.

Bills must be passed by both houses of Congress

House must originate revenue bills

Neither house may adjourn for more than three days without the consent of the other house

All journals are to be published

Legislative Responsibilities

Passing bills

Broad taxing and spending power

Regulating interstate commerce

Controlling the federal budget

Borrowing money on the credit of the United States

Sole power to declare war and to support and regulate the military

Overseeing and making rules for the government and its officers to follow

Defining the jurisdiction of the federal judiciary by law in cases not specified by the Constitution
Ratifying treaties
Sole power of impeachment and trial of impeachments
Executive Branch Checks on the Legislature and the Judiciary
Checks on the Legislature
Veto Power
Vice President is President of the Senate
Commander in chief of the military
Recess appointments
Emergency calling into session of one or both houses of Congress
May force adjournment when both houses cannot agree on adjournment
Compensation cannot be diminished
Checks on the Judiciary
Power to appoint judges
Pardon power
Checks on the Executive
Vice President and Cabinet can vote that the President is unable to discharge his duties
Executive Responsibilities:
The President is the commander-in-chief of the armed forces
Executes the instructions of Congress
May veto bills passed by Congress
Executes the spending authorized by Congress
Declares states of emergency, publishes regulations and executive orders
Makes executive agreements and signs treaties
Makes appointments to the federal judiciary, federal executive departments, and other posts
Can grant reprieves and pardons for offenses against the United States, except in cases of impeachment.
Judicial Branch Checks on the Legislature
Checks on the Legislature
Judicial review
Seats are held on good behavior
Compensation cannot be diminished
The Judicial Branch's Responsibilities
Determining which laws Congress intended to apply to any given case

Determining how Congress meant the law to apply to disputes

Determining how a law acts to determine the disposition of prisoners

Determining how a law acts to compel testimony and the production of evidence

Determining how laws should be interpreted to assure uniform policies through the appeals process

Reviewing the constitutionality of laws through judicial review

Notwithstanding, an oligarchy has emerged in American politics. It looks a little different than those of the past and that is only because societies have become very complex and our model of government under the Constitution was very innovative. The trend of an oligarchy in America consists of globally minded elitists in the democratic and republican parties, called progressives or globalists, that want open borders and a single government for the world. Socialism and communism have failed worldwide, the globalists think it can work if there are no countries, only one people and one government. Which is in effect enslaving the world population. The globalists and the compliant mainstream media continually attack America because they cannot initiate a one world government as long as there are superpowers. America must go first, the strongest and most influential, then Russia and China. Their belief is that, for the most part "We The People" are not qualified and are too naive for self-government. Globalist believe that only they know what is best for the masses, and only they are capable of running the government. This is what President John Kennedy meant when he said, "There's a plot in this country to enslave every man, woman, and child. Before I leave this high and noble office, I intend to expose this plot." Seven days later he was assassinated. There are six major media companies that control 90 percent of what you read, watch and listen to, in 1983 there were 50 media companies. Today 232 media executives' control what 277 million Americas receive as news and entertainment, with an income of 275 Billion dollars. Many of whom are globalists and ensure that their message comes across to Americans in the news, movies, TV, and radio. The six major media companies are: Comcast's whose notable properties are, NBC, Universal Pictures and Focus Features. Newscorp's notable properties are, Fox, Wall Street Journal and the New York Post. Disney's notables are, ABC, ESPN, Pixar, Miramax, and Marvel Studios. Viacom notables are, MTV, Nick Jr, SET, CMT and Paramount Pictures. Time Warner's notables are, CNN, HBO, Time, Warner Bros. CBS's notables are, Showtime, Smithsonian Channel, NFL.Com, and 60 Minutes.

The oligarchy in America, better known as, "globalists" have a centric power source that self-perpetuates by giving the illusion to the American people that they are in charge of the government, when in fact we work to support them. "We the People," keep them in money and in power. The globalist is driven by any and all programs that increase their wealth and power, by taking wealth from "We The People". Whoever controls the money controls the people; which is why there is no end to their incessant desire for the accumulation of wealth and quest for more power. This is why we have in large part gone from a single income to two-income families to support a single household. The nations of the world are paying a billion dollars a day to stop global warming, which is another scam to accumulate money and power, under the pretense of redistributing the wealth. You might ask yourself, where does the money go? I suspect the money is used to pay the individuals needed to influence, lobby and implement Agenda 21/30 across the globe.

In 1992 178 heads of state met in Rio de Janeiro at the UN Conference on Environment and Development. The conference produced five documents for, "a comprehensive plan of action to be taken globally, nationally and locally by organizations of the United Nations system, government, and major groups, in every area in which humans have an impact." The end result of the conference was five documents to be implemented by all nations to ensure "Sustainable Development," of all societies. The master document is called "Agenda for the 21st Century, and because not all of it has been implemented it is now called Agenda 30. Meaning it should be in place by 2030 as long as the 2021 deadline was missed. Agenda 21/30 is a political movement designed to control the world's economy, development, capture and redistribute the world's wealth on a national, state, and local lever. The precursor for implementing Agenda 21 is climate change, this is supposed to be the apocalypse that will befall all humanity and justifies the extreme measures needed under Agenda 21/30 to save the world. When climate change was debunked in 2009 under, "Climategate." The hoax was rebranded as "global warming."

In 2019 the Supreme Court in British Colombia threw out a lawsuit filed by Michael Mann against Dr. Tim Ball who had challenged Mann's study results on global warming. Mann's climate study is the one used by the UN as the premise for the urgent need for the implementation of Agenda 21/30 to stop global warming. The lawsuit was thrown out because Mann would not provide to the court his data that lead to his conclusions on global warming. Mann's graph was referred to as the

341

"hockey stick graph" because it shows steady temperatures from the year 1000 to today which is represented by a sudden rise in global temperatures over the last approximately hundred years. Dr. Ball's research, for which he provided documentation, showed a history of high temperatures, and some even higher than todays from the years 1150 to 1350.[41] Mann was ordered to pay all court costs, and face a possible criminal investigation in the U.S. Mann not unlike many scientists fudge their results to say what they want it to say, he just got caught. Global warming, climate change, like evolution are a fanciful hoax perpetuated by globalists world-wide in an attempt to achieve world dominance under a one world government, governing all people.

The other documents produced at the UN conference were the "Biodiversity Treaty," that declares hundreds of millions of acres of land should be designated as off limits to human development. Another was the, "Rio Declaration," which called for the eradication of poverty throughout the world by the redistribution of wealth. Which was to be financed through global warming funds, inequitable trades agreements, such as; NAFTA, and TTP (Trans-Pacific Partnership). The TTP involved: Australia, Brunel, Canada, Chile, Japan, Malaysia, Mexico, Vietnam, New Zealand, Peru, Singapore, and the United States, however, President Trump refused to sign, and the treaty fell apart. Another document was the, "Convention on Forest Principles," which mandated international management of the world's forest.

How will the control of every aspect of our existence be controlled by the UN? The U.S. Government will not stand for it, we will not give up our sovereignty. Most democrats and some republicans are compliant, they like to refer to themselves as progressives, which actually translates into globalists and it is the globalists that are enacting Agenda 21/30. The means of implementing the elements of Agenda 21/30 in the U.S. is through the Presidential Council on Sustainable Development, created under President Bill Clinton and carried forward by George Bush and Obama. Members of the council include; The Sierra Club, The Nature Conservancy, National Wildlife Federation, and the World Resource Institute, termed NGOs, non-governmental agencies. They are unelected officials, with no accountability to "We The People," and should have no jurisdiction over Americans. Six members from these organizations are

---

[41] As reported by the Gateway Pundit on August 26, 2019, "Hockey Stick Broken! "Scientist" Michael Mann loses in Court, Forced to Pay Court Costs – Global Warming Hoax Hit Hardest"

part of the twelve council secretaries and they work directly with the UN to establish policy. These are the groups that sue over development because said development will endanger, an owl species, or turtles, or a type of mussels. They are currently fighting against farmers in the west using water, during the drought, for irrigation, because that will endanger the smelt. There is also a myriad of regional government agencies set up to implement Agenda 21/30. Most municipalities are strapped for cash, these regional agencies extract compliance to their demands by offering grants to local governments. The agencies are set up so that the regulations can be put in place circumventing congress. Three of the regulatory agencies that span from Maine to Louisiana are: The Northern Border Regional Commission, The Delta Regional Authority, and the Appalachian Regional Commission. All of which have been defunded by President Trump.

George Bush Sr. signed off on Agenda 21[42] telling the conference, "It is the sacred principles enshrined in the United Nations Charter to which the American people will henceforth pledge their allegiance." Bush Sr. was the first president to use the term, "New world order." The problem with these treaties is that once you sign off on them, they evolve over time, you are still committed to the treaty and the changes, even if they become detrimental to the U.S. in the future. That is why President Trump un-signed the UN Small Arms Treaty and would not participate in the Paris Climate Accord. The trade deal NAFTA signed into law by Bill Clinton, the following year, cost America 600,000 jobs and closed 70,000 factories in America. Our trading with Mexico under NAFTA went from a $1.7 billion U.S. surplus to a $54 billion deficit. President Trump re-negotiated the NAFTA Treaty and rolled back the rules limiting carbon emissions and those regulating fossil fuel producers, which was all part of Agenda 21/30. President Trump also, reversed Obama's war on coal. He also opened up federal lands to oil and gas exploration which had been severely restricted under Obama, again part of compliance to Agenda 21/30. The U.S. has (had) an $800-billion trade deficit which means our $800 billion flows to other countries and does not come back to the U.S. We have lost that money, in the redistribution of wealth. That is how China has become a world superpower since NAFTA was signed. China is not a part of NAFTA

---

[42]   http://www.agenda21course.com/defining-agenda-21-and-how-america-has-been-made-to-accept-sustainable-development/ Agenda 21 lesson 1 – 10

but at the same time they became members of the World Trade Organization. Our largest trade deficits are with China, Germany, Mexico, Canada, South Korea, and Japan. Under Obama We had 95 million Americans out of work in a nation of 310 million. That is 30.6 percent unemployment, not the 5% the globalists with its media allies, continued to tell the public. We had a 54% unemployment rate in the inner city, do we really need to wonder why there was such a high crime rate? Agenda 21/30 and all of the corresponding regulations was all undertaken to weaken our sovereignty as a nation and bring us under control of the dictates of the UN Agenda 21/30. In addition to gutting our military. All actions to undercut Americas standing in the world and given more time America would have been neutralized. This is why there are such rigorous attempts to remove President Trump from office. It is no longer about democrats and republicans; it is about nationalists and globalists. We should also, halt all immigration until we have 100% employment for Americans and all U.S. children, veterans and the needy are out of poverty. Illegal immigration costs the U.S. taxpayer 132 billion dollars every year. The only exception to an immigration ban should be for people who will contribute to American society, with a preference for persecuted Christians, and those that are willing to acclimate to our way of life. The European Union is an exercise in globalism under Agenda 21/30 with open borders and a governing body in Brussels for the twenty-seven nation members.

Nationalism is about protecting your borders, that is why the political legislatures with a globalist agenda in America are trying to prevent the border wall. ICLEI, the International Committee for Local Environmental Initiatives is charged with implementing Agenda 21/30 in all levels of our local government. When the vice-chair of ICLEI was asked about individual rights he replied, "Individual rights take a back seat to the collective." In the U.S. government we have globalist legislators and judges that support Agenda 21/30 which is in direct violation of the U.S. Constitution and the Bill of Rights, to which they have taken an oath to defend. When a person violates their oath of office, they should be removed from that office and charged with sedition and treason.

The reason we are in the state we are in is because of bad science: in evolution and global warming, bad government: crooked politician, payoffs, and abuse of powers along with regional governmental agencies. A poor theology brought about on June 17, 1963, the U.S. Supreme Court concluded that any Bible reciting or prayer, in public schools, was deemed unconstitutional. A Supreme Court that makes law displaying overreach and an abuse of powers which is unconstitutional, needs to be under a new set of checks and balances. A distorted worldview held by some of those in power, especially the globalists, and their numerous means to circumvent the U.S. Constitution are having an effect on America's sovereignty and the freedom of its citizens. And we have a globalist news media that hides the truth from the American people, that is why so few people know about Agenda 21/30. It started in and is as old as the Garden of Eden. In Luke 19:14 we read; "But the citizens hated him, and sent a delegation after him saying, "We do not desire this one to reign over us." Herein lies the crux of the issue; worldviews. The Founding Fathers all had a Christian worldview, in spite of what historical revisionists would have you believe. Remember the Mayflower Compact, written and signed on Nov 11, 1620, on the Mayflower ship as it laid at anchor off America's shores stating, "...Haueing vndertaken for ye glorie of God and the aduancemente of ye Christian faith...a voyage to plant ye first colonie in ye Northerne parts of Virginia..." I think I know why Noah Webster thought he had to standardize the English langue.

The Mayflower Compact was the first agreement for self-government to be created and enforced as the great American experiment. However, the blueprint for our self-rule that can be traced back to God, Moses and the Ten Commandments. Conversely, the globalists have a worldview that eliminates God. This is why globalists so desperately cling to the theory of evolution, despite all of the evidence to the contrary. It is a worldview that tries to be completely autonomous and will not answer to a higher authority. If they did, they could not do what they do. Scripture says there will be a day of judgement[43] and it is not just about sin. Judgment is also about what we did or did not do according to God's commandments, statutes, ordinances and judgments. Scripture says we will be judged for our deeds.[44] A "deed" is not necessarily a sin it can be just a wrong committed by someone. This is a scrutiny some people do not want to endure. Nonetheless, ignoring God, does not make Him irrelevant or His judgments less real. Within the context of man's relationship to God there are basically two worldviews. The Christian worldview says God created the heavens, the earth, and man in His image; also, that man has fallen and is in need of a Savior. The afterlife is either an eternal reward or an eternal punishment. The evolutionary, globalists worldview states there is

---

[43] Romans 14:10
[44] Jeremiah 17:10

no God; man evolved from a single cell and man's significance comes from what he accomplishes while alive on earth, to the benefit or detriment of everyone else, survival of the fittest. The afterlife is death, so, there are no consequences for our behavior. The deceptive philosophies of the evolutionists turned globalists are that without God, there are no moral restraints that would inhibit one's accomplishments, and there is no accountability for one's actions; hence, those in power are able to do whatever they wish, funded and supported by the lesser class. People who do not report to a higher authority are capable of some extremely horrendous acts. The Christian worldview is that created man has a fallen nature and has a proclivity for evil, and therefore is in need of moral restraint. The global progressive worldview is that man is an evolved creature that is basically good and does not need external restraints on his behavior. If man is basically good, why is their evil in the world? This is what has gone wrong, we have allowed the globalists to throw God out of our government, our schools and out of our culture, effectively removing or suppressing religion and morality from our culture, the intended restraint on man's behavior of the Founding Fathers.

I had a job a while ago where the owner took his managers to events in other states for meetings and some recreation, which was usually golf. The culture was such in this company that while the guys were out of town they would engage in adultery, and as long as they were doing that, the wives back home could do likewise. I would participate in the daily events and after dinner I would go up to my room. I eventually was fired from this job because I didn't fit in; because I didn't participate, I was making the guys feel like they were doing something wrong. My moral restraint exemplified an accountability to a higher authority, which made others uncomfortable as they had to consider the consequences of their behavior. Just like the globalists that push evolution, the more that believe as they do the less isolated, they feel. That's why we do not go to Scripture to verify our morality, we take a poll. If a lot of people are doing it, it must be okay. Polls are notoriously unreliable as questions are structured to achieve a desired outcome.

Romans 1:18-25 (NASB) "For the wrath of God is revealed from heaven against all ungodliness and unrighteousness of men who suppress the truth in unrighteousness, because that which is known about God is evident within them; for God made it evident to them. For since the creation of the world His invisible attributes, His eternal power and divine nature, have been clearly seen, being understood through what has been made, so that they are without excuse. For even though they knew God, they did not honor Him as God or give thanks, but they became futile in their speculations, and their foolish heart was darkened. Professing to be wise, they became fools, and exchanged the glory of the incorruptible God for an image in the form of corruptible man... Therefore, God gave them over in the lusts of their hearts to impurity, so that their bodies would be dishonored among them. For they exchanged the truth of God for a lie and worshiped and served the creature rather than the Creator, who is blessed forever."

Romans 1:28 (NASB) "And just as they did not see fit to acknowledge God any longer, God gave them over to a depraved mind, to do those things which are not proper, being filled with all unrighteousness, wickedness, greed, evil; full of envy, murder, strife, deceit, malice; *they are* gossips, slanderers, haters of God, insolent, arrogant, boastful, inventors of evil, disobedient to parents, without understanding, untrustworthy, unloving, unmerciful; and although they know the ordinance of God, that those who practice such things are worthy of death, they not only do the same, but also give hearty approval to those who practice them."

Romans Ch 2:1 (NASB) "Therefore you have no excuse, every one of you who passes judgment, for in that which you judge another, you condemn yourself; for you who judge practice the same things. And we know that the judgment of God rightly falls upon those who practice such things. But do you suppose this, O man, when you pass judgment on those who practice such things and do the same *yourself,* that you will escape the judgment of God? Or do you think lightly of the riches of His kindness and tolerance and patience, not knowing that the kindness of God leads you to repentance? But because of your stubbornness and unrepentant heart you are storing up wrath for yourself in the day of wrath and revelation of the righteous judgment of God, who WILL RENDER TO EACH PERSON ACCORDING TO HIS DEEDS: to those who by perseverance in doing good seek for glory and honor and immortality, eternal life; but to those who are selfishly ambitious and do not obey the truth, but obey unrighteousness, wrath and indignation. *There will be* tribulation and distress for every soul of man who does evil, of the Jew first and also of the Greek, but glory and honor and peace to everyone who does good, to the Jew first and also to the Greek. For there is no partiality with God."

The evolution theory will erase God from our culture. If we do not need God, we do not need a Savior, the government will be all you need. Without God there are no unalienable rights. Without unalienable rights, the only rights we have will be those given by man. Any right given by a man can be taken away by a man. Wisdom should tell us that fallen man cannot be his own lawgiver and judge.

Those who exchange the truth for the lie do so because their life motivation is lust for greed, money, power, and influence, "the lust of the flesh"[45] and to satisfy the selfish hunger of their egos. They cannot tell you that is what drives them, or they will be rejected, so they subscribe to the religion of evolution, global warming, and political correctness so that you cannot say what you think. Can you hear the hiss of the snake? The progressive globalists have to subscribe to the theory of evolution because they cannot just come out and say we do not believe in God. (Although, that is exactly what they are saying.) They will not submit to a higher authority because then they cannot do the things they want to do. They lie, because their deeds are evil. Liberty, man's freedom, which the globalists are trying to take, is a right from God.

So, this is their worldview and they see everything through this prism. Even though it is a lie they must profess the lie to accomplish world dominion. This rationale is no different than that of Islam, where any lie is permissible as long as it advances the goal of an Islamic dominated world. The ends justify any means. Their approach is not limited to their attempt to negate God, but extends to maintaining that the constitution is outdated, and thereby usurping the rule of law. A republic is governed by the rule of law, not by an individual, a monarchy, or by elitists and the law is derived from God's law, not man's self-assumed position of authority. A government under the rule of law assures equal justice for all of its citizenry.

Globalists and historical revisionists espouse that many of the Founding Fathers were nothing but criminals, however, they do not qualify that sentiment, and it is true many were locked up for their Protestant views. They were also branded criminals and traitors because they were in rebellion against the crown. One such criminal was William Penn, a Quaker, who was imprisoned for his beliefs. Penn negotiated his way out of prison by traveling to America. He established a colony in Pennsylvania as a "religious experiment", with an emphasis on religious freedom and

---

[45] 1 John 2:16

democracy. He was also well known for establishing good relations with the Lenape American Indians. Compare that to a quote by Jeremy Rifkin, atheist, American economist; "We no longer feel ourselves to be guests in someone else's home and therefore obligated to make our behavior conform with a set of preexisting cosmic rules. It is our creation now. We make the rules. We establish the parameters of reality. We create the world, and because we do, we no longer feel beholden to outside forces. We no longer have to justify our behavior, for we are now the architects of the universe. We are responsible to nothing outside ourselves, for we are; the kingdom, the power, and the glory forever and ever." We do not see things as they are, we see things as we are. Are you beginning to understand What the Hell Went Wrong?

WHAT THE HELL WENT WRONG

*"**F**or we are opposed around the world by a monolithic and ruthless conspiracy that relies on covert means for expanding its sphere of influence - on infiltration instead of invasion, on subversion instead of elections, on intimidation instead of free choice, on guerrillas by night instead of armies by day. It is a system which has conscripted vast human and material resources into the building of a tightly knit, highly efficient machine that combines military, diplomatic, intelligence, economic, scientific and political operations."* John F Kennedy

The answer to the question of, *"What the Hell Went Wrong,"* is we lost our moral compass, and now we have a crisis of morality. Government officials without morals seek to establish their own morality, which has no stability and will change based on who has the next power base. However, the artificial morality already in place will only worsen as the next layer is laid on by the next liberal globalists elected to power. This is what leads to a downward spiral of morality, the inevitable decadence leads to the collapse of a republic.

The colonies were established on the Founder's wisdom that good government would come from good people. However, they also understood man has a proclivity for significance, which often leads to unsuitable behavior to obtain that significance. The first form of checks and balances would have to be on man. Being that all of the founders were Christian it was natural for them to see the Christian religion and Judeo-Christian values as the basis for moral conduct. God's commandments, ordinances, statutes and judgments were all based on absolute truth, as they originate from the Creator, and espouse the judicial treatment of your

350

fellow man. The Founders desire was to establish a government, free from the perils of past and present governments.

In the first half of the 1500s John Calvin emerged as the successor to Martin Luther as the preeminent Protestant theologian for Reformed theology. Not all protestants subscribed to Calvin's theology, which became known as, "Calvinism." However, his influence can be seen in the extreme significance the Founders placed on Religion and Morality as essential for self-restraint. One of the five doctrines of Calvinism, was "the total depravity of man." Calvin held that man was completely depraved and incapable of any good or responding to God without God's grace. Calvin thought that even man's will was totally depraved aside from the grace of God. If man is totally depraved all the more reason for man to be held accountable to God. Eighteen of the signors of The Declaration of Independence were Calvinists.

The Founders idea was that the government would have to have few restraints to allow Americans maximum freedom and liberty, but also have the ability to govern. They decided the universal truths are from God expressed in His revealed law and that will be the bases of the written document for the new nation, and its laws. A written document just as with contracts, written down so that with the passage of time people would not forget what they had agreed to. A constitution based on God's Law, with its inherent dictates for morality, governing man's behavior. It is imperative that the government be based on God's Law because everyone is accountable to God and this would be the only means of insuring self-restraint over human nature, accountability to God.

"The religion which has introduced civil liberty is the religion of Christ and His Apostles. To this we owe our free Constitutions of government." Noah Webster

It is a matter of human nature that even the best of men in authority are liable to be corrupted, temptation, greed, power, need for influence, the need for significance. Scripture is replete with examples of Godly men, once in power becoming corrupted by that power; King Saul, King David, King Solomon, to mention a few. Once in power and becoming successful, Scripture says they forgot God and thought they were responsible for all of their success, "by my own hand." God's commandments, judgments and ordinances, the Law of God, established over all His creation does not change, any honest person can see their inherent value for governing a society. What the Founders did not anticipate was that in another eight-three years an ideology would evolve that would denounce God's existence, removing the primary restraints on man's behavior, religion and morality. The globalists when in power make every effort to weaken America, politically, militarily, economically, and to destroy our religious liberty. To understand the push for socialism by the left is to understand that socialism is not a share the wealth program, but in reality, it is a program for the globalists to consolidate and control the wealth. Whoever controls the money controls the people. An excellent work on how money is controlled and manipulated for world dominance is a book called, *"None Dare Call It Conspiracy,"* by Gary Allen and Larry Abraham.

Consider thoughtfully the wisdom and foresight of some of our Founders.

Noah Webster, "The Christian religion, in its purity, is the basis, or rather the source of all genuine freedom in government...and I am persuaded that no civil government of a republican form can exist and be durable in which the principles of that religion have not a controlling influence."

James Wilson, signor of the Declaration of Independence and original Justice of the U. S. Supreme Court, "Human law must rest its authority ultimately upon the authority of that law which is Divine."

John Quincy Adams, "Is it not that the Declaration of Independence first organized the social compact on the foundation of the Redeemer's mission upon earth? – that is laid the cornerstone of human government upon the first precepts of Christianity?"

James Madison, 4th President of the US, "Before any man can be considered as a member of civil society, he must be considered as a subject of the Governor of the Universe."

George Washington, "While we are zealously performing the duties of good citizens and soldiers, we certainly ought not to be inattentive to the higher duties of religion. The distinguished character of Patriot, it should be our highest glory to add the more distinguished character of Christian."

John Adams, "We have no government armed with power capable of contending with human passions unbridled by morality and religion. Our Constitution was made only for a moral and religious people. It is wholly inadequate to the government of any other."

Thomas Jefferson, "And can the liberties of a nation be thought secure when we have removed their only firm basis, a conviction in the minds of the people that these liberties are of the gift of God? That they are not to be violated but with His wrath?

John Hancock, "Resistance to tyranny becomes the Christian and social duty of each individual...Continue steadfast and, with a proper sense of your dependence on God, nobly defend those rights which heaven gave, and no man ought to take from us."

Benjamin Franklin, "That the most acceptable service we render to Him is in doing good to His other children. That the soul of man is immortal and will be treated with justice in another life respecting its conduct in this."

The religion of our Protestant Founders from the Mayflower Compact, to with "a firm reliance on the protection of Divine Providence" to "the laws of nature and of Nature's God entitled them to be "endowed by their Creator," to "in the Year of our Lord," to the Declarations in the state constitutions. To the Supreme Courts findings in 1892; the Church of the Holy Trinity Vs United States, "Our laws and our institutions must necessarily be based upon and embody the teachings of the Redeemer of mankind. It is impossible that it should be otherwise: and in this sense and to this extent our civilization and our institutions are emphatically Christian. ...This is a religious people. This is historically true. From the discovery of this continent to the present hour, there is a single voice making the affirmation...we find everywhere a clear recognition of the same truth...These, and many other matters which might be noticed, add a volume of unofficial declarations to the mass of organic utterances that this is a Christion nation." It is obvious that we are a Christian Nation, these are our roots, and this is our heritage.

The religious tolerance implied in our founding documents as to our religious forbearance is for the many Christian denominations. From within the framework of the Christian faith we find our Judeo-Christian values, our morality. It was never the intent of the Founders to be inclusive of any other religion. Each religion has its own set of believes and their own morality. The Founders explicitly meant by religion, the Christian faith and by morality, they explicitly meant morality from our Judeo-Christian values. We can never compromise on the fundamentals of our faith. Compromise is the art of give and take, compromise on fundamentals is surrender, it is all give and no take. The fundamentals of Christianity and Christian morality cannot be compromised by merging belief systems.

The Founders challenge was to create a government with limited power and securing the rights promised in the Declaration of Independence while preserving a republican form of government that reflected the consent of the governed. They would establish a government with three equal branches that would have the ability to restrain the actions of each other. Abuse of power occurs when that power becomes consolidated in a single entity. The constitution is designed to limit the power of government exemplified by three equal branches, and restrictions, "shall make no law…" The overriding principle of the government would be government by the consent of the governed. And if the government was not protecting the rights of the individual citizens, or not governing by the values of the citizens, they would have the right, and the duty, to replace the government. All three branches would be accountable to the people for the laws they pass and the activities they or they allow the government to be involved in. Laws will have their origin, and all would be in accordance with God's revealed law. This is why so many of the Founders professed that the Republic just formed, "was only good for a religious and a moral people, and it is wholly inadequate for any other."

So, one of the things that has gone wrong is that we have legislators and executives that have agendas that do not represent the majority of the population. They listen to and are influence by lobbyists, special interest groups and the globalist agenda. When a member of congress wants to be on a committee or to chair a committee, he or she must pay a fee to their respective parties (greed) of anywhere from $250,000 to $500,000. They will have to hold a fundraiser to collect the money for the fee. Lobbyists, special interests, and companies with business in front of that committee all show up with their checkbooks. They often have bills they have written and all the representative need to is claim it as his/her bill. Now the representative is beholding to all that contributed funds to them, representing your interests has fallen by the wayside. It is no different than the indulgences, "I have to accept the money so I can continue to do good for you." When was the last time your legislator asked your opinion on an issue? Forty years ago, when you wrote your representative, regardless of their party affiliation or yours you would receive a competent, coherent response. Today, my last two correspondences with my representatives, from one, I received a propaganda sheet, completely ignoring my inquire. The next did not bother to respond. The third; I had signed a petition against proposed gun legislation in Minnesota. I received an unsolicited response justifying new legislation with some examples of anti-gun sentiment. Her letter failed to mention FBI reports from 2017 that showed 33 times in mass shooting events, armed citizens, were successful in stopping the active shooter 75 percent of the time and that there were no citizens harmed or killed by their intervention. The Clinton Justice Department research found that guns are used 1.5 million times per year for self-defense. In 200,000 of those instances a woman fended off an attacker. Less than 8 percent of the time, a citizen will kill or wound his/her attacker.[46] However, the bigger issue here, and one of our problems, is that the Constitution says that, "A well regulated militia, being necessary to the security of a free state, the right of the people to keep and bear arms, shall not be infringed." The proposed legislation was an infringement on the rights of Minnesotans to keep and bear arms. This representative had taken an oath to protect and defend the Constitution, her actions are in direct violation of her oath, and she should be removed from office. In a Republic, the law should govern, not the intent of a legislator. When lawmakers want to ban assault weapons, they want us to have smoothbore muskets, while the army has rifles. The point is the militia should have the same weapons as the military, who may be defending the take down of a government that has abandoned its people.

Before assuming office: public servants, police, military, politicians, judges all take an oath of office. An oath is a solemn, formal calling upon God to witness to the truth of what one says or to witness that one sincerely intends to do what one says in their oath. In the U.S. the oath of office is a promise to carry out the duties set forth in the U.S. Constitution. This is why, when taking the oath, one places their hand on the Holy Bible. People that have no intention of carrying out that oath request that they be sworn in on the Qú ran, a Dr Seuss book or anything but the Bible, which of course, should prevent them from taking office. When a person takes the oath of office, if their intentions are anything else, this is taking God's name in vain, for which Scripture says will not go unpunished.[47]

"I, AB, do solemnly swear (or affirm) that I will support and defend the Constitution of the United States against all enemies, foreign and domestic; that I will bear true faith and allegiance to the same; that I take this obligation freely, without any mental reservation *or purpose of evasion*, and that I will well and faithfully discharge the duties of the office on which I am about to enter. So help me God."

Minnesota's oath of office reads as follows: I, _____ do solemnly swear or affirm that I will support the Constitution of the United States and the Constitution of the State of Minnesota, and that I will discharge faithfully the duties of

---

[46] http://thinkaboutnow.com/2016/06/study-guns-stop-crime-2-5-million-times-each-year/

[47] Exodus 20:7

_____, the State of Minnesota, to the best of my ability and judgement. Signature.

Violating one's oath of office occurs so frequently it has become routine with little or no consequences. The oath of office is another check and balance that needs to be addressed in light of politician's lack of religion and morality. Violating one's oath of office needs to be legislated as a felony, punishable by a fine equal to one year's salary and five years in prison. If you will not take an oath or will not take it with your right hand on The Holy Bible you cannot hold the office. Without accountability to an oath of office the oath is meaningless, which is probably how politicians want it. Accountability will have to happen by executive order, current politicians will never pass an oath accountability law.

There are liberal globalists that profess the Constitution is outdated and should be replaced. The Constitution should be enforced as originally intended. What needs to be revised is our checks and balances to compensate for politicians that have abandoned their Christian religion and Christian morality. As politicians and judges have become more corrupt, and without the restraint of religion and morality, they are more in need of orchestrated restraint. Why bother with the oath if it is not going to be honored or enforced, this is part of what has gone wrong. There are legislators that do not represent the will of the people, nor do they honor the oath they have taken, and we fail to hold them accountable by removing them from office.

James Madison said, "It will be of little avail to the people that the laws are made by men of their own choice if the laws be so voluminous that they cannot be read, or so incoherent that they cannot be understood." The Declaration of Independence 1,458 words. The Constitution of the United States has 4,543 words. State Constitutions average 27,000 and Obamacare was 11,588,500 million words. Remember, "We have to pass it to see what is in it."

So, what the hell went wrong? Schools were built in every colonial settlement so that children could learn to read, so they could read the Bible and develop a relationship with the Trinity and understand morality. In the colonies, if you wanted to run for office, you had to sign a pledge professing your Christian faith.

We have allowed judges to set law; they have overridden God's Law, they have thrown God out of schools, and the public arena. So, the problem is a Gallup Poll says 75.2 percent of US Citizens consider themselves Christian. A PBS Poll says 70 percent of Americans are

Christian. If the vast majority of Americans considers themselves Christian how does the government, ruled by the consent of the people, justify eliminating God from our culture. An immense problem is liberal judges passing laws that are anti-God in intent and meaning. Judges are not supposed to pass laws, that is a breach of the separation of powers, and is unconstitutional, for which they should be removed from office. 71 percent of Republicans consider themselves Christian, whereas only 51 percent of Democrats claim to be Christian. There are 29 percent of Republicans and 49 percent of Democrats that undermine the Founders belief that for the Constitution to work, we must be a religious and moral people. In 2019 the Democratic National Committee professed to be the party of no God and no religion. Judges are supposed to be non-partisan, it is quite obvious they are not. They must identify themselves on the ballot as either conservative or liberal and their religious affiliation so "We The People" know who we are sending to the bench. At a minimum their faith and political ideology must be a part of their opening statement in their confirmation hearing. This election of secrecy is what perpetuates godless men and women in the judiciary.

American sovereignty rests with "We The People," through elected representatives within Constitutional constraints. We have a representative republic, in which we vote for representatives who enact laws on our behalf, and the validity of those laws, and the process by which thy are enacted, are subject to a written Constitution. The only means by which we can maintain the original intent of the Founders is to subscribe to their belief that the government and its people must be religious and moral, the best way to ensure that is to have religious and moral legislators. We need public servants to identify themselves as Christians before they are able to hold office, as they did in the colonies, or else we are going to have to abandon the Constitution and our current form of government or, "it is their right, it is their duty, to throw off such government, and to provide new Guards for their future security."

"It is the duty as well as the privilege and interest of our Christian nation to select and prefer Christians for our rulers." John Jay 1st Supreme Court Justice.

What went wrong, we abandoned the concept of a religious and moral people, especially those serving in government. 90 percent of news people are liberal, democrats and subscribe to the globalist's ideology, their bias feeds this counter Christianity perception and pushes the concept of a post-Christian America, which could not be further from the truth.

What do we do with freedom of the press when the press gives out misinformation, distorts the truth, refuses to air some stories and outright lies about stories that are being covered, in order to press forth their agenda? We need strict libel laws for the news media. Malcolm X said, "The media is the most powerful entity on earth. They have the power to make the innocent guilty and to make the guilty innocent, and that is power, because they control the minds of the masses."

All these items under what went wrong are eroding our unalienable rights. The Constitution is not outdated and should be replaced we should go back to its original meaning and intent. This is all very serious, no republic has ever lasted very long. The American Experience so far has had the best chance, but we have to go back to our original ideals of a Constitution based on God's law and a representative from of government. Lobbyist have to be outlawed, as well as special interest groups from interacting with legislators. Representatives must be limited to two terms and annual financial audits for representatives and biennial for senators. All Presidential Councils on Sustainable Development, regional government agencies and all NGOs, involved in government affairs, must be eliminated. Governmental agencies that impose rules and regulations on American citizens and then impose fees and fines, which is in fact taxation without representation, agencies such as the EPA should be eliminated. All laws and regulation must originate in congress subject to presidential vetoes. The Supreme Court must no longer legislate. When an extremely important issue arises, an issue that will affect our culture, we must put it on the ballot. We also must ensure that our elections are not rigged, that the vote count and voter registration records are accurate, along with mandated voter ID.

Today we have unelected judges, therefore unaccountable to "We The People," that overstep their bounds for political reasons not because of the rule of law or as a means of enforcing checks and balances. Federal Judges have issued 42 injunctions against President Trump, that is more than issued against the first 42 presidents combined, all from blue states, and all politically motivated. Chief Justice Roberts has stated judges are not politically motivated. That kind of naivete, irrational thought, and denial of reality has no place in any court.

Attorney General William Barr said, "Nationwide injunctions undermine the democratic process, depart from history and tradition, violate constitutional principles, and impeded sound judicial administration, all at the cost of public confidence in our institutions and particularly in our courts as political-makers dispassionately applying objective law." A Federal judge should be limited to his/her jurisdiction only, not national jurisdiction, that should be left to the Supreme Court. This is another violation of our checks and balances, the legislature is to set the jurisdiction of the federal judiciary. No judge may render an interpretation that will result in a de facto law without deferring the courts findings to the House of Representatives.

The current democratic majority House of Representatives is in defiance of the rule of law, due process, abuse of power and the legitimate exercise of checks and balances. The republican senate has betrayed "We The People" and the Constitution by abandoning their sworn duty in the checks and balance process by not checking the house democrats abuse of power and overreach, allowing a concentration of power. The Mueller investigation found no collusion between candidate Trump and the Russian government. They also found no obstruction of justice. Yet, the house continues to investigate and move ahead with efforts to impeach the President. The grounds for impeachment are; "treason, bribery, high crimes and misdemeanors." The impeachment must be upheld in the senate by a two thirds majority. President Trump was acquitted of any wrongdoing. The motivation behind the attempts to remove President Trump are to continue the implementation of Agenda 21/30 with no boarders and a one world government, with all citizens slaves to the elite; you work, they tax. President Trump is a stumbling block to the globalist's Agenda 21/30, that is why they continue to attempt to remove him from office. The globalists know they cannot defeat President Trump in the next election, so they are desperately trying to remove him from office. In a country ruled by the rule of law a person is innocent until proven guilty, not assumed to be guilty and then go looking for a crime.

After God is removed from society, the state will provide for everyone. Socialism and communism have proven that those systems do not work; however, the benefits of those systems are still taught in today's colleges. Abraham Lincoln said, "The philosophy in the school room in one generation, will be the philosophy of the government in the next." He also said, "We the people are the rightful masters of both the congress and the courts, not to overthrow the constitution but to overthrow the men who pervert the constitution."

The theory now is that if socialism does not work in a country it will work in a global application, one government and one people, no borders, then it will work. Hillary Clinton was to pick up where Obama left off with the implementation of Agenda 21/30.

Man is capable of horrific evil, I spent a year in the war in Vietnam, I have seen this evil first-hand.[48] It was this knowledge that prompted the Founders to establish, "One Nation Under God" and a preponderance of emphasis of religion and morality. Annuit Coeptis is on the Great Seal of the United States, which is Latin for, "He approves the undertaking." The only realistic means for man to restrain his behavior is to know that he is accountable to God for his actions. Scripture is meant to be the plumb line for, people, society and government. As a nation "We The People," have the right to define what kind of a nation we want to be, and as in the beginning we are and should be a Christian Nation. Even if that means only electing Christians to office, as was the case in the colonies, if we do not, we will lose what this country was founded to be, "for the glory of God and the advancement of the Christiaan faith." A free and independent people to enjoy the fruits of their labor under a just and fair government. This is also the best assurance we have that we will stop putting crooks, criminals and crazies into office.

In one of my other books: *Things To Come: A Brief History of the Bible,* I write about external influences. Ephesians 6:10, "Finally, be strong in the Lord and in the strength of His might. Put on the full armor of God, so that you will be able to stand firm against the schemes of the devil. For our struggle is not against flesh and blood, but against the rulers, against the powers, against the world forces of this darkness, against the spiritual forced of wickedness in the heavenly places. Therefore, take up the full armor of God, so that you will be able to resist in the day of evil, and having done everything to stand firm. Stand firm therefore, having girded your loins with truth, and having put on the breastplate of righteousness, and having shop your feet with the preparation of the Gospel of peace; in addition to all, taking up the shield of faith with which you will be able to extinguish all the flaming arrows of the evil one. And take the helmet of salvation, and the sword of the Spirit, which is the word of God. With all prayer and petition pray at all times in the Spirit, and with this in view, be on the alert with all perseverance and petition for all the saints."

In April of 1968, I was an infantry paratrooper with the 101st Airborne Division in Vietnam as we advanced on a village in the northeast portion of 1 Corp, the trooper next to me struck a wasp's nest with the butt

---

[48] Just War: A Soldier's Revelation by Tom Newman

of his rifle. The wasps swarmed on me and stung me eleven times in the head. I was evacuated by helicopter to the MASH unit at LZ Sally. By the time we arrived, my facial features had completely disappeared because of the swelling from the stings. As they carried me into the emergency room, the doctor looked at me and said, "What in the hell happened to him?" I realized I had bitten one of the wasps that had stung me in the mouth; I removed the wasp from my mouth and offered it up for anyone to see. I then went into anaphylactic shock and suffered cardiac arrest and complete respiratory failure. As soon as I flat lined, my spirit and soul left my body. I just floated above the operating table and watched the efforts to revive me. I was aware of my existence. I was fully conscious, and I knew I was still "me." As I looked at my body I thought, that's the glove, I'm the hand. The surgical team withdrew blood from one arm and put new blood into my other arm. As soon as they resuscitated me, I returned into my body.

The next day, in the recovery room, I was thinking about the supernatural phenomena that had just occurred and was wondering how I could empirically verify my experience. The ER orderly came in and said, "Oh, I see you are coming around."

I asked him, "Why were you guys putting blood in one arm and taking it out of the other?"

With a very surprised look, he replied, "How the hell did you know we did that? You were gone."

When you go from believing in life after death to knowing, it changes everything. Satan is not omnipresent, he is a single entity, so he can only be one place at a time. Given his limited scope, although he does have the aid of a third of the angels, he must focus his efforts on where it will be most effective. Which will be people of influence, and people who are not Christian: judges, legislators, those in the media and the entertainment industry. We are told in Scripture that Christians are indwelt by the Holy Spirit and that "greater is He that is in you, than he that is in the world."[49] This does not make one immune from satanic influences but it does give us the power to overcome temptation, self-restraint. It is even believed by some that those involved in satanic worship have made a deal with Satan for: fame, wealth, power and influence.

America has had, and still has many enemies. Nikita Khrushchev said communism would take over America, not through war but from

---

[49] 1 John 4:4

within. The Communist Manifesto was written as the blueprint for how this would be done. Below are some of the items from the list of 45 ways to defeat America. It may no longer represent a communist takeover, however, based on the number of items already in play, the globalists, and others may be borrowing from that playbook.

"We will not take America under the label of communism; we will not take it under the label of socialism. These labels are unpleasant to the American people and have been speared too much. We will take the United States under labels we have made very lovable; we will take it under liberalism, under progressivism, under democracy. But take it, we will!"

-Alexander Trachtenberg, National Convention of Communist Parties, 1944

On Jan. 10, 1963, Congressman Albert S. Herlong Jr. of Florida read a list of 45 Communist goals into the Congressional Record.

At Mrs. Nordman's request, I include in the RECORD, under unanimous consent, the following "Current Communist Goals," which she identifies as an excerpt from "The Naked Communist," by Cleon Skousen:

11. Promote the U.N. as the only hope for mankind. If its charter is rewritten, demand that it be set up as a one-world government with its own independent armed forces.

13. Do away with all loyalty oaths.

15. Capture one or both of the political parties in the United States.

16. Use technical decisions of the courts to weaken basic American institutions by claiming their activities violate civil rights.

17. Get control of the schools. Use them as transmission belts for socialism and current Communist propaganda. Soften the curriculum. Get control of teachers' associations. Put the party line in textbooks.

18. Gain control of all student newspapers.

19. Use student riots to foment public protests against programs or

organizations which are under Communist attack.

20. Infiltrate the press. Get control of book-review assignments, editorial writing, policy-making positions.

21. Gain control of key positions in radio, TV, and motion pictures.
24. Eliminate all laws governing obscenity by calling them "censorship" and a violation of free speech and free press.

25. Break down cultural standards of morality by promoting pornography and obscenity in books, magazines, motion pictures, radio, and TV.

26. Present homosexuality, degeneracy and promiscuity as "normal, natural, healthy."

27. Infiltrate the churches and replace revealed religion with "social" religion. Discredit the Bible and emphasize the need for intellectual maturity, which does not need a "religious crutch."

28. Eliminate prayer or any phase of religious expression in the schools on the ground that it violates the principle of "separation of church and state."

29. Discredit the American Constitution by calling it inadequate, old-fashioned, out of step with modern needs, a hindrance to cooperation between nations on a worldwide basis.

30. Discredit the American Founding Fathers. Present them as selfish aristocrats who had no concern for the "common man.
"
31. Belittle all forms of American culture and discourage the teaching of American history on the ground that it was only a minor part of the "big picture." Give more emphasis to Russian history since the Communists took over.

32. Support any socialist movement to give centralized control over any part of the culture--education, social agencies, welfare programs, mental health clinics, etc.

33. Eliminate all laws or procedures which interfere with the operation of the Communist apparatus.

34. Eliminate the House Committee on Un-American Activities.

35. Discredit and eventually dismantle the FBI.

40. Discredit the family as an institution. Encourage promiscuity and easy divorce.

41. Emphasize the need to raise children away from the negative influence of parents. Attribute prejudices, mental blocks and retarding of children to suppressive influence of parents.

42. Create the impression that violence and insurrection are legitimate aspects of the American tradition; that students and special-interest groups should rise up and use ["]united force["] to solve economic, political or social problems.

44. Internationalize the Panama Canal.

45. Repeal the Connally reservation so the United States cannot prevent the World Court from seizing jurisdiction [over domestic problems. Give the World Court jurisdiction] over nations and individuals alike.

Included in the list of those who hate America and want to see it destroyed, are those that have declared war on America and consider the U.S. the great Satan, Islam. They also have prepared a blueprint for taking over America.

In August of 2004, a Maryland Transportation Authority Police officer witnessed a female in traditional Islamic clothing videotaping the support structure of the Chesapeake Bay Bridge. In the ensuing traffic stop it was discovered she had an outstanding warrant. The FBI executed a search warrant on her home and found a document from the Muslim Brotherhood in North America. The document, "An Explanatory

Memorandum,"[50] made clear their objectives to implement Islamic law in America and re-establishing a global caliphate. The complete document can be found in the link below.

The first statement in the memorandum states, "One: The Memorandum is derived from: 1 – The general strategic goal of the Group in America which was approved by the Shura Council and the Organization Conference for the year 1987 is "Enablement of Islam in North America, meaning: establishing an effective and a stable Islamic Movement led by the Muslim Brotherhood which adopts Muslims' causes domestically and globally, and which works to expand the observant Muslim base, aims at unifying and directing Muslim; efforts, presents Islam as a civilization alternative, and supports the global Islamic State wherever it is."

4 – Understanding the role of the Muslim Brother in North America:The process of settlement (occupation) is a "Civilization-Jihadist Process" with all the word means. The Ikhwan (Muslim Brotherhood) must understand that their work in America is a kind of a grand Jihad in eliminating and destroying the Western civilization from within and "sabotaging" its miserable house by their hands and the hands of the believers so that it is eliminated and God's religion is made victorious over all other religions. Without this level of understanding, we are not up to this challenge and have not prepared ourselves for Jihad yet. It is a Muslim's destiny to perform Jihad and work wherever he is and wherever he lands until the final hour comes, and there is no escape from that destiny except for those who chose to slack. But, would the slackers and the Mujahedeen be equal."

14 – Adopting a written "jurisprudence" that includes legal and movement bases, principles, policies and interpretations which are suitable for the needs and challenges of the process of settlement."

The Immigration and Nationality Act passed June 27, 1952, became Public Law 414, established both the law and the intent of Congress regarding the immigration of Aliens to the U.S. and remains in effect today. In Chapter 2 Section 212, is the prohibition of entry to the U.S. if the Alien belongs to an organization seeking to overthrow the government of the United States by "force, violence, or other unconstitutional means." The law prohibits entry of "Aliens who the consular officer or the Attorney General knows or has reason to believe seek to enter the United States solely, principally, or incidentally to engage

---

[50] https://clarionproject.org/Muslim_Brotherhood_Explanatory_Memorandum/

in activities which would be prejudicial to the public interest, or endanger the welfare, safety, or security of the United States." It also prohibits the entry of Aliens who are members of or affiliated with any organization that advocates or teaches, the overthrow by force, violence, or other unconstitutional means of the US or of all forms of law, and Aliens who publish, circulate and distribute materials teaching or advocating the overthrow by force, violence or other unconstitutional means of the US Government or of all forms of law.

The stated objectives of the "Explanatory Memorandum" are in direct violation of the U.S. Immigration and Nationality Act. A natural course of action would be for the U.S. Department of Citizenship and Immigration Services to employ extreme vetting for Muslims seeking entry into the Unites States and prohibiting any member of the Muslim Brotherhood from entry and deport any that are already here. Another major issue with what has gone wrong, is when members of congress ignore their responsibility to exercise, they duty under the oath of office to execute the responsibilities in the checks and balances process. And when the executive branch, the president, violates the law and his oath of office by not enforcing the law. The law states that aliens who are affiliated with any "organization that advocates the overthrow of our government are prohibited from entry into the United States. The law categorically prohibits members of the Muslim Brotherhood from entry into the Unites States. It could also be reasoned that any Muslim that adheres to the teachings of the Qú ran, Sharia Law, and the Hadith which, all of which require complete submission to Islam, be barred from entry into the Unites States, as all of these Muslim writings are antithetical to the U.S. Government, the Constitution and to our Republic. A circuit judge blocked, nationally, President Trumps travel ban, his actions violated the Immigration and Nationality Act and prohibited the President from performing his Constitutional duties. This illegal violation of checks and balances cannot be tolerated in a Republic governed by the rule of law.

During the Obama administration there was blatant disregard for the law and the U.S. Constitution. Once in the White House, Obama chose members of the Muslim Brotherhood to be a part of his administration. Mazen al-Asbahi, an American lawyer of Arab origin, was appointed as an adviser on education and to make sure Islam was integrated into U.S. textbooks, although schools are prohibited from teaching Christianity. In a court proceeding Justice Phyllis Hamilton issued a ruling condemning the Ten Commandments while endorsing banners in front of a school that state, "There is one God, Allah, and Mohammed is his prophet." This is her ruling, upheld by the Ninth Circuit:[51] she should be removed from office, for violating her oath and violating U.S. law. The Ten Commandments inscribed on the front of the Supreme Court building, as well as in courtrooms and classrooms, are a reminder of the very foundation of our laws. Other members of administration with connections to the Muslim Brotherhood include Arif AliKhan, Assistant Secretary of Homeland Security. Judicial Watch has released hundreds of pages of FBI memos and other documents revealing that, in 2012, the agency purged its anti-terrorism training curricula of material determined by an undisclosed group of "Subject Matter Experts" (SME) to be "offensive" to Muslims. The excised material included references linking the Muslim Brotherhood to terrorism, tying al Qaeda to the 1993 World Trade Center and Khobar Towers bombings, and suggesting that "young male immigrants of Middle Eastern appearance ... may fit the terrorist profile best."[52] Mohammed al-byari, a member of the National Consultative Council for Security, who studied the ideas of Sayyid Qutb –founder of the muslim brotherhood, Hussain Rashad, the US special envoy for the organization of the Islamic Conference, Imam Muhammad Majid, President of the Islamic Society of North America, Eboo Patel, a member of the Obama Advisory Council, Dalia Mogahed, who was appointed to manage the Internal Security Advisory Council, and Rashad Hussain, whose work focused on national security and the new media as well as science and technology issues. [53]

"In 2008 there were 1,349,000 Muslims in the U.S. By 2012 there were 2.6 million. Because of Obama's policy of only Muslim immigration since 2012 the number has grown by 76 percent to an estimated 7 million through 2015. Greek Catholic sources have said more than 300,000 Christians are among the refugees...but neither the UN nor Obama have shown a willingness to resettle Christians in the U.S."[54] When Obama took office there were 200 mosques in America when he left office there were

---

[51] http://www.renewamerica.com/columns/shroder/100603

[52] https://www.judicialwatch.org/press-releases/documents-obtained-by-judicial-watch-reveal-fbi-training-curricula-purged-of-material-deemed-offensive-to-muslims/

[53] Excellent books on Islamic takeover of America by Anis Shorrosh, Islam Revealed and The True Furgan

[54] https://drrichswier.com/2015/02/02/obamas-massive-resettlement-6-million-muslims-u-s/

2,106. Prior to 1992, Muslims could not hold congressional offices, legislatively this was changed by Nancy Pelosi, Diane Feinstein, John Kerry and John McCain. The Muslim immigrants were located in select geographical regions where their population density would give them an advantage when they ran for U.S. Government offices.

One of the most controversial elements of the Obama administration is Huma Mahmoud Abdeen who was born in Kalamazoo, Michigan. She moved with her family to Jeddah, Saudi Arabia at the age of two. Abdeen began working as an intern at the White House in 1996 and was assigned to Hillary Clinton to work in the State Department in 2010.

In 2012, accusations against Huma came to the fore because of her relationship with the Muslim Brotherhood. The most important U.S. officials who asked to investigate this matter were members of Congress: Michele Bachmann,[55] Trent Franks, Louie Gohmert, Tom Rooney and Westmoreland Lane. They sent a letter to the inspector general requesting him to investigate the association of Huma with the Muslim Brotherhood, and to investigate the infiltration of the US government by the group, as well as the arrival of Hassan Abdeen, brother of Huma who held a senior position in the U.S. administration.[56] Globalists Senator McCain gave a passionate speech supporting Islam and condemning Representative Bachmann. Representative Bachmann did not seek reelection, we lost a true patriot, and one of the very few that are willing to fight for America and the U.S. Constitution. In failing to support this effort representatives and senators failed in their duty and oath to uphold the constitution, they failed the American people and should have been removed from office. A dishonest media and a complacent citizenry ignored the illegalities and reelected the globalist back into power. American failed to vote McCain out of office, and to retain the services of Representative Bachmann. If you do not take a stand in situations of injustice, you have become one of the oppressors.

The most compelling, what is wrong with America is we have abandoned most of what the Founders fought for, built and who pledged: "Our Lives, Our Fortunes, And Our Honor." We have senators, representatives, judges and executives that have abandoned America, abandoned "We The People," and all it stands for.

---

55   https://www.newsmax.com/Newsmax-Tv/Michele-Bachmann-Muslim-Brotherhood-jihad/2014/09/10/id/593881/
56   https://circanada.com/2019/02/08/barack-obamas-support-for-the-muslim-brotherhood/

"Remember the height from which you have fallen! Repent and do the things you did at first. If you do not repent, I will come and remove your lampstand from its place."

New   American   Standard   Revelation   2:5

EPILOGUE

❝ *A revolution is coming: a revolution which will be peaceful if we are wise enough, compassionate if we care enough, successful if we are fortunate enough – but a revolution which is coming whether we will it or not. We can affect it's character, we cannot alter it's inevitability."*

-John F. Kennedy

In the broadest terms, what the hell went wrong is that we have politicians and judges that are trying to undermine everything that America stands for and sell us out to world domination to the new world order. On January 27, 1838, Abraham Lincoln, while serving as a state representative told a young male audience, "All the armies of Europe, Asia and Africa combined, with all the treasures of the earth in their military chest; with Buonaparte for a commander, could not by force, take a drink from the Ohio, or make a track on the Blue Ridge, in a trial of a thousand years. At what point then is the approach of danger to be expected? I, answer, if it ever reach us, it must spring up amongst us. It cannot come from abroad. If destruction be our lot, we must ourselves be its author and finisher. As a nation of freemen, we must live through all time, or die by suicide."

Our Founders repeatedly stressed the importance of Religion and Morality if the American experiment were to work. Darwin's theory changed the way a lot of people think, the idea of not being created but that our existence was by accident, without a creator, why subscribe to His rules? Darwin's dogma began to erode Judeo-Christian ethics and values. These ethics and values are taken from the Jewish Scripture in the Old Testament and the moral foundations revealed in Judaism are upheld in Christianity. If creation, as recorded in Genesis, is wrong, then what about the rest of the Bible? Judeo-Christian values upheld the sanctity of human life, denounced the taking of innocent life, murder, infanticide, abortion and

370

even suicide. They profess good will to your fellow citizen and an attitude of love your neighbor. The values expressed in Christianity profess the equality of all, that moral law, found in Scripture, assures justice and dignity of human life for all and professes behavioral parameters between individuals and within the community. There was an importance to human life, as well as significance in death. As the rejection of God allowed many to disregard what was once morally right, these same people no longer saw any justification for their government to be subject to God's moral laws, and we have voted many of them into office. Anything and everything can be justified once you remove God.

Aldous Huxley, an English philosopher said, "Those who detect no meaning in the world generally do so because, for one reason or another, it suits their purpose that the world should be meaningless...For myself, as, no doubt, for most of my contemporaries, the philosophy of meaninglessness was essentially an instrument of liberation. The liberation we desired was... liberation from a certain system of morality. We objected to the morality because it interfered with our sexual freedom."

This rational gave us the LGBTQ movement seeking civil rights as some are explicable antithetical to God's law. Those, in power, without religion and morality perpetuate this Godless ideology and force it on the rest of society. There is no outcry, or warning, from the media because they are complicit with a Godless society.

The ominous threat here is who continues in power. If we continue to elect globalists and people sympathetic to the political ideology of Islam, we will continue to surrender our sovereignty. This is no small task; we certainly cannot rely on the media for an accurate appraisal of the candidates. And American polls have become a vehicle to sway public opinion. Political candidate debates are hosted by jaded journalists with their own globalist's agenda and should be done away with altogether. Each candidate should be given 30 minutes of airtime on TV and computer to address the top ten issues facing the nation.

It is time for the average American citizen to step up to the plate and assume the responsibility of citizenship. There are reliable news sources online,[57] and before we vote for anyone, we should check their voting record.[58] The days of going to work and coming home to watch TV programming, there is a reason they call it programming, are over. The news, the story narrative of shows and movies are designed to program

---

[57] The Gateway Pundit, The Daily Caller, Hot Air, WND
[58] https://votesmart.org/

thinking, to a way to desensitize viewers to the globalist agenda and chip away and the morality of our culture. Globalist do not talk or report on Agenda 21/30, because true Americans would be vehemently opposed to all of its provisions. However, aspects of Agenda 21/30 are discussed in terms that make it sound like a good and the right thing to do, political correctness. Mainstream Media, for the most part is dishonest, "Fake News," is apparent as 90 percent of all news coverage about President Trump is negative, because he is trying to stop the globalists agenda. Yet he has accomplished more for "We The People" than any other president in my lifetime. You will have to get involved in your school, what are the schools teaching your children, what are they not teaching? What will you have to teach them? Set up a neighborhood classroom so the adults can rotate instruction: academics, theology and morality. Get involved in politics and the issues of the day, make your voice heard.

"If we do not advocate a love of country to our children and the generations to come, then why would our children grow up to fight for our country's founding principles and moral truth?"

First Lady Melania Trump

"Every civil government is based upon some religion or philosophy of life. Education in a nation will propagate the religion of that nation. In America, the foundational religion was Christianity, and it was sewn in the hearts of Americans through the home, private, and public schools for centuries. Our liberty, growth, and prosperity were the result of a Biblical philosophy of life. Our continued freedom and success are dependent upon our educating the youth of America in the principles of the Christian religion. " Noah Webster

As in the colonial days, I think every home should have a firearm for defense. I also encourage friends and family to carry a concealed weapon and to become proficient with whatever firearm they choose. Do not believe the globalists news and globalists politicians about gun violence. Anywhere from 1.5 to 2.5 million crimes are prevented by armed citizens each year, a quarter of a million of those are women fending off attackers.[59]

Justice Clarence Thomas' argument that the Supreme Court needs to stop this erosion of Americans' Second Amendment rights. As Thomas recently wrote, "The Framers made a clear choice: They reserved to all Americans the right to bear arms for self-defense. I do not think we should

---

[59] https://gunowners.org/sk0802htm/

stand by idly while a State denies its citizens that right, particularly when their very lives may depend on it."

I would not be surprised to find out that all of the mass shootings are staged by elements of the globalists, all in an effort to pass gun control legislation. Socialists are notorious for killing their citizens, for the good of the collective. 1,771 babies are aborted every day in America, denying them their unalienable right to life, what's another 20 more when the ends justify the means. Godless people are capable of anything. If you think the good of the collective supersedes the rights of the individual. In 1776, the British found out they were unable to subjugate an armed populace. The globalists know full well that their agenda, programs, regulation, and subversions constitute: a long train of abuses and usurpations, pursuing invariably the same Object evinces a design to reduce them under absolute Despotism..." It seems that when there is news destructive to the globalist agenda, we have a mass shooting and the globalist media shifts the narrative away from the globalists to the shooting and gun control. It is very important to remember the party in power decides the definitions, that is why gun control legislation is extremely dangerous. There is talk of "Red Fag," laws, which means that if you think someone is a potential threat the authorities will confiscate a person's firearms without due process. Then the person will have to prove to the court they are not a threat. Once these laws pass definitions continue to change eroding more and more of our rights, "we are only adding to an already existing law." Just as abortion has evolved since Roe Vs Wade to late term abortions. If Red Flag laws fail, they will resurface under a different name. In 2009, President Obama's Department of Homeland Security classified returning U.S. Veterans as terror threats. "the return of military veterans facing challenges reintegrating into their communities could lead to the potential emergence of terrorist groups or lone wolf extremists capable of carrying out violent acts." Red Flag, camouflage and subterfuge, they are setting the stage to disarm the militia.

Under President Trump veterans are national heroes. It is not that the black helicopters flying around at night are necessarily an ominous threat, it all depends on who is in the White House.

The globalists and the Islamic sympathizers, at every turn, try to prevent President Trump from moving ahead with his agenda of America First and undoing Agenda 21/30, restoring Christian liberty and returning the government to "We The People." While the members of congress and other globalists in the government enrich themselves and sell out the

American people; the Green New Deal is taken right from the pages of Agenda 21/30. President Trump is the only recent politician, "with a firm reliance on the protection of divine Providence," has pledged his live, his fortune and his sacred Honor.

Pope Francis, who is a globalist, signed an agreement with Iman of the Islamic faith stating that both sects worship the same God. Both ideologies seek to dominate the world. This reminds me of the pack between Hitler and Stalin at the outset of World War II. They would conquer all of Europe then split it up amongst themselves. However, paranoia and mistrust; Hitler was not sure why Stalin was assembling a million man army in southwestern Europe, so he decided to invade Russia.

President John Kennedy said, "Today we need a nation of minute men; men who are not only prepared to take up arms, but citizens who regard the preservation of freedom as a basic purpose of their daily life."

So, we, as a nation, are at a precipice, the American experiment, a republican form of government, based on the rule of law, and the consent of the governed, will be restored, or gone forever. Ruled by the rule of law so that we are not misguided by the passions of men. All violations of the law must be prosecuted, or you are not governed by the rule of law.

"A nation ceases to be a republic only when the will of the majority ceases to be the law,"   Thomas Jefferson

We all know what happened in Benghazi on September 11, 2012, here is my take. U.S. Ambassador Christopher Stevens and U.S. Foreign Services Officer Sean Smith were murdered at the U.S. Embassy in Libya. Tyrone Woods and Glen Doherty, CIA contractors were killed one and a half miles away in a mortar attack on the U.S. Annex. Ten others were wounded. Hillary Clinton said the attack was the result of a video that insulted Islam. Hours later she told her daughter that it was actually a terrorist attack by terrorist organization Ansar al-Sharia. Susan Rice that following Sunday appeared on five morning talk shows reaffirming the video lie. During the attack U.S. military personal were told to stand down and not to go to the aid of the Embassy. FEST (Foreign Emergency Support Team) specifically deployed around the world as key responders were never called. A Commando team in Italy was told to stand down. It was reported they arrived too late to deploy, another lie. Hillary was using Stevens for gun running from the weapons in Libya, after she orchestrated Ghedaffi's murder, to arm Syrian rebels, ISIS and al-Qaida in support of the administration and to enrich the Clinton Foundation. Hillary said on national TV, "We came, we saw, Ghedaffi died." Ghedaffi was cooperating with U.S. policy, his removal was a crime. Hillary lied to congress about her involvement in gun running. The above can be verified through WikiLeaks information and from Judicial Watch reports. My point is one person cannot perpetuate this type of a cover-up without a lot of help from others in the government. No one was punished for any of this and four Americans were murdered. It cannot be said that the American people did nothing. We no longer have a representative form of government. Christian America is well aware of all that has gone wrong, we have been waiting for an honest leader for "We The People," or the inevitable, whichever comes first. Those in power committed the crimes and those in power covered it up.

After Saddam Hussein was removed from power, John Brennen took over as the governor of Iraq. He told the Iraqi army they could not be trusted so they should disband. They bled into the countryside becoming ISIS. The President of Turkey recently stated the U.S. through Libya supplied rebel forces in Syria with 30,000 truckloads of munitions. U.S. Code 2381.Treason – "Whoever, owing allegiance to the United States, levies war against them or adheres to their enemies, giving them aid and comfort within the United States or elsewhere, is guilty of treason and shall suffer death…"

Lying to congress and lying under oath, as occurred under the Benghazi investigation, is occurring today in the coup (overthrow of an existing government by non-democratic means) attempt on President Trump. Comey lied under oath, Clinton, and McCabe lied under oath and so far with no repercussions. For a Republic governed by the rule of law, this is very serious business.

People that lie and compound that by lying under oath are breaking God's Law. "You shall not bear false witness…"[60] thereby using God's name in vain. They are also breaking their oath, and they are breaking U.S. law. If we cannot maintain the basic requirements of the law, basic elements of morality, we have lost the Republic. Lying destroys trust and trust is the glue that holds everything together. The book of Revelation reminds us that all liars go to hell.[61]

What the Hell Went Wrong we lost our Republic. "We The People" let criminal politicians, corrupt government officials, seditious judges, completely bastardize the rule of law. Without the rule of law, we do not

---

[60] Exodus 20:16, Proverbs 19:5, 9
[61] Revelation 21:8

have a Republic, we have an oligarchy run by criminals, the very thing the Founders tried so very hard to prevent. That early colonists fought and died for. When you change our history, you change the significance of all this, and you change who we are as Americans.

We have one last chance, and I mean one last chance, to redeem or Republic. We all know there was an attempted coup against the duly elected President of the United States. Because President Trump is trying to restore the government to; "We The People," weed out corruption, restore religious liberty, and stop the implementation of Agenda 21/30. With a firm reliance on the Providence of God as, "God governs in the affairs of men." And with enough support from "We The People" President Trump can succeed. If not…

So, the bottom-line as to What the Hell Went Wrong, is that "We The People," abandoned the basic premise of a religious and moral people. We allowed corrupt politicians, and judges contrary to 72 percent of the Americans professing to be Christians, to legislate and judicate God out of our society and completely ignore the basic premise of our Constitutional Republic that it is for a Religious and Moral people, by electing godless and immoral people into office, with the help of a corrupt and dishonest news media and entertainment industry. "We The People," let true crusaders, like Michelle Bachman, get beat out by the system.

The Founding Fathers called this new venture in Government the "American Experiment." They were setting up a radical new form of government, democracies and republics of the past had failed and in their view nothing current was working. These are the ideals and models they grappled with. The revolutionary thought process was that a civilization needs to be ordered and provide for the security and freedom of its citizens. Man is fallen and prone to yield to his passions and has a proclivity to yield to temptations. Hence a government must be structured to safeguard the citizens against these vulnerabilities. The idea they came up with was the creation of a government that would allow broad liberties to the people and limit the coercive power of the government by establishing three branches of government with checks and balances on each other so that power could never become concentrated in any one area. Also, because of man's fallen nature he could never be trusted to be his own lawgiver and judge. The only foundation for this government would have to be God's law, universally just and never changing. A major caveat is that man would have to be able to self-govern, that is be able to restrain his proclivity for passion and idiosyncratic appetites. The only way to accomplish this is to hold man to a moral standard and the moral standard must come from man's creator, to whom we all are accountable. That is why so many of the Founders held that a written Constitution based on God's law is "only good for a religious and moral people and wholly inadequate for anyone else." Three branches of government accountable to "We The People," and all ultimately accountable to our creator.

We are endowed by our Creator with certain unalienable rights and as with any right comes responsibility. God's laws are the fundamental principles of life. You cannot compromise on the fundamentals or else you have no firm footing, on which to stand, on which to build, on which to establish principles of morality. The basic fundamental of life, the single source for our morality is our Creator and as His creations we are accountable to the Creator and He has revealed His law and His morality to us, that to which we are to be held accountable. Man's judgements, laws, and interpretations are only valid and just when they are in conformity to the revealed laws, commandments, ordinances, judgments and statutes of God. It is from these that all of our laws should flow and have their foundation.

From the Mayflower Compact to our state Constitutions to our Protestant Founders to the U.S. Constitution and the findings of the Supreme Court in 1892 in the Church of the Holy Trinity Vs United States who found: "Our laws and our institutions must necessarily be based upon and embody the teachings of the Redeemer of mankind. It is impossible that it should be otherwise; and in this sense and to this extent our civilization and our institutions are emphatically Christian...This is a religious people. This is historically true. From the discovery of this continent to the present hour, there is a single voice making this affirmation...we find everywhere a clear recognition of the same truth...These, and many other matters which might be noticed, add a volume of unofficial declarations to the mass of organic utterances that this is a Christian nation." It is obvious that we are a Christian Nation, those are our roots and that is our heritage.

"A nation which does not remember what it was yesterday does not know what it is today, nor what it is trying to do. We are trying to do a futile thing if we do not know where we came from or what we have been about." Woodrow Wilson.

Within the provisions for checks and balances in our government is authorization for the Supreme Court to reverse itself for previous errors made in the court's decision. The court needs to review anti-God rulings

377

starting with the 1962 in Engel Vs Vitale prohibiting prayer in the classroom and in 1963 the Supreme Court in Murray Vs Curlett the court's decision prohibited prayer and Bible reading in the classroom. The court jurists declared prayer and Bible reading were violations of the establishment clause of the Constitution. The establishment clause forbids the government from establishing an official religion. It also prohibits government actions that unduly favor one religion over another. It also prohibits the government from unduly preferring religion over non-religion, or non-religion over religion. However, in these decisions the court is establishing a religion of secular humanism. The supreme court favored a godless religion violating the establishment clause. Using an argument of separation of church and state, which is not in the Constitution, to negate the 1st Amendment of the Constitution which prevents the government from establishing a religion. God, prayer and the Bible were the original intent of the classroom, to teach Scripture and morality. How is this now unconstitutional? The courts have also found that secular humanism is a religion under the equal protection clause and our tax dollars pay for this to be taught in our public schools. In a country ruled by law these injustices cannot be allowed to stand. Our standard is still God's law, not the whimsical and capricious ideations of fallen man.

The Supreme Court has almost single handedly destroyed America, religious liberty, the American Experiment, and the whole idea of a religious and moral people. The justices have judicated God out of the public sector, destroying our religious liberty and the preeminent position of religion and morality. In direct violation of the Constitution they have made secular humanism the state religion. In their arrogance they have destroyed everything the Founding Fathers, the colonists sacrificed and endured to establish, a government based on liberty. A new check and balance to be considered is term limits for justices, competency tests and the ability for a special court to be able to try judges for sedition and treason punishable by death.

So given the question, What the Hell Went Wrong?

In its most fundamental position, I have said when seeking the truth in seeking answers we must view our conundrum with considerations from both provisional and foundational reality. As spiritual and physical beings we live, right now, within both of these realities. Therefore, a complete answer can only come by a solution that encompasses considerations from both realities. Before Darwin and his provisional explanation of life everyone lived a more foundational existence. They lived life, as it were,

Coram Deo. Coram Deo is a Latin phrase that means something that takes place in the presence of an omnipresent God, always under His gaze. As such, Coram Deo is living one's life in the presence of God, under the sovereignty and authority of God, to His glory and honor. To answer the question, What the Hell Went Wrong? We have far too many people that have abandoned Coram Deo, but instead have chosen to live Coram Me, abandoning the requirement or even the desire of being religious and moral.

Is there a remedy for What the Hell Went Wrong? The first thing we must do is reestablish our government under the premise of a religious and moral people. We first accomplish this by individually adopting a philosophy of life of Coram Deo. If you want to get to know someone, you spend time with them. If you want a relationship with your personal Savior or with the Holy Spirit shut off the TV and read your Bible.[62]

"Do not love the world nor the things in the world. If anyone loves the world, the love of the Father is not in him.[63] Trust in the Lord with all your heart and do not lean on your own understanding.[64]And do not be conformed to this world, but be transformed by the renewing of your mind, so that you may prove what the will of God is, that which is good and acceptable and perfect."

Martin Luther's crusade was for every man woman and child to have their own Bible to read. That they could then develop a personal relation with Christ based on the dictates of their conscience. If you try to develop this relationship without reading Scripture, God is who you think He is, and that is worshipping an idol.

Secondly, Christian America must realize that we are involved in a Revolutionary War. It may be the most crucial war in our nation's history. It is a war for preeminence and control of America. The problem is Christian Americans, nationalists, do not even realize they are in a war for the heart and soul of America with the godless, immoral globalists. Presently this is not a war of rifles and smoothbores it is a war of ideologies, of ideas, of values and beliefs. If Christian America does not become actively involved in the current revolutionary war it will, inevitably, evolve into one of armed conflict.

"Prudence, indeed, will dictate that Governments long established should not be changed for light and transient causes; and accordingly, all

---

[62] Things To Come: A Brief History of the Bible
[63] 1 John 2:15

experience hath shewn, that mankind are more disposed to suffer, while evils are sufferable, than to right themselves by abolishing the forms to which they are accustomed. But when a long train of abuses and usurpations, pursuing invariably the same Object evinces a design to reduce them under absolute Despotism, it is their right, it is their duty, to throw off such Government, and to provide new Guards for their future security." Do we have enough Patriots, do we have enough minuteman?

"Resistance to tyranny becomes the Christian and social duty of each individual...Continue steadfast and, with a proper sense of your dependence upon God, nobly defend those rights which heaven gave, and no man ought to take from us." John Hancock

The addendum for *America* contains a legal brief presented to the US Supreme Court by fellow Christian Chris Gates, which they have not acted upon. It will only be acted upon if enough pressure can be exerted upon Congress and the US Supreme Court from "We the People." The addendum reads in part, "In 1879, the U.S. Supreme Court illegally altered the writing of the Constitution and changed it. How? First, the court declared in U.S. v Reynolds that the Constitution did not define the term "religion." On that basis, that court then went on to make its own definition of that term. And the court chose a broad rendering; it adopted a plural meaning for the term "religion." Hence, they changed the writing of the First Amendment Religion Clause to, in fact, read as follows: "Congress shall make no law respecting an establishment of religions or prohibiting the free exercise thereof."

We were founded as a Christian nation, singular. The religious tolerance implied in our founding documents as to our religious forbearance is for the many Christian denominations. From within the framework of the Christian faith we find our Judeo-Christian values, our morality. It was never the intent of the Founders to be inclusive of any other religion. Each religion has its own set of believes and their own morality. The Founders explicitly meant by religion, the Christian faith and by morality, they explicitly meant morality from our Judeo-Christian values. We can never compromise on the fundamentals of our faith. Compromise is the art of give and take, compromise on fundamentals is surrender, it is all give and no take. The fundamentals of Christianity and Christian morality cannot be compromised by merging belief systems. This is another grievous err made by the supreme court that must be reversed.

"It is the duty of nations as well as men, to own their dependence upon the overruling power of God to recognize the sublime truth announced in the Holy Scripture and proven by all history that those nations only are blessed whose God is the Lord."   Abraham Lincoln

FINALS

It came to mind one day in 2016 as I was reading Isiah 45, that President Trump is the 45th President of the United States, and I deliberated, that God is involved in the affairs of men.

Isiah 45: 1-7: "Thus says the Lord to Cyrus His anointed, Whom I have taken by the right hand, To subdue nations before him, And to loose the lions of kings; To open doors before him so that gates will not be shut: I will go before you and make the rough places smooth; I will shatter the doors of bronze, and cut through their iron bars. And I will give you the treasures of darkness, And hidden wealth of secret places. In order that you may know that it is I, The Lord, the God of Israel, who calls you by name. For the sake of Jacob My Servant, And Israel My chosen one, I have also called you by name; I have given you a title of honor Though you have not known Me. I am the Lord, and there is no other; Besides Me there is no God. I will gird you, though you have not known Me; That men may know from the rising to the setting of the sun That there is no one besides Me. I am the Lord, and there is no other, The One forming light and creating darkness, Causing well-being and creating calamity; I am the Lord who does all this."

Tom Fitton, President of Judicial Watch is a tremendous source of truth and an organization that is truly fighting for the truth and the rights of American citizens, like no other organization, congress included. I would encourage you to watch his weekly reports and support the ministry of Judicial Watch. [65]

---

[65] https://www.judicialwatch.org/

An interesting side note, earlier I footnoted a reference to [1] http://thinkaboutnow.com/2016/06/study-guns-stop-crime-2-5-million-times-each-year/   I went back to this site, and was told the site could not be found, it offered a link using the same words, I clicked on it and all of the search results took me to google which displayed articles that were anti-gun from liberal sources. I copied the link into duckduckgo and the original site came with other pro-gun studies and sites. I located a new site[66] with the same information I referenced above.

If You found **AMERICA: WHAT THE HELL WENT WRONG** to be of merit please tell your friends it is available on Amazon, and please write a review on Amazon.

Usa.life – conservative alternate to Facebook

1776free – conservative alternate search engine to google

---

[66] https://gunowners.org/sk0802htm/

ADDENDUM

AMERICA'S HERITAGE: A CHRISTIAN NATION, LIGHT FOR THE WHOLE WORLD

By Chris Gates

"The highest glory of the American Revolution was this: It connected in one **indissoluble** bond the principles of civil government with the principles of Christianity". – President John Adams

Forward

A Christian nation, simply, is a nation whose laws and actions are in concord with the teachings of Jesus Christ, a nation where laws promote and foster Jesus-like behavior in society. As the first Virginia State Constitution states," it is the mutual duty of all to practice Christian forbearance, love and charity towards each other." A Christian nation requires no religious duties of its members other than <u>good civil behavior</u> - no stealing, no killing, no sexual immorality, etc. The religious duties of loving, serving, worshipping and promoting God, on the other hand, is a personal choice and that duty is a matter between the individual and God.

Jeremiah 1.10 says (New American Standard Bible), "See I have appointed you this day over the nations and over the kingdoms, to pluck up and to break down, to destroy and to overthrow, to build and to plant." In this writing you will find a pulling down of the status quo and a building of the founding fathers' paradigm. Therefore, the current powers-at-be will find this writing frightening because it destroys their bogus right to lead the people in the direction and fashion as they have.

"Do not separate text from historical background. If you do, you will have perverted and subverted the Constitution, which can only

end in a distorted, bastardized form of illegitimate government." - President James Madison, Author of the Constitution

The bottom line to this writing is: Jesus Christ taught that the greatest among you SHALL BE a servant of all. America, without doubt, is mandated to exercise the commands of Christ by their founding law as you will see. Therefore, America has a moral duty to be a Servant to the whole world. Likewise, Jesus commands one to lay down one's life for the betterment of their brother. Therefore, America must also lay down its life for the life of the World. That is its national duty.

It is my sincere hope America will fulfill its divine destiny as a self-sacrificing servant to the world at large. No man is deserving of the freedom we have here, unless he is willing to fight for and secure another man's freedom. "The kingdom of heaven suffers violence and the violent take it by force." Matthew 11.12

SECTIONS:
-Introduction to how the U.S. Supreme Court illegally altered the writing of the Constitution and changed it: p284
-The Analytical Framework and Governing Case Law that aids in understanding the Constitution: p286
-The literal meaning of "religion" in the First Amendment speaks of one, and only one, particular religion, even though no religion is specified therein: p287
-Deriving the lawfully practical application of the Religion Clause using the literal definition of one exclusive religion for the term 'religion': p288
-The U.S. Constitution identifies the unstated religion of the First Amendment to be the teachings of Jesus Christ: p290
-The applicable laws at the time of drafting and ratifying the Constitution and the words and terms used then all clearly corroborate the obvious Christian meaning of the words "our Lord" used in Article 7 of the Constitution: p291
-The intent of Religion Clause is to expunge the sectarianism that plagues the Christian religion: p295
-Critiquing the Reynolds's Decision: p288

Introduction

In 1879 the U.S. Supreme Court illegally altered the writing of the Constitution and changed it. How? First, the court declared in U.S. v

Reynolds[67] that the Constitution did not define the term "religion". On that basis, that court then went on to make its own definition of that term. And the court chose a broad rendering; it adopted a plural meaning for the term "religion". Hence, they CHANGED the writing of the First Amendment Religion Clause to, in fact, read as follows: "Congress shall make no law respecting an establishment of <u>religions</u> or prohibiting the free exercise thereof."

America is a Constitutional Republic, and the Law is king.

Consequently, where the 'Law" goes; so, goes this Nation.

True law is eternal, consistent, and unchanging - like the law of gravity. The American Constitutional Republic is supposed to seek and install true social law that is eternal, consistent and unchanging for all generations. And its laws are not supposed to be a reflection of the ever-changing desires of the majority or some power group. President Calvin Coolidge stated that "Men do not make laws. They do but discover them. Laws must be justified by something more than the will of the majority. They must rest on the eternal foundation of righteousness. That State is most fortunate in its form of government which has the aptest instruments for the discovery of law."

Our Nation is currently mired in corruption and division that is unprecedented in its history. So, if America is to be a better nation, the Law, and the interpretation of law, must become better. And adopting the true interpretation of the First Amendment Religion Clause will make America a better Nation.

In 1993 in case no. 92-8104, I brought a matter before the Supreme Court that simply said that the 1879 declaration that the Constitution did not define "religion" was absolutely and undeniably wrong: And if the text of the religion clause is parsed according to the rules of grammar, logical reasoning implies a clear and certain definition for the term "religion". The court in 1993 chose to remain with the 1879 declaration in spite of clear and convincing proof that any honest and honorable person would agree with, and they ruled against the truth presented to them without any explanation as to why they decided to remain with the Reynolds precedence.

The court's behavior in 1993 is despicable and criminal. They have acted with total disregard to truth and have consciously misinterpreted the Constitution with a complete understanding of it. The court here is

---

[67] <u>Reynolds v. U.S.</u>, 98 U.S. 145, 162 (1879)

suppressing truth and this is an impeachable offense under Article 3 and 6 of the Constitution. Justice Anthony Scalia warned the American public in dissenting opinions in 1996, that the court "day by day, case by case, is busy designing a constitution for a country he does not recognize and that a lawyer -trained elite is determined to foist its smug assurances and counter majoritarian preferences onto a helpless and unwitting nation."

After you read through the following clear and convincing truth, I hope you become stirred to rise up and answer 'Justice Scalia's call for help, because now is the time for all the good, the just, the courageous MEN in America to stand up in defense of our Constitution. Together, we must pledge our lives, our fortunes, and our sacred honor in defense of our legal rights, which were purchased with blood, for our children's sake. We must stand and defend our Constitution, the bulwark of our Nation, from those who are destroying it. We must spread the truth of our Constitution. We must put an end to the social corruption, chaos and filth that plague our land and restore a love for truth, honor and respect for one another. We must do our DUTY as required of by THE DECLARATION OF INDEPENDCE, that being: when government becomes abusive (and corrupt) it is the right and the DUTY of the people to throw off such Government and to provide new guards for their future security.

<u>The Analytical Framework and Governing Case Law that aids in understanding the Constitution</u>

The Constitution is what 'IT' says it is and its mandates and instruction therein are self-evident and obvious to a reasonable mind. Moreover, no court has the right to use tortured logic to alter the obvious meanings and directives therein.

The true meaning of the religion clause becomes evident through the reasonable application of the following: The first is a reasonable rendering of the terms in the text of the religion clause. The second is a logical application the rules of grammar governing the text of the religion clause. The third is accurate application of the rules for interpretation of law generated through specific case law. These three criteria will make the absolute truth regarding the First Amendment Religion Clause apparent.

Case Law has developed a number of parameters to aid in coming to an understanding of what the Constitution means, and they are:

a) The intention of the instrument is to prevail; this intention must be collected from its words; its words are to be understood in that sense in which they are generally used by those for whom the instrument was intended; its provisions are neither to be restricted into insignificance, nor extended to objects not comprehended in them, nor contemplated by its framers. Ogden v. Saunders (1827) 12 Wheat 332.

b) "The spirit of an instrument, especially of a constitution, is to be respected not less than its letter, yet the spirit is to be collected chiefly from its words." We have no need in this case to go beyond the plain, obvious meaning of the words in those provisions of the Constitution which, it is contended, must control our decision. Jacobson v. Massachusetts (1904) 197 U.S. 22.

c) Chief Justice Marshall said : "As men, whose intentions require no concealment, generally employ the words which most directly and aptly express the ideas they intend to convey, the enlightened patriots who framed our constitution, and the people who adopted it, must be understood to have employed words in their natural sense, and to have intended what they have said." Gibbons v. Ogden (1824) 9 Wheat 188.

d) No word or clause can be rejected as superfluous or meaningless, but each word must be given it due force and appropriate meaning. Knowlton v. Moore (1899) 178 U.S. 87.

e) Where any particular word is obscure, or of doubtful meaning, taken by itself, its obscurity or doubt may be removed by reference to associated words, and meaning of a term may be enlarged or restrained by reference to object of whole clause in which it is used. Virginia v. Tennessee (1893) 148 U.S. 503, 37 L. Ed. 537, 13 S. Ct. 728.

f) Supreme Court is bound to interpret Constitution in light of the law as it existed at time it was adopted, not as reaching out for new guaranties of rights of citizen. Mattox v. United States (1895) 156 U.S. 237, 39 L. Ed. 409, 15 S. Ct. 337.

g) Framers of Constitution employed words in their natural sense, and where they are plain and clear, resort to collateral aids to interpretations is unnecessary and cannot be indulged in to narrow or enlarge the text. McPherson v. Blacker (1892) 146 U.S. 1, 36 L. Ed. 869, 13 S. Ct. 3.

h) The Constitution must receive a practical construction. Railroad Co. v. Peniston ( ) 18 Wall 31.

i) Words in a constitution are always to be given the meaning they have in common use unless there are strong reasons to the contrary. Tennessee v. Whitworth (1885) 117 U.S. 147.

j) That which is implied is as much part of the constitution as what is expressed. Ex Parte Yarbourgh (1884) 110 U.S. 651, 28 L. Ed. 274, 4 5. Ct. 152.

k) An amended constitution must be read as a whole and as if every part of it had been adopted at the same time and as one law. Badger v. Hoidale, C.C.A. 88 F 2d 208 (1937), 109 A.L.R. 798.

The literal meaning of "religion" in the First Amendment speaks of one, and only one, particular religion, even though no religion is specified therein

In 1879 the U.S. Supreme Court illegally altered the writing of the Constitution and changed it. The court declared in U.S. v Reynolds that the Constitution did not, in fact, define the term "religion" at all – either expressly or implicitly. And on that basis, the court then went on to make up its own definition for that term. The court chose to adopt a broad and plural meaning for the term "religion". And they CHANGED the normal singular meaning of the First Amendment Religion Clause to, in fact, read as follows: "Congress shall make no law respecting an establishment of religions or prohibit the free exercise thereof."

With case law specifying that: the intention of the instrument is to prevail, and this intention is to be collected chiefly from its words understood in their ordinary sense, and although the spirit of an instrument is to be respected not less than its letter, yet the spirit is to be collected chiefly from its words, let us examine the letter of the First Amendment.

The First Amendment of U.S. Constitution states:

"Congress shall make no law respecting an establishment of religion or prohibiting the free exercise thereof."

Note, here that the word 'religion' is in the single case form rather than the plural form (religions); therefore, it literally means a single religious belief by grammatical rule. When we consider the plural rendering of the single case form, which is atypical, there needs to exist some word modifying religion, such as: 'a' or 'any' to change its ordinary meaning. And here, none exists. Therefore, it can be unequivocally stated from this analysis: that the literal meaning of 'religion' in the First Amendment means one particular albeit-unidentified religion.

Deriving the lawfully practical application of the Religion Clause using the literal definition of one exclusive religion for the term 'religion'

When judges look at new law and they seek to apply it to a case, there is a presumption that the drafters of the law made a reasonable law. And this new law can be applied in a practical, common sense way. And this practical way is in accord to the common meaning of the words used in the law. Furthermore, each word used therein is to be given its full force in defining that law.

The First Amendment Religion Clause reads as follows: CONGRESS SHALL MAKE NO LAW respecting an establishment of religion OR prohibiting the free exercise thereof.

This clause contains two provisions. The first part of the clause is called the establishment provision. The second part of the clause is called the free exercise provision. These two provisions are joined by the conjunction 'or". And according to the rules of grammar, the use of the conjunction 'or" means that the two provisions are equal in importance and can exchange places without changing any meaning. It could have been written - Congress shall make no law prohibiting the free exercise of religion or respecting an establishment thereof- and mean exactly the same thing as it reads above.

In general, the Religion Clause is a total prohibition leveled at the U.S. Congress. Congress can make no law." This is a direct command. It is final and absolute in nature. But what exactly is Congress eternally prohibited from doing?

Looking at the Free Exercise Provision alone, it reads as follows - Congress shall make no law prohibiting the free exercise of religion. What does this mean? Literally, this provision applies to every living soul in the American society - man, woman, child, business, governmental body. And it gives everyone and every group the right to practice religion freely without any restraint. It creates a total freedom of expression for religion for everyone.

This provisional absolute, however, is only practical in an environment where there is only one religious belief being acted out in the general society. The Free Exercise Provision does not work in an environment where there is more than one religious belief being acted out in society. The reason is in a society with multiple religions practicing, differing religions will eventually clash with other religions over their religiously mandated behaviors. And when that happens, a judge will curtail the religious exercise of one of the clashing religions in order to bring civil peace. But the Free Exercise Provision specifically forbids any kind of interference with religious exercise, period. Governmental power is absolutely banned from such action.

The following example shows this multiple religion problem clearly: Consider a controversy between devout Hindus and devout Jews. Hindus worship cattle and do them no harm. Jews, however, sacrifice and eat them. It is easily seen that a fight will break out between these opposing beliefs. And to settle this dispute, the courts will restrict some party in their religious freedom so as to bring peace. But the courts cannot do that as the Free Exercise Provision is written. (Currently, the courts are restricting religious practices without any Constitutional authority to do so. This is absolutely illegal, and the court has no RIGHT under law to do so.)

In an environment of only one religious' belief in society, a religious exercise is either right or wrong when it is measured against doctrine. Therefore, if an exercise is correct, the religious exercise cannot be curtailed; however, if it is incorrect it can be restricted lawfully. In this scenario of the Free Exercise Provision, religious controversies are easily resolved. For example, sacrificing a fish is either right or wrong according to Jewish doctrine.

Now, looking at the Establishment Provision alone, it reads as follows - Congress shall make no law respecting an establishment of religion. On the face in the broadest of meaning, this provision compels government to restrict all expression of religion in society. It, therefore, creates a society devoid of any religion. However, this type of definition is absolutely contrary to the definition of the Free Exercise Provision where every person and institution is granted total freedom to practice religion. There is now an inescapable, inherent contradiction here between the broad definitions of the Free Exercise and Establishment Provisions. The Supreme Court says this is the true situation with the provisions in the case of Walz v. Tax Commission (1969) 397 U.S. 668, 669 which states, "The court has struggled to find a neutral course between the two religion clauses, both of which are cast in absolute terms and either of which, if expanded to a logical extreme, would tend to clash with the other. In other words, the two provisions are at natural odds. However, logically, that cannot be the case. First, no one in their right mind would construct an absurd law that has no logical application ever. That is totally unthinkable, especially if you consider the brilliance of the forefathers who designed our society. Secondly, and more importantly, such a notion goes against the fundamental legal presumption that the drafters of a law created a practical law in the first place. Therefore, in the name of practicality, there must be a more limited meaning to the term establish. And this limited meaning is in harmony with the concept of total religious freedom.

Since the First Amendment is addressing the powers of Congress only, the establishment of religion restriction applies only to the religious freedoms of the Congress and does not extended out to reach the religious freedoms of the other members of society. The working model of this is: the American society has everyone and every group practicing religion and establishing religion throughout the whole of society except for Congress. Congress is prohibited by law from the one particular religious exercise of establishing a national religious institution like in England where the church and state were wedded.

However, Congress can perform every other form of religious practice that is available to them like giving thanks to God (i.e. - Thanksgiving Day National Holiday), opening a session of Congress with a prayer, portraying religious saying on government property, etc. (All of these examples occur now in government circles). Another way to look at it and see the practical application of the Religion Clause is to see a wholly religious society with many communities therein. And then see the government as a subset community in the larger society, practicing religion with all of the other members it organizes. And further see government having no part in managing religious affairs therein.

Therefore, according to the above analysis, the First Amendment is only, I repeat, only practical is a society that acts out the mandates of one and exclusively one religion; the clause is ridiculous otherwise.

The U.S. Constitution identifies the unstated religion of the First Amendment to be the teachings of Jesus Christ

The Preamble to the Bill of Rights begins with "The Conventions of a number of the States having at the time of their adopting the Constitution, expressed a desire, <u>in order to prevent misconstruction or abuse of its powers</u>, that **further declaratory and restrictive clauses should be added**:" With the use of the words 'further declaratory and restrictive clauses (to prevent misconstruction), this charge superimposes the Bill of Rights on the initial constitution and makes the Bill of Rights the heart, and preeminent part, of the Constitution, clarifying the Constitution in a greater and more definite way; and implies a finished work that is wholly reasonable and congruent with the Constitution.

Now that the literal text of the First Amendment is certain in meaning of one and only one unique religion and the amendment does not identify that one religion, one must conclude and assume that the main text to which the amendment has been attached contains that necessary identification.

History shows that the U.S. Constitution was completed on September 17, 1787. And on March 4, 1789 the federal government was inaugurated in New York under the new constitution. And on September 25, 1789 the first Congress, under the new constitution, adopted the first ten amendments, Bill of Rights, to the constitution, which came to force two years later on December 15, 1791.

The fore mentioned case law states that: where any particular word or sentence is obscure or of doubtful meaning, taken by itself (which is what there is here), its obscurity may be removed by comparing it with the words and sentences with which it stands connected. But there are none. Therefore, case law deems further that: an amended constitution must be read as a whole and as if every part of it had been adopted at the same time and as one law. All of which leads to the main text of the Constitution.

In examination of the Constitution, there are only two other provisions that have any religious intonation in them: Article 7 and Article 6, both of which precede the First Amendment in time.

For this analysis case law stipulates that: no word or clause can be rejected as superfluous or meaningless, but each word must be given it due force and appropriate meaning, reference is to be had to the literal meaning of the words to be expounded, their connection with other words, and the general objects to be accomplished. But, more importantly, logical assumption has disposed us to seek any meaningful word to identify the unstated religion of the first amendment.

Article 6 of the U.S. Constitution states:

"No religious test shall ever be required as a qualification to any office or public trust under the United States."

Here, there exists no meaningful word which identifies religion. However, Article 7 of the U.S. Constitution states:

(This new constitution is)"Done in convention by the unanimous consent of the states present the seventeenth day of September in the year of our Lord one thousand seven hundred and eighty seven and of the independence of the United States of America the twelfth." (This marks the date the Constitutional Convention completed and signed the new constitution.)

And here it can be clearly seen from the words "Done in convention by the unanimous consent of the States present" that the signers totally assented to the whole contents of the document, the Constitution, as written. And this obviously includes the words "in the year of our Lord" which is a clear inference to Jesus Christ of Nazareth, the founder of the Christian religion. So, in writing "our Lord" verses "the Lord", a mere demarcation of time, the framers literally declared their corporate religious belief to be the teachings of Christ in using the plural possessive "our." Thus, religion is identified, and it is the teaching of Jesus Christ. Therefore, the American society is a Christian Nation that is legally mandated to act out the teaching of Jesus Christ in all aspects.

Even if the signers had used the term "the Lord", the historical record would have confirmed the religious identification to be the teachings of Jesus Christ beyond any doubt. The historical record shows that the country was first a Christian society, which over time grew into a Christian nation. This fact is undeniably true. In 1891 the Supreme Court in its examination of the historical record a century after the country was founded stated unequivocally that the United States is a "Christian Nation" in the case of Holy Trinity v. U.S.

<u>The applicable laws at the time of drafting and ratifying the Constitution and the words and terms used then all clearly corroborate the obvious Christian meaning of the words "our Lord" used in Article 7 of the Constitution</u>

Case law states that words and terms are to be taken in the sense in which they were used and understood at common law and at the time the constitution and amendments were adopted.

In examining the following state constitutions which were applicable at the time of drafting and ratifying of the new federal Constitution and the Bill of Rights, it is found that all sanctioned, advocated, protected, and fostered the exercise of the Christian religion to the affairs of state and man, and granted religious freedom and rights only within the context of such:

Article 22 of the 1776 Delaware Constitution, which was controlling of the five signing state representatives sent to the 1787 U.S. Constitutional Convention, states that: Every person who shall be chosen a member of either house, or appointed to any office or place of trust, before taking his seat, or entering upon the execution of his office, shall take the following oath .... " A.B., do profess faith in God the Father, and in Jesus Christ his only son, and in the Holy Ghost, one God, blessed for evermore; and I do acknowledge the Holy Scriptures of the Old and New Testament to be given by divine inspiration.

Article 6 of the 1777 Georgia Constitution, which was controlling of the two signing state representatives sent to the 1787 U.S. Constitutional Convention, states that: The representatives shall be ... of the Protestant religion

Article 35 of the 1776 Maryland Constitution, which was controlling of the three signing state representatives sent to the 1787 U.S. Constitutional Convention, states that: No other test or qualification ought to be required, on admission to any office of trust or profit, than such oath of support and fidelity to this state, ... and a declaration of a belief in the Christian religion

Chapter 6, Article 1 of the 1780 Massachusetts Constitution, which was controlling of the two signing state representatives sent to the 1787 U.S. Constitutional Convention, states that:

Any person chosen governor, lieutenant-governor, ... , or representative, and

accepting the trust, shall ... make and subscribe the following declaration, "I, A.B., do declare that I believe the Christian religion and have a firm persuasion of its truth."

Article 3 of the 1778 South Carolina Constitution, which was controlling of the four signing state representatives sent to the 1787 U.S. Constitutional Convention, states that: No person shall be eligible to sit the House of Representatives unless he be of the Protestant religion

Article 32 of the 1776 North Carolina Constitution, which was controlling of the three signing state representatives sent to the 1787 U.S. Constitutional Convention, states that: No person, who shall deny the being of God or the truths of the Protestant religion, or the divine authority either of the Old or New Testaments ... shall be capable of holding any office or place of trust.

Article 19 of the 1776 New Jersey Constitution, which was controlling of the four signing state representatives sent to the 1787 U.S. Constitutional Convention, states that: There shall be no establishment of any one religious sect in this province, in preference to another; and that no Protestant inhabitant of this colony shall be denied the enjoyment of any civil right, merely on account of his religious principles; but that all persons, professing a belief in the faith of any Protestant sect who shall demean themselves peaceably under the government shall be capable of being elected into any office of profit or trust.

Section 10 of the Pennsylvania Constitution, which was controlling of the seven signing state representatives sent to the 1787 U.S. Constitutional Convention, states that: Each member, before he takes his seat, shall make and subscribe the following declaration: I do believe in one God, the Creator and Governor of the Universe, the Rewarder of the good and the Punisher of the wicked. And I do acknowledge the scriptures of the Old and New Testament to be given by divine inspiration.

Article 6 of the Bill of Rights of the 1784 New Hampshire Constitution, which was controlling of the two signing state representatives sent to the U.S. Constitutional Convention, states that: As morality and piety, rightly grounded on evangelical principles, will give the best and greatest security to government, and will lay in the hearts of men the strongest obligations to due subjection, ... Therefore, to promote those important purposes, the people of this state have a right to impower, and do hereby fully impower the legislature ... to make adequate provision ... for the support and maintenance of public Protestant teachers of piety, religion, and morality ... and every denomination of Christians demeaning themselves quietly, and as good subjects of the state, shall be equally under the protection of the law and no subordination of any one sect or denomination to another, shall ever be established by law.

Section 16 of the Bill of Rights of the 1776 Virginia Constitution, which was controlling of the three signing state representatives sent to the 1787 U.S. Constitutional Convention, states that: religion, or duty which we owe to our creator, and the manner of discharging it, can be directed only by reason and conviction, not by force of violence; and therefore all men are equally entitled to the free exercise of religion, according to the dictates of conscience; and that it is the mutual duty of all to practice Christian forbearance, love, and charity towards each other."

Article 38 of the 1777 New York Constitution, which was controlling of the signing state representative sent to the 1787 U.S. Constitutional Convention, states that:

Whereas we are required, by the benevolent principles of rational liberty, not only to expel civil tyranny, but also to guard against that spiritual oppression and intolerance wherewith the bigotry and ambition of weak and wicked priests and princes have scourged mankind, this convention doth further ordain, determine, declare, that the free exercise and enjoyment of religious profession and worship, without discrimination or preference, shall forever hereafter be allowed to all mankind.

Article 39 states that: And whereas the ministers of the Gospel are, by their profession, dedicated to the service of God and the care of souls, and ought not be diverted from their great duties of their function; therefore, no minister of the Gospel, or priest of any denomination whatsoever shall, at any time hereafter, under any pretense or description whatever, be eligible to, or capable of holding, any civil or military office or place.

The preamble of the 1776 Connecticut Constitution, which adopts the organic English Charter as its constitutional base and was controlling of the two signing state representative sent to the 1787 U.S. Constitutional Convention, states that: The people of this state, being by the providence of God, free and independent, have the sole and exclusive right of governing themselves as a free, sovereign, and independent state and forasmuch as the free fruition of such liberties and privileges as humanity, civility and Christianity call for as is due to every man in his place and proportion.

No state representative was sent to the 1787 U.S. Constitutional Convention from Rhode Island. However, they would have been subject to Rhode Island's constitutional authority, namely: the 1663 English Charter, which states that: Charles the Second, by the grace of God, Defender of the Faith ... that all and every person and persons may ... bee in the better capacity to defend themselves, in their just rights and liberties against all the enemies of the Christian faith.

All of the signing delegates, by their state constitutions, had a fiduciary duty to uphold the truths and duties of the Christian religion. And 29 of the 36 signing delegates to the constitution were required by their state constitution to affirmatively testify to such in some fashion. Furthermore, 24 of the delegates were trained ministers of the Christian Religion.

Additionally, the representatives of the state legislatures that ratified the new federal Constitution and First Amendment had a fiduciary duty to uphold the Christian religion by their state constitutions, which were controlling at the time under the Federal Articles of Confederation and new Constitution, respectively And therefore when the legislatures ratified those propositions, one must conclude that the representatives perceived those propositions to be congruent with their fiduciary duty to uphold Christian principles, mandated by their state constitution. Otherwise, the representatives would have struck down the ratification of those propositions because of a moral and official imperative. And this sober duty of the state representatives is particularly underscored by their religious text in Matthew 7:21-23 (New American Standard Bible), which warns that:

Not everyone who says to me (Jesus), "Lord, Lord, will enter the kingdom of heaven; but he who does the will of My Father who is in heaven. Many will say to Me on that day, 'Lord', 'Lord', did we not prophesy in Your name, and in Your name cast out demons, and in Your name perform many miracles? And then I will declare to them, I never knew you; depart from Me, you who practice lawlessness.

And this would have a tremendous sobering affect upon a faithful practitioner.

Moreover, the Northwest Ordinance of 1787, which was drafted by Congress on July 13, 1787 at the same time the Constitutional Convention was meeting and drafting our current U.S. Constitution, further enhances the sense of the words and terms as they were used and understood at common law at that time and establishes more applicable law that aids interpretation:

Para. 1: "Be it ordained by the United States, in congress assembled, that the said territory, for the purpose of temporary government "

Para. 13: "And for extending the fundamental principles of civil and religious liberty, which form the basis whereon these republics, their laws and constitutions, are erected to fix and establish those principles as the basis of all laws, constitutions, and governments, which forever hereafter shall be formed in the said territory... ."

Art. 3: " morality, and knowledge being necessary to good government and the happiness of mankind, schools and means of education shall forever be encouraged.

Closing salutation: "Done by the United States, in Congress assembled, the 13th day of July, in the year of our Lord one thousand seven hundred and eighty seven and of their sovereignty and independence the 12th."

Therefore, in this analysis, the applicable laws at the time of drafting and ratifying the Constitution and the words and terms used then all clearly corroborate the obvious Christian meaning of the words "our Lord" used in the Constitution.

Much more can be said, collaterally speaking, further underscoring the above, but case law stipulates that where <u>the meaning is plain and clear, resort to collateral aids to interpretations is unnecessary and cannot be indulged in to narrow or enlarge the text</u>. Consequently, none will follow. Clearly, then, the unstated religion of the First Amendment is the teachings of Jesus Christ.

Before moving on, the following declarations of the U.S. Supreme Court and its members and President John Adams, further, certifies the above conclusion:

In 1833 Rev. Jasper Adams, college president, wrote a pamphlet on the relations of Christianity to civil government in the U.S. that contested the view "Christianity had no connection with our civil constitutions" and contended the "concept of a national religion with it being the foundation for their civil government."

Chief Justice John Marshall wrote Rev. Adams a letter in regard to his pamphlet and stated, speaking for the U.S. Supreme Court,

"The American Population is entirely Christian, and with us Christianity and religion are identified."

Justice Joseph Story, a member of the Marshall Supreme Court, wrote also a letter to Rev. Adams regarding his pamphlet and stated:

"I have read it with uncommon satisfaction. I think its tone and spirit excellent. My own private judgment has long been (and every day's experience more and more confirms me in it) that government cannot long exist without an alliance with religion; and that Christianity is indispensable to true interests and solid foundations of free government,

And the U.S. Supreme Court in 1891 in Holy Trinity v. U.S (143 U.S. 457) states:

"If we examine the constitutions of the various states, we find in them a constant recognition of religious obligations. Every constitution of every one of the 48 states contains language which either directly or by clear implications recognizes a profound reverence for religion and an assumption that its influence in all human affairs is essential to the wellbeing of the community. p468 There is no dissonance in these declarations. There is a universal language pervading them all, having one meaning; they affirm and reaffirm that there is a religious nation. These are not individual sayings; they are organic utterances. p470 These, and many other matters which might be noticed, add a volume of unofficial declarations to the mass of organic utterances that this is a Christian nation." p471

President John Adams stated that "The highest glory of the American Revolution was this: it connected in one indissoluble bond the Principles of Civil Government with the Principles of Christianity.

The intent of Religion Clause is to expunge the sectarianism that plagues the Christian religion

Preceding the Constitutional Convention that met and created our Constitution, the principle architect of our federal constitution and chairman of the committee that drafted the First Amendment, James Madison published a paper against a bill establishing provision for teachers of Christianity in the State of Virginia. It was called "Memorial and Remonstrance".

Para. 1 states: "It is the duty of every man to render to the creator such homage and such only as he believes to be acceptable to him. This duty is precedent, both in order of time and in degree of obligation, to the claims of society. Before any man can be considered as a member of civil society, he must be considered as a subject of the governour of the universe."

Para. 2 therein states: "Because if religion be exempt from authority of the society at large, still less can it be subject to that of the legislative body. The latter are but creatures and vicegerents of the former. Their jurisdiction is both derivative and limited."

Para. 6 states: "Because the establishment proposed by the bill is not requisite for the support of the Christian religion. To say that it is, is a contradiction to the Christian religion itself, for every page of it disavows a dependence on the powers of this world: It is a contradiction to fact; for it is known that this religion both existed and flourished, not only without the support of human laws, but in spite of every opposition from them, and not only during the period of miraculous aid, but long after it had been left to its own evidence and ordinary care of providence. Nay, it is a contradiction in terms; for a religion not invented by human policy, must have pre—existed and been supported, before it was established by human policy. It is moreover to weaken in those who profess this religion a pious confidence in its innate excellence and the patronage of its author."

Para. 7 states: "Because experience witnesseth that ecclesiastical establishments, instead of maintaining the purity and efficacy of religion, have had a contrary operation. During almost fifteen centuries has the legal establishment of Christianity been on trial. What have been its fruits? ... Pride and indolence in the clergy, ignorance and servility in the laity, in both supersition, bigotry and persecution."

Para. 8 states: "A just government will be best supported by protecting every citizen in the enjoyment of his religion with the same equal hand which protects his person and his property; by neither invading the equal rights of any sect, nor suffering any sect to invade those of another."

Para. 3 states: "Who does not see that the same authority which can establish Christianity, in exclusion of all other religions, may establish with the same ease any particular sect of Christians, in exclusion of all other sects?";

From the above paragraph one gleans that Madison saw true society as a manifestation of the teachings of Jesus Christ (something initially the original 13 colony-states constitutionally established); however, he was concerned about the failings and pitfalls of history's prior attempts at establishing religion in society by legal decree. And this perspective gives us the key to understanding the wording of the First Amendment Religion Clause and what it intends to accomplish.

Madison was undoubtedly a brilliant man and one can assume that he knew that the sectarianism that existed then was contrary to the teachings of Jesus Christ, according to John 17.22-23. (Jesus said his followers are to be "one" like he and his Father in Heaven are "one".) One is assured this fact when one considers the letter to Ezra Styles by Thomas Jefferson, Madison's co-leader in the religious liberty movement of that time and author of the misinterpreted and misapplied statement" Wall of separation of Church and State". Jefferson writes "we should all be one sect, doers of good and eschewers of evil. No doctrines of his lead to schism. It is the speculations of crazy theologists which have made a babel of a religion the most moral and sublime ever preached to man, and calculated to heal, and not create differences."

Under our initial federal constitutional instrument, the Articles of Confederations, there was no provision for reconciling the religious sectarianism that existed in the 13 states and this insured a measure of permanent domestic turmoil. This repugnant fact, among other things, drove our forefathers to form a new federal constitution. And this desire to form a more perfect union and ensure domestic tranquility is clearly expressed in the Preamble to the current Constitution.

Madison, obviously, figured that logic and reason is the sufficient counter measure to the speculations of theologians and their resulting schisms. And he carefully drafted the Free Exercise provision in the double-negative sense. (The first negative-make NO law; the second negative- PROHIBITING free exercise of religion) This way of the Religion Clause is the logical equivalent of an affirmative drafting [- (-1) = + 1] and means same as if Madison wrote into law every one of the numerous teachings of Jesus Christ that was to govern society. However, in using the double negative, he escapes the pitfall of a decree in the affirmative, which also could be used to declare a particular sect above all the other sects.

One also sees that the double-negative construction of the Free Exercise Provision superimposes religious law upon society at large because no religious expression of Jesus' teaching can be prohibited. This then makes society a derivative of religion as Madison stated, "society must be" in his "Memorial and Remonstrance."

The brilliance and purpose of the double negative structure is found in the principle that government has a fundamental right to make and pass law and to control behavior. With the double negative structure of the First Amendment, no specific religious doctrine is listed, only the general description of "Teaching of Jesus Christ" is implied to in our legal foundation. This subtle fact has enormous repercussions, however, because it requires every Christian sect to factually and logically establish their religious practice. It requires them to trace their practices back through all of times religious texts and prove their practice is indeed a command of Jesus Christ. If the sects cannot do this, their practice is not protected by the Constitution and it can be restricted by the government. (To paraphrase Luke 21.15, Jesus said that he would give his true followers wisdom that could not be refuted or resisted when they came against enemies of truth.)

Now the brilliance of the Religion Clause double-negative construction is seen because, over time, all ill-founded doctrinal positions causing sectarianism that Jefferson cried against will be exposed. And when remedied, unity and more domestic tranquility will arise, which will create a more perfect union. And then the intent of the Preamble will be achieved.

Critiquing the Reynolds's Decision

The Preamble to the Bill of Rights begins with "The Conventions of a number of the States having at the time of their adopting the Constitution, expressed a desire, <u>in order to prevent misconstruction or abuse of its powers</u>, that **further declaratory and restrictive clauses should be added**:"

Before examining the Reynolds decision, let us identify the absolute, inviolate rights and the governmental restrictions contained within First Amendment. Defining such first, will aid in the judging Reynolds more quickly and will show the obvious error in their justifying argument.

The First Amendment in its entirety reads:

"Congress shall make no law respecting (1) an establishment of religion, or (2) prohibiting the free exercise thereof; or (3) abridging the freedom of speech, or (4) of the press; or (5) the right of the people peaceably to assemble, and (6) to petition the government for a redress of grievances."

The First Amendment contains one governmental restriction, namely #1, and five rights, namely #2- #6. Right #3, the freedom of Speech, is the right to think - and believe what you think – and, then, the right to act out, by speaking out on what you think, no matter the topic; therefore this right is the right that protects one's religious ideas and opinions. Right#2, the freedom to exercise your religious belief, is the right to physically act on and act out a religiously held belief. In other words, one can commit overt acts that are religiously based, **differing from speaking out**, and the government cannot restrict any of those actions at all.

The pertinent portion of the Reynolds decision follows; criticism will show by bold, center-formatted sentences:

"Congress cannot pass a law for the government of the Territories which shall prohibit the free exercise of religion. The first amendment to the Constitution expressly forbids such legislation. Religious freedom is guaranteed everywhere throughout the United States, so far as congressional interference is concerned. The question to be determined is, whether the law now under consideration comes within this prohibition.

The court correctly interpreted the freedom to exercise one's religion here.

The word 'religion' is not defined in the Constitution.

This statement is false because it implies to a religion.

We must go elsewhere, therefore, to ascertain its meaning, and nowhere more appropriately, we think, than to the history of the times in the midst of which the provision was adopted. The precise point of the inquiry is, 'what is the religious freedom which has been guaranteed?'

The legal question is identified.

Before the adoption of the Constitution, attempts were made in some of the colonies and States to legislate not only in respect to the establishment of religion, but in respect to its doctrines and precepts as well. The people were taxed, against their will, for the support of religion, and sometimes for the support of particular sects to whose tenets they could not and did not subscribe. Punishments were prescribed for a failure to attend upon public worship, and sometimes for entertaining [US. 145. 163] heretical opinions. The controversy upon this general subject was animated in many of the

403

States but seemed at last to culminate in Virginia. In 1784, the House of Delegates of that State having under consideration 'a bill establishing provision for teachers of the Christian religion,' postponed it until the next session, and directed that the bill should be published and distributed, and that the people be requested 'to signify their opinion respecting the adoption of such a bill at the next session of assembly.'

This brought out a determined opposition. Amongst others, Mr. Madison prepared a 'Memorial and Remonstrance,' **(shown earlier herein)** which was widely circulated and signed, and in which he demonstrated 'that religion, or the duty we owe the Creator,' was not within the cognizance of civil government. Semple's Virginia Baptists, Appendix. At the next session the proposed bill was not only defeated, but another, 'for establishing religious freedom,' drafted by Mr. Jefferson, was passed. 1 Jeff Works, 45; 2 Howison, Hist. of Va. 298.

In the next segment the court sets their definition of "religious freedom".

In the preamble of this act (12 Hening's Stat. 84) religious freedom is defined; and after a recital 'that to suffer the civil magistrate to intrude his powers into the field of opinion, and to restrain the profession or propagation of principles on supposition of their ill tendency, is a dangerous fallacy which at once destroys all religious liberty,' it is declared 'that it is time enough for the rightful purposes of civil government for its officers to interfere when principles break out into overt acts against peace and good order.'

This is the correct working of the amendment as shown earlier herein.

In these two sentences is found the true distinction between what properly belongs to the church and what to the State.

This conclusion, Premise 1, is ridiculous and false.

In a little more than a year after the passage of this statute the convention met which prepared the Constitution of the United States.' Of this convention Mr. Jefferson was not a member, he being then absent as minister to France. As soon as he saw the draft of the Constitution proposed for adoption, he, in a letter to a friend, expressed his disappointment at the absence of an express declaration insuring the freedom of religion (2 Jeff Works, 355), but was willing to accept it as it was, trusting that the good sense and honest intentions of the people would bring about the necessary alterations. [98 U.S. 145, 164] 1 Jeff Works 79. Five of the States, while adopting the Constitution, proposed amendments. Three - New Hampshire, New York, and Virginia – included, in one form or another, a declaration of religious freedom in the changes they desired to have made, as did also North Carolina, where the convention at first declined to ratify the Constitution until the proposed amendments were acted upon. Accordingly, at the first session of the first Congress the amendment now under consideration was proposed with others by Mr. Madison. It met the views of the advocates of religious freedom and was adopted.

Jefferson's Wall of Separation Metaphor is next
Mr. Jefferson afterwards, in reply to an address to him by a committee of the Danbury Baptist Association (8 id. 113), took occasion to say: 'Believing with you that religion is a matter which lies solely between man and his God; that he owes account to none other for his faith or his worship; that the legislative powers of the government reach actions only, and not opinions,-I contemplate with sovereign reverence that act of the whole American people which declared that their legislature should 'make no law respecting an establishment of religion or prohibiting the free exercise thereof,' **thus building a wall of separation between church and State**. Adhering to this expression of the supreme will of the nation in behalf of the rights of conscience, I shall see with sincere satisfaction the progress of those sentiments **which tend to restore man to all his natural rights**, convinced he has no natural right in opposition to his social duties.' Coming as this does from an acknowledged leader of the advocates of the measure, it may be accepted almost as an authoritative declaration of the scope and effect of the amendment thus secured.

Congress was deprived of all legislative power over mere opinion,

This is a correct interpretation of the Amendment.

but was left free to reach actions which were in violation <u>of social duties or subversive of good order</u>.

This statement that court is inferring in its absolute sense is false because all overt-RELIGIOUSLY INSPIRED-action is protected under the free exercise of religion right, #2. Congress's reach only goes to non-religious actions, and those only; the only exception to this is restriction is a hostile controversy between parties asserting religious reasons, in which case, the court will decide the reasonableness of their so called religious actions. The rest of the opinion from hereon is corrupted because of the false foundation. For the court to rule on this controversy, it must prove that polygamy

in not a true religious expression as defined by the teaching of Jesus Christ, The Lord.

Polygamy has always been odious among the northern and western nations of Europe, and, until the establishment of the Mormon Church, was almost exclusively a feature of the life of Asiatic and of African people. At common law, the second marriage was always void (2 Kent, Com. 79), and from the earliest history of England polygamy has been treated as an offence against society. After the establishment of the ecclesiastical [U.S. 145, 165] courts, and until the time of James I., it was punished through the instrumentality of those tribunals, not merely because ecclesiastical rights had been violated, but because upon the separation of the ecclesiastical courts from the civil the ecclesiastical were supposed to be the most appropriate for the trial of matrimonial causes and offences against the rights of marriage, just as they were for testamentary causes and the settlement of the estates of deceased persons.

By the statute of 1 James I. (c. 11), the offence, if committed in England or Wales, was made punishable in the civil courts, and the penalty was death. As this statute was limited in its operation to England and Wales, it was at a very early period re-enacted, generally with some modifications, in all the colonies. In connection with the case we are now considering, it is a significant fact that on the 8th of December, 1788, after the passage of the act establishing religious freedom, and after the convention of Virginia had recommended as an amendment to the Constitution of the United States the declaration in a bill of rights that 'all men have an equal, natural, and unalienable right to the free exercise of religion, according to the dictates of conscience,' the legislature of that State substantially enacted the statute of James I., death penalty included, because, as recited in the preamble, 'it hath been doubted whether bigamy or polygamy be punishable by the laws of this Commonwealth.' 12 Hening's Stat. 691. From that day to this we think it may safely be said there never has been a time in any State of the Union when polygamy has not been an offence against society, cognizable by the civil courts and punishable with more or less severity. In the face of all this evidence, it is impossible to believe that the constitutional guaranty of religious freedom was intended to prohibit legislation in respect to this most important feature of social life. Marriage, while from its very nature a sacred obligation, is nevertheless, in most civilized nations, a civil contract, and usually regulated by law. Upon it society may be said to be built, and out of its fruits spring social relations and social obligations and duties, with which government is necessarily required to deal. In fact, according as monogamous or polygamous marriages are allowed, do we find the principles on which the government of U.S. 145, 166] the people, to a greater or less extent, rests. Professor, Lieber says, polygamy leads to the patriarchal principle, and which, when applied to large communities, fetters the people in stationary despotism, while that principle cannot long exist in connection with monogamy. Chancellor Kent observes that this remark is equally striking and profound. 2 Kent, Com. 81, note (e). An exceptional colony of polygamists under an exceptional leadership may sometimes exist for a time without appearing to disturb the social condition of the people who surround it; but there cannot be a doubt that, unless restricted by some form of constitution, it is within the legitimate scope of the power of every civil government to determine whether polygamy or monogamy shall be the law of social life under its dominion.

In our opinion, the statute immediately under consideration is within the legislative power of Congress. It is constitutional and valid as prescribing a rule of action for all those residing in the Territories, and in places over which the United States have exclusive control. This being so, the only question which remains is, whether those who make polygamy a part of their religion is excepted from the operation of the statute. If they are, then those who do not make polygamy a part of their religious belief may be found guilty and punished, while those who do, must be acquitted and go free. This would be introducing a new element into criminal law. Laws are made for the government of actions, and while they cannot interfere with mere religious belief and opinions, they may with practices. Suppose one believed that human sacrifices were a necessary part of religious worship, would it be seriously contended that the civil government under which he lived could not interfere to prevent a sacrifice? Or if a wife religiously believed it was her duty to burn herself upon the funeral pile of her dead husband, would it be beyond the power of the civil government to prevent her carrying her belief into practice?

So here, as a law of the organization of society under the exclusive dominion of the United States, it is provided that plural marriages shall not be allowed.

Can a man excuse his practices to the contrary because of his religious belief? [U.S. 145, 167] To permit this would be to make the professed doctrines of religious belief superior to the law of the land, and in effect to permit every citizen to become a law unto himself. Government could exist only in name under such circumstances." (end of opinion)

In regard to the closing paragraph, the court is wrong in thinking that government cannot truly exist being subservient to religious beliefs. James Madison, the author of our Constitution and Chairman of the committee that <u>drafted the First Amendment</u>, specifically states in Para. 2 of his "Memorial and Remonstrance", p13 herein, that "society and government" are nothing but <u>creatures</u> and vicegerents [deputy administrators] of religion and <u>their jurisdictions are both derived from religion and limited by religion</u>. Furthermore, in Para. 1, Madison states that a person's religious duty is <u>precedent</u>, both in order of time and in degree of obligation, to the claims of society. He says that "before any man can be considered as a member of civil society, he must be considered as a subject of the governour of the universe." True religious beliefs are not subjective or caprice in nature but are in fact universally applicable to all parties; they are verifiable and wholly reasonable in nature and are based on eternal religious precepts and principles.